PROFESSIONAL WINDOWS® 8 PROGR

Y0-BRD-599

PROFESSIONAL

Windows® 8 Programming

PROFESSIONAL

Windows® 8 Programming

APPLICATION DEVELOPMENT WITH C# AND XAML

Nick Lecrenski
Doug Holland
Allen Sanders
Kevin Ashley

John Wiley & Sons, Inc.

Professional Windows® 8 Programming: Application Development with C# and XAML

Published by
John Wiley & Sons, Inc.
10475 Crosspoint Boulevard
Indianapolis, IN 46256
www.wiley.com

ISBN: 978-1-118-20570-9
ISBN: 978-1-118-22852-4 (ebk)
ISBN: 978-1-118-24082-3 (ebk)
ISBN: 978-1-118-26569-7 (ebk)

Manufactured in the United States of America

10 9 8 7 6 5 4 3 2 1

For general information on our other products and services please contact our Customer Care Department within the United States at (877) 762-2974, outside the United States at (317) 572-3993 or fax (317) 572-4002.

Wiley publishes in a variety of print and electronic formats and by print-on-demand. Some material included with standard print versions of this book may not be included in e-books or in print-on-demand. If this book refers to media such as a CD or DVD that is not included in the version you purchased, you may download this material at http://booksupport .wiley.com. For more information about Wiley products, visit www.wiley.com.

Library of Congress Control Number: 2012947694

This book is dedicated to my remarkably patient family, my wife Kristie and daughters Tabetha and Cheyenne for once again tolerating another year-long book authoring process!

—NICK LECRENSKI

Thanks to my wife Wendi and our children Mekella, Jaimee, Andrew, and Jake for their love and support.

—DOUG HOLLAND

To Olga, my father Gregory, my mother Vera, and to all of you for reading this book. Enjoy!

—KEVIN ASHLEY

ABOUT THE AUTHORS

NICK LECRENSKI is a developer with over 10 years of experience in a wide range of Microsoft technologies including Silverlight, XAML, C#, VB.NET, ASP.NET, C++, Java, HTML, MVVM, SQL Server, and more. He has a BS in Computer Science and has worked in various fields from biometrics to financial services. He is also the founder and lead developer of `MyFitnessJournal` `.com,` an online fitness tracking site that utilizes the latest web development technologies including ASP.NET MVC and JQuery.

DOUG HOLLAND is an architect with Microsoft's Developer & Platform Evangelism team. He works with Microsoft's strategic ISV partners to help them bring new and exciting experiences to consumers on Windows 8 and Windows Phone 8. Before joining Microsoft DPE, he was awarded both the Microsoft MVP (Visual C#) and Intel Black Belt Developer awards and holds an M.Sc. in Software Engineering from Oxford University.

ALLEN SANDERS is an architect at Teksouth Corporation and co-owner of LiquidKey, LLC. He provides expertise from the UX (user experience) to the database for LOB (line of business), Windows 8, and Windows Phone solutions.

KEVIN ASHLEY (`@kashleytwit`) is an architect evangelist at Microsoft, author of top Windows 8 and Windows Phone apps (`http://wpcardgames.com`), code junkie and a part-time ski instructor. Prior to Microsoft, Kevin founded a successful cloud-based business intelligence startup and worked in finance. In his role as a senior software developer and architect, Kevin developed grid, data warehousing and real-time trading solutions for Fortune 500 companies and hedge funds worldwide: US, UK, Europe and Asia. Kevin has degrees in Mathematics, Computer Science and has an MBA in Finance. He enjoys writing about software and technology on his blog: `http://kevinashley.com`.

ABOUT THE TECHNICAL EDITORS

JOHN BOX has almost 30 years of experience in the computer industry. Currently, he is finishing his seventh year at Microsoft as a senior technical evangelist in the Developer & Platform Evangelism organization (DPE). In past lifetimes, Jon has been a developer, architect, software manager, consultant, instructor, and a general manager of a consulting office. Today, he is working with customers in the central US build Windows 8 applications for the Windows Store. You can find more background at his blog (`http://blogs.msdn.com/jonbox`) or on Twitter (@jonbox).

FRANK LA VIGNE works for Microsoft as a public sector technical evangelist and Windows 8 Champ. Prior to joining Microsoft, Frank was a Tablet PC MVP and co-authored a book on Silverlight 4. He has been in software development since the days of Visual Basic 3. Frank blogs regularly about Windows 8 development at `www.FranksWorld.com/blog`.

DON REAMEY is an architect/principal engineer for TIBCO Software working on TIBCO Spotfire business intelligence analytics software. Prior to TIBCO, Don spent 12 years with Microsoft corporation as software development engineer working on SharePoint, SharePoint Online and InfoPath Forms Service. Don has also spent 10 years writing software in the financial service industry for capital markets.

CREDITS

ACQUISITIONS EDITOR
Mary James

PROJECT EDITOR
Maureen Spears

TECHNICAL EDITORS
John Box
Frank La Vigne
Don Reamey

PRODUCTION EDITOR
Daniel Scribner

COPY EDITOR
San Dee Phillips

EDITORIAL MANAGER
Mary Beth Wakefield

FREELANCER EDITORIAL MANAGER
Rosemarie Graham

ASSOCIATE DIRECTOR OF MARKETING
David Mayhew

MARKETING MANAGER
Ashley Zurcher

BUSINESS MANAGER
Amy Knies

PRODUCTION MANAGER
Tim Tate

VICE PRESIDENT AND EXECUTIVE GROUP PUBLISHER
Richard Swadley

VICE PRESIDENT AND EXECUTIVE PUBLISHER
Neil Edde

ASSOCIATE PUBLISHER
Jim Minatel

PROJECT COORDINATOR, COVER
Katie Crocker

PROOFREADERS
Jennifer Bennett, Word One
Josh Chase, Word One
Scott Klemp, Word One

INDEXER
Robert Swanson

COVER DESIGNER
LeAndra Young

COVER IMAGE
@archana bhartia/iStock

ACKNOWLEDGMENTS

WHEN YOU AUTHOR A BOOK and you get to the process of writing any acknowledgments it is a very good day. It means you are finally at the end of a very long journey that has many ups and downs. From late nights working through coding issues, to scouring the web for any new information on the topics you are trying to write about, getting here requires a lot of help. First and foremost, I want to thank Maureen Spears for once again leading me through this journey and keeping me sane when deadlines were missed or things just didn't work the way I wanted them to. I also need to thank Mary James for keeping all of us on track and taking care of the various project management details of which there were many, given the number of authors involved. Finally, I want to thank Paul Reese who initiated this entire process quite some time ago and got the entire ball rolling!

—NICK LECRENSKI

THANKS TO MY WIFE for her love and support throughout this project, and thanks also to my managers, Leslie Pickering and Matt Thompson, for their support in writing this book. Windows 8 has been completely re-imagined, as has the associated developer platform. As such, I owe a debt of gratitude to numerous people within Microsoft's Developer Platform & Evangelism (DPE) team, the Developer Division, as well as the Windows team. Their time and expertise was invaluable as the book was researched and written. Thanks to Jon Box and Kevin Ashley for their attention to detail during the technical edit, and a special thank you to Mary James and Maureen Spears at Wiley.

—DOUG HOLLAND

THANKS TO OLGA for all her support and love, and her family. Thanks to my mother Vera and my father Gregory; your dedication to Physics will always be my inspiration. Special thanks to Warren Wilbee and the team at Microsoft—all of you made many dreams possible.

—KEVIN ASHLEY

CONTENTS

INTRODUCTION

IT SEEMS LIKE YESTERDAY that Microsoft announced at its first annual BUILD conference the upcoming game-changing operating system: Windows 8. In the Microsoft world for the first time, Windows 8 was to provide an operating system that could create an ecosystem of apps that ran among phones, desktop computers, and tablets. Developers would be closer to writing an app for one device and, with few-to-no modifications, having it run on additional devices. Now that Windows 8 is finally here, it's time for you, the developer, to get on board and understand some of the vast changes involved in creating Windows-based apps. *Professional Windows 8 Programming* is designed as your guide to all the changes and to get you on the fast track of developing your own apps for the new Windows Store.

In this book, you learn all about the new development features of Windows 8 and how best to use them in apps for both the PC and tablet. You see how to use XAML and C# to create a new style of app that emphasizes content rather than chrome. Windows Store apps are different from traditional Windows desktop apps because they run full screen and without all the traditional menu systems that have historically taken up valuable screen real estate. In addition to a new style of app through the new WinRT development platform, Windows 8 gives you easy access to various hardware features such as sensors and geolocation. This book walks you through making use of these new features in your own apps.

Finally, you should be aware that Windows 8 brings massive change in the area of app distribution. With the release of Windows 8, developers can now access an online app store where they can easily distribute and sell apps to the massive Windows 8 audience. Step by step, this book shows you how to leverage Visual Studio 2012 to prepare your apps for deployment in the Windows Store. The new Windows Store gives you a great way to generate revenue as well as free online distribution for your apps.

It is an exciting time to be a Microsoft developer, and now that Windows 8 is out in the wild, you'll see a massive increase in the demand for quality, content-rich apps in the Windows Store. These apps must target the PC and tablet, as well as the soon-to-be-released Windows Phone 8. *Professional Windows 8 Programming* will guide you through all this, ensuring that you have the knowledge and tools necessary to create these in-demand apps.

WHO THIS BOOK IS FOR

This book is designed for the professional-level developer who has previous experience writing applications for both Windows and the web. It assumes a familiarity with the following technologies:

- ➤ Visual Studio
- ➤ .NET Runtime

- ➤ C#
- ➤ XAML
- ➤ WPF

Although this book provides some introductory coverage of XAML and how it pertains to creating user interfaces for Windows Store apps, it isn't a primer on all the detailed aspects of XAML. If you have done any Silverlight or WPF development in the past, you should be fine.

This book also assumes not only that you are familiar with C#, but also that you are proficient in it. It discusses several new features to the language added in the new .NET 4.5 run time and WinRT, but does not include introductory text explaining the fundamental concepts of programming in C#.

If you have been reading the various blogs and information technology websites lately, you probably know that Windows 8 enables you to create apps using the language of your choice, including HTML/CSS/JavaScript. All this is true — you can create complete Windows 8 solutions using all your favorite web technologies. However, this book does not delve into detail on this method of development, but rather focuses specifically on creating Windows Store apps with XAML and C# as your primary programming language. The book has some basic introductory information about how to use HTML/CSS/JavaScript to write Windows Store apps, but it does not go into great detail.

WHAT THIS BOOK COVERS

This book covers how to write rich content-driven Windows Store apps using XAML and C#. You see how to make use of the new improvements to Visual Studio 2012, including several new application templates that help you jump-start your Windows Store app development. The following is an overview of the various chapters and content associated with them:

- ➤ **Chapter 1:** "A Glimpse into the Future" — Provides a brief overview of Windows 8 history. You are introduced to Visual Studio 2012 and create your first Windows Store app.

- ➤ **Chapter 2:** "What Is XAML?" — Offers a brief introduction to the XAML user interface language and how to use Visual Studio 2012 to design your apps.

- ➤ **Chapter 3:** "Enhancing Your Apps with Control Styles, Data Binding, and Semantic Zoom" — With a solid XAML foundation, you can now become familiar with some of the advanced XAML topics.

- ➤ **Chapter 4:** "Windows 8 User Interface Final Touches" — Introduces you to many of the new XAML controls available in WinRT and Windows 8.

- ➤ **Chapter 5:** "Application Life Cycle" — Windows Store apps have a different life cycle compared to traditional Windows applications. This chapter shows you how to handle the required events for when your app is suspended and activated as opposed to simply being shut down like a standard desktop app.

➤ **Chapter 6:** "Handling Data, Files, and Networking" — Become familiar with the changes to File IO, Data Access, and networking in the WinRT run time.

➤ **Chapter 7:** "Sensors" — Learn how to access and make use of the various sensor hardware included on Windows 8 tablet devices.

➤ **Chapter 8:** "Geolocation" — Provides an introduction to Windows 8 support for geolocation services and how to best incorporate this feature in your own apps.

➤ **Chapter 9:** "Application Contracts and Extensions" — Windows 8 introduces a new concept called contracts. These enable your app to become part of a shared feature ecosystem in which features in your app can be made accessible to other apps installed on the system. This chapter walks you through the process to open your app up to further use by alternative apps.

➤ **Chapter 10:** "Windows Store Application Architecture" — Learn how to best organize the code structure a Windows Store app. You also learn how to use the new MVVM design pattern that reduces code and complexity in your apps.

➤ **Chapter 11:** "Windows Store and Monetization" — After you start completing Windows Store apps, you must find out how to potentially start making money with them. This chapter introduces you to the new Windows Store concept and provides guidance on the supported monetization strategies the store can offer.

➤ **Chapter 12:** "Putting It All Together: Building a Windows Store Application" — After you understand all the core Windows 8 development concepts, you create a full-blown Windows Store app from start to finish. This chapter walks you through the design and implementation of a fully fledged Windows Store app and shows you how to incorporate features of the cloud with SkyDrive support.

WHAT YOU NEED TO USE THIS BOOK

To follow the examples in this book, you need the following software requirements:

➤ Visual Studio 2012 (Express, Professional, or Ultimate)

➤ Windows 8 RTM (Final Release)

CONVENTIONS

To help you get the most from the text and keep track of what's happening, a number of conventions are used throughout the book.

> **WARNING** *Warnings hold important, not-to-be-forgotten information directly relevant to the surrounding text.*

> **NOTE** *Notes indicate tips, hints, tricks, or asides to the current discussion.*

As for styles in the text:

➤ We *italicize* new terms and important words when we introduce them.

➤ We show keyboard strokes like this: Ctrl+A.

➤ We show filenames, URLs, and code within the text like so: `persistence.properties`.

➤ We present code in two different ways:

```
We use a monofont type with no highlighting for most code examples.
```

We use bold to emphasize code that's particularly important in the present context.

SOURCE CODE

As you work through the examples in this book, you may choose either to type in all the code manually or to use the source code files that accompany the book. All the source code used in this book is available for download at `http://www.wrox.com`. You find the code snippets from the source code are accompanied by a download icon and note indicating the name of the program, so you know it's available for download and can easily locate it in the download file. At the site, simply locate the book's title (either by using the Search box or by using one of the title lists) and click the Download Code link on the book's detail page to obtain all the source code for the book.

> **NOTE** *Because many books have similar titles, you may find it easiest to search by ISBN; this book's ISBN is 978-1-118-20570-9.*

After you download the code, decompress it with your favorite compression tool. Alternatively, you can go to the main Wrox code download page at `http://www.wrox.com/dynamic/books/download.aspx` to see the code available for this book and all other Wrox books.

ERRATA

We make every effort to ensure that there are no errors in the text or in the code. However, no one is perfect, and mistakes do occur. If you find an error in one of our books, such as a spelling mistake or faulty piece of code, we would be grateful for your feedback. By sending in errata you may save another reader hours of frustration, and at the same time you can help us provide even higher quality information.

To find the errata page for this book, go to `http://www.wrox.com` and locate the title using the Search box or one of the title lists. Then, on the book details page, click the Book Errata link. On this page you can view all errata that has been submitted for this book and posted by Wrox editors.

> **NOTE** *A complete book list including links to each book's errata is also available at* `www.wrox.com/misc-pages/booklist.shtml`.

If you don't spot "your" error on the Book Errata page, go to `www.wrox.com/contact/techsupport.shtml` and complete the form there to send us the error you have found. We'll check the information and, if appropriate, post a message to the book's errata page and fix the problem in subsequent editions of the book.

P2P.WROX.COM

For author and peer discussion, join the P2P forums at `p2p.wrox.com`. The forums are a web-based system for you to post messages relating to Wrox books and related technologies and interact with other readers and technology users. The forums offer a subscription feature to e-mail you topics of interest of your choosing when new posts are made to the forums. Wrox authors, editors, other industry experts, and your fellow readers are present on these forums.

At `http://p2p.wrox.com` you can find a number of different forums that help you not only as you read this book, but also as you develop your own applications. To join the forums, follow these steps:

1. Go to `p2p.wrox.com` and click the Register link.

2. Read the terms of use and click Agree.

3. Complete the required information to join and any optional information you want to provide, and click Submit.

4. You will receive an e-mail with information describing how to verify your account and complete the joining process.

> **NOTE** *You can read messages in the forums without joining P2P, but to post your own messages, you must join.*

After you join, you can post new messages and respond to messages other users post. You can read messages at any time on the web. If you want new messages from a particular forum e-mailed to you, click the Subscribe to this Forum icon by the forum name in the forum listing.

For more information about how to use the Wrox P2P, be sure to read the P2P FAQs for answers to questions about how the forum software works as well as many common questions specific to P2P and Wrox books. To read the FAQs, click the FAQ link on any P2P page.

PROFESSIONAL

Windows® 8 Programming

A Glimpse into the Future

WROX.COM CODE DOWNLOADS FOR THIS CHAPTER

You can find the wrox.com code downloads for this chapter in code file 205709 C01.zip at `http://www.wrox.com/remtitle.cgi?isbn=1118205707` on the Download Code tab.

THE GAME CHANGER

In a developer's life, you have a handful of moments in which a new "game-changing" technology release actually lives up to the hype. This could be new hardware or software, but it is especially game-changing when it's for new operating systems. Often a new OS is just a more reliable working version of the one that came before it with several new visual upgrades. It is rare that an OS release changes the game so much that developers must reboot their knowledge and think about creating apps in a "different" way. This happened with the original release of Windows, which gave MS developers a graphical user interface with a windowed environment. It happened again with Windows 95 with the introduction of the 32-bit operating system and with Internet Explorer that hosted new computing features, including better support for windowed gaming through DirectX and more memory, larger hard drives, and more powerful programs overall.

Now with the pending release of Windows 8, developers are on the forefront of yet another major evolution in programming and user interface design. Instead of creating applications that appeal only to a PC, you now have the option to create apps that run on a myriad of devices, including PCs, cell phones, tablets, TVs, and more. Windows 8 and WinRT help you get there in ways that simply were previously not possible. The new convergence of devices and programming support coming from Microsoft for Windows 8 provide opportunities for developers to create innovative solutions, which includes new, improved user interfaces that target multiple devices while using similar or, in many cases, the same underlying code base.

WHAT MAKES WINDOWS 8 DIFFERENT?

Although Windows 8 concepts are now rapidly being applied throughout the Microsoft ecosystem, they've actually been around for some time. More than likely, if you were a first-generation Zune software owner, you noticed how drastically different the user interface was for both the Zune hardware and the software. In Figure 1-1 you can quickly see the stark difference between a standard Windows application and the Zune software that first started to show the Windows 8 design principles that are now showcased in Windows Phone and ultimately across the entire Windows product line with the release of Windows 8.

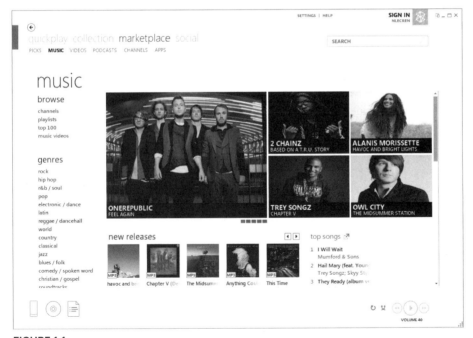

FIGURE 1-1

Understanding Windows 8: The Zune Concept

Although the Zune hardware never did catch on with the mass markets with the success that the iPod from Apple did, the software internally left a lasting mark at Microsoft. What the Zune software did well was place emphasis on application content rather than on the chrome. The Zune software didn't have hundreds of menu options and toolbars spread throughout the app. You also didn't see multiple windows that users could drag across the screen. Instead you had album artwork, song titles, meta data about the music, and controls specific to the actual function you were using. The software was easy to use, and many of the more complex functions were handled with a simple right-click context menu and a modal dialog, as shown in Figure 1-2, so users could always get back to where they started.

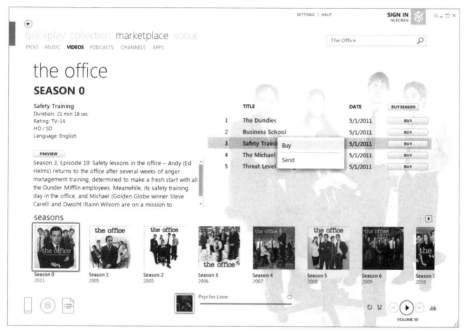

FIGURE 1-2

Compared to a traditional Windows application, this was definitely a different way to do things. With the iPod cruising and the iPhone on its way, Microsoft needed a way to get into the exploding mobile market and to differentiate itself from both Android and iOS competition. Instead of making small changes to the existing Windows mobile platform, Microsoft looked to the Zune software for its design principles to achieve its goals in the mobile space. The Zune software team essentially created a new way to look at the user interface and the design behind it: Windows 8.

To stand out from the crowd, Microsoft used the Windows 8 design concepts in its upcoming release of the new Windows Phone 7. However, this platform was not just a direct copy of Zune; Microsoft took the Windows 8 design concept even further by creating an entirely new way to develop applications that focused on content over chrome.

Microsoft invested research time and money into *gestures* that gave the best overall experience on a mobile device, and it determined how to apply those gestures to the user interface for phone apps. This led to some groundbreaking controls and concepts. An example is the panorama control that shows a horizontally scrolling user interface, giving users a basic preview of available content when they scroll.

Windows Phone 7 Carry-overs

Windows Phone 7 introduced several new user interface concepts that have carried over into Windows 8. Live tiles is an example of this and is now an integral part of the newly enhanced Start screen in Windows 8. *Live tiles* gives users several customizable tiles that continuously update with the latest relevant information for the application that they represent. This could be an e-mail application that always displays the latest count of unread e-mail messages or the latest tweet from a preferred Twitter user. Microsoft offers many different possibilities for these tiles and gives guidance on how your application should attempt to use tiles, a topic covered in Chapter 4, "Windows 8 User Interfaces." Figure 1-3 shows the new Windows 8 start screen and several live tiles, which continuously update with information downloaded in the background through various web services.

FIGURE 1-3

GETTING AROUND IN WINDOWS 8

Typically, it's simple to get up to speed on new versions of Windows. Most of the familiar operating system tools and interactions don't change. However, because Windows 8 is geared to a wide range of devices, Microsoft made significant changes to the way the user interface and navigation operating systems work. As a Windows 8 developer, you need to know how to get around Windows 8 and how it affects the applications you create and deploy. This section covers some of these navigational changes.

The Login Screen

The first thing you notice is that the standard login screen is different than previous versions of Windows. The new startup screen offers icons that enable you to quickly see information before logging in. The number of icons and type of information change depending on which applications are currently running (if they support this feature). For example, if you have the default Mail application running and then lock the computer, you can see a Mail icon along with the number of currently unread e-mails. This new feature is not only restricted to default Windows Store applications; you can also integrate your applications with the startup screen so that a meaningful icon displays and reflects data from your app.

The Start Screen

You can quickly see that gestures play a big role in Windows 8 whether you use them on a tablet or a PC. To actually get past the initial screen and move to the login screen, you simply click anywhere on the screen. Once logged in you are presented with the new Start screen. You can notice that:

➤ The new Start screen is essentially a full-blown replacement for the traditional Windows Start menu.

➤ Tiles represent applications, which are written using WinRT and Windows 8, as well as traditional Windows 7 or earlier-based desktop applications.

➤ Windows Store applications are presented as live tiles that can change dynamically.

➤ Desktop applications are small static tiles with the name of the applications and an icon to represent them.

➤ Any installed desktop or Windows 8-based application has an icon added to the Start screen.

This means that when you develop apps for Windows 8, you must carefully consider how your app appears on this screen. You must ensure that you use a solid-looking icon and design live tiles that give the user information about the app. In traditional Windows desktop development, you simply ensured that your application appeared on the Start menu — and if you packaged your application correctly, it most likely was not a problem. You certainly didn't spend a ton of time worrying about how your application looked on the Start menu. With Windows 8 you need to pay attention to those details because you want your application tile to stand out on this screen.

Users can easily customize the Start menu by dragging and dropping tiles into the various tile groups. The user can also remove tiles by right-clicking a tile to select it, and then choosing Unpin from the new App Bar that appears at the bottom of the screen. Figure 1-4 shows the App Bar along with some options for managing the selected tiles.

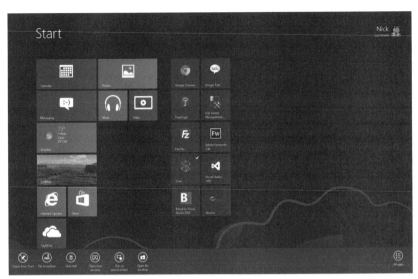

FIGURE 1-4

Although the right-click is a valid operation on the PC, it obviously won't work on a tablet. The equivalent operation for the tablet is a new gesture: swiping from the bottom of the screen to the center.

The Search Feature

So what if you want to start a program that isn't currently on the Start screen? Rather than hunt down the application, as you would have under the traditional Start menu, you simply bring up the new Windows 8 search feature. From a PC you type the name of the application, and the search screen appears with the best matches (see Figure 1-5).

FIGURE 1-5

On a tablet you swipe from the right side to enable the new Charm bar, which is shown in Figure 1-6, and then touch the Search icon that displays.

FIGURE 1-6

Application Life Cycle

Another important thing about Windows 8 is how the life cycle of applications differs from traditional desktop applications. For example, in a traditional desktop app, you have Minimize, Maximize, and Close icons at the top-right corner of the window. With Windows Store apps you won't have those options. As you will learn later in the book in Chapter 5, "Application Life Cycle," Windows Store apps follow a life cycle similar to apps on the Windows Phone platform. They don't typically close but instead are suspended until you need them again. If, however, you do want to close an application, you have several options:

➤ **You can bring up the Task Manager and simply kill the application.** This is the same as you would do in any previous version of Windows (see Figure 1-7).

➤ **There is a close gesture that works on both the PC and the tablet.** But to perform the gesture, you need to move your hand/mouse to the top of the screen, hold the left mouse button/finger down, and then drag the app toward the bottom of the screen. As you move the app toward the bottom of the screen, you let go and the app closes.

➤ **If all else fails, on a PC, you always have the Alt+F4 keyboard shortcut.** This forces the currently open Windows Store app to close. On a PC, keyboard shortcuts are often the easiest way to access features in Windows 8. Although all the gestures developed for Windows 8 were created with touch interfaces in mind, they all have equivalent mouse operations, but the keyboard is the fastest way for Windows 8 power users to access features.

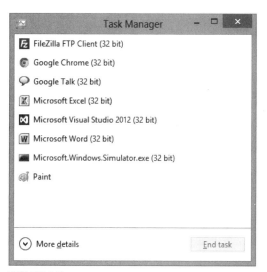

FIGURE 1-7

Accessing Desktop Mode

While developing apps and using Visual Studio, you're primarily in desktop mode. You need to become familiar with several mouse gestures to navigate the desktop mode quickly and efficiently. In desktop mode, moving the mouse to the corners of the screen brings up various Windows 8 feature allowing you to:

➤ **View currently running Windows Store applications:** In desktop mode traditional Windows applications that are currently running appear in the taskbar as they have with previous versions of Windows. However, Windows Store apps do not appear here. To view and switch between available Windows Store apps, you can move the mouse to the top left of any connected display to see the next available app that you can run.

➤ **View a full list of running Windows Store apps:** Simply move the mouse to the top-left corner and then move the mouse downward slightly. This brings up a bar with icons for all the running Windows Store apps. Figure 1-8 shows that after you perform the gesture, you can switch between both the calendar and messaging application that are currently running.

A bar showing all running windows Store apps

FIGURE 1-8

➤ **View a shortcut to go back to the Start screen.** By bringing the mouse over to the bottom-left corner, you can return to the Start screen.

➤ **View a list of common power user tasks.** You can do this by right-clicking the icon for the Start screen, which you can find at the bottom-left corner of the display (see Figure 1-9). This is helpful during development.

➤ **View the outline of the Charms bar.** You can view this if you bring the mouse to the top right of the primary display. This works only on the primary display and not on any secondary display. If you drag the mouse down slightly, the Charms bar comes into full view so that you can easily access Search, Share, Start, Devices, and Settings.

FIGURE 1-9

Although this has in no way been an in-depth look at all the new user interface features of Windows 8, it should be enough to help you quickly navigate to the features that are the most important during the development process.

In all cases, if you have a mouse gesture on the PC that brings up a feature in Windows 8, you also have a corresponding touch gesture that does the same on a tablet or touch-based device. Table 1-1 is a quick reference — a list of the common touch gestures with the mouse equivalents that you need to know during development. This can come in handy when you deploy and test your apps on touch-based Windows 8 devices such as tablets.

TABLE 1-1: Common Windows 8 Touch Gestures

ACTION	TABLET	PC/MOUSE
Display the Charm Bar.	Swipe from the right side of screen.	Hover the mouse on the top-right side of the monitor.
Display a list of running programs, which enables you to switch programs.	Swipe from the left side of screen and then back.	Hover the mouse on the top-left side of the monitor, and then move mouse down.
Show the next application to which you can switch; similar to traditional Alt+Tab behavior from previous Windows versions.	Swipe from the left side of the screen toward the center.	Hover the mouse on the top-left side of the monitor.
Close the running Windows Store application.	Swipe and pull from the top of the running Windows Store app screen toward the bottom of the display.	Hover the mouse on the top of the screen until a hand appears, and then left-click and hold while dragging the Windows Store app toward the bottom of the display.
Bring up additional application menus or the context menu.	Swipe slightly from the top or bottom of the display when the Windows Store app is running.	Right-click with the mouse.
Perform a zoom operation in a running Windows Store app or start a semantic zoom of visible tiles if you're currently on the Start screen.	Pinch.	Ctrl+Mouse Wheel.

Often developers are power users who tend to do as much as possible with the keyboard; they consider moving the mouse around to perform these gestures wasteful movement. Table 1-2 shows the most commonly used keyboard shortcuts available in Windows 8, along with the action that the shortcut performs.

TABLE 1-2: Commonly Used Windows 8 Keyboard Shortcuts

KEYBOARD COMBO	ACTION
Win+C	Open the Charm bar.
Win+D	Go to the desktop.
Win+E	Start Windows Explorer.
Win+F	Open Search under the Charm bar with files as the default filter.
Win+H	Open Share Charm.
Win+I	Open Setting the Charm.
Win+J	Switch between the snapped and full version of the Windows Store app.
Win+K	Open the Devices Charm.
Win+L	Lock the PC.
Win+Q	Open the Search Charm.
Win+R	Run.
Win+W	Open Charm Search with the settings filter enabled.
Win+Z	Open the app bar or menu.
Alt+Tab	Cycle through currently running apps or windows.

WINDOWS STORE APP DEVELOPMENT

Windows Store application development begins with Visual Studio 2012. You'll spend a considerable amount of time in this program. Lucky for you, it is considered an industry-standard IDE for developers. Previous users of Visual Studio 2010 or earlier will notice some big aesthetic changes. Even if you work on a desktop application, you'll find the look and feel of Visual Studio 2012 in line with the new Windows 8 style apps. When in Visual Studio, you see the familiar Start screen, as shown in Figure 1-10. From here, you can easily open recent projects, take a look at some MSDN article links, and, of course, start new projects.

Visual Studio comes with several new project templates that help you start writing Windows Store apps for Windows 8. It also boasts many new productivity enhancements that come in handy during

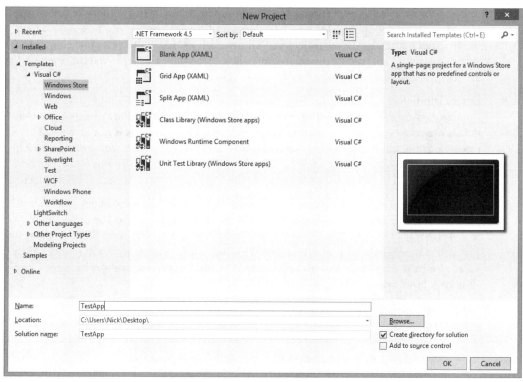

FIGURE 1-10

the course of development. The following is a list of the most useful improvements made to this latest version of Visual Studio:

➤ **Page Inspector:** Enables you to view and manipulate currently running HTML code. This great, new enhancement gives developers a way to view DOM objects. You can also run JavaScript from the IDE when you debug sites — it's like having Firebug built into Visual Studio.

➤ **IntelliSense:** You have full IntelliSense when you work with JavaScript. For example, pressing the Period button after typing the name of a string variable displays all available methods and properties for that string. No more painful Google lookups for every JavaScript operation you want to perform; most important, you reduce typos.

➤ **Image preview:** You no longer need to right-click an image in your project and open it using a third-party tool to see what it is. Visual Studio now includes a cool, new feature that enables you to simply move the mouse over the filename of a given image to instantly see a thumbnail preview of that image.

➤ **Browser Switcher:** When developing in HTML, it is imperative that you preview your pages in all the major browsers. When you debugged in previous versions of Visual Studio, it was somewhat of a pain unless you used third-party extensions. Often, this required you to right-click and select the Browse With option, select a browser, cancel the operation, and finally start debugging. In this latest version of Visual Studio, you now have a new toolbar that automatically loads icons of all installed browsers. To test your changes while debugging with a different browser, simply click the icon of the preferred browser, and you are ready to go.

➤ **Device simulator:** Visual Studio now has one of the most powerful and productive device simulators available for mobile development. The new version includes a simulator that makes it easy to try your application in tablet form. The simulator is not just a visual representation, but it also mimics several hardware features such as rotation and touch events. If you develop mobile apps for Windows Phone, it enables you to easily perform preliminary testing of your apps without deploying to an actual Windows Phone device.

➤ **App Store support:** Another major new Windows 8 feature (discussed later in Chapter 12, "Putting It All Together: Building a Windows Store Application,") is the inclusion of the new App Store. The App Store is where you must deploy any Windows Store application that you want to make available to other Windows users. Visual Studio now includes full support for the App Store and makes it simple to build, package, and deploy newly created Windows Store apps to the Store from the IDE.

➤ **Existing project support:** In previous versions of Visual Studio, if you wanted to open a project from an earlier version, you were forced to upgrade the raw project files. Often, this process made it difficult to open the project again from the previous version. In Visual Studio 2012, you can now open any project or solution file created in a previous version of Visual Studio, and those files remain compatible with the version in which you created them.

➤ **Goto definition:** If you've previously developed in Visual Studio using C# or other .NET languages, no doubt you found the right-click option that goes directly to a method or property definition — a useful feature. Unfortunately, this feature was not available for JavaScript development, which meant you had to perform long, tedious searches or scroll to find method declarations in potentially long JavaScript files. Now in Visual Studio 2012, the *Goto definition* feature works perfectly, even for JavaScript source code files.

➤ **Drag and Drop JavaScript references:** Another great, new feature is the ability to drag and drop a JavaScript source file into an HTML file and have Visual Studio automatically add the appropriate reference to that file.

➤ **CSS improvements:** Visual Studio 2012 has also added many improvements to CSS editing and management. This includes using the toolbar to more easily comment and uncomment large sections of CSS code, as well as finally creating collapsible regions of CSS in situations in which you have extremely large CSS files and are forced to scroll for long periods of time to find CSS code blocks.

➤ **3-D model preview:** In addition to the cool image preview thumbnails now available, Visual Studio has also added a basic 3-D model viewer that helps game developers view models without going outside of the IDE to review them or to make small changes to existing models that they've added to the project.

Throughout this book you see many of these new features used during the course of Windows Store app development.

HELLO WINDOWS 8

Regardless of language, traditionally when you write a development book, you introduce a new topic with a Hello World application. Not wanting to upset the status quo, you do the same here. At this point, you have some basic knowledge about Windows 8, and Visual Studio 2012, so now is a great time to get your feet wet developing your first Windows Store app. Because you can write a Windows Store app in the language of your choice, start by picking a language in which you're most comfortable working.

> **NOTE** *This book includes C#, C++, and JavaScript examples whenever possible. As always, the full code for all the apps and examples is available from* `http://www.wrox.com` *for all three languages.*

Selecting a Language and Default Folders

To start, follow these steps:

1. Fire up Visual Studio, and select File ⇨ New ⇨ Project. This launches the Project Template dialog.

2. For the language of your choice, find the Windows Store template.

3. In Figure 1-10, you can see the full list of available Windows Store app templates. Select Blank App and give the project a name, such as **Hello Windows 8,** and click OK to continue. Visual Studio creates a new project with all the required files for a basic Windows Store full-screen app. With the C# version in the Solution Explorer, you can see several directories and files. Table 1-3 covers for which task each file is responsible at a high level.

TABLE 1-3: Default Project Files

FILE	TASK
MainPage.xaml	The initial page that loads in your application. You must create your user interface with this file.
MainPage.xaml .cs	The code behind the file for the default page. In this file, you can add code to handle control events or page navigation events.
App.xaml	Contains a globally available `ResourceDictionary` object. To style various user interface controls, you must declare styles in this file, which are automatically available to any page in your application.
App.xaml.cs	This code-behind file contains event handlers for important application events such as launched, suspending, and others. This file is also where you set `MainPage.xaml` as the first page to load upon application startup. To change which page displays first, you can modify the `OnLaunched` event handler to point to the wanted page.

continues

TABLE 1-3 *(continued)*

FILE	TASK
`Assets\Logo.png`	This image is the default logo that appears on your application's tile and that displays on the Start screen. Replace this file with a 150 x 150 .png image if you want to use a different logo on the tile.
`Assets\SmallLogo.png`	If your tile includes dynamic text in addition to an icon, you must ensure you replace this file with a 30 x 30 .png image.
`Assets\SplashScreen.png`	This is the default splash screen that displays when the application starts. To replace it, you must use a 620 x 300 .png image. In addition to the image, you must select a background color for the splash screen display. You can set this by using the project properties editor.
`Assets\StoreLogo.png`	This is the icon that represents your app in the Windows Store App Store. To change this default, you must replace it with a 50 x 50 .png icon image.
`Common\StandardStyles.xaml`	This file is similar to `App.xaml` in that it also contains control styles for the application. This resource dictionary contains a default set of tested and proven styles that you should use in controls and pages throughout your application. Normally, you don't need to modify these styles but it's recommended to inherit from them using the XAML `BasedOn` syntax (see in Chapter 3, "Enhancing Your Apps with Control Styles, Data Binding, and SemanticZoom). For now, remember that before you style text or other controls in your app, you should check this file for an available standard style to use instead. Remember, Windows Store apps should have a common look and feel, so where possible, make use of the standard styles to keep the user interface consistent with other published Windows Store apps.
`Package.appxmanifest`	This file contains all the settings and App Store information for your app. Here, you can change the display name of your app, set the logo files, set supported orientations, and define what capabilities your app requires. Double-clicking this file brings up the applications property configuration window and is the preferred way to make modifications to this file.

If you have done any WPF or Silverlight development in the past, the files in Table 1-3 should look familiar. In many cases, Windows Store apps borrow from the application designs and frameworks of WPF and Silverlight. If, however, you come from a Windows Forms-based or ASP.NET-based development background, some of these XAML concepts and files will be new to you.

Building a Simple Windows Store App

This first simple Windows Store app you build has only one purpose, which is to display the words "Hello Windows 8" on the screen, ideally centered and in a nice, large font. The main page that launches at application startup is the `MainPage.xaml`. By default, Windows Store apps work similar to Silverlight navigation apps in that each new screen inherits from the Page class. Listing 1-1 shows you the code behind for MainPage and includes the OnNavigatedTo event handler just like it would in Silverlight. This event handler gives you a place to run code as soon as the page displays to the user.

LISTING 1-1: MainPage.xaml.cs

```
using System;
using System.Collections.Generic;
using System.IO;
using System.Linq;
using Windows.Foundation;
using Windows.Foundation.Collections;
using Windows.UI.Xaml;
using Windows.UI.Xaml.Controls;
using Windows.UI.Xaml.Controls.Primitives;
using Windows.UI.Xaml.Data;
using Windows.UI.Xaml.Input;
using Windows.UI.Xaml.Media;
using Windows.UI.Xaml.Navigation;

// The Blank Page item template is documented at
http://go.microsoft.com/fwlink/?LinkId=234238

namespace HelloWindows
{
    /// <summary>
    /// An empty page that can be used on its own or navigated to within a Frame.
    /// </summary>
    public sealed partial class MainPage : Page
    {
        public MainPage()
        {
            this.InitializeComponent();
        }

        /// <summary>
        /// Invoked when this page is about to be displayed in a Frame.
        /// </summary>
        /// <param name="e">Event data that describes how this
        /// page was reached.  The Parameter
        /// property is typically used to configure the page.</param>
        protected override void OnNavigatedTo(NavigationEventArgs e)
        {
        }
    }
}
```

At this point, the user interface file for the application resides in the BlankPage.xaml file and, as you can see in Listing 1-2, contains only an empty Grid control.

LISTING 1-2: MainPage.xaml

```
<Page
    x:Class="HelloWindows.MainPage"
    xmlns="http://schemas.microsoft.com/winfx/2006/xaml/presentation"
    xmlns:x="http://schemas.microsoft.com/winfx/2006/xaml"
    xmlns:local="using:HelloWindows"
    xmlns:d="http://schemas.microsoft.com/expression/blend/2008"
    xmlns:mc="http://schemas.openxmlformats.org/markup-compatibility/2006"
    mc:Ignorable="d">

    <Grid Background="{StaticResource ApplicationPageBackgroundThemeBrush}">
    </Grid>
</Page>
```

Now all you need to do to make this simple app work is add the "Hello Windows 8" text. Because this is a C#/XAML based application, you can use all the great XAML-based user interface controls. To simply display text on the screen, you can make use of the `TextBlock` control. The `TextBlock` control has a property called `Text` that you can set to `"Hello Windows 8"`. So to finish up this app, you simply add that control inside the current `Grid` tag, and the text appears in the app. The following is the updated version of the code with the `TextBlock` control.

LISTING 1-3: MainPage.xaml

```
<Page
    x:Class="HelloWindows.MainPage"
    xmlns="http://schemas.microsoft.com/winfx/2006/xaml/presentation"
    xmlns:x="http://schemas.microsoft.com/winfx/2006/xaml"
    xmlns:local="using:HelloWindows"
    xmlns:d="http://schemas.microsoft.com/expression/blend/2008"
    xmlns:mc="http://schemas.openxmlformats.org/markup-compatibility/2006"
    mc:Ignorable="d">

    <Grid Background="{StaticResource ApplicationPageBackgroundThemeBrush}">
        <TextBlock Text="Hello Windows 8" VerticalAlignment="Center"
HorizontalAlignment="Center" />      </Grid>
</Page>
```

Note in the previous code how a couple of properties were added to the `TextBlock` to ensure that the text centers both vertically and horizontally and appears in a large-sized font. All XAML controls have similar properties that you can adjust to affect elements common to all controls, such as alignments, fonts, size, and so on. You can see more of that in Chapter 2, "What is XAML?," which covers XAML and the available controls extensively.

Setting App Capabilities

The last thing you must do before running the application is ensure you've set up any device capabilities that your app requires. In Windows Store, apps don't have the abilities you've taken for granted with other forms of Windows development. For example, you can't simply make API calls to download information from the Internet without first declaring that your app requires this functionality.

This allows Windows Store apps running on a tablet to inform the user about what kinds of permissions the app need to run. If you've used any Android or iOS-based device, by now you've seen the permission request screen pop up before an application performs an action. Most App Stores now also list the required permissions and capabilities on the application download page so that users can make an informed decision as to whether they will purchase or download the app. Windows 8 is no different in that respect and your app needs to follow the same rules. Although a "Hello Windows" app realistically doesn't need many device features, pretend it at least requires Internet access, and see how to configure that for the app before running:

1. Find the `Package.appxmanifest` file in the Solution Explorer.

2. Double-click to bring up the application configuration screen, as shown in Figure 1-11.

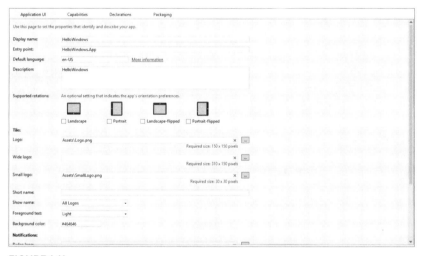

FIGURE 1-11

As you can see, you have several application properties that you can set from this initial screen, including the name and description of the app. You can use these to give the end user information about your app in the Windows Store App Store. You can also set the supported orientations for your app when you're running on a tablet. These include:

➤ Landscape

➤ Portrait

➤ Landscape-Flipped

➤ Portrait-Flipped

By default the initial orientation is Landscape.

3. The Application UI tab also gives you an easy way to change the logo files associated with your app and the overall background color of your app. Because you want the "Hello Windows 8" app to have Internet access, you must display the list of available Capabilities to choose from. Click the Capabilities tab to see the full list, as shown in Figure 1-12.

FIGURE 1-12

Depending on what features your app implements, you have various device capabilities for which you potentially need to request permission. Table 1-4 gives a brief description of what these capabilities provide for your app.

TABLE 1-4: Device Capabilities

CAPABILITY	DESCRIPTION/FEATURE
Documents Library	Can add/edit/create/delete documents in the Documents Library on the file system.
Enterprise Authentication	Performs domain credential authentication typically on a corporate LAN network.
Internet (Client & Server)	Downloads and uploads information to/from the Internet via Wi-Fi or cellular data connections.
Internet (Client)	Downloads information from the Internet via Wi-Fi or cellular data connections.
Location	Acquires location information through Wi-Fi/Cell Triangulation or GPS.
Microphone	Makes use of the built-in microphone where available.
Music Library	Gives apps access to music files that are indexed and stored in the Music Library on the file system.

Pictures Library	Gives apps access to picture files that are stored in the Pictures Library on the file system.
Private Networks (Client & Server)	Sends/receives data through private/home network firewall configurations.
Proximity	Sends/receives information to other devices within a close proximity of the originating device.
Removable Storage	Gives application and programmatic access to any connected external hard drives.
Shared User Certificates	Uses software/hardware certificates that may exist on alternative devices such as smartcards.
Videos Library	Gives apps access to video files that are indexed and stored in the Videos Library on the file system.
Webcam	Makes use of built-in webcam on device.

> **NOTE** *By default, every Windows Store app has the Internet capability set to true, so for this app you don't need to change any of the default settings.*

4. With the Capabilities and app properties set, your app is finally ready to launch. If you start the debugger, you should see your application running in full-screen mode on the primary display.

5. By default, the application runs in full screen on your primary display. But what if you want to see how this looks on a tablet? To find out, all you need to do is run the app in the simulator included in Visual Studio. To do this, just select the simulator from the debugging drop-down shown in Figure 1-13, and run the app again in the debugger.

FIGURE 1-13

Now when the app is run, the simulator takes over, and you have a full-blown tablet environment in which to preview your application, complete with the touch gestures and rotation enabled. Figure 1-14 shows the same "Hello Windows 8" app running under the simulator.

FIGURE 1-14

As you can see it's simple to create and run a basic Windows Store app and preview it both on the PC and on a tablet environment. Now what if your preferred language is C++? Well, then it gets even better. The same user interface code you used for the C# version works in a C++ environment. C# and C++ Windows Store apps both use XAML for the primary user interface code. If you go back and create the same "Hello Windows 8" project under the C++ language environment, the same `MainPage.xaml` file is created. The only difference is instead of a C# code behind, you get a C++ version of that same code behind like the one shown in Listing 1-4.

LISTING 1-4: MainPage.xaml.cpp

```
//
// MainPage.xaml.cpp
// Implementation of the MainPage class.
//

#include "pch.h"
#include "MainPage.xaml.h"
```

```
using namespace HelloWindowsC__;

using namespace Platform;
using namespace Windows::Foundation;
using namespace Windows::Foundation::Collections;
using namespace Windows::UI::Xaml;
using namespace Windows::UI::Xaml::Controls;
using namespace Windows::UI::Xaml::Controls::Primitives;
using namespace Windows::UI::Xaml::Data;
using namespace Windows::UI::Xaml::Input;
using namespace Windows::UI::Xaml::Media;
using namespace Windows::UI::Xaml::Navigation;

// The Blank Page item template is documented at
http://go.microsoft.com/fwlink/?LinkId=234238

MainPage::MainPage()
{
    InitializeComponent();
}

/// <summary>
/// Invoked when this page is about to be displayed in a Frame.
/// </summary>
/// <param name="e">Event data that describes how this page was reached.
/// The Parameterproperty is typically used to configure the page.
///</param>
void MainPage::OnNavigatedTo(NavigationEventArgs^ e)
{
    (void) e;    // Unused parameter
}
```

This code shows that you still have the same `OnNavigatedTo` event handler created in case you want to run some code when the page is presented to the user. The only thing that changes is that you use C++ instead of C#. The user interface stays the same.

What About HTML Developers?

In addition to C#/C++/VB.NET, you have the option to create Windows Store apps using HTML/CSS/JS. Although this book focuses primarily on C#/XAML development, this section takes a quick look at what the "Hello Windows 8" looks like if you came from the web development world and want to join the growing list of Windows developers.

For starters, if you use the blank application template shown in the previous C#/C++ examples, you can notice that the default files that you add to the project are slightly different. There are far fewer files in the HTML/JS version of the "Hello Windows 8" app. However, many of the same application features are still implemented in the default files, but instead of required C# code to perform operations, you can handle several using CSS and JavaScript. Table 1-5 defines what each of the default files is responsible for.

TABLE 1-5: Default HTML/JS files

FILE	TASK
`default.html`	The start screen for the app. You can chose another HTML file to be the first page in the app by modifying the application configuration settings.
`default.css`	Holds all the default style information for the page, including CSS for handling Full Screen and snapped views of the app.
`logo.png, smalllogo .png, splashscreen .png, storelogo.png`	Images are used as icons for tiles and the App Store.
`default.js`	Instead of having a direct code behind for the page as in ASP.NET or C#/C++ Windows Store apps, HTML/JS-based Windows Store apps rely on JavaScript files for event handling logic. `default.js` contains the event handler's equivalent to the C#/C++ `App.xaml.cs` and `App.xaml .cpp`, respectively. For the most part, you use this file to add application startup and shutdown code.

Now with the default files in place, you don't need to do much to add the required "Hello Windows 8" text to display. Just as you would in standard HTML programming, you can simply add a DIV tag and the text. Listing 1-5 shows the updated version of `default.html` that includes your "Hello Windows 8" text.

LISTING 1-5: default.html

```
<!DOCTYPE html>
<html>
<head>
<meta charset="utf-8" />
<title>HelloWindowsJS</title>

<!-- WinJS references -->
<link href="//Microsoft.WinJS.1.0/css/ui-dark.css" rel="stylesheet" />
<script src="//Microsoft.WinJS.1.0/js/base.js"></script>
<script src="//Microsoft.WinJS.1.0/js/ui.js"></script>

<!-- HelloWindowsJS references -->
<link href="/css/default.css" rel="stylesheet" />
<script src="/js/default.js"></script>
</head>
<body>
    <div>Hello Windows 8</div>
</body>
</html>
```

In the C#/XAML version, the text is centered on the screen. You can still do this with the HTML version simply by using standard CSS code. Adding a class or id to the DIV tag and appropriate margin code does the trick. This changes the DIV to the following:

```
<div class="centered">hello Windows 8</div>
```

In the `default.css` file, you can add CSS to center the text. Listing 1-6 shows the updated `default.css` file.

LISTING 1-6: css\default.css

```
body {
}

@media screen and (-ms-view-state: fullscreen-landscape) {
}

@media screen and (-ms-view-state: filled) {
}

@media screen and (-ms-view-state: snapped) {
}

@media screen and (-ms-view-state: fullscreen-portrait) {
}

.centered {
    text-align: center;
}
```

If you build and run the app at this point, you'll see the same app as before with text centered horizontally on the screen but not vertically. This is no different than any other types of web development because there is still no solid way to do vertical centering through CSS alone. However, you have CSS additions for Windows 8/IE 10 development that enable you to duplicate the grid-based layout of the XAML app created in the previous code that let you add the vertical centering of the text.

TYPES OF WINDOWS STORE APPS

When you start a Windows 8 development project, Visual Studio has several different project templates from which to choose. Depending on the type of app you plan to create, these templates can give you a great starting point for layout and coding best practices. These templates include the following:

➤ **Blank app:** Just an empty Windows Store app template that gives you only the basic shell required to run an app.

➤ **Grid app:** Creates a grid based user interface for your app where content is grouped in a grid. You can access detailed information and perform additional actions by having the user interact with the groups.

➤ **Split app:** Provides a different take on the grid-based application. This type of application has a split view of both the grid content and the detailed content at the same time.

Before doing any Windows Store app development, the thing you need to decide is the type of application you plan to build and which of the previous templates to use for your starting point. The following sections take an in-depth look at the Grid and Split templates and how they might best serve particular types of Windows Store apps.

Grid Applications

The goal of the grid application template is to give you an easy way to present collections of information that the user navigates within a group. For example, if your app intends to present something such as a music collection, you might use this template to show particular genres, followed by artists that fall into that genre. This template also enables the user to touch or click on a particular genre or artist and view additional information about that artist while enabling the user to seamlessly navigate between artists and ultimately back to the starting point. Now modify the project that this template creates to do just that: Create a new C#/XAML Windows Store project in Visual Studio called ArtistBrowser, and select the Grid App template.

After the project is created, you have several new files added to the Solution Explorer. Table 1-6 covers these at a high level.

TABLE 1-6: Default Grid Template Files

FILE	TASK
GroupedItemsPage .xaml	The start page for the app, this shows a scrolling list of groups along with group items.
GroupDetailPage .xaml	If the user clicks a group header from the Start page, the app navigates to this page, which displays all the items from the group.
ItemDetailPage .xaml	This final page is responsible for showing detailed information for an item that the user selected on the group on the previous screen.
DataModel\ SampleData Source.cs	Contains classes that hold the sample data. In this file, there are classes for Items, Groups, and the overall Group collection. There is also a class that populates the default data with sample information. Data binding is used extensively in the app, and the classes in this file are the main objects being bound to.

Setting the App's Start Page

In this example, the app starts with the GroupedItemsPage, which is the top-level collection of groups. As you saw previously, the default starting page is set in the App.xaml.cs file, as shown in Listing 1-7.

LISTING 1-7: App.xaml.cs

```
using ArtistBrowser.Common;

using System;
using System.Collections.Generic;
using System.IO;
using System.Linq;
using Windows.ApplicationModel;
using Windows.ApplicationModel.Activation;
using Windows.Foundation;
using Windows.Foundation.Collections;
using Windows.UI.Xaml;
using Windows.UI.Xaml.Controls;
using Windows.UI.Xaml.Controls.Primitives;
using Windows.UI.Xaml.Data;
using Windows.UI.Xaml.Input;
using Windows.UI.Xaml.Media;
using Windows.UI.Xaml.Navigation;

// The Grid App template is documented at
// http://go.microsoft.com/fwlink/?LinkId=234226

namespace ArtistBrowser
{
    /// <summary>
    /// Provides application-specific behavior to supplement
    ///the default Application class.
    /// </summary>
    sealed partial class App : Application
    {
        /// <summary>
        /// Initializes the singleton Application object.
        /// This is the first line of authored code
        /// executed, and as such is the logical equivalent
        /// of main() or WinMain().
        /// </summary>
        public App()
        {
            this.InitializeComponent();
            this.Suspending += OnSuspending;
        }

        /// <summary>
        /// Invoked when the application is launched normally by
        /// the end user.       Other entry points
        /// will be used when the application is launched to
        /// open a specific file, to display
```

continues

LISTING 1-7 *(continued)*

```
/// search results, and so forth.
/// </summary>
/// <param name="args">Details about the launch request
/// and process.</param>
protected override async void OnLaunched(LaunchActivatedEventArgs args)
{
    Frame rootFrame = Window.Current.Content as Frame;

    // Do not repeat app initialization when the
    // Window already has content,
    // just ensure that the window is active

    if (rootFrame == null)
    {
        // Create a Frame to act as the navigation
        // context and navigate to the first page
        rootFrame = new Frame();
        //Associate the frame with a SuspensionManager key
        SuspensionManager.RegisterFrame(rootFrame, "AppFrame");

        if (args.PreviousExecutionState ==
ApplicationExecutionState.Terminated)
        {
            // Restore the saved session state only when appropriate
            try
            {
                await SuspensionManager.RestoreAsync();
            }
            catch (SuspensionManagerException)
            {
                //Something went wrong restoring state.
                //Assume there is no state and continue
            }
        }

        // Place the frame in the current Window
        Window.Current.Content = rootFrame;
    }
    if (rootFrame.Content == null)
    {
        // When the navigation stack isn't restored
        // navigate to the first page,
        // configuring the new page by passing required
        // information as a navigation
        // parameter
        if (!rootFrame.Navigate(typeof(GroupedItemsPage), "AllGroups"))
        {
            throw new Exception("Failed to create initial page");
        }
    }
        // Ensure the current window is active
```

```
                    Window.Current.Activate();
        }

        /// <summary>
        /// Invoked when application execution is being suspended.
        /// Application state is saved
        /// without knowing whether the application will be
        /// terminated or resumed with the contents
        /// of memory still intact.
        /// </summary>
        /// <param name="sender">The source of the suspend request.</param>
        /// <param name="e">Details about the suspend request.</param>
        private async void OnSuspending(object sender, SuspendingEventArgs e)
        {
            var deferral = e.SuspendingOperation.GetDeferral();
            await SuspensionManager.SaveAsync();
            deferral.Complete();
        }
    }
}
```

Again you can set the default start page in the `OnLaunched` event handler by changing the parameter of the `Navigate` method for the main `Frame` object, as shown in the following code:

```
    if (!rootFrame.Navigate(typeof(GroupedItemsPage), "AllGroups"))
```

You see more about what the `Frame` object is in Chapter 4, but for now think of it in terms of web browsing in that the `Frame` simply offers you methods that control what page is currently visible using browsing type constructs such as `Navigate`, `Back`, `Forward`, and so on.

Setting Scrolling and Layout Controls

The `GroupedItemsPage.xaml` page contains the user interface for displaying the scrolling collection of groups. In the code for the page shown in Listing 1-8, you can see that XAML layout controls such as the `Grid` and `ScrollViewer` take care of the overall layout, while internally has a `GridView` control that uses data binding to take care of the individual group item display.

LISTING 1-8: **GroupedItemsPage.xaml**

```
<common:LayoutAwarePage
    x:Name="pageRoot"
    x:Class="ArtistBrowser.GroupedItemsPage"
    DataContext="{Binding DefaultViewModel, RelativeSource={RelativeSource Self}}"
    xmlns="http://schemas.microsoft.com/winfx/2006/xaml/presentation"
    xmlns:x="http://schemas.microsoft.com/winfx/2006/xaml"
    xmlns:local="using:ArtistBrowser"
    xmlns:data="using:ArtistBrowser.Data"
    xmlns:common="using:ArtistBrowser.Common"
    xmlns:d="http://schemas.microsoft.com/expression/blend/2008"
    xmlns:mc="http://schemas.openxmlformats.org/markup-compatibility/2006"
    mc:Ignorable="d">
```

continues

LISTING 1-8 *(continued)*

```
<Page.Resources>

<!--
    Collection of grouped items displayed by this page, bound to a subset
    of the complete item list because items in groups cannot be virtualized
-->
    <CollectionViewSource
        x:Name="groupedItemsViewSource"
        Source="{Binding Groups}"
        IsSourceGrouped="true"
        ItemsPath="TopItems"
        d:Source="{Binding AllGroups, Source={d:DesignInstance
Type=data:SampleDataSource, IsDesignTimeCreatable=True}}"/>
    </Page.Resources>

<!--
    This grid acts as a root panel for the page that defines two rows:
    * Row 0 contains the back button and page title
    * Row 1 contains the rest of the page layout
-->
    <Grid Style="{StaticResource LayoutRootStyle}">
        <Grid.RowDefinitions>
            <RowDefinition Height="140"/>
            <RowDefinition Height="*"/>
        </Grid.RowDefinitions>

        <!-- Horizontal scrolling grid used in most view states -->
        <GridView
            x:Name="itemGridView"
            AutomationProperties.AutomationId="ItemGridView"
            AutomationProperties.Name="Grouped Items"
            Grid.RowSpan="2"
            Padding="116,137,40,46"
            ItemsSource="{Binding Source={StaticResource
groupedItemsViewSource}}"
            ItemTemplate="{StaticResource Standard250x250ItemTemplate}"
            SelectionMode="None"
            IsSwipeEnabled="false"
            IsItemClickEnabled="True"
            ItemClick="ItemView_ItemClick">

            <GridView.ItemsPanel>
                <ItemsPanelTemplate>
                    <VirtualizingStackPanel Orientation="Horizontal"/>
                </ItemsPanelTemplate>
            </GridView.ItemsPanel>
            <GridView.GroupStyle>
                <GroupStyle>
                    <GroupStyle.HeaderTemplate>
                        <DataTemplate>
                            <Grid Margin="1,0,0,6">
                                <Button
```

```xml
                                                   AutomationProperties.Name="Group
Title"
                                                   Click="Header_Click"
                                                   Style="{StaticResource
TextPrimaryButtonStyle}" >

                                                   <StackPanel Orientation="Horizontal">
                                                       <TextBlock Text="{Binding Title}"
Margin="3,-7,10,10" Style="{StaticResource GroupHeaderTextStyle}" />
                                                       <TextBlock Text="{StaticResource
ChevronGlyph}" FontFamily="Segoe UI Symbol" Margin="0,-7,0,10"
Style="{StaticResource GroupHeaderTextStyle}"/>
                                                   </StackPanel>
                                               </Button>
                                           </Grid>
                                       </DataTemplate>
                                   </GroupStyle.HeaderTemplate>
                           <GroupStyle.Panel>
                               <ItemsPanelTemplate>
                                   <VariableSizedWrapGrid Orientation="Vertical"
Margin="0,0,80,0"/>
                               </ItemsPanelTemplate>
                           </GroupStyle.Panel>
                       </GroupStyle>
                   </GridView.GroupStyle>
           </GridView>

           <!-- Vertical scrolling list only used when snapped -->
           <ListView
               x:Name="itemListView"
               AutomationProperties.AutomationId="ItemListView"
               AutomationProperties.Name="Grouped Items"
               Grid.Row="1"
               Visibility="Collapsed"
               Margin="0,-10,0,0"
               Padding="10,0,0,60"
               ItemsSource="{Binding Source={StaticResource groupedItemsViewSource}}"
               ItemTemplate="{StaticResource Standard80ItemTemplate}"
               SelectionMode="None"
               IsSwipeEnabled="false"
               IsItemClickEnabled="True"
               ItemClick="ItemView_ItemClick">

               <ListView.GroupStyle>
                   <GroupStyle>
                       <GroupStyle.HeaderTemplate>
                           <DataTemplate>
                               <Grid Margin="7,7,0,0">
                                   <Button
                                       AutomationProperties.Name="Group Title"
                                       Click="Header_Click"
Style="{StaticResource
TextPrimaryButtonStyle}">

                                       <StackPanel Orientation="Horizontal">
                                           <TextBlock Text="{Binding Title}"
```

continues

LISTING 1-8 *(continued)*

```xml
Margin="3,-7,10,10" Style="{StaticResource GroupHeaderTextStyle}" />
                                        <TextBlock Text="{StaticResource
ChevronGlyph}" FontFamily="Segoe UI Symbol" Margin="0,-7,0,10"
Style="{StaticResource GroupHeaderTextStyle}"/>
                                        </StackPanel>
                                    </Button>
                                </Grid>
                            </DataTemplate>
                        </GroupStyle.HeaderTemplate>
                    </GroupStyle>
                </ListView.GroupStyle>
            </ListView>

            <!-- Back button and page title -->
            <Grid>
                <Grid.ColumnDefinitions>
                    <ColumnDefinition Width="Auto"/>
                    <ColumnDefinition Width="*"/>
                </Grid.ColumnDefinitions>
                <Button x:Name="backButton" Click="GoBack"
IsEnabled="{Binding Frame.CanGoBack, ElementName=pageRoot}"
Style="{StaticResource BackButtonStyle}"/>
                    <TextBlock x:Name="pageTitle" Text="{StaticResource AppName}"
Grid.Column="1" IsHitTestVisible="false" Style="{StaticResource
PageHeaderTextStyle}"/>
            </Grid>

            <VisualStateManager.VisualStateGroups>

            <!-- Visual states reflect the application's view state -->
                <VisualStateGroup x:Name="ApplicationViewStates">
                    <VisualState x:Name="FullScreenLandscape"/>
                    <VisualState x:Name="Filled"/>

                    <!-- The entire page respects the narrower 100-pixel
                        margin convention for portrait -->
                    <VisualState x:Name="FullScreenPortrait">
                        <Storyboard>
                            <ObjectAnimationUsingKeyFrames
Storyboard.TargetName="backButton" Storyboard.TargetProperty="Style">
                                <DiscreteObjectKeyFrame KeyTime="0"
Value="{StaticResource PortraitBackButtonStyle}"/>
                            </ObjectAnimationUsingKeyFrames>

                            <ObjectAnimationUsingKeyFrames
Storyboard.TargetName="itemGridView" Storyboard.TargetProperty="Padding">
                                <DiscreteObjectKeyFrame KeyTime="0"
Value="96,137,10,56"/>
                            </ObjectAnimationUsingKeyFrames>
                        </Storyboard>
                    </VisualState>
```

```
                    <!-- The back button and title have different styles
                         when snapped, and the list representation is substituted
                         for the grid displayed in all other view states
                    -->
                    <VisualState x:Name="Snapped">
                        <Storyboard>
                            <ObjectAnimationUsingKeyFrames
    Storyboard.TargetName="backButton" Storyboard.TargetProperty="Style">
                                <DiscreteObjectKeyFrame KeyTime="0"
    Value="{StaticResource SnappedBackButtonStyle}"/>
                            </ObjectAnimationUsingKeyFrames>
                            <ObjectAnimationUsingKeyFrames
    Storyboard.TargetName="pageTitle" Storyboard.TargetProperty="Style">
                                <DiscreteObjectKeyFrame KeyTime="0"
    Value="{StaticResource SnappedPageHeaderTextStyle}"/>
                            </ObjectAnimationUsingKeyFrames>

                            <ObjectAnimationUsingKeyFrames
    Storyboard.TargetName="itemListView" Storyboard.TargetProperty="Visibility">
                                <DiscreteObjectKeyFrame KeyTime="0" Value="Visible"/>
                            </ObjectAnimationUsingKeyFrames>
                            <ObjectAnimationUsingKeyFrames
    Storyboard.TargetName="itemGridView" Storyboard.TargetProperty="Visibility">
                                <DiscreteObjectKeyFrame KeyTime="0"
    Value="Collapsed"/>
                            </ObjectAnimationUsingKeyFrames>
                        </Storyboard>
                    </VisualState>
                </VisualStateGroup>
            </VisualStateManager.VisualStateGroups>
        </Grid>
    </common:LayoutAwarePage>
```

Grouping Items

Because the default data isn't terribly useful when the application starts, now tackle that problem. If you look at the SampleDataSource.cs file, you might notice something different about that file.

1. Double-clicking the file expands only the file further, which is not typical Visual Studio behavior. Visual Studio 2012 offers a great feature that actually splits multiple classes that have been defined in one source file into multiple objects in the Solution Explorer. In Figure 1-15 you can see that all four defined classes have their own clickable area to help you quickly navigate to the defined class.

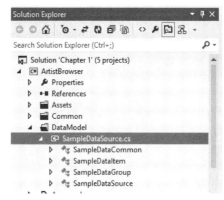

FIGURE 1-15

2. The default data is defined in the `SampleDataSource` class. Because this sample becomes an ArtistBrowser, for this example, change some of the groups and items to reflect something more meaningful such as musical genres and artists within those genres. Replace the `SampleDataSource` class code in the `SampleDataSource.cs` file with the following code:

```
public SampleDataSource()
{
    String ITEM_CONTENT = String.Format("Item Content:
{0}\n\n{0}\n\n{0}\n\n{0}\n\n{0}\n\n{0}\n\n{0}",
"Curabitur class aliquam vestibulum nam curae maecenas sed");

    var group1 = new SampleDataGroup("Rock",
"Group Title: Rock",
"Group Subtitle: Rock Bands",
"Assets/DarkGray.png",
"Group Description: Lorem ipsum dolor sit amet, consectetur
    adipiscing elit. ");
    group1.Items.Add(new SampleDataItem("Aerosmith",
"Item Title: Aerosmith",
"Item Subtitle: ",
"Assets/LightGray.png",
"Item Description: Pellentesque porta, mauris quis interdum
vehicula, urna sapien ultrices velit.",
ITEM_CONTENT,
group1));
    group1.Items.Add(new SampleDataItem("Guns N Roses",
"Item Title: Guns N Roses",
"Item Subtitle: ",
"Assets/DarkGray.png",
"Item Description: Pellentesque porta, mauris quis interdum vehicula.",
ITEM_CONTENT,
group1));
    group1.Items.Add(new SampleDataItem("KISS",
"Item Title: KISS",
"Item Subtitle: ",
"Assets/MediumGray.png",
"Item Description: Pellentesque porta, mauris quis interdum
vehicula, urna sapien ultrices velit.",
ITEM_CONTENT,
group1));

    this.AllGroups.Add(group1);

    var group2 = new SampleDataGroup("Metal",
"Group Title: Metal",
"Group Subtitle: Heavy Metal Bands",
"Assets/LightGray.png",
"Group Description: Lorem ipsum dolor sit amet, consectetur
    adipiscing elit.");
    group2.Items.Add(new SampleDataItem("Iron Maiden",
"Item Title: Iron Maiden",
"Item Subtitle: ",
"Assets/DarkGray.png",
"Item Description: Pellentesque porta, mauris quis interdum vehicula.",
ITEM_CONTENT,
group2));
```

```
      group2.Items.Add(new SampleDataItem("Metallica",
"Item Title: Metallica",
"Item Subtitle: ",
"Assets/MediumGray.png",
"Item Description: Pellentesque porta, mauris quis interdum
vehicula, urna sapien ultrices velit.",
ITEM_CONTENT,
group2));
      group2.Items.Add(new SampleDataItem("Megadeth",
"Item Title: Megadeth",
"Item Subtitle: ",
"Assets/LightGray.png",
"Item Description: Pellentesque porta, mauris quis interdum vehicula.",
ITEM_CONTENT,
group2));
    this.AllGroups.Add(group2);

    var group3 = new SampleDataGroup("Country",
"Group Title: Country",
"Group Subtitle: Country Music Bands",
"Assets/MediumGray.png",
"Group Description: Lorem ipsum dolor sit amet, consectetur
    adipiscing elit.");
      group3.Items.Add(new SampleDataItem("Garth Brooks",
"Item Title: Garth Brooks",
"Item Subtitle: ",
"Assets/MediumGray.png",
"Item Description: Pellentesque porta, mauris quis interdum
vehicula, urna sapien ultrices velit.",
ITEM_CONTENT,
group3));
      group3.Items.Add(new SampleDataItem("Kenny Chesney",
"Item Title: Kenny Chesney",
"Item Subtitle: ",
"Assets/LightGray.png",
"Item Description: Pellentesque porta, mauris quis interdum vehicula.",
ITEM_CONTENT,
group3));
    group3.Items.Add(new SampleDataItem("Darius Rucker",
"Item Title: Darius Rucker",
"Item Subtitle: ",
"Assets/DarkGray.png",
"Item Description: Pellentesque porta, mauris quis interdum vehicula.",
ITEM_CONTENT,
group3));
    group3.Items.Add(new SampleDataItem("Rascal Flatts",
"Item Title: Rascal Flatts",
"Item Subtitle: ",
"Assets/LightGray.png",
"Item Description: Pellentesque porta, mauris quis interdum vehicula.",
ITEM_CONTENT,
group3));

    this.AllGroups.Add(group3);
}
```

3. You still leave some of the Lorum Ipsum text as filler, and in this case you do not update the images because this is just a quick sample.

4. If you build and run the app, on the Start page you can see the rock, metal, and country groups with the associated artists displayed, as shown in Figure 1-16.

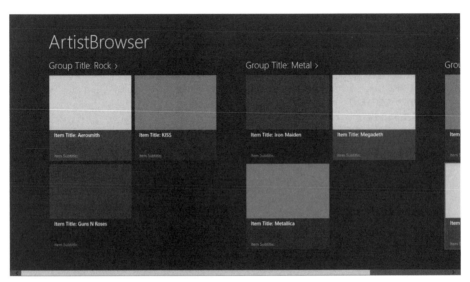

FIGURE 1-16

5. If you touch or click the genre heading, the GroupDetailPage displays, as shown in Figure 1-17, which provides additional group details, including a larger image for the group and a scrolling list of artists.

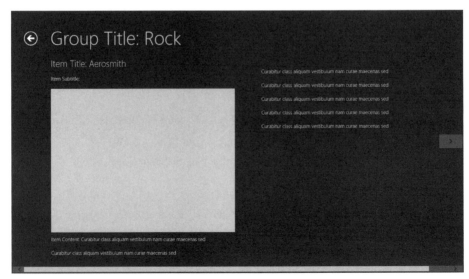

FIGURE 1-17

6. Use similar `Grid`, `ScrollViewer`, and `GridView` controls on this page to display the genre and artist information but in a more detailed format. Listing 1-9 shows the XAML source code.

LISTING 1-9: GroupDetailPage.xaml

```xaml
<common:LayoutAwarePage
    x:Name="pageRoot"
    x:Class="ArtistBrowser.GroupDetailPage"
DataContext="{Binding DefaultViewModel, RelativeSource={RelativeSource Self}}"
    xmlns="http://schemas.microsoft.com/winfx/2006/xaml/presentation"
    xmlns:x="http://schemas.microsoft.com/winfx/2006/xaml"
    xmlns:local="using:ArtistBrowser"
    xmlns:data="using:ArtistBrowser.Data"
    xmlns:common="using:ArtistBrowser.Common"
    xmlns:d="http://schemas.microsoft.com/expression/blend/2008"
    xmlns:mc="http://schemas.openxmlformats.org/markup-compatibility/2006"
    mc:Ignorable="d">

    <Page.Resources>

    <!-- Collection of items displayed by this page -->
    <CollectionViewSource
        x:Name="itemsViewSource"
        Source="{Binding Items}"
        d:Source="{Binding AllGroups[0].Items,
Source={d:DesignInstance Type=data:SampleDataSource,
IsDesignTimeCreatable=True}}"/>
    </Page.Resources>

    <!--
        This grid acts as a root panel for the page that defines two rows:
        * Row 0 contains the back button and page title
        * Row 1 contains the rest of the page layout
    -->
    <Grid
        Style="{StaticResource LayoutRootStyle}"
        DataContext="{Binding Group}"
        d:DataContext="{Binding AllGroups[0],
Source={d:DesignInstance Type=data:SampleDataSource,
IsDesignTimeCreatable=True}}">

        <Grid.RowDefinitions>
            <RowDefinition Height="140"/>
            <RowDefinition Height="*"/>
        </Grid.RowDefinitions>

        <!-- Horizontal scrolling grid used in most view states -->
        <GridView
            x:Name="itemGridView"
            AutomationProperties.AutomationId="ItemGridView"
            AutomationProperties.Name="Items In Group"
            TabIndex="1"
```

continues

LISTING 1-9 *(continued)*

```
                Grid.RowSpan="2"
                Padding="120,126,120,50"
                ItemsSource="{Binding Source={StaticResource itemsViewSource}}"
                ItemTemplate="{StaticResource Standard500x130ItemTemplate}"
                SelectionMode="None"
                IsSwipeEnabled="false"
                IsItemClickEnabled="True"
                ItemClick="ItemView_ItemClick">

                <GridView.Header>
                    <StackPanel Width="480" Margin="0,4,14,0">
                        <TextBlock Text="{Binding Subtitle}" Margin="0,0,18,20"
Style="{StaticResource SubheaderTextStyle}" MaxHeight="60"/>
                        <Image Source="{Binding Image}" Height="400"
Margin="0,0,18,20" Stretch="UniformToFill"
AutomationProperties.Name="{Binding Title}"/>
                        <TextBlock Text="{Binding Description}"
Margin="0,0,18,0" Style="{StaticResource BodyTextStyle}"/>
                    </StackPanel>
                </GridView.Header>
                <GridView.ItemContainerStyle>
                    <Style TargetType="FrameworkElement">
                        <Setter Property="Margin" Value="52,0,0,10"/>
                    </Style>
                </GridView.ItemContainerStyle>
            </GridView>

            <!-- Vertical scrolling list only used when snapped -->
            <ListView
                x:Name="itemListView"
                AutomationProperties.AutomationId="ItemListView"
                AutomationProperties.Name="Items In Group"
                TabIndex="1"
                Grid.Row="1"
                Visibility="Collapsed"
                Padding="10,0,0,60"
                ItemsSource="{Binding Source={StaticResource itemsViewSource}}"
                ItemTemplate="{StaticResource Standard80ItemTemplate}"
                SelectionMode="None"
                IsSwipeEnabled="false"
                IsItemClickEnabled="True"
                ItemClick="ItemView_ItemClick">

                <ListView.Header>
                    <StackPanel>
                        <TextBlock Text="{Binding Subtitle}"
Margin="10,0,18,20" Style="{StaticResource TitleTextStyle}" MaxHeight="60"/>
                        <Image Source="{Binding Image}" Margin="10,0,18,0"
MaxHeight="160" Stretch="UniformToFill"
AutomationProperties.Name="{Binding Title}"/>
                        <TextBlock Margin="10,20,18,30"
Text="{Binding Description}" Style="{StaticResource BodyTextStyle}"/>
                    </StackPanel>
```

```
                    </ListView.Header>
            </ListView>

            <!-- Back button and page title -->
            <Grid>
                    <Grid.ColumnDefinitions>
                          <ColumnDefinition Width="Auto"/>
                          <ColumnDefinition Width="*"/>
                    </Grid.ColumnDefinitions>
                    <Button x:Name="backButton" Click="GoBack" IsEnabled="{Binding
Frame.CanGoBack, ElementName=pageRoot}" Style="{StaticResource
BackButtonStyle}"/>
                          <TextBlock x:Name="pageTitle" Text="{Binding Title}"
Style="{StaticResource PageHeaderTextStyle}" Grid.Column="1"
IsHitTestVisible="false"/>
            </Grid>

            <VisualStateManager.VisualStateGroups>

            <!-- Visual states reflect the application's view state -->
                    <VisualStateGroup x:Name="ApplicationViewStates">
                          <VisualState x:Name="FullScreenLandscape"/>
                          <VisualState x:Name="Filled"/>

                          <!-- The entire page respects the narrower
                                100-pixel margin convention for portrait -->
                          <VisualState x:Name="FullScreenPortrait">
                                <Storyboard>
                                      <ObjectAnimationUsingKeyFrames
Storyboard.TargetName="backButton" Storyboard.TargetProperty="Style">
                                            <DiscreteObjectKeyFrame KeyTime="0"
Value="{StaticResource PortraitBackButtonStyle}"/>
                                      </ObjectAnimationUsingKeyFrames>

                                      <ObjectAnimationUsingKeyFrames
Storyboard.TargetName="itemGridView" Storyboard.TargetProperty="Padding">
                                            <DiscreteObjectKeyFrame KeyTime="0"
Value="100,126,90,0"/>
                                      </ObjectAnimationUsingKeyFrames>
                                </Storyboard>
                          </VisualState>

                          <!--
                                The back button and title have different
                                styles when snapped, and the list representation
                                is substituted
                                for the grid displayed in all other view states
                          -->
                          <VisualState x:Name="Snapped">
                                <Storyboard>
                                      <ObjectAnimationUsingKeyFrames
Storyboard.TargetName="backButton" Storyboard.TargetProperty="Style">
                                            <DiscreteObjectKeyFrame KeyTime="0"
Value="{StaticResource SnappedBackButtonStyle}"/>
                                      </ObjectAnimationUsingKeyFrames>
```

continues

LISTING 1-9 *(continued)*

```
                              <ObjectAnimationUsingKeyFrames
Storyboard.TargetName="pageTitle" Storyboard.TargetProperty="Style">
                              <DiscreteObjectKeyFrame KeyTime="0"
Value="{StaticResource SnappedPageHeaderTextStyle}"/>
                              </ObjectAnimationUsingKeyFrames>

                              <ObjectAnimationUsingKeyFrames
Storyboard.TargetName="itemGridView" Storyboard.TargetProperty="Visibility">
                              <DiscreteObjectKeyFrame KeyTime="0"
Value="Collapsed"/>
                              </ObjectAnimationUsingKeyFrames>
                              <ObjectAnimationUsingKeyFrames
Storyboard.TargetName="itemListView" Storyboard.TargetProperty="Visibility">
                              <DiscreteObjectKeyFrame KeyTime="0"
Value="Visible"/>
                              </ObjectAnimationUsingKeyFrames>
                        </Storyboard>
                    </VisualState>
                </VisualStateGroup>
          </VisualStateManager.VisualStateGroups>
    </Grid>
</common:LayoutAwarePage>
```

> **NOTE**   *All these pages inherit from the* LayoutAwarePage *class, as discussed earlier. This ensures support for orientation changes as well as notification for when you should use the snapped view for the layout.*

7.   Touch or click one of the individual artists, either from the Start page or from the group details page, to see the item detail page, as shown in Figure 1-18, which in this case is potentially a more detailed look at the artist.

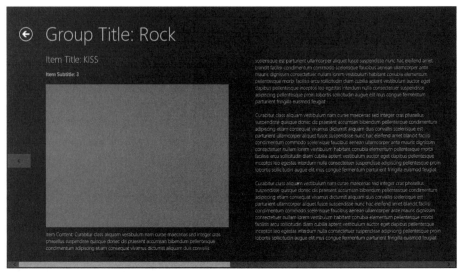

FIGURE 1-18

This page is unique because it uses a control called the `FlipView`, which enables the user to scroll through additional artists without having to navigate back to the group view. Of course, users always have the option to go back using the back arrow or the header navigation, but the `FlipView` is nice because any artist information for that group is available no matter which artist is actually touched or clicked. Listing 1-10 shows the code containing the `FlipView` bound to the same collection of artists that the group page uses when binding to the `GridView` control.

LISTING 1-10: ItemDetailPage.xaml

```xml
<common:LayoutAwarePage
    x:Name="pageRoot"
    x:Class="ArtistBrowser.ItemDetailPage"
    DataContext="{Binding DefaultViewModel, RelativeSource={RelativeSource Self}}"
    xmlns="http://schemas.microsoft.com/winfx/2006/xaml/presentation"
    xmlns:x="http://schemas.microsoft.com/winfx/2006/xaml"
    xmlns:local="using:ArtistBrowser"
    xmlns:data="using:ArtistBrowser.Data"
    xmlns:common="using:ArtistBrowser.Common"
    xmlns:d="http://schemas.microsoft.com/expression/blend/2008"
    xmlns:mc="http://schemas.openxmlformats.org/markup-compatibility/2006"
    mc:Ignorable="d">

    <Page.Resources>

        <!-- Collection of items displayed by this page -->
        <CollectionViewSource
            x:Name="itemsViewSource"
            Source="{Binding Items}"
            d:Source="{Binding AllGroups[0].Items,
Source={d:DesignInstance Type=data:SampleDataSource,
IsDesignTimeCreatable=True}}"/>
    </Page.Resources>

    <!--
        This grid acts as a root panel for the page that defines two rows:
        * Row 0 contains the back button and page title
        * Row 1 contains the rest of the page layout
    -->
    <Grid
Style="{StaticResource LayoutRootStyle}"
DataContext="{Binding Group}"
d:DataContext="{Binding AllGroups[0], Source={d:DesignInstance
Type=data:SampleDataSource, IsDesignTimeCreatable=True}}">

        <Grid.RowDefinitions>
            <RowDefinition Height="140"/>
            <RowDefinition Height="*"/>
        </Grid.RowDefinitions>

        <!--
            The remainder of the page is one large FlipView that
            displays details for one item at a time, allowing the
```

continues

LISTING 1-10 *(continued)*

```
                    user to flip through all items in the chosengroup
            -->
            <FlipView
                x:Name="flipView"
                AutomationProperties.AutomationId="ItemsFlipView"
                AutomationProperties.Name="Item Details"
                TabIndex="1"
                Grid.RowSpan="2"
                ItemsSource="{Binding Source={StaticResource itemsViewSource}}">

                <FlipView.ItemContainerStyle>
                    <Style TargetType="FlipViewItem">
                        <Setter Property="Margin" Value="0,137,0,0"/>
                    </Style>
                </FlipView.ItemContainerStyle>

                <FlipView.ItemTemplate>
                    <DataTemplate>

                    <!--
                        UserControl chosen as the templated item because it
                        supports visual state management Loaded/unloaded events
                       explicitly subscribe to view state updates from the page
                    -->
                        <UserControl Loaded="StartLayoutUpdates"
Unloaded="StopLayoutUpdates">
                            <ScrollViewer x:Name="scrollViewer"
Style="{StaticResource HorizontalScrollViewerStyle}" Grid.Row="1">

                                <!-- Content is allowed to flow across as
many columns as needed -->
                                    <common:RichTextColumns
x:Name="richTextColumns" Margin="117,0,117,47">
                                        <RichTextBlock x:Name="richTextBlock"
Width="560" Style="{StaticResource ItemRichTextStyle}"
IsTextSelectionEnabled="False">
                                            <Paragraph>
                                                <Run FontSize="26.667"
FontWeight="Light" Text="{Binding Title}"/>

                                                <LineBreak/>
                                                <LineBreak/>
                                                <Run FontWeight="Normal"
Text="{Binding Subtitle}"/>
                                            </Paragraph>
                                            <Paragraph
LineStackingStrategy="MaxHeight">

                                                <InlineUIContainer>
                                                    <Image x:Name="image"
MaxHeight="480" Margin="0,20,0,10" Stretch="Uniform" Source="{Binding Image}"
AutomationProperties.Name="{Binding Title}"/>

                                                </InlineUIContainer>
                                            </Paragraph>
                                            <Paragraph>
                                                <Run FontWeight="SemiLight"
```

```
Text="{Binding Content}"/>
                                                    </Paragraph>
                                          </RichTextBlock>

                                          <!-- Additional columns are created
from this template -->
                                          <common:RichTextColumns.
ColumnTemplate>
                                              <DataTemplate>
                                                  <RichTextBlockOverflow
Width="560" Margin="80,0,0,0">
                                                <RichTextBlockOverflow.
RenderTransform>
                                                      <TranslateTransform X="-1"
Y="4"/>
                                                </RichTextBlockOverflow.
RenderTransform>
                                                  </RichTextBlockOverflow>
                                              </DataTemplate>
                                          </common:RichTextColumns.
ColumnTemplate>
                                      </common:RichTextColumns>

        <VisualStateManager.VisualStateGroups>

        <!-- Visual states reflect the application's view state inside
the FlipView -->
                <VisualStateGroup x:Name="ApplicationViewStates">
                    <VisualState x:Name="FullScreenLandscape"/>
                    <VisualState x:Name="Filled"/>

                    <!-- Respect the narrower 100-pixel margin convention
for portrait -->
                    <VisualState x:Name="FullScreenPortrait">
                        <Storyboard>
                            <ObjectAnimationUsingKeyFrames
Storyboard.TargetName="richTextColumns" Storyboard.TargetProperty="Margin">
                                <DiscreteObjectKeyFrame KeyTime="0"
Value="97,0,87,57"/>
                            </ObjectAnimationUsingKeyFrames>
                            <ObjectAnimationUsingKeyFrames
Storyboard.TargetName="image" Storyboard.TargetProperty="MaxHeight">
                                <DiscreteObjectKeyFrame KeyTime="0"
Value="400"/>
                            </ObjectAnimationUsingKeyFrames>
                        </Storyboard>
                    </VisualState>

                    <!-- When snapped, the content is reformatted and
scrolls vertically -->
                    <VisualState x:Name="Snapped">
                        <Storyboard>
                            <ObjectAnimationUsingKeyFrames
Storyboard.TargetName="richTextColumns" Storyboard.TargetProperty="Margin">
                                <DiscreteObjectKeyFrame KeyTime="0"
```

continues

LISTING 1-10 *(continued)*

```
Value="17,0,17,57"/>
                                    </ObjectAnimationUsingKeyFrames>
                                    <ObjectAnimationUsingKeyFrames
Storyboard.TargetName="scrollViewer" Storyboard.TargetProperty="Style">
                                        <DiscreteObjectKeyFrame KeyTime="0"
Value="{StaticResource VerticalScrollViewerStyle}"/>
                                    </ObjectAnimationUsingKeyFrames>
                                    <ObjectAnimationUsingKeyFrames
Storyboard.TargetName="richTextBlock" Storyboard.TargetProperty="Width">
                                        <DiscreteObjectKeyFrame KeyTime="0"
Value="280"/>
                                    </ObjectAnimationUsingKeyFrames>
                                    <ObjectAnimationUsingKeyFrames
Storyboard.TargetName="image" Storyboard.TargetProperty="MaxHeight">
                                        <DiscreteObjectKeyFrame KeyTime="0"
Value="160"/>
                                    </ObjectAnimationUsingKeyFrames>
                                </Storyboard>
                            </VisualState>
                        </VisualStateGroup>
                    </VisualStateManager.VisualStateGroups>
            </ScrollViewer>
        </UserControl>
    </DataTemplate>
    </FlipView.ItemTemplate>
</FlipView>

<!-- Back button and page title -->
<Grid>
    <Grid.ColumnDefinitions>
        <ColumnDefinition Width="Auto"/>
        <ColumnDefinition Width="*"/>
    </Grid.ColumnDefinitions>
    <Button x:Name="backButton" Click="GoBack" IsEnabled="{Binding
Frame.CanGoBack, ElementName=pageRoot}" Style="{StaticResource
BackButtonStyle}"/>
    <TextBlock x:Name="pageTitle" Text="{Binding Title}" Style="{StaticResource
PageHeaderTextStyle}" Grid.Column="1" IsHitTestVisible="false"/>
</Grid>

<VisualStateManager.VisualStateGroups>

        <!-- Visual states reflect the application's view state -->
        <VisualStateGroup x:Name="ApplicationViewStates">
            <VisualState x:Name="FullScreenLandscape"/>
            <VisualState x:Name="Filled"/>

        <!-- The back button respects the narrower 100-pixel
margin convention for portrait -->
        <VisualState x:Name="FullScreenPortrait">
            <Storyboard>
                <ObjectAnimationUsingKeyFrames
Storyboard.TargetName="backButton" Storyboard.TargetProperty="Style">
                    <DiscreteObjectKeyFrame KeyTime="0"
```

```
                    Value="{StaticResource PortraitBackButtonStyle}"/>
                                </ObjectAnimationUsingKeyFrames>
                            </Storyboard>
                        </VisualState>

                        <!-- The back button and title have different styles
when snapped -->
                        <VisualState x:Name="Snapped">
                            <Storyboard>
                                <ObjectAnimationUsingKeyFrames
Storyboard.TargetName="backButton" Storyboard.TargetProperty="Style">
                                    <DiscreteObjectKeyFrame KeyTime="0"
Value="{StaticResource SnappedBackButtonStyle}"/>
                                </ObjectAnimationUsingKeyFrames>
                                <ObjectAnimationUsingKeyFrames
Storyboard.TargetName="pageTitle" Storyboard.TargetProperty="Style">
                                    <DiscreteObjectKeyFrame KeyTime="0"
Value="{StaticResource SnappedPageHeaderTextStyle}"/>
                                </ObjectAnimationUsingKeyFrames>
                            </Storyboard>
                        </VisualState>
                </VisualStateGroup>
            </VisualStateManager.VisualStateGroups>
    </Grid>
    </common:LayoutAwarePage>
```

Again don't stress over the details of the code just yet; the next chapter has a solid primer on all these different XAML controls and constructs. For now just try to get a feel for how some of these layout controls might work and how the pages in this particular template interact with each other.

Supporting a Snapped View

Earlier, there was a reference to all Windows Store apps being required to support a snapped view. This is covered in greater detail in the next chapter but for now:

1. Build and run the app.

2. Drag from the top of the screen, and pull the app to the left or right side; then let go of the mouse or your finger. The app snaps into place and a new user interface displays. Figure 1-19 shows what the snapped version of the Grid Application template looks like alongside the default Windows 8 Weather app.

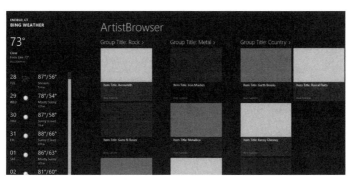

FIGURE 1-19

As you can see, the displayed information is still relevant and useful without inhibiting the user from actively working on the Calendar app as well.

SPLIT APPLICATIONS

Another template available to build standard Windows Store apps is the Split App template. This template creates an app that displays groups of data. However, rather the user navigating to the grouped items page and then an item details page, this type of app simply displays the list of group items along with the selected items detailed in a 50/50 window split.

Creating a Split Application

To illustrate the split application:

1. Create a new C#/XAML Split App in Visual Studio called **ArtistBrowserSplit**.

2. After the project is created, you can see mostly the same files as the Grid app you built in this chapter but with a couple exceptions. Table 1-7 shows the files included with this type of project along with the task for which they are responsible.

TABLE 1-7: Default Split Application Files

FILE	TASK
SampleData Source.cs	Sample data for application; same usage as in the Grid Application template.
App.xaml	Contains application-wide control styles. Here you should store any user-created styles that must be available across multiple pages.
App.xaml.cs	The code-behind page that contains main application startup code along with distinguishing which page will become the Startup page. In Split Application template you set the start page to ItemsPage.xaml.
SplitPage.xaml	The items detail page that shows a list of items in a group on a split screen along with the detailed information for the currently selected item.
SplitPage.xaml.cs	The code behind to add control event handlers or handle page navigation events.
ItemsPage.xaml	The user interface for the Start page that shows a collection of groups.
ItemsPage.xaml.cs	The code behind to add control event handlers or handle page navigation events.
Package. appxmanifest	The application settings file.

3. Before running this application you should grab the `SampleDataSource.cs` file from the previous Grid version of the `ArtistBrowser` and replace the current Split app's version with that content. If you build and run the application with the simulator, the first page that displays is the `ItemsPage`, as shown in Figure 1-20, where the available music genres display to the user.

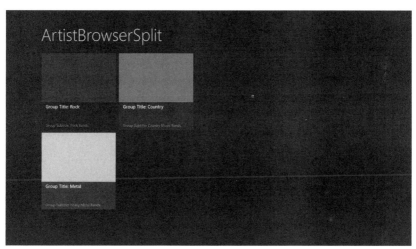

FIGURE 1-20

As you can see, this user interface is simpler and doesn't require horizontal scrolling because only the group information displays — not any of the individual items as in the Grid sample application template. However, the `ItemsPage` code shown in Listing 1-11 does rely on many of the same user interface controls that the Grid application required.

LISTING 1-11: ItemsPage.xaml

```
<common:LayoutAwarePage
    x:Name="pageRoot"
    x:Class="ArtistBrowserSplit.ItemsPage"
    DataContext="{Binding DefaultViewModel, RelativeSource={RelativeSource Self}}"
    xmlns="http://schemas.microsoft.com/winfx/2006/xaml/presentation"
    xmlns:x="http://schemas.microsoft.com/winfx/2006/xaml"
    xmlns:local="using:ArtistBrowserSplit"
    xmlns:data="using:ArtistBrowserSplit.Data"
    xmlns:common="using:ArtistBrowserSplit.Common"
    xmlns:d="http://schemas.microsoft.com/expression/blend/2008"
    xmlns:mc="http://schemas.openxmlformats.org/markup-compatibility/2006"
    mc:Ignorable="d">

    <Page.Resources>

        <!-- Collection of items displayed by this page -->
        <CollectionViewSource
```

continues

LISTING 1-11 *(continued)*

```xml
                    x:Name="itemsViewSource"
                    Source="{Binding Items}"
                    d:Source="{Binding AllGroups, Source={d:DesignInstance
    Type=data:SampleDataSource, IsDesignTimeCreatable=True}}"/>
        </Page.Resources>

        <!--
            This grid acts as a root panel for the page that defines two rows:
            * Row 0 contains the back button and page title
            * Row 1 contains the rest of the page layout
        -->
        <Grid Style="{StaticResource LayoutRootStyle}">
            <Grid.RowDefinitions>
                <RowDefinition Height="140"/>
                <RowDefinition Height="*"/>
            </Grid.RowDefinitions>

            <!-- Horizontal scrolling grid used in most view states -->
            <GridView
                x:Name="itemGridView"
                AutomationProperties.AutomationId="ItemsGridView"
                AutomationProperties.Name="Items"
                TabIndex="1"
                Grid.RowSpan="2"
                Padding="116,136,116,46"
                ItemsSource="{Binding Source={StaticResource itemsViewSource}}"
                ItemTemplate="{StaticResource Standard250x250ItemTemplate}"
                SelectionMode="None"
                IsSwipeEnabled="false"
                IsItemClickEnabled="True"
                ItemClick="ItemView_ItemClick"/>

                <!-- Vertical scrolling list only used when snapped -->
                <ListView
                    x:Name="itemListView"
                    AutomationProperties.AutomationId="ItemsListView"
                    AutomationProperties.Name="Items"
                    TabIndex="1"
                    Grid.Row="1"
                    Visibility="Collapsed"
                    Margin="0,-10,0,0"
                    Padding="10,0,0,60"
                    ItemsSource="{Binding Source={StaticResource itemsViewSource}}"
                    ItemTemplate="{StaticResource Standard80ItemTemplate}"
                    SelectionMode="None"
                    IsSwipeEnabled="false"
                    IsItemClickEnabled="True"
                    ItemClick="ItemView_ItemClick"/>

                    <!-- Back button and page title -->
                    <Grid>
                        <Grid.ColumnDefinitions>
```

```xml
                                <ColumnDefinition Width="Auto"/>
                                <ColumnDefinition Width="*"/>
                            </Grid.ColumnDefinitions>
                            <Button x:Name="backButton" Click="GoBack"
IsEnabled="{Binding Frame.CanGoBack, ElementName=pageRoot}"
Style="{StaticResource BackButtonStyle}"/>
                            <TextBlock x:Name="pageTitle" Grid.Column="1"
Text="{StaticResource AppName}" IsHitTestVisible="false"
Style="{StaticResource PageHeaderTextStyle}"/>
                        </Grid>

                        <VisualStateManager.VisualStateGroups>

                        <!-- Visual states reflect the application's view state -->
                        <VisualStateGroup x:Name="ApplicationViewStates">
                            <VisualState x:Name="FullScreenLandscape"/>
                            <VisualState x:Name="Filled"/>

                        <!-- The entire page respects the narrower
100-pixel margin convention for portrait -->
                            <VisualState x:Name="FullScreenPortrait">
                                <Storyboard>
                                    <ObjectAnimationUsingKeyFrames
Storyboard.TargetName="backButton" Storyboard.TargetProperty="Style">
                                        <DiscreteObjectKeyFrame KeyTime="0"
Value="{StaticResource PortraitBackButtonStyle}"/>
                                    </ObjectAnimationUsingKeyFrames>
                                    <ObjectAnimationUsingKeyFrames
Storyboard.TargetName="itemGridView" Storyboard.TargetProperty="Padding">
                                        <DiscreteObjectKeyFrame KeyTime="0"
Value="96,136,86,56"/>
                                    </ObjectAnimationUsingKeyFrames>
                                </Storyboard>
                            </VisualState>

                            <!--
                                The back button and title have
different styles when snapped, and the list representation is substituted
for the grid displayed in all other view states
                                -->
                            <VisualState x:Name="Snapped">
                                <Storyboard>
                                    <ObjectAnimationUsingKeyFrames
Storyboard.TargetName="backButton" Storyboard.TargetProperty="Style">
                                        <DiscreteObjectKeyFrame KeyTime="0"
Value="{StaticResource SnappedBackButtonStyle}"/>
                                    </ObjectAnimationUsingKeyFrames>
                                    <ObjectAnimationUsingKeyFrames
Storyboard.TargetName="pageTitle" Storyboard.TargetProperty="Style">
                                        <DiscreteObjectKeyFrame KeyTime="0"
Value="{StaticResource SnappedPageHeaderTextStyle}"/>
                                    </ObjectAnimationUsingKeyFrames>

                                    <ObjectAnimationUsingKeyFrames
```

continues

LISTING 1-11 *(continued)*

```
             Storyboard.TargetName="itemListView" Storyboard.TargetProperty="Visibility">
                                        <DiscreteObjectKeyFrame KeyTime="0"
Value="Visible"/>
                                    </ObjectAnimationUsingKeyFrames>
                                    <ObjectAnimationUsingKeyFrames
             Storyboard.TargetName="itemGridView" Storyboard.TargetProperty="Visibility">
                                        <DiscreteObjectKeyFrame KeyTime="0"
Value="Collapsed"/>
                                    </ObjectAnimationUsingKeyFrames>
                                </Storyboard>
                            </VisualState>
                        </VisualStateGroup>
                    </VisualStateManager.VisualStateGroups>
            </Grid>
        </common:LayoutAwarePage>
```

SUMMARY

This chapter discussed some of the important changes coming to the Windows development environment including Windows Store application principals, WinRT, the App Store, and more. You saw how some great, new additions to Visual Studio greatly enhance developer productivity for Windows Store app creation as well as traditional ASP.NET MVC or ASP.NET site development.

Windows Store apps are designed to be fully immersive; in a break from traditional windowed environments, they always display in full-screen mode without the typical chrome and toolbars displaying. Windows Store apps are also designed with the touch experience first in mind, and the apps provide users with a great experience on a wide variety of both touch screen devices and PCs.

In this chapter, you also saw that you have several different ways to create Windows Store apps, and you have a choice of what language you want to pursue without losing any functionality. You can create Windows Store app user interfaces with XAML or HTML, and you can create backend/code- behind logic with C#, C++, and JavaScript. This opens up new doors to existing web developers from other platforms that may not have been familiar with WPF/Silverlight/ASP.NET or Windows Forms. Existing web developers from other platforms can use HTML/CSS/JS skills combined with the WinRT API to create fully immersive Windows Store apps and generate revenue from those apps
in the upcoming Windows App Store.

It is yet another exciting time to be a Windows developer; Windows is installed on millions of PCs and, soon, millions of tablets. With the launch of Windows 8, developers will create Windows Store apps for Windows and sell them in the App Store. This gives you an unprecedented opportunity to make money using your development skills. The upcoming chapters can solidify your skills in Windows Store app development so that you can fully take advantage of this rare opportunity to become involved in a platform during its initial launch.

What Is XAML?

WROX.COM CODE DOWNLOADS FOR THIS CHAPTER

You can find the wrox.com code downloads for this chapter in the code file 205709 C02.zip at www.wrox.com/remtitle.cgi?isbn=1118205707 on the Download Code tab.

You can develop Windows Store Apps in several different ways. Windows 8 enables you to use whatever programming language you may be the most familiar with to do your development. As stated in Chapter 1, "A Glimpse into the Future," the WinRT API has been designed and built to work with HTML/JavaScript, XAML/VB.NET, XAML/C++, and XAML/C#. For the first time if you don't have knowledge of Microsoft programming languages, you can still write apps for Windows 8 by making use of solely HTML, CSS, and JavaScript. The API calls and User Interface controls used in Windows 8 development are available to all these language combinations with no major restrictions. This book focuses on development of Windows Store apps using XAML as the user interface language and C# for the application logic. This chapter offers a brief tutorial on XAML and how it is used to create dynamic user interfaces. The XAML language is a powerful markup language that you can use to create complex screens as well as fluid and dynamic Windows 8 user interfaces.

Now, if you have a background in Microsoft development and have been developing line-of-business applications over the last few years, it is highly likely that you have used Silverlight.

Silverlight is a Microsoft technology that provides great improvements in streaming media over the Internet as well as gives developers a first look at XAML and a new way to create web applications with a strong emphasis on line-of-business features. If you have developed applications using Silverlight or WPF recently, some content is redundant in this chapter and you could jump ahead; however, some important differences exist between traditional XAML development with Silverlight/WPF and how it is used in Windows 8 with WinRT as the backbone. If you are interested in those differences or just need an overall refresher in how everything works, this chapter is for you.

A QUICK XAML HISTORY LESSON

XAML pronounced (ZAMEL) at its core is a markup language similar to XML used to design user interfaces. It started in Windows Presentation Foundation (WPF) development. For years thick client Windows applications were designed with a basic forms editor and some code behind each form to handle basic control interactions. The resulting user interfaces were not slick and looked boring overall, having a myriad of similar controls and generating a good deal of confusion about best practices when developers designed the user interface for a Windows application.

When Windows Vista came out with the new Aero desktop, it provided new interfaces that could be leveraged for much richer user interfaces in Windows applications. Microsoft went back to the drawing board and created XAML, which not only provided more powerful and better designed user interfaces for applications, it also simplified the overall control set that was available to developers. Using just a handful of controls and concepts, you could develop rich user interfaces learning complicated APIs, such as DirectX, which were traditionally used for writing Windows game software. When WPF was unleashed, it was not a far jump for Microsoft to take a look at how web development was done. Most Microsoft-based web development was performed using ASP.NET and Web Forms, which were basically a web-based version of the Win Forms technology that developers had at their disposal for full-blown thick client Windows apps.

Microsoft soon created a plug-in called Silverlight, which made full use of XAML. Developers could create user interfaces and could access some of the powerful API calls in the .NET framework that were traditionally only available for desktop client software. With Silverlight supporting a large chunk of the features included in the .NET framework as well as running in the context of the web browser, XAML and Silverlight quickly became a popular choice for replacing existing ASP.NET line-of-business apps. There was no doubt that performance and ease of user interface creation combined with a simple deployment strategy would quickly rocket Silverlight to the top of preferred web development technologies.

XAML-based solutions solved one problem that haunted Microsoft web developers for years: how to make a user interface look consistent across multiple browsers and browser versions. HTML and CSS had their strengths but because each browser handled things — such as layout and positioning — slightly different, this often resulted in web developers coding completely different versions of sites depending on the browser. Silverlight and XAML eliminated that by running as a plug-in. User interfaces written in XAML looked the same in IE 6, 7, 8, Firefox, Chrome, Safari, PC, and MAC. The beginnings of a write-once-run-anywhere scenario suddenly came to an abrupt end.

Just as Silverlight and XAML were poised to conquer the world's mobile devices, mobile app development started to absolutely explode. Websites weren't anywhere near as cool as having an "app" for your phone. Before long Android and iPhone devices were everywhere; to complicate matters, the iPad was released, and there was yet another form factor to develop against. Although Silverlight worked well on the PC and Mac, it was clear early on in the mobile wars that plug-ins were not going to be treated well on mobile devices. And Apple did not even allow the popular Adobe Flash plug-in to run on the iPhone.

So now there was this great technology for development but a totally new category of devices that you couldn't use it on due to restrictions in place on the various systems. Unfortunately, without the capability to support mobile devices, it appeared that Silverlight was heading toward the end of its boom. When Microsoft released its new mobile platform in Windows Phone 7, the Silverlight plug-in was also not included. However, developers who invested their time in learning XAML or who developed apps using XAML had some good news: Although not making use of the actual Silverlight plug-in, Windows Phone 7 did make XAML the primary user interface development technology, which dramatically reduced the learning curve for Windows Mobile development for existing Silverlight/XAML developers.

Although it appears that the Silverlight plug-in may be heading toward the same path as almost all the other web plug-ins, the technology and development practices that resulted from it, such as XAML, Data Binding, and Model-View-View-Model (MVVM), are destined to live on in Windows 8. When you compare Windows 8 to other development platforms and languages, the combination of XAML and your preferred .NET language means you have the tools to quickly create rich user experiences. When you pair this with the new design principles of Windows 8, you can create new types of apps that give your end users unparalleled views into the content that they truly care about while providing the performance required for additional devices, such as the new Surface tablets and the upcoming new version of the Windows Phone platform.

Now with that brief history lesson out of the way, you'll jump into some real-life XAML code and start to see exactly how easy it is to create user interfaces for Windows Store apps.

XAML BASICS

Controls in XAML have several common concepts and properties across most of the controls. For example, just like the ID tag in HTML elements or ASP.NET server controls, XAML provides a way to reference a control using the syntax x:Name=. So if you were to have a control responsible for displaying a phone number, you could use syntax similar to the following:

```
<TextBlock x:Name="PhoneNumber" />
```

The Name attribute is available for all XAML controls but is not required. If you do not need to access the control from code, as is common with controls that are only responsible for layout, you can simply omit the Name from the control declaration.

In addition to the `Name` attribute, most XAML controls also provide various `Brush` objects that you can manipulate to change the foreground and background colors of the control. Using a `Button` control you can add options for the `Foreground` and `Background` brush directly in XAML as follows:

```
<Button Content="Button" Foreground="#FFCC0620" Background="#FF191818"/>
```

The `Brush` color attributes are typically defined using an ARGB format, which is set of hexadecimal values similar to how HTML color codes are often defined. The `Foreground` and `Background` properties of controls are not just restricted to simple colors. Both properties are actually instances of a `Brush` object that XAML creates in the background. When using a simple color, you can actually create a `SolidColorBrush`. In addition, there are `Brush` objects that handle gradients and images. These additional `Brush` objects are typically defined as child properties in XAML code. For example, a simple gradient background could be applied to the `Button` control using the following:

```
<Button Content="Button">
    <Button.Background>
        <LinearGradientBrush EndPoint="0.5,1" StartPoint="0.5,0">
            <GradientStop Color="Black"/>
            <GradientStop Color="White" Offset="1"/>
        </LinearGradientBrush>
    </Button.Background>
</Button>
```

You can also use several different attributes to modify how the control appears overall in the layout of the page. These include `Visibility`, `Margin`, `Padding`, `HorizontalContentAlignment`, `VerticalContentAlignment`, `HorizontalAlignment`, `VerticalAlignment`, `Height`, and `Width`. Again all these attributes are simply added to the control declaration. For example, the following code declares the same `Button` control again, but this time adds some additional padding, as well as a specific `Height` and `Width` and `Margins`:

```
<Button Content="Button" HorizontalContentAlignment="Left"
Margin="5,5,10,10" Height="20" Width="100">
```

The `Height` and `Width` attributes are self-explanatory, but the `Margin` property works slightly different than it does for CSS margins (if you're familiar with them). The XAML `Margin` attribute starts with the `Top` margin and works its way clockwise, so you have `Top`, `Right`, `Bottom`, and `Left`. Like a typical CSS margin, you can also simply set `Margin="5"` to make all the control margins equal to 5. Or you can set two of the settings to apply to their counterparts. Use the `HorizontalContentAlignment` to affect the alignment of the text located inside of the `Button` control. By default it is centered, but this code actually changes it to be left-aligned. When working with XAML controls, you can use the `HorizontalAlignment` and `VerticalAlignment` to align the control relative to its container, whereas the `HorizontalContentAlignment` and `VerticalContentAlignment` attributes always affect the actual content inside of the control.

Another important property and concept of XAML controls is the `Content` property. You may have noticed that the `Button` control used in the previous examples uses the `Content` property to display text. In ASP.NET, the text for the `Button` is set using the `Text` property and is limited to string-based content. In XAML that's no longer the case; you can use the `Content` property to hold any valid XAML control along with static text. In the control declaration, static text is automatically converted to a simple `TextBlock` control, and the text displays; however, XAML, such as the following, is just as legal and works without any special coding:

```
<Button>
    <CheckBox Content="CheckBox"/>
</Button>
```

In this case (which isn't particularly useful) a `CheckBox` control is added inside the declaration of the `Button` control. Because there is no `Content` attribute specifically declared, the `CheckBox` becomes the `Content` of the `Button` and displays inside the context of the `Button` control. Even though there is a `CheckBox` sitting inside the `Button`, when the application runs, the `Button` still retains all the capabilities you would expect, such as firing events when a user touches or clicks it. In addition, you also see the `CheckBox` being updated to reflect the touch or click. The ability to add any XAML control as the `Content` of another control becomes an important concept when you create more complicated user interfaces, and it provides a level of flexibility that would have required complicated custom controls in previous Windows development scenarios.

XAML IN VISUAL STUDIO 2012

In previous versions of Visual Studio or if you developed using Silverlight/WPF, it was typically faster (and in many ways easier) to work with raw XAML when you created your user interfaces and pages. With Visual Studio 2012, however, you now have an extremely powerful WYSIWYG editor to work with XAML controls and create pages for your app. As you develop more complex Windows Store applications, it's beneficial to understand the details of how XAML works. It is always a good idea to look at raw XAML code to help troubleshoot problems, so this section looks at what Visual Studio 2012 has to offer for designing powerful XAML user interfaces. If you fire up Visual Studio 2012 and open a XAML page in the designer, you CAN see there are several features that make it easy to create user interfaces.

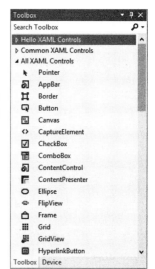

FIGURE 2-1

➤ **Toolbox:** By default, this is located in the top-left corner of the screen. From here you see a list of all the available XAML controls for your apps, as shown in Figure 2-1:

At the top, the Toolbox has a Search Toolbox bar, which makes it easy for you to quickly filter the view, so you can quickly access the control you need. To make use of a XAML control in the Toolbox, simply drag it out of the Toolbox and onto the designer for the page on which you're working.

➤ **Document Outline:** Shown in Figure 2-2, this enables you to quickly see the hierarchy of controls as they are laid out on a given page. By clicking a control in the outline, you can automatically set the focus to that control and can easily modify its properties. Or you can drag and drop from within this view to rearrange various controls.

FIGURE 2-2

➤ **Properties pane:** By far however the most used area of the designer is the Properties pane located by default on the lower-right side of the screen. After you select a control from the Document Outline pane or from the page view, you can quickly and easily alter any of the control's properties. Figure 2-3 shows the Properties pane for a basic Button control. Notice how you can modify the Foreground, Background, Margins, Content, and more easily without actually writing a single line of XAML code.

➤ **XAML tab:** When you develop apps for Windows 8, you can simply drag and drop controls onto the designer and then manipulate their properties using the Properties pane. When you run into a situation in which you need more control and require direct editing of the XAML, you can simply click the XAML tab, as shown in Figure 2-4, that appears directly below the designer view of the page you are building.

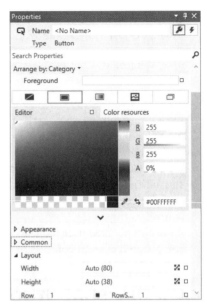

FIGURE 2-3

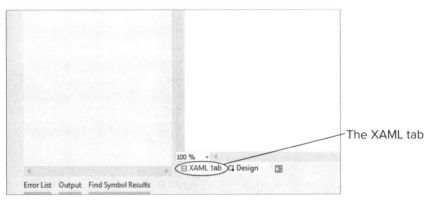

FIGURE 2-4

CONTROLS FOR WINDOWS 8

In Chapter 1, you were introduced to some of the Windows 8 project templates available in Visual Studio 2012. You also got your feet wet by looking at some actual XAML code. When you get the hang of things, you can see that there are only a handful of core concepts critical to understanding user interface development using XAML. Almost everything starts with the Windows 8 control stack. Several categories of controls can help you with layout, handling user interactions as well as the display of content and data. Let's take a look at what controls are available from each of these categories to help you make great Windows Store apps.

Layout Controls

One of the most important concepts in user interface design is layout. If you create an app using HTML or CSS, you may start by adding <div> tags on your page and then add content to those tags. After you set the structure of your page, you go to a CSS style sheet file and define attributes that better position elements on the page as well as setup margins, padding, background images, and so on. When writing a Windows Store app, you don't need to worry about making your pages work across multiple browsers but it can still be tricky to get things positioned correctly, even using the latest HTML 5 techniques. In contrast, XAML provides several layout controls that make positioning content and additional controls a breeze. When you create a page for your Windows Store app, XAML offers a Grid, StackPanel, and Canvas for handling layout. Now take a look at how to use all three of these controls.

Grid

The Grid control offers a flexible table-like approach to layout. A Grid control has both a collection of rows and columns that you can use to create all sorts of arrangements. In the simplest form a Grid control in XAML looks like the following:

```
<Grid x:Name="MainGrid">
</Grid>
```

Because the Grid works similarly to a table, you can add rows and columns by simply adding RowDefinition and ColumnDefinition objects to the XAML code like the following:

```
<Grid>
    <Grid.RowDefinitions>
        <RowDefinition />
        <RowDefinition />
    </Grid.RowDefinitions>
    <Grid.ColumnDefinitions>
        <ColumnDefinition />
        <ColumnDefinition />
        <ColumnDefinition />
        <ColumnDefinition />
    </Grid.ColumnDefinitions>
</Grid>
```

In this case a Grid control with two rows and four columns is created. Notice how you can add RowDefinition and ColumnDefinition objects to the Grid by making use of the RowDefinitions and ColumnDefinitions collections, respectively. Also notice that the way you access those collections is to actually use Grid.RowDefinitions. The RowDefinitions property is called an *attached property*, which is an important concept to understand because it's used throughout XAML development. The way these work is that a parent control, in this case the Grid, may have a collection object defined for use. In other words if you were doing this in C# code, you might see something like the following:

```
Grid.RowDefinitions = new List<RowDefinitions>();
```

That is a standard way to access the property of the Grid; however, to access that property in XAML, you need to declare it as attached so that it effectively becomes a static property in the markup that you can instantiate and use to add new objects, such as the RowDefinition and ColumnDefinition. The Grid control also makes use of attached properties to allow the controls added to the Grid to determine what row and column they should sit in. Basically, you can think of attached properties as any property in the parent object that you need to make available to children for direct manipulation. For example, if you were to add a Button control to this Grid and you wanted it to reside in the second row and second column, your XAML markup would use the Row and Column attached properties of the Grid from the Button control.

```
<Grid>
    <Grid.RowDefinitions>
        <RowDefinition />
        <RowDefinition />
    </Grid.RowDefinitions>
    <Grid.ColumnDefinitions>
        <ColumnDefinition />
        <ColumnDefinition />
        <ColumnDefinition />
        <ColumnDefinition />
    </Grid.ColumnDefinitions>
    <Button x:Name="MainButton" Grid.Row="1" Grid.Column="1" />
</Grid>
```

Even though the Button control does not actually contain a property called Row or Column (because the Grid control marks those as attached properties), they are made accessible to all child controls sitting in the Grid so that in this case the Button can be placed precisely in the Grid where you want it.

Now that you can see how to add controls to the Grid as well as how to add columns and rows, how about sizing? Well, to understand how to specify a size for the various rows and columns in the Grid, you need to understand the overall general concept of sizing in XAML. Unlike traditional HTML-based tables, the Grid control gives you several options for sizing rows and columns that enable complex fluid layouts, which in HTML/CSS would require complicated floating DIV tags and positioning code.

The Grid control offers three main ways to declare the height and width of a row and column.

➤   **You can directly set the height and width using a pixel-based format such as the following.** This results in a Grid with one row 100 pixels in height, regardless of the content displayed, and a column 200 pixels wide.

```
<Grid>
    <Grid.RowDefinitions>
        <RowDefinition Height="100" />
    </Grid.RowDefinitions>
    <Grid.ColumnDefinitions>
        <ColumnDefinition Width="200" />
    </Grid.ColumnDefinitions>
</Grid>
```

➤ **You can use the Auto sizing mode.** Setting the `Height` or `Width` to `Auto` can result in the `Grid` control setting the `Width` and `Height` internally to give exactly enough space to display the content placed in it. This mode is perhaps the easiest to work with because it takes the guess work out of determining the exact pixels required to have enough room for the `Grid` content.

➤ **The Grid control also provides you with the ability to use Star sizing.** This sizing concept is what gives the `Grid` the ability to create fluid layouts with ease. The basis of Star sizing is that the row and column that has a value of * for its `Height`, or `Width` uses all the remaining available space to place its content. For example, say you want a `Grid` with a header row that has a fixed height of 100 pixels, but then you want all the rest of your content to take up the remainder of the page. In that case, you might end up with the following XAML:

```
<Grid>
    <Grid.RowDefinitions>
        <RowDefinition Height="100" />
        <RowDefinition Height="*" />
    </Grid.RowDefinitions>
</Grid>
```

The `Star` sizing concept becomes truly powerful if you need a complex layout. Say you now want a header row, a content row, and then another content row that is exactly twice the height of the first content row. You would need to create the following XAML:

```
<Grid Margin="0" Grid.Row="1">
    <Grid.RowDefinitions>
        <RowDefinition Height="100"/>
        <RowDefinition Height="*"/>
        <RowDefinition Height="2*"/>
    </Grid.RowDefinitions>
    <Rectangle Fill="#FFF4F4F5" Margin="0" Grid.Row="1" Stroke="Black"/>
    <Rectangle Fill="#FFF4F4F5" Margin="0" Grid.Row="2" Stroke="Black"/>
    <TextBlock HorizontalAlignment="Center" Margin="0" Grid.Row="1"
VerticalAlignment="Center" Foreground="#FF000000" FontSize="20"
Text="This text resides in a 1* sized row" />
    <TextBlock HorizontalAlignment="Center" Margin="0" Grid.Row="2"
VerticalAlignment="Center" FontSize="20"
Text="This text resides in a 2* sized row" Foreground="#FF000000"/>
</Grid>
```

Looking at the XAML, you can see that to get the third row of the `Grid` control to be twice the size of the middle row, you added the 2* value for the `Height`. This makes it easy to create fluid table-like `Grid` layouts. You can apply the same concepts to columns as well.

The `Grid` control is most likely the most commonly used layout control in your apps. The primary goal of Windows 8-based apps is to get content to the user; flexible `Grid`-based layouts often are the preferred way to do that, so you must master some of these key concepts for XAML `Grid` controls. The following is an exercise to help you get a feel for the Visual Studio 2012 designer, how to work with the `Grid`, control and how to place child controls:

1. Open Visual Studio 2012 and create a new Windows Store application called `Grid` in C# using the blank application template.

2. Open up the MainPage.xaml file and use the Visual Studio 2012 designer to drag and drop several controls onto the screen. Figure 2-5 shows the user interface that you are trying to create.

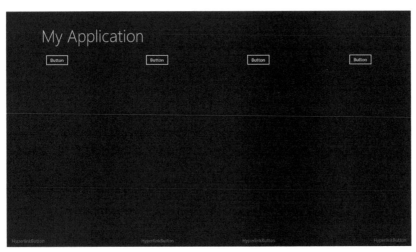

FIGURE 2-5

3. Drag a Grid control from the Toolbox and drop it in the center of the page. When dropped the Grid is the default with some automatic sizing and margins associated with it.

4. This parent Grid must take up all the remaining space, so go to the Properties pane to set any Margin values to zero.

5. Ensure the size of the Grid is set to auto for both Height and Width using the property pane as shown in Figure 2-6.

FIGURE 2-6

> **NOTE** *For the* VerticalAlignment *and* HorizontalAlignment *properties, the last icon is selected. This last icon represents a value of* Stretch. *Any XAML control can have its alignment properties set to* Left, Center, Right, *and* Stretch. Stretch *mode forces the control to resize itself to fill all the available space in its container. In some cases the* Auto *sizing properties can take care of that, but by default an* Auto *sized* Grid *control takes up only as much room as required by its contents. In this case you want the* Grid *to take up all available space in its container regardless of the actual* Grid *content.*

6. Define the columns and rows. If you move the cursor just over the Grid, you can see yellow outlines. If you move across the top of the Grid, the yellow lines represent a guide to where you can create a new column. If you click the yellow line, you see the outline of a new column added to the Grid.

7. Repeat step 4 two more times to create the four columns required for this user interface.

8. With that complete you may notice that the columns seem to be all different widths — unless of course you have perfect vision and placed perfectly equal columns. Because you want equal columns, this is a good candidate for the Star sizing discussed earlier. You want all four columns to use the value of * for the width. Although you can easily do this in XAML, the Visual Studio 2012 designer also gives you a visual way to accomplish this task. If you hover the cursor over the size displayed for any column, as shown in Figure 2-7, you can click in the size area and select from Pixel, Auto, and Star. You can also enter the actual width value you want. In this case for each column, you want to select Star sizing with the value equal to * or 1* — either one will work. After you do this, you should see that all four columns now are equal in width.

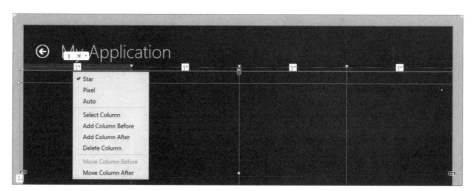

FIGURE 2-7

9. You must do something similar to define the two rows required. By default you have one row already available in the Grid; so all you need to do is hover over the left side of the Grid until the yellow guideline appears, and click to create the second row.

10. The goal of the first row is to auto adjust to the height of the content. Make sure that row is set to Auto by hovering over the current height and selecting Auto from the menu.

11. Add some content to adjust the row height to. Drag and drop a Button control from the Toolbox, and place it somewhere in that first row or column of the Grid.

12. After the Button control drops, clear any predefined Margin and set the HorizontalAlignment to Center using the Properties pane.

13. Force the first row to be Auto sized by simply grabbing the visible row line and dragging it straight up toward the Button. Because the Auto mode for Height was selected, the guideline does not let you continue sizing past the Button control.

14. Now that your rows and columns are properly sized, you can simple add the remaining three `Button` controls into the appropriate columns. Use the Properties pane to adjust the `Button` controls to be `Center`-aligned in their respective columns.

15. Add some `HyperlinkButton` controls to the second row, but this time set the `VerticalAlignment` to `Bottom` for all of them.

If you have done any HTML or CSS development and wanted to align items across the bottom of the screen, it always seems to be an adventure depending on what browser you develop for, which usually involves tricky absolute positioning. As you can see, accomplishing the same task in XAML using the `Grid` control is a breeze.

After you finish adding the `HyperlinkButton` controls, if you switch to the XAML view of the page, you should see XAML code similar to following:

```
<Grid Background="{StaticResource ApplicationPageBackgroundThemeBrush}">
    <Grid.RowDefinitions>
        <RowDefinition Height="Auto"/>
        <RowDefinition/>
    </Grid.RowDefinitions>
    <Grid.ColumnDefinitions>
        <ColumnDefinition/>
        <ColumnDefinition/>
        <ColumnDefinition/>
        <ColumnDefinition/>
    </Grid.ColumnDefinitions>
    <Button Content="Button" HorizontalAlignment="Center" Margin="0"
VerticalAlignment="Center" d:IsHidden="True"/>
    <Button Content="Button" Grid.Column="1" HorizontalAlignment="Center"
Margin="0" VerticalAlignment="Center" d:IsHidden="True"/>
    <Button Content="Button" Grid.Column="2" HorizontalAlignment="Center"
Margin="0" VerticalAlignment="Center" d:IsHidden="True"/>
    <Button Content="Button" Grid.Column="3" HorizontalAlignment="Center"
Margin="0" VerticalAlignment="Center" d:IsHidden="True"/>
    <HyperlinkButton Content="HyperlinkButton" HorizontalAlignment="Left"
Margin="0" Grid.Row="1" VerticalAlignment="Bottom" d:IsHidden="True"/>
    <HyperlinkButton Content="HyperlinkButton" HorizontalAlignment="Center"
Margin="0" Grid.Row="1" VerticalAlignment="Bottom" Grid.Column="1"
d:IsHidden="True"/>
    <HyperlinkButton Content="HyperlinkButton" HorizontalAlignment="Center"
Margin="0" Grid.Row="1" VerticalAlignment="Bottom" Grid.Column="2"
d:IsHidden="True"/>
    <HyperlinkButton Content="HyperlinkButton" HorizontalAlignment="Right"
Margin="0" Grid.Row="1" VerticalAlignment="Bottom" Grid.Column="3"
d:IsHidden="True"/>
</Grid>
```

At this point, building and running the app should give you an initial screen that looks like the prototype from Figure 2-5. Although this app doesn't have any logic, you should know how to navigate around the Visual Studio 2012 page designer to see how easy it is to make fluid and complex table-like user interfaces using the `Grid` control. The following section moves on to a few of the other layout controls that you need to use in your apps starting with the `StackPanel`.

StackPanel

In addition to the Grid control, you can also use a StackPanel control to help with the placement and layout of other controls. The StackPanel essentially is a container that "stacks" objects vertically or horizontally. There are no columns or rows to deal with in this control. The StackPanel is simple because when you add it to the page, you can set the Orientation property to either Vertical or Horizontal, and controls added to the StackPanel are automatically laid out accordingly.

Because the StackPanel simply places controls next to each other, you normally must make adjustments to the Margin properties of the controls the StackPanel contains to create some space between controls.

Declaring a StackPanel in XAML looks like the following:

```
<StackPanel Orientation="Horizontal">
    <Button Margin="5" Content="Inside StackPanel" />
    <Button Margin="5" Content="Inside StackPanel" />
</StackPanel>
```

By default, the StackPanel can place objects in the vertical Orientation. So the only time you need to set this value is if you use Horizontal. As with the Grid control, you now can create a sample project that uses the StackPanel following these steps:

1. Create a new blank metro project called StackPanel.

2. Use the Visual Studio 2012 Designer to re-create the user interface, as shown in Figure 2-8. To this end:

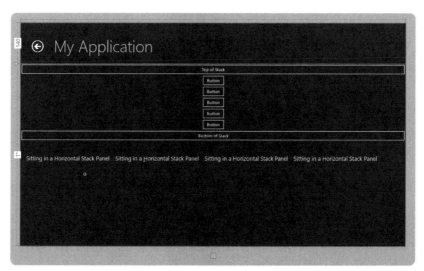

FIGURE 2-8

A. Drag a StackPanel control from the Toolbox over to the main Grid control and set its Height/Width to Auto and clear out any existing Margin properties.

B. Set the HorizontalAlignment and VerticalAlignment to Stretch.

C. Add some Button controls to the StackPanel and notice how they are automatically added below each other because of the default Orientation value for the StackPanel.

D. Use the Properties pane to manipulate the alignments and margins required to make the buttons look as they do in Figure 2-10.

3. Drag another StackPanel inside of the first StackPanel, and set it to Auto height/width and Stretch for alignment. It can be tricky to drop the StackPanel inside of another so you may want to verify that this was done correctly by looking at the Document Outline or by checking the XAML code to be sure the new StackPanel has been properly nested. This time in the Properties pane, find the Orientation property and set it to Horizontal.

4. You can now start dragging TextBlock controls into this StackPanel; they should automatically line up horizontally.

5. Again adjust the Margin properties of each TextBlock accordingly to match the figure. When everything is complete you have XAML similar to the following:

```
<StackPanel Margin="0" Grid.Row="1">
    <Button Content="Top of Stack" HorizontalAlignment="Stretch"/>
    <Button Content="Button" HorizontalAlignment="Center"/>
    <Button Content="Button" HorizontalAlignment="Center"/>
    <Button Content="Button" HorizontalAlignment="Center"/>
    <Button Content="Button" HorizontalAlignment="Center"/>
    <Button Content="Button" HorizontalAlignment="Center"/>
    <Button Content="Bottom of Stack"
HorizontalAlignment="Stretch"
VerticalAlignment="Stretch"/>
    <StackPanel Orientation="Horizontal">
        <TextBlock Text="Sitting in a Horizontal Stack Panel"
Margin="20,50,0,50"
FontSize="20"/>
        <TextBlock Text="Sitting in a Horizontal Stack Panel"
Margin="20,50,0,50"
FontSize="20"/>
        <TextBlock Text="Sitting in a Horizontal Stack Panel"
Margin="20,50,0,50"
FontSize="20"/>
        <TextBlock Text="Sitting in a Horizontal Stack Panel"
Margin="20,50,0,50"
FontSize="20"/>
    </StackPanel>
</StackPanel>
```

The StackPanel provides you with another tool to assist for layouts of controls where you may not need actual rows and columns. Many times an initial Grid control is used as the top-level layout control and then StackPanel controls are added to handle internal positioning of controls. It can also be useful to use the StackPanel control to align a group of controls to the right or left of the screen easily.

Canvas

So far, both of the main layout controls in XAML that you have seen use a form of relative positioning. This type of positioning enables fluid table-like layouts that properly adjust based on screen size without you needing to do any additional work. However, sometimes you may find a particular need to use an approach closer to absolute positioning of your controls. In this case, you want to drag and drop a control and have it stay there regardless of what happens to the screen size or other objects around it. For example, you may be creating a painting program and need to allow a specific drawing of objects on the screen. Obviously, a `Grid` or `StackPanel` cannot provide you with the capabilities you want.

For these absolute positioning type scenarios, use the `Canvas` control, which is a simple control that works like a paint canvas. Instead of relying on the `Margin` and various alignment properties of the controls that are dropped on it, the `Canvas` uses `Top` and `Left` to determine where the objects should display on the screen. In Figure 2-9 you see that several `TextBlock` controls have been dropped onto a `Canvas` control. Both the `Top` and `Left` properties position the objects exactly where you want on the screen.

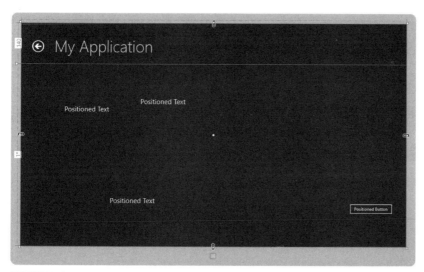

FIGURE 2-9

The following code shows the required XAML for this layout. You can use the attached properties `Canvas.Top` and `Canvas.Left` to actually position the objects inside of the `Canvas`.

```
<Canvas Grid.Row="1">
    <Button Content="Positioned Button" Canvas.Left="1165" Canvas.Top="478"/>
    <TextBlock Canvas.Left="154" Text="Positioned Text"
Canvas.Top="142" FontSize="24"/>
    <TextBlock Canvas.Left="425" Text="Positioned Text"
Canvas.Top="116" FontSize="24"/>
    <TextBlock Canvas.Left="317" Text="Positioned Text"
Canvas.Top="458" FontSize="24"/>
</Canvas>
```

Another potential use for the `Canvas` control is if you want to create a simple game for Windows 8. The `Canvas` control gives you an easy area to place shapes and images, and because of the attached `Left` and `Top` properties, it also gives you an easy way to move them in code.

ScrollViewer

The final layout control to cover is the `ScrollViewer`, which is self-explanatory; it simply acts as a container for any content that may overflow the visible part of the screen. If an overflow occurs a scrollbar is added to the user interface, and the user can scroll content contained in the `ScrollViewer` into position.

The `ScrollViewer` can handle scrolling content vertically or horizontally depending on your preferences. This control comes into play when you add large amounts of content to your application; depending on the device used, you may want the content to scroll vertically or horizontally. Like the previous two layout controls, you can add your content in between the opening and closing of the `ScrollViewer` tag with one key difference. With the `Canvas`, `StackPanel`, and `Grid`, you can add any number of controls as children without issue. For the `ScrollViewer`, however, you can add only one control as a child. If you want to scroll multiple controls hosting content, the main child of the `ScrollViewer` must be one of the other layout controls, such as a `Canvas`, `StackPanel`, or `Grid`. Then that child control can host as many controls as desired.

To get a feel for how to work with the `ScrollBar`, let's work through another sample:

1. Create another project in Visual Studio 2012 called `ScrollBar`.

2. In the MainPage.xaml file drag and drop a `ScrollViewer` control from the Toolbox onto the main `Grid` control in the designer.

3. As you have before force the `ScrollViewer` to take up all available space in the parent `Grid` control, and then add a `StackPanel` to the `ScrollViewer`.

4. The `StackPanel` holds a collection of button controls so that you can create a need for horizontal scrolling. You can change the `Orientation` of the `StackPanel` to `Horizontal` and then simply copy and paste button controls until they start to appear off the screen.

5. So that things look cleaner, you can also add a `Top`, `Left`, and `Right Margin` value of 50. When everything is complete you should have something similar to Figure 2-10.

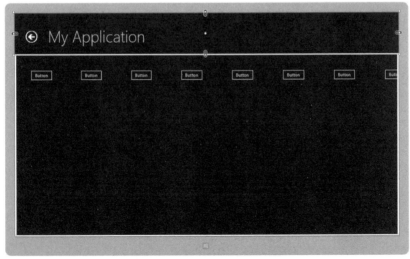

FIGURE 2-10

6. By default if you build and run the app in the Simulator, you see that only a vertical scrollbar appears, and you can't do any horizontal scrolling to reach the buttons that are off the screen. This isn't particularly useful for your app, so you need to set the ScrollViewer properties to enable horizontal scrolling and not vertical. To do this, go to the Properties pane and search for a property called VerticalScrollBarVisibility.

7. When that property displays, set it to Disabled. This eliminates the vertical scrollbar that appears when the application launches because you don't need it.

8. Search for the HorizontalScrollBarVisibility property and set that to Visible. Setting this value ensures that the correct scrollbar appears on the screen.

9. Build and run the app. You should see a horizontal scrollbar, and the vertical scrollbar should no longer be visible.

10. The scrollbar now enables you to scroll to the right to see the remaining hidden button controls; however, it does not seem to work if you simply try to scroll using the mouse wheel. This behavior occurs because although the correct scrollbar displays, the correct scrolling mode has not yet been set. ScrollViewer requires that you set both the visibility of the appropriate scrollbar and the appropriate mode. You can set the scrolling mode using the HorizontalScrollMode and VerticalScrollMode properties. In this particular case you want to enable the horizontal mode and disable the vertical mode.

11. To make it easier to see the ScrollViewer in this example, you can set the BorderThickness property to 5 and the BorderBrush to White. You can do this in XAML or by using the Properties pane in the designer. This just makes it a little easier to see exactly where the ScrollViewer boundaries are as you scroll so that you can see the effect.

When this is done you should have XAML code similar to the following:

```
<ScrollViewer Margin="0" Grid.Row="1" VerticalScrollBarVisibility="Hidden"
HorizontalScrollBarVisibility="Visible" HorizontalScrollMode="Enabled"
VerticalScrollMode="Disabled" BorderThickness="5" BorderBrush="White">
    <StackPanel Orientation="Horizontal">
        <Button Content="Button" VerticalAlignment="Top" Margin="50,50,50,0"/>
        <Button Content="Button" VerticalAlignment="Top" Margin="50,50,50,0"/>
        <Button Content="Button" VerticalAlignment="Top" Margin="50,50,50,0"/>
        <Button Content="Button" VerticalAlignment="Top" Margin="50,50,50,0"/>
        <Button Content="Button" VerticalAlignment="Top" Margin="50,50,50,0"/>
        <Button Content="Button" VerticalAlignment="Top" Margin="50,50,50,0"/>
        <Button Content="Button" VerticalAlignment="Top" Margin="50,50,50,0"/>
        <Button Content="Button" VerticalAlignment="Top" Margin="50,50,50,0"/>
        <Button Content="Button" VerticalAlignment="Top" Margin="50,50,50,0"/>
        <Button Content="Button" VerticalAlignment="Top" Margin="50,50,50,0"/>
        <Button Content="Button" VerticalAlignment="Top" Margin="50,50,50,0"/>
        <Button Content="Button" VerticalAlignment="Top" Margin="50,50,50,0"/>
        <Button Content="Button" VerticalAlignment="Top" Margin="50,50,50,0"/>
        <Button Content="Button" VerticalAlignment="Top" Margin="50,50,50,0"/>
        <Button Content="Button" VerticalAlignment="Top" Margin="50,50,50,0"/>
    </StackPanel>
</ScrollViewer>
```

If you build and run the application, you should see that the correct scrollbars appear. Mouse wheel support is working again allowing you to easily scroll to see the hidden Button controls.

In addition, the `ScrollViewer` has features that enable you to handle pan and zoom effects that give you more options for displaying content to the user. The pan and zoom effects of the `ScrollViewer` are covered in the next chapter when you learn more about semantic zoom and how it is useful to support it for content in Windows Store applications.

Action Controls

After you master how to incorporate the various layout controls in XAML, you should move to some of the controls that your users can interact with, such as the `Button`, `TextBlock`, `TextBox`, `ComboBox`, and more. Because Windows Store applications should have a consistent user experience, all the controls you need are available in WinRT. If you come from a WinForms background or an ASP.NET background, you are already familiar with the concept of a code behind page. The code behind page is where you put event handlers for the various interactive controls and put the logic required to manipulate those controls.

In XAML you also have the same concept of a code behind file to place your control event handling code. However in Chapter 8, "Geolocation," you can see a new way to handle control events that was made popular with Silverlight development and has become an integral part of creating Windows Store apps as well called Model-View-View-Model (MVVM). This way to program is only available to user interface languages that support the concept of Data Binding, which you can see more of in the next chapter. MVVM development has become popular because it separates your user interface code or XAML from the actual business logic even further than the code behind concept does. It also provides you with a way to automatically update and refresh the user interface without writing traditional event handlers. For now, though, we'll look at the default behavior of interacting with XAML controls using the code behind page and see what types of interactive controls are available from WinRT.

TextBlock

The `TextBlock` control is probably the most basic control available in XAML. It has one purpose, which is to display basic text on the screen. It is the XAML equivalent of a plain old `<div>` tag or `Label` control in ASP.NET. Although most XAML controls rely on the `Content` property to determine what appears, the `TextBlock` control uses a `Text` property instead because the only valid output for this control is text. Here is the XAML code for declaring a basic `TextBlock`:

```
<TextBlock Text="This is some text" />
```

TextBox

The `TextBox` control is a data input control that enables you to capture keyed input from the user. Like the `TextBlock` this control uses the `Text` property instead of the Content property to display the entered text. The `Text` property is read/write, but you often simply capture input in this control and use it elsewhere. Here is the XAML code to create a basic `TextBox` control:

```
<TextBox Text="" />
```

Button

The Button control (that you have already seen in this chapter) enables the user to click or touch to perform an action. When declaring an instance of a Button control in XAML, you can use the Content property to determine what text appears in the Button. The following code declares a basic XAML Button control:

```
<Button x:Name="StandardButton" Content="Create Message" />
```

The main purpose to use a Button control is usually to perform some kind of user interface action. Specifically, you can handle the Click event of the Button control and perform some logic in the code behind event handler. To see all the various user interface events available for the Button and other controls, click the Lightning Bolt icon in the Properties pane of Visual Studio, as shown in Figure 2-11.

After you bring up the list of events, you can find the Click event and either double-click to auto-generate an event handler in the code behind or type in the name of the method you want to use to handle the event. You can use a Button Click event to manipulate another area of the user interface.

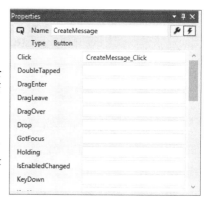

FIGURE 2-11

Now we'll look at another simple example of this:

1. In Visual Studio create a new project called ActionControls and add a new page called Controls.xaml using the Basic Page item template. After doing this you should see a warning that several necessary files will be automatically added to the project. Go ahead and allow this as these files are required to provide things like basic page navigation that you will be using in this example. This page can host sample code for all the various controls you see throughout the rest of the chapter. Don't forget to set this page to load on the application startup in the App.xaml.cs file by modifying the OnLaunched event handler.

2. So that you have a good layout, add a StackPanel control to the main content row of the Grid that exists on the page.

3. Set the Orientation to Horizontal and then drag the following controls into the StackPanel in the correct order: TextBlock, TextBox, Button, and TextBlock.

4. After the controls have been dropped, look at the XAML view of the code to make sure it looks like the following code:

```
<StackPanel Margin="0,20,0,0" Orientation="Horizontal"
VerticalAlignment="Top" Grid.Row="1">
    <TextBlock HorizontalAlignment="Center" TextWrapping="Wrap"
Text="Enter your name:"
VerticalAlignment="Center" FontSize="20"
Margin="20,0,0,0"/>
    <TextBox x:Name="FullName" HorizontalAlignment="Center"
TextWrapping="Wrap" VerticalAlignment="Center"
Width="200" Margin="20,0,0,0"/>
```

```
        <Button x:Name="CreateMessage" Content="Create Message"
HorizontalAlignment="Center"
VerticalAlignment="Center"
Margin="20,0,0,0" Click="CreateMessage_Click"/>
        <TextBlock x:Name="MessageText" HorizontalAlignment="Center"
TextWrapping="Wrap" VerticalAlignment="Center"
FontSize="20"
Margin="20,0,0,0"/>
    </StackPanel>
```

This code provides you with a TextBox control so that your users can enter their name. You also have a TextBlock control ready to display the results of that input after the Button Click event is processed.

5. For this example, you must link the Click event to a handler called CreateMessage_Click in the code behind file Controls.xaml.cs. Go to that file now and add the following code in to implement the method:

```
private void CreateMessage_Click(object sender, RoutedEventArgs e)
{
    MessageText.Text = String.Format("Welcome {0}", Name.Text);
}
```

All that is required of this code is to grab the text that was entered using the Text property of the TextBox control and create a message to display in the TextBlock control — simple event handling code but it forms the basis of how to write code to manipulate the user interface in Windows Store apps. If you are familiar with WPF/Silverlight or ASP.NET/WinForms development, nothing is new here; event handling is the same as it was in those environments but with different controls.

CheckBox

Another user interface control that you will no doubt make use of is the CheckBox. The CheckBox control (like the Button) offers a Content property that you can use to add descriptive text. By default the CheckBox supports your typical checked and unchecked states. You can also set the CheckBox, however, to behave in three state modes that give you Checked, Unchecked, and Indeterminate. This is sometimes useful when you want to force the user to make a selection instead of defaulting to unchecked. Declaring a CheckBox control that uses all three states looks like the following XAML code:

```
<CheckBox x:Name="MainCheck" Content="CheckBox"
Checked="MainCheck_Checked"
Unchecked="MainCheck_Unchecked" IsThreeState="True"/>
```

In this declaration, notice that you set the IsThreeState attribute to true to allow for all three checked states to be valid. You also declare three separate event handlers to handle all three potential state changes. The CheckBox control fires Checked, Unchecked, and Indeterminate events depending on the state of the control. The following code shows the three event handlers updating a TextBlock control with the result of the action:

```
private void MainCheck_Checked(object sender, RoutedEventArgs e)
{
    CheckState.Text = "CheckBox State: Checked";
```

```
    }

    private void MainCheck_Unchecked(object sender, RoutedEventArgs e)
    {
        CheckState.Text = "CheckBox State: Unchecked";
    }

    private void MainCheck_Indeterminate(object sender, RoutedEventArgs e)
    {
        CheckState.Text = "CheckBox State: Indeterminate";
    }
```

HyperlinkButton

The `HyperlinkButton` is a control that works similar to the standard `Button` control but can actually navigate to another page in your app or to an external link depending on what logic you place in the code behind event handler. Like the `Button` control, it uses its `Content` property to determine what text displays. In addition, you can implement the `Click` event handler to actually setup the destination of the hyperlink. To declare a `HyperlinkButton` you can use the following XAML:

```
<HyperlinkButton x:Name="InnerLink" Content="Go to linked page" />
```

What the `HyperlinkButton` navigates to is entirely under your control and is usually manipulated in the code behind with a `Click` event handler. The first scenario, which is navigating to another page in the app, requires you to access the current page's `Frame` object to perform the actual navigation. Now look at a quick example.

1. Open up the Controls.xaml file that you've been using in the `ActionControls` project and add another row to the content Grid.

2. Again add a `StackPanel` with a `Horizontal Orientation` set.

3. Add a `HyperlinkControl` and be sure the XAML code looks like the following:

```
<HyperlinkButton x:Name="InnerLink" Content="Go to linked page"
Click="InnerLink_Click"/>
```

4. Add a new `Page` to the project called HyperlinkedPage.xaml using the Basic Page template. On this page, you simply want to change the title and add a centered `TextBlock` control so that you know the page has changed after navigating, as shown in the following code:

```
<common:LayoutAwarePage
    x:Name="pageRoot"
    x:Class="ActionControls.Controls"
    DataContext="{Binding DefaultViewModel,
RelativeSource={RelativeSource Self}}"
    xmlns="http://schemas.microsoft.com/winfx/2006/xaml/presentation"
    xmlns:x="http://schemas.microsoft.com/winfx/2006/xaml"
    xmlns:local="using:ActionControls"
    xmlns:common="using:ActionControls.Common"
    xmlns:d="http://schemas.microsoft.com/expression/blend/2008"
    xmlns:mc="http://schemas.openxmlformats.org/markup-compatibility/2006"
    mc:Ignorable="d">
```

```xml
<Page.Resources>

    <!-- TODO: Delete this line if the key AppName is
              declared in App.xaml -->
    <x:String x:Key="AppName">My Application</x:String>
</Page.Resources>

<!--
This grid acts as a root panel for the page that defines two rows:
* Row 0 contains the back button and page title
* Row 1 contains the rest of the page layout
-->
<Grid Style="{StaticResource LayoutRootStyle}">
    <Grid.RowDefinitions>
        <RowDefinition Height="140"/>
        <RowDefinition Height="*"/>
    </Grid.RowDefinitions>

    <!-- Back button and page title -->
    <Grid>
        <Grid.ColumnDefinitions>
            <ColumnDefinition Width="Auto"/>
            <ColumnDefinition Width="*"/>
        </Grid.ColumnDefinitions>
        <Button x:Name="backButton" Click="GoBack"
IsEnabled="{Binding Frame.CanGoBack, ElementName=pageRoot}"
Style="{StaticResource BackButtonStyle}"/>
        <TextBlock x:Name="pageTitle" Grid.Column="1"
Style="{StaticResource PageHeaderTextStyle}" Text="Hyperlinked Page"/>
    </Grid>
    <TextBlock Margin="0,20,0,0" Grid.Row="1" TextWrapping="Wrap"
Text="This page contains the linked content" FontSize="20"
HorizontalAlignment="Center" VerticalAlignment="Top"/>

    <VisualStateManager.VisualStateGroups>

    <!-- Visual states reflect the application's view state -->
        <VisualStateGroup x:Name="ApplicationViewStates">
            <VisualState x:Name="FullScreenLandscape"/>
            <VisualState x:Name="Filled"/>

            <!-- The entire page respects the narrower
100-pixel margin convention for portrait -->
            <VisualState x:Name="FullScreenPortrait">
                <Storyboard>
                    <ObjectAnimationUsingKeyFrames
Storyboard.TargetName="backButton"
Storyboard.TargetProperty="Style">
                        <DiscreteObjectKeyFrame KeyTime="0"
Value="{StaticResource PortraitBackButtonStyle}"/>
                    </ObjectAnimationUsingKeyFrames>
                </Storyboard>
            </VisualState>

            <!-- The back button and title have different styles
when snapped -->
```

```
<VisualState x:Name="Snapped">
    <Storyboard>
        <ObjectAnimationUsingKeyFrames
Storyboard.TargetName="backButton" Storyboard.TargetProperty="Style">
            <DiscreteObjectKeyFrame KeyTime="0"
Value="{StaticResource SnappedBackButtonStyle}"/>
        </ObjectAnimationUsingKeyFrames>
        <ObjectAnimationUsingKeyFrames
Storyboard.TargetName="pageTitle" Storyboard.TargetProperty="Style">
            <DiscreteObjectKeyFrame KeyTime="0"
Value="{StaticResource SnappedPageHeaderTextStyle}"/>
        </ObjectAnimationUsingKeyFrames>
    </Storyboard>
</VisualState>
                    </VisualStateGroup>
                </VisualStateManager.VisualStateGroups>
        </Grid>
</common:LayoutAwarePage>
```

5. With the new page added to the project, you must add the code for the `HyperlinkButton` `Click` event. In the following code you are simply making use of the `Navigate` method of the current `Frame` object to create an instance of the `HyperlinkedPage` and then navigate to it.

```
private void InnerLink_Click(object sender, RoutedEventArgs e)
{
    this.Frame.Navigate(typeof(HyperlinkedPage));
}
```

You can see more about how this `Navigate` method works and what the `Frame` control is in Chapter 4, "Windows 8 User Interfaces Final Touches," where you learn about the WinRT page navigation system. For now, just know that this code can load up the new page and redirect the user to it. If you build and run the app in the simulator, you should see your `HyperlinkButton` control. Click the `HyperlinkButton` with the mouse, and you will be redirected to the new page, as shown in Figure 2-12.

FIGURE 2-12

In addition to linking to internal pages in your application you can also use the HyperlinkButton to load content from an external resource. If you scan the various properties available for the `HyperlinkButton`, you see one called `NavigateUri`. In Silverlight-based applications, simply setting this property to a valid URL was all that was required to redirect to an external page. Because Silverlight applications were always running in the context of a browser, this worked just fine. In a Windows Store app, however, you are not running in a browser but in the context of a full-blown thick client app. Setting a URL in this property will not get you what you want. Instead just as before you must handle the `Click` event of the `HyperlinkButton` and manually redirect the user. This time you must make use of a concept called a `Launcher`.

The `Launcher` you want to work with in this case is the default system `Launcher`, which provides a method called `LaunchUriAsync`. You can use this method to redirect the user to any valid external URL resource. It does so by launching an instance of the default web browser and loading up the specified page. In the following code, this method sends the user to `http://www.wiley.com` via the default browser.

```
private void Outerlink_Click(object sender, RoutedEventArgs e)
{
     LaunchBrowser();
}

private async void LaunchBrowser()
{
     var success = await Windows.System.Launcher.LaunchUriAsync(new
Uri("http://www.wiley.com"));
}
```

You may wonder about the syntax used in this example. Because the `LaunchUriAsync` method is asynchronous in nature, you need to make use of the new `await` keyword and encapsulate the `Launcher` call in a method marked async. The `await` keyword essentially enables you to make an asynchronous call but code it in a synchronous way. Instead of implementing complex asynchronous callback methods that are fired when the operation is complete, the `await` keyword forces the system to perform the asynchronous method and wait for its completion before moving on in the code. The other major benefit to this, aside from code that is much easier to read and follow, is that the user interface can accept user input because no actual blocking method call takes place. The `await` keyword internally creates all the code needed for the standard asynchronous callback mechanism and simply returns the result of the method in a synchronous manner.

ComboBox

The `ComboBox` control provides you with an easy way to give your users a choice of options to select from. Almost all development environments provide some form of this control, whether it is a `<select>` tag in HTML or the `DropDownList` control in ASP.NET. Like those other implementations the `ComboBox` consists of the control with a collection of item controls or in this case `ComboBoxItem` objects. Use the following XAML code to declare an instance of a `ComboBox` that contains several option choices:

```
<ComboBox x:Name="MainCombo">
    <ComboBoxItem Content="ASP.NET"/>
    <ComboBoxItem Content="WPF"/>
    <ComboBoxItem Content="Silverlight"/>
    <ComboBoxItem Content="WinForms"/>
    <ComboBoxItem Content="WinRT"/>
    <ComboBoxItem Content="Select Item" IsSelected="True"/>
</ComboBox>
```

Notice how the ComboBoxItem objects make use of the Content property to determine what displays upon selection. To determine which item should be selected by default, you can set the IsSelected property to true for the appropriate ComboBoxItem object. Now if you want to be notified when a selection has been made and need to perform logic when that happens, you can hook up an event handler for the SelectionChanged event. This event handler provides you with an AddedItems collection that you can use to extract the selected ComboBoxItem. The following code shows how you can update the user interface with the selected ComboBox option:

```
private void BasicCombo_SelectionChanged(object sender,
SelectionChangedEventArgs e)
{
    ComboBoxItem selected = e.AddedItems[0] as ComboBoxItem;

    if (selected != null && SelectedComboItem != null)
        SelectedComboItem.Text = String.Format("Selected Item: {0}",
selected.Content);
}
```

When a user makes a selection in the ComboBox control, the selected item that is extracted is of type object. This is slightly different from how other ComboBox style controls are done in ASP.NET and WinForms. In this case because you are statically declaring the content as ComboBoxItems, you can safely cast the selection to that type and use the Content property to display the selected string. However, the ComboBox is even more flexible than that. The reason the AddedItems collection returns object types is because it enables the collection of items to be any kind of business class. This means you can set the list of ComboBoxItems to your own business objects and configure the ComboBox to display a certain property of that class for the text shown to the user. Now look at a simple example. Say you have a class called Book with several properties such as ID, Author, and Title. You will probably end up with the following code:

```
public class Book
{
    public int ID { get; set; }
    public string Author { get; set; }
    public string Title { get; set; }
}
```

Now say that you want the ComboBox control to present to the user a collection of Books, but you want the text displayed to the user to be the Title of the book. You would follow these steps:

1. You need a collection of Book items, which can be built with the following code somewhere in the constructor of the page.

```
private void LoadBooks()
{
    List<Book> books = new List<Book>();

    books.Add(new Book { Author = "", Title = "Please Select A Book",
ID = -1 });
    books.Add(new Book { Author = "Nick Lecrenski",
Title = "Silverlight 4.0 Problem Design Solution", ID = 1 });
    books.Add(new Book { Author = "Doug Holland",
Title = "Professional Windows 8 Metro Development", ID = 2 });

}
```

At this point you have a collection of `Book` objects complete with a dummy object that represents the default selection that simply tells the users they need to select a book.

2. You give that object an `ID` of –1 so that you can easily differentiate it from a valid `Book` object.

3. You need to tell the `ComboBox` to use this collection of objects and to make sure that the dummy `Book` object is selected by default. In the following code you can do this by setting the `ItemsSource` property to the collection of `Book` objects and the `SelectedIndex` to the correct `Book` in the collection.

```
AdvancedCombo.ItemsSource = books;
AdvancedCombo.SelectedIndex = 0;
```

4. You need to tell the `ComboBox` control what property of the `Book` class it should use as the content to display to the user. Do this using the `DisplayMemberPath` property directly in the XAML declaration for the `ComboBox`. The following code shows the updated XAML for this:

```
<ComboBox x:Name="AdvancedCombo" DisplayMemberPath="Title"
SelectionChanged="AdvancedCombo_SelectionChanged" />
```

Because you probably want to perform some logic when a selection is made, there is an event handler also wired up in the previous code. The `DisplayMemberPath` is a powerful mechanism that makes it easy for you to use your own custom business objects to populate the `ComboBox`. As you see in the next chapter, the concept can be taken even further using data binding to further reduce the setup code.

5. All that is left now is to take a look at how to grab the selected `Book` when a selection is made. In the following event handler code, the `AddedItems` collection again is used to grab the selected `ComboBoxItem`; however, it can safely be cast as a `Book` type. Now that you have a `Book` object, you can access the `ID` property to make sure a valid `Book` was selected and then update the user interface to alert the user of the selection that was made.

```
private void AdvancedCombo_SelectionChanged(object sender,
SelectionChangedEventArgs e)
{
    Book selected = e.AddedItems[0] as Book;

    if (selected.ID > 0)
```

```
                AdvancedComboSelectedValue.Text =
        String.Format("Selection: Title - {0} Author - {1}", selected.Title,
        selected.Author);
            else
                AdvancedComboSelectedValue.Text = "";
    }
```

RadioButton

The RadioButton control is similar to the ComboBox control in that it provides the user with a set of choices/options. Unlike the ComboBox control, which displays only a selected option, a set of RadioButton controls usually present all available options on the screen at the same time. The following code shows the basic XAML required to add a RadioButton to your user interface.

```
<RadioButton Content="Option 1" IsChecked="True"/>
```

Like most XAML controls, the Content property determines what text should display to the user along with the actual RadioButton control. The RadioButton also provides an IsChecked property to set up the default selection state. Although it is perfectly valid to present only a single choice with a RadioButton, the control is useful when you add a group of them to the screen. The most common scenario for a group of RadioButtons is to provide a list of options to the user but allow only for one valid selection at a time. This means if the user selects another RadioButton control, whatever RadioButton is currently selected should become deselected. This is fully supported in the XAML RadioButton and is done by making use of the GroupName property. In the following XAML code, three RadioButton controls are added to the user interface, and by setting the GroupName property to the same value, only one choice is allowed across all three RadioButton controls.

```
<RadioButton Content="Option 1" GroupName="RadioOptions" IsChecked="True"/>
<RadioButton Content="Option 2" GroupName="RadioOptions"/>
<RadioButton Content="Option 3" GroupName="RadioOptions"/>
```

Slider

The Slider control is a useful control in your user interface when you want to increment/decrement a particular value. When declaring a Slider control, you want to set the Minimum and Maximum properties to values that make sense for your scenario. By default, these are set to 0 and 100, respectively. The following XAML code shows a basic Slider control declared that uses a range of 0 to 500.

```
<Slider x:Name="MainSlider" Minimum="0" Maximum="500" />
```

To capture the actual value that users select when they complete moving the slider, you can implement an event handler for the ValueChanged event. In the following code the Value property determines what position the Slider stops at. Because, by default, the Value property is a double type, you can simply cast it to an int if you don't require measurements that precise.

```
private void MainSlider_ValueChanged(object sender,
RangeBaseValueChangedEventArgs e)
{
    SliderValue.Text = String.Format("Slider Value: {0}", (int)MainSlider.Value);
}
```

The Slider control also includes several properties that can alter the appearance of the control. For example, if you want the Slider to show tick marks as the user interacts with the control, set the TickFrequency property to a value other than zero. You can also control where the tick marks appear with the TickPlacement property. Values for this include Inline, TopLeft, BottomRight, and Outside.

Image

You can use the Image control to display images in your app. These images can reside internally in your application or can also display from external resources. The Image control uses its Source property to determine what to display. The following XAML code displays the cover art for this book using no stretching:

```
<Image Source="Assets/book.png" Stretch="None"/>
```

The Source property in this case looks for a file called book.png in the Assets folder of your project. The Stretch property offers several possible values including None, Fill, Uniform, and UniformToFill. If you simply want to display the image at its default size, you use the Stretch option of None. If, however, you have a larger container, you can set the Stretch property to one of the alternative fill options, and the image will stretch to fill the remaining space in the container. The Image control can also display an external resource by simply setting the Source property to a valid URL such as the following:

```
<Image Source="http://media.wiley.com/product_data/coverImage/82/11180126/
1118012682.jpg" Stretch="None"/>
```

MediaElement

In addition to the Image control, the MediaElement control provides you with a quick and easy way to add multimedia to your app. This powerful control can play all sorts of media ranging from assets included in your project to external resources on the Web. When using the MediaElement control the Source property is where the magic happens. You can set the source to an internal asset using the drop-down box in the Properties pane, or you can simply type a URL to use. The following code shows a MediaElement that links to an existing Channel 9 video.

```
<MediaElement Margin="20,0,0,0" Source="http://media.ch9.ms/ch9/bf13/
ff35aa0d-534b-4302-94d0-cf7fd2b4bf13/TWC9July132012_Source.wmv"
Volume="0.05"/>
```

The Source points to the URL of the resource you want to include. In addition to the Source attribute, the Volume property is set to 0.05 to slightly decrease the default volume that the clip is played at. If you build and run the code using this MediaElement, you can see that the video clip starts playing as soon as it is available. This may be the behavior you want, but you can change it by setting the AutoPlay property to true or false depending on when you want the media to start playing.

Referring to the figure, although the video clip is visible and playing, there are not any actual playback controls available. The MediaElement is a powerful video player control but does not provide a user interface to actually control the media. It does however offer several methods that can easily create your own playback functionality. The following code shows updated XAML that adds several playback buttons to the user interface to control the MediaElement playback. Each Button control uses an event handler to call the appropriate method on the MediaElement for each required playback option.

```xml
<MediaElement x:Name="MainMedia"  Source="http://media.ch9.ms/ch9/bf13/
ff35aa0d-534b-4302-94d0-cf7fd2b4bf13/TWC9July132012_Source.wmv"
Volume="0.05" AutoPlay="False"/>
    <StackPanel VerticalAlignment="Top" HorizontalAlignment="Left"
Margin="20,0,0,0">
        <Button x:Name="Play" Content="Play" VerticalAlignment="Top"
Margin="0,0,0,10" Width="120" Click="Play_Click"/>
        <Button x:Name="Stop" Content="Stop" VerticalAlignment="Top"
Margin="0,0,0,10" Width="120" Click="Stop_Click"/>
        <Button x:Name="Rewind" Content="Rewind"
VerticalAlignment="Top" Margin="0,0,0,10"
Width="120" Click="Rewind_Click"/>
        <Button x:Name="FastForward" Content="Fast Forward"
VerticalAlignment="Top" Margin="0,0,0,10"
Click="FastForward_Click"/>
</StackPanel>
```

Now that you have some Button controls created and wired to the appropriate event handlers, you need code to implement each of these actions on the MediaElement. The following code shows the code behind for each of these methods. For the Fast Forward and Rewind operations, you must first check the CanSeek property before attempting to move the current Position of the media because not all media files support seeking operations.

```csharp
private void Play_Click(object sender, RoutedEventArgs e)
{
    MainMedia.Play();
}

private void Stop_Click(object sender, RoutedEventArgs e)
{
    MainMedia.Stop();
}

private void Rewind_Click(object sender, RoutedEventArgs e)
{
    if (MainMedia.CanSeek)
        MainMedia.Position = MainMedia.Position.Subtract(new TimeSpan(0, 0, 10));
}

private void FastForward_Click(object sender, RoutedEventArgs e)
{
    if (MainMedia.CanSeek)
        MainMedia.Position = MainMedia.Position.Add(new TimeSpan(0, 0, 10));
}
```

SUMMARY

With this chapter complete, if you have never seen or heard of XAML, you should have a good idea of how to start using XAML to create powerful Windows 8 user interfaces. If you've used XAML in the past, hopefully you got a quick refresher in some of the basics. This chapter displayed some of the basic WinRT controls that you can create in XAML as well as the event handling mechanism used to manipulate the controls and user interface.

In addition to understanding the various basic controls that you can use in your interfaces, you should also have a good understanding of the layout controls such as the `Grid`, `StackPanel`, and `Canvas`. Understanding the `Grid` control is critical to creating user interfaces going forward in this book. You should know how to add rows and columns to the `Grid` and how to properly size them depending on the controls that the `Grid` contains. You saw how the `Grid` control supports `Auto`, `Pixel`, and `Star` based sizing algorithms that give you plenty of flexibility to create fluid tables such as layouts. You also saw that when you need to create a layout that makes use of an absolute positioning mechanism the `Canvas` control is much better suited than the `Grid`.

The next chapter and the remainder of the book require you to understand the basics of XAML, control event handling, and the various layout controls. You'll see even more powerful controls available in WinRT and Windows Store apps, and you'll be introduced to the concept of Data Binding, which can help you to cut back further on the amount of code required in the code behind. You will see how to use several of the Windows 8 data controls to help you present content to your users from various data sources.

If you feel confident in your XAML abilities at this point, charge ahead; if not don't hesitate to refer to some of the samples in this chapter to get a solid feel for how to utilize things, such as the `Button`, `TextBlock`, `Grid`, `StackPanel`, and `TextBox` controls. This will form a basis for the user interfaces you will create going forward.

3

Enhancing Your Apps with Control Styles, Data Binding, and Semantic Zoom

WHAT'S IN THIS CHAPTER?

- ➤ Understanding control styling
- ➤ Hooking your user interface controls with Data Binding
- ➤ How to use the various Data Binding controls
- ➤ Using the Semantic Zoom for a large number of items
- ➤ How to create your own custom control

WROX.COM CODE DOWNLOADS FOR THIS CHAPTER

You can find the wrox.com code downloads for this chapter in the code file 205709 C03.zip at www.wrox.com/remtitle.cgi?isbn=1118205707 on the Download Code tab.

CUSTOMIZING YOUR APPS

In the previous chapter, you were introduced to the XAML user interface language and were shown how to create basic user interfaces using the standard Windows 8 XAML controls. You should now be familiar with how to use the various layout controls such as the Grid, StackPanel, and Canvas. You should also understand how to work with the various control events through the appropriate control event handler methods in the code-behind files. This chapter takes all these basic concepts a few steps further and introduces you to some additional features of XAML that both help you to reduce the amount of code you write and provide more powerful user interfaces for your Windows Store apps.

In this chapter you see how to customize the standard controls using control styles. It also introduces you to the topic of data binding, which enables you to create user interfaces that are dynamic and data centric with minimal amounts of code. After you have a good handle on data binding concepts, you'll create custom controls that you can use in addition to the standard Windows 8 controls. Knowing how to build custom controls allows you to easily reuse common user interface elements and even support custom data binding to the control properties where applicable.

After you have a good handle on control styling, data binding, and custom controls, you see how to make use of the new data controls in Windows 8. Controls, like the `ListView` and `GridView`, were designed for data presentation using powerful data binding to make it easy for you, the developer, to present lists of data and information to your users. Finally you see how to add SemanticZoom features to your `GridView` that helps give your users an easy way to navigate through large lists of data.

STYLING CONTROLS

When you start creating user interfaces for Windows 8, you usually place a layout control, such as a `Grid` or `StackPanel`, onto the design area and add some basic controls to the screen. You may add a `TextBlock` to display some static text or a `TextBox` to collect some user input. You may have noticed that after dropping the controls onto the design area they all default to a certain look and feel. In the previous chapter, you used the Properties pane in Visual Studio 2012 to adjust various properties, such as the `Font`, `FontSize`, `Margin`, and so on. Doing this for a few controls in a simple demo application is no big deal and not time-consuming. Trying to do this for complex user interfaces with many different pages becomes a tedious task quickly.

If you have any kind of web development background, you surely are familiar with *Cascading Style Sheets* (CSS) and their ability to apply various styles to controls and elements on a particular web page. The beauty of CSS is that you can create a style of attributes and quickly apply them to all HTML elements on a page that match a given selector, such as a class or id. XAML provides a similar concept with control styles. *Control styles* work similar to CSS in that you can create a style and apply it to a particular XAML control instance, or you can create it in such a way that it is generic to all instances of a given XAML control. This section examines a basic example of control styling.

Understanding Basic Styling

Figure 3-1 shows a simple user interface consisting of a couple of `TextBlock` and `TextBox` controls. Both the `TextBox` controls must have the same width and the `FontSize` of the `TextBlock` controls have been adjusted higher.

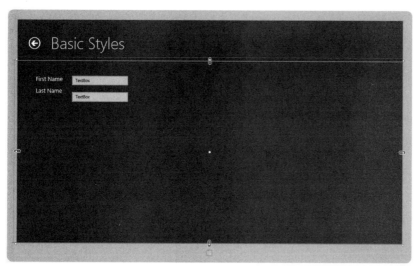

FIGURE 3-1

In addition to the font size and overall width of the controls, there are also other common things — such as the text color, alignment, and even `Margin` properties for the `TextBlock` and `TextBox` controls here. In this case the full XAML declaration for this set of controls looks like the following:

```
<Grid Margin="0" Grid.Row="1">
    <TextBlock HorizontalAlignment="Left" Margin="65,53,0,0"
TextWrapping="Wrap" Text="First Name" VerticalAlignment="Top"
FontSize="20"/>
    <TextBox HorizontalAlignment="Left" Margin="193,53,0,0"
TextWrapping="Wrap" Text="TextBox" VerticalAlignment="Top"
Width="200"/>
    <TextBlock HorizontalAlignment="Left" Margin="65,93,0,0"
TextWrapping="Wrap" Text="Last Name" VerticalAlignment="Top"
FontSize="20"/>
    <TextBox HorizontalAlignment="Left" Margin="193,109,0,0"
TextWrapping="Wrap" Text="TextBox" VerticalAlignment="Top"
Width="200"/>
</Grid>
```

As you can see, there are a lot of common property values here like the `TextWrapping`, `VerticalAlignment`, `HorizontalAlignment`, and so on. Now if you want to add another data entry form to a different page in the app and you want it to also have similar characteristics, such as the `Width` of the `TextBox` controls, for example, you would again need to adjust all these values or minimally copy and paste the previous code to at least get you a head start. Using control styles, however, makes the entire process much simpler.

Control styles are basically a collection of properties like CSS attributes that reside in the Resources section of either the file you are working with or the `App.xaml` file. Style definitions can also be located in a separate resource file called a `ResourceDictionary`. You can include them in the app by adding a line in the `App.xaml` file. This behavior is close to how HTML style sheets are included in the `Head` area of the HTML document. As far as where to place the style definitions, that depends on a few things:

➤ If you need only the styles for controls on a particular page, you can simply add them to that page between the following Resource tags:

```
<Page.Resources>

<!-- TODO: Delete this line if the key AppName is declared in App.xaml -->
</Page.Resources>
```

➤ If you think you need to reuse the style information across multiple pages or if you want a particular style to apply to all instances of a given XAML control type, you need to include it either in App.xaml or a `ResourceDictionary` file.

For the following example, assume that you need only these styles for this particular page of the app. In this case you can add the style information to the `Page.Resources` section. In doing so, you end up with the code shown in Listing 3-1.

LISTING 3-1: Chapter 3\ControlStyling\BasicStyles.xaml

```
<common:LayoutAwarePage
    x:Name="pageRoot"
    x:Class="ControlStyling.BasicStyles"
    DataContext="{Binding DefaultViewModel, RelativeSource={RelativeSource Self}}"
    IsTabStop="false"
    xmlns="http://schemas.microsoft.com/winfx/2006/xaml/presentation"
    xmlns:x="http://schemas.microsoft.com/winfx/2006/xaml"
    xmlns:local="using:ControlStyling"
    xmlns:common="using:ControlStyling.Common"
    xmlns:d="http://schemas.microsoft.com/expression/blend/2008"
    xmlns:mc="http://schemas.openxmlformats.org/markup-compatibility/2006"
    mc:Ignorable="d">

<Page.Resources>

    <!-- TODO: Delete this line if the key AppName is declared in App.xaml -->
    <x:String x:Key="AppName">Basic Styles</x:String>

    <Style x:Key="BasicTextBlockStyle" TargetType="TextBlock">
        <Setter Property="HorizontalAlignment" Value="Left"/>
        <Setter Property="VerticalAlignment" Value="Top"/>
        <Setter Property="TextWrapping" Value="Wrap"/>
        <Setter Property="FontSize" Value="20"/>
    </Style>

    <Style x:Key="BasicTextBoxStyle" TargetType="TextBox">
        <Setter Property="HorizontalAlignment" Value="Left"/>
```

```
            <Setter Property="VerticalAlignment" Value="Top"/>
            <Setter Property="TextWrapping" Value="Wrap"/>
            <Setter Property="Width" Value="200"/>
        </Style>

</Page.Resources>

<!--
This grid acts as a root panel for the page that defines two rows:
* Row 0 contains the back button and page title
* Row 1 contains the rest of the page layout
-->
<Grid Style="{StaticResource LayoutRootStyle}">
     <Grid.RowDefinitions>
         <RowDefinition Height="140"/>
         <RowDefinition Height="*"/>
     </Grid.RowDefinitions>

     <!-- Back button and page title -->
     <Grid>
         <Grid.ColumnDefinitions>
             <ColumnDefinition Width="Auto"/>
             <ColumnDefinition Width="*"/>
         </Grid.ColumnDefinitions>
         <Button x:Name="backButton" Click="GoBack"
IsEnabled="{Binding Frame.CanGoBack, ElementName=pageRoot}"
Style="{StaticResource BackButtonStyle}"/>
         <TextBlock x:Name="pageTitle" Grid.Column="1"
Text="{StaticResource AppName}" Style="{StaticResource
PageHeaderTextStyle}"/>
     </Grid>
     <Grid Margin="0" Grid.Row="1">
         <TextBlock Margin="65,53,0,0" Text="First Name" Style="{StaticResource
BasicTextBlockStyle}" />
         <TextBox Margin="193,53,0,0"  Text="TextBox" Style="{StaticResource
BasicTextBoxStyle}"/>
         <TextBlock Margin="65,93,0,0" Text="Last Name" Style="{StaticResource
BasicTextBlockStyle}"/>
         <TextBox Margin="193,109,0,0" Text="TextBox" Style="{StaticResource
BasicTextBoxStyle}"/>
     </Grid>

     <VisualStateManager.VisualStateGroups>

         <!-- Visual states reflect the application's view state -->
             <VisualStateGroup x:Name="ApplicationViewStates">
                 <VisualState x:Name="FullScreenLandscape"/>
                 <VisualState x:Name="Filled"/>

                 <!-- The entire page respects the narrower 100-pixel margin
convention for portrait -->
                 <VisualState x:Name="FullScreenPortrait">
                     <Storyboard>
                         <ObjectAnimationUsingKeyFrames
Storyboard.TargetName="backButton" Storyboard.TargetProperty="Style">
```

```xml
                                        <DiscreteObjectKeyFrame KeyTime="0"
Value="{StaticResource PortraitBackButtonStyle}"/>
                                    </ObjectAnimationUsingKeyFrames>
                                </Storyboard>
                            </VisualState>

                            <!-- The back button and title have different styles when
snapped -->
                            <VisualState x:Name="Snapped">
                                <Storyboard>
                                    <ObjectAnimationUsingKeyFrames
Storyboard.TargetName="backButton" Storyboard.TargetProperty="Style">
                                        <DiscreteObjectKeyFrame KeyTime="0"
Value="{StaticResource SnappedBackButtonStyle}"/>
                                    </ObjectAnimationUsingKeyFrames>
                                    <ObjectAnimationUsingKeyFrames
Storyboard.TargetName="pageTitle" Storyboard.TargetProperty="Style">
                                        <DiscreteObjectKeyFrame KeyTime="0"
Value="{StaticResource SnappedPageHeaderTextStyle}"/>
                                    </ObjectAnimationUsingKeyFrames>
                                </Storyboard>
                            </VisualState>
                        </VisualStateGroup>
                    </VisualStateManager.VisualStateGroups>
            </Grid>
    </common:LayoutAwarePage>
```

Now with the style information extracted out and shared, the original code example is reduced to the following code:

```xml
<Grid Margin="0" Grid.Row="1">
    <TextBlock Margin="65,53,0,0" Text="First Name" Style="{StaticResource
BasicTextBlockStyle}" />
    <TextBox Margin="193,53,0,0"  Text="TextBox" Style="{StaticResource
BasicTextBoxStyle}"/>
    <TextBlock Margin="65,93,0,0" Text="Last Name" Style="{StaticResource
BasicTextBlockStyle}"/>
    <TextBox Margin="193,109,0,0" Text="TextBox" Style="{StaticResource
BasicTextBoxStyle}"/>
</Grid>
```

As you can see in the Page.Resources section, the following code declares the styles necessary to achieve the effect:

```xml
<Style x:Key="BasicTextBlockStyle" TargetType="TextBlock">
    <Setter Property="HorizontalAlignment" Value="Left"/>
    <Setter Property="VerticalAlignment" Value="Top"/>
    <Setter Property="TextWrapping" Value="Wrap"/>
    <Setter Property="FontSize" Value="20"/>
</Style>

<Style x:Key="BasicTextBoxStyle" TargetType="TextBox">
    <Setter Property="HorizontalAlignment" Value="Left"/>
```

```
            <Setter Property="VerticalAlignment" Value="Top"/>
            <Setter Property="TextWrapping" Value="Wrap"/>
            <Setter Property="Width" Value="200"/>
        </Style>
```

The `Style` tag in XAML starts the declaration of a new set of styles to apply to a particular control or set of controls. By adding the `x:Name` attribute you create a named style. That means that the style applies only to the controls set up to use that specific style. This was done in the previous example by setting the `Style` property of the `TextBlock` or `TextBox` with the following code:

```
    Style="{StaticResource BasicTextBoxStyle}"
```

The `StaticResource` syntax is basically telling the system to look for a `Style` declaration named "BasicTextBoxStyle" and apply it to this control. The system searches the `Page.Resources` section for the `Page` the control currently resides in and then the App.xaml file and any embedded `ResourceDictionary` files.

> **NOTE** *In addition to the* `x:Name` *attribute, the* `TargetType` *attribute is also set to the type of control the* `Style` *should be applied to. In this example, these were set to* TextBlock *and* TextBox, *but you can also create styles for any of the other standard XAML controls, such as* Button, Grid, *and* StackPanel. *When setting the* `TargetType` *to a particular type of XAML control, remember to include only property settings for properties that actually exist for that control. For example if you were to have a* `TargetType` *of* Button *and attempt to add a setting for the* Text *property, your app would crash if you ran it because the* Button *control uses the* Content *property instead of* Text *to determine what displays.*

You can also use the `TargetType` attribute to apply a style globally to all instances of a particular control. For example, if you want all `TextBox` controls to have the previous style applied, you can rewrite the style omitting the `x:Name` attribute like this:

```
    <Style TargetType="TextBox">
        <Setter Property="HorizontalAlignment" Value="Left"/>
        <Setter Property="VerticalAlignment" Value="Top"/>
        <Setter Property="TextWrapping" Value="Wrap"/>
        <Setter Property="Width" Value="200"/>
    </Style>
```

Now, just remove the `Style` assignment from the `TextBox` controls in your XAML code, and the `Style` will automatically apply. If for some reason you want one particular `TextBox` to stand out, you can still add another named `Style` and add the `Style` assignment on that instance of the control, and the `Style` would apply. When using class-based styles versus id-based styles, this works almost the same way as CSS does. In XAML, the main difference is that you don't need to add anything to the instances of the controls if you want unnamed `Style` definitions to apply to those controls.

Referencing Styles Across an App

In your app, you may need to create many different styles for your controls, and in doing so you most likely need to reference them across your app and not just a single page. You have several options for this:

➤ **Using the App.xaml file:** Adding the wanted styles to the `App.xaml` file, by default, makes them available across your app.

➤ **Add the styles to a custom `ResourceDictionary`.** This is sometimes one of the better ways to reference styles. This type of file is designed to hold style information. You can easily include it to provide global access in your app to the resources stored in it. In addition to control styles, it is also common to put string resources for globalization in a `ResourceDictionary`. This makes it easy to swap one language for another while the app runs or if you simply need to support different environments.

Using the previous example, again, make these styles global to the application by adding them to a `ResourceDictionary`. To create a new `ResourceDictionary`, follow these steps:

1. Right-click the `Project` node in Solution Explorer, and select Add New File.

2. When the dialog appears, choose the `ResourceDictionary` option, as shown in Figure 3-2, and give your `ResourceDictionary` a name.

FIGURE 3-2

3. After this process finishes, simply open the new file and copy/paste any control styles you may have that you want to include. In Listing 3-2 you can see an updated `ResourceDictionary` file that contains the `TextBox` and `TextBlock` styles used previously.

LISTING 3-2: Chapter 3\ControlStyling\BasicStyleDictionary.xaml

```
<ResourceDictionary
    xmlns="http://schemas.microsoft.com/winfx/2006/xaml/presentation"
    xmlns:x="http://schemas.microsoft.com/winfx/2006/xaml"
    xmlns:local="using:ControlStyling">

    <Style x:Key="BasicTextBlockStyle" TargetType="TextBlock">
        <Setter Property="HorizontalAlignment" Value="Left"/>
        <Setter Property="VerticalAlignment" Value="Top"/>
        <Setter Property="TextWrapping" Value="Wrap"/>
        <Setter Property="FontSize" Value="20"/>
    </Style>

    <Style x:Key="BasicTextBoxStyle" TargetType="TextBox">
        <Setter Property="HorizontalAlignment" Value="Left"/>
        <Setter Property="VerticalAlignment" Value="Top"/>
        <Setter Property="TextWrapping" Value="Wrap"/>
        <Setter Property="Width" Value="200"/>
</Style>

</ResourceDictionary>
```

4. Now that the styles are included in a `ResourceDictionary`, you must include the dictionary in the app before these styles are globally available. If you open up the App .xaml file, you can see a section called `Application.Resources`. In this section you can add any `ResourceDictionary` files you need by placing them to the `ResourceDictionary` .MergedDictionaries collection. Listing 3-3 shows an `App.xaml` file that contains the new `ResourceDictionary` and the `StandardStyles` file that is automatically added to the project by the project template.

LISTING 3-3: Chapter 3\ControlStyling\App.xaml

```
<Application
    x:Class="ControlStyling.App"
    xmlns="http://schemas.microsoft.com/winfx/2006/xaml/presentation"
    xmlns:x="http://schemas.microsoft.com/winfx/2006/xaml"
    xmlns:local="using:ControlStyling">

    <Application.Resources>
        <ResourceDictionary>
            <ResourceDictionary.MergedDictionaries>
```

```
        <!--
            Styles that define common aspects of the platform look and feel
            Required by Visual Studio project and item templates
        -->
            <ResourceDictionary Source="Common/StandardStyles.xaml"/>
            <ResourceDictionary Source="BasicStyleDictionary.xaml"/>
        </ResourceDictionary.MergedDictionaries>

    </ResourceDictionary>
  </Application.Resources>
</Application>
```

Using Microsoft's Default Styles

As you can imagine referencing styles across an app opens up many possibilities for styling controls
and reusing those styles throughout your application. The Windows 8 project templates typically
include many recommended `Style` definitions that you can use across the various controls. To keep
a consistent user interface across Windows Store apps, Microsoft provides these default styles and
encourages you use them with standard controls whenever possible. Listing 3-4 shows some of the
default styles for Windows 8 controls that you can use. These styles are automatically added to
your project in the Common\StandardStyles.xaml file if you add a new `Page` to your app using the
`BasicPage` item template.

LISTING 3-4: Chapter 3\ControlStyling\Common\StandardStyles.xaml

```
<!--
This file contains XAML styles that simplify application development.

These are not merely convenient, but are required by most Visual Studio
project and item templates.
Removing, renaming, or otherwise modifying the content of these files may
result in a project that
does not build, or that will not build once additional pages are added.
If variations on these
styles are desired it is recommended that you copy the content under a
new name and modify your
private copy.
-->

<ResourceDictionary
    xmlns="http://schemas.microsoft.com/winfx/2006/xaml/presentation"
    xmlns:x="http://schemas.microsoft.com/winfx/2006/xaml">

    <!-- Non-brush values that vary across themes -->

    <ResourceDictionary.ThemeDictionaries>
        <ResourceDictionary x:Key="Default">
            <x:String x:Key="BackButtonGlyph">&#xE071;</x:String>
            <x:String x:Key="BackButtonSnappedGlyph">&#xE0BA;</x:String>
        </ResourceDictionary>
```

```xml
            <ResourceDictionary x:Key="HighContrast">
                <x:String x:Key="BackButtonGlyph">&#xE0A6;</x:String>
                <x:String x:Key="BackButtonSnappedGlyph">&#xE0C4;</x:String>
            </ResourceDictionary>
        </ResourceDictionary.ThemeDictionaries>

    <!-- RichTextBlock styles -->

    <Style x:Key="BasicRichTextStyle" TargetType="RichTextBlock">
        <Setter Property="Foreground" Value="{StaticResource
ApplicationForegroundThemeBrush}"/>
        <Setter Property="FontSize" Value="{StaticResource
ControlContentThemeFontSize}"/>
        <Setter Property="FontFamily" Value="{StaticResource
ContentControlThemeFontFamily}"/>
        <Setter Property="TextTrimming" Value="WordEllipsis"/>
        <Setter Property="TextWrapping" Value="Wrap"/>
        <Setter Property="Typography.StylisticSet20" Value="True"/>
        <Setter Property="Typography.DiscretionaryLigatures" Value="True"/>
        <Setter Property="Typography.CaseSensitiveForms" Value="True"/>
    </Style>

    <Style x:Key="BaselineRichTextStyle" TargetType="RichTextBlock"
BasedOn="{StaticResource BasicRichTextStyle}">
        <Setter Property="LineHeight" Value="20"/>
        <Setter Property="LineStackingStrategy" Value="BlockLineHeight"/>
        <!-- Properly align text along its baseline -->
        <Setter Property="RenderTransform">
            <Setter.Value>
                <TranslateTransform X="-1" Y="4"/>
            </Setter.Value>
        </Setter>
    </Style>

    <Style x:Key="ItemRichTextStyle" TargetType="RichTextBlock"
BasedOn="{StaticResource BaselineRichTextStyle}"/>

    <Style x:Key="BodyRichTextStyle" TargetType="RichTextBlock"
BasedOn="{StaticResource BaselineRichTextStyle}">
        <Setter Property="FontWeight" Value="SemiLight"/>
    </Style>

    <!-- TextBlock styles -->

    <Style x:Key="BasicTextStyle" TargetType="TextBlock">
        <Setter Property="Foreground" Value="{StaticResource
ApplicationForegroundThemeBrush}"/>
        <Setter Property="FontSize" Value="{StaticResource
ControlContentThemeFontSize}"/>
        <Setter Property="FontFamily" Value="{StaticResource
ContentControlThemeFontFamily}"/>
        <Setter Property="TextTrimming" Value="WordEllipsis"/>
        <Setter Property="TextWrapping" Value="Wrap"/>
```

```xml
            <Setter Property="Typography.StylisticSet20" Value="True"/>
            <Setter Property="Typography.DiscretionaryLigatures" Value="True"/>
            <Setter Property="Typography.CaseSensitiveForms" Value="True"/>
    </Style>

    <Style x:Key="BaselineTextStyle" TargetType="TextBlock"
BasedOn="{StaticResource BasicTextStyle}">
            <Setter Property="LineHeight" Value="20"/>
            <Setter Property="LineStackingStrategy" Value="BlockLineHeight"/>
            <!-- Properly align text along its baseline -->
            <Setter Property="RenderTransform">
                <Setter.Value>
                    <TranslateTransform X="-1" Y="4"/>
                </Setter.Value>
            </Setter>
    </Style>

    <Style x:Key="HeaderTextStyle" TargetType="TextBlock"
BasedOn="{StaticResource BaselineTextStyle}">
            <Setter Property="FontSize" Value="56"/>
            <Setter Property="FontWeight" Value="Light"/>
            <Setter Property="LineHeight" Value="40"/>
            <Setter Property="RenderTransform">
                <Setter.Value>
                    <TranslateTransform X="-2" Y="8"/>
                </Setter.Value>
            </Setter>
    </Style>

    <Style x:Key="SubheaderTextStyle" TargetType="TextBlock"
BasedOn="{StaticResource BaselineTextStyle}">
            <Setter Property="FontSize" Value="26.667"/>
            <Setter Property="FontWeight" Value="Light"/>
            <Setter Property="LineHeight" Value="30"/>
            <Setter Property="RenderTransform">
                <Setter.Value>
                    <TranslateTransform X="-1" Y="6"/>
                </Setter.Value>
            </Setter>
    </Style>

    <Style x:Key="TitleTextStyle" TargetType="TextBlock"
BasedOn="{StaticResource BaselineTextStyle}">
            <Setter Property="FontWeight" Value="SemiBold"/>
    </Style>

    <Style x:Key="ItemTextStyle" TargetType="TextBlock"
BasedOn="{StaticResource BaselineTextStyle}"/>

    <Style x:Key="BodyTextStyle" TargetType="TextBlock"
BasedOn="{StaticResource BaselineTextStyle}">
            <Setter Property="FontWeight" Value="SemiLight"/>
    </Style>
```

DATA BINDING

When using XAML controls, another important concept in your Windows Store app user interface is Data Binding. In the previous chapter you saw how to build a basic data entry form. When the user enters data you presumably would write some code in the code behind to extract the data from the controls and ultimately store it in a database somewhere. Then when it's time to load that data back to the user interface, you would go through the tedious process to gain access to an instance of each control and appropriate property to the value of the data being loaded. Naturally this process becomes more complex when you start using larger data entry forms.

Data binding in XAML provides you a better way to hook your user interface controls to the underlying data being displayed or manipulated. By making use of data binding, you not only eliminate all the direct control access code traditionally required to update the user interface, but you also get some additional benefits, such as having your user interface automatically update when the data changes. For example, in the standard data entry form setting, any time you load the data from the back end you need to add code to set properties on every user interface control that is responsible to display the data. With data binding, you simply refresh the data source, and the data binding automatically handles refreshing the user interface to reflect the changes. The rest of this section looks at a simple example of basic data binding and how easy it is to get set up in XAML.

Understanding Basic Data Entry

Figure 3-3 shows a basic data entry form consisting of a first name, a last name, and an email field. Now assume you want to populate it with data from a `Person` class loaded from a database somewhere. Listing 3-5 shows the code for the `Person` class.

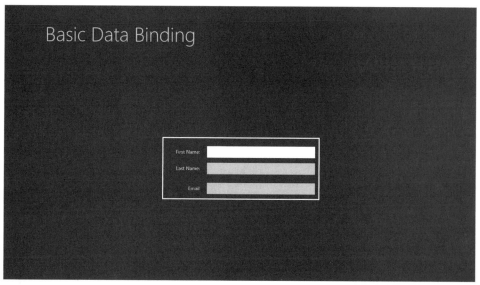

FIGURE 3-3

LISTING 3-5: Chapter 3\BasicDataBinding\Data\Person.cs

```
namespace BasicDataBinding.Data
{
    public class Person
    {
        public string FirstName { get; set; }
        public string LastName { get; set; }
        public string Email { get; set; }
    }
}
```

Here you have a basic business object class, and when populated from the database, you must set the controls in the user interface to the values of a particular instance of this Person class. The XAML code for the user interface consists of three TextBox controls to hold the value of FirstName, LastName, and Email and looks like the following:

```
<TextBox x:Name="FirstName" />
<TextBox x:Name="LastName" />
<TextBox x:Name="Email" />
```

When you have an instance of the Person class with the data, you can add the following code in the code behind to actually populate the TextBox controls:

```
FirstName.Text = person.FirstName;
LastName.Text = person.LastName;
Email.Text = person.Email;
```

Next, if you allow editing of these fields and want to store the changes made back to the database, you need more code to collect the new values and create another instance of a Person object to store the data. To do this you need the following code somewhere in the code-behind file.

```
Person person = new Person { FirstName = FirstName.Text, LastName =
LastName.Text, Email = Email.Text };

SaveChanges(person);
```

Binding Objects to the User Interface

Although the code is not terrible for simple examples like this one, you can see how quickly it spirals into requiring quite a bit of boilerplate code just to collect values from a form and save them or load them to or from a database. Data binding, however, simplifies this entire process by enabling you to create an instance of a Person object and "bind" it to the user interface, which effectively means the user interface automatically loads the current values of the Person object even if the values change as the program runs. For Two-Way binding, it even updates the Person object if the user makes any changes in the TextBox controls in an attempt to manipulate the values of the Person object. Listing 3-6 shows an updated version of the user interface that uses the data binding syntax of XAML to tell the TextBox controls which property of the Person class it is responsible to manage the data for.

LISTING 3-6: Chapter 3\BasicDataBinding\Home.xaml

```xml
<common:LayoutAwarePage
    x:Name="pageRoot"
    x:Class="BasicDataBinding.Home"
    IsTabStop="false"
    xmlns="http://schemas.microsoft.com/winfx/2006/xaml/presentation"
    xmlns:x="http://schemas.microsoft.com/winfx/2006/xaml"
    xmlns:local="using:BasicDataBinding"
    xmlns:common="using:BasicDataBinding.Common"
    xmlns:d="http://schemas.microsoft.com/expression/blend/2008"
    xmlns:mc="http://schemas.openxmlformats.org/markup-compatibility/2006"
    mc:Ignorable="d">

    <Page.Resources>

    </Page.Resources>

    <!--
        This grid acts as a root panel for the page that defines two rows:
        * Row 0 contains the back button and page title
        * Row 1 contains the rest of the page layout
    -->
    <Grid Style="{StaticResource LayoutRootStyle}">
        <Grid.RowDefinitions>
            <RowDefinition Height="140"/>
            <RowDefinition Height="*"/>
        </Grid.RowDefinitions>

        <!-- Back button and page title -->
        <Grid>
            <Grid.ColumnDefinitions>
                <ColumnDefinition Width="Auto"/>
                <ColumnDefinition Width="*"/>
            </Grid.ColumnDefinitions>
            <Button x:Name="backButton" Click="GoBack" IsEnabled="{Binding
Frame.CanGoBack, ElementName=pageRoot}" Style="{StaticResource BackButtonStyle}"/>
            <TextBlock x:Name="pageTitle" Grid.Column="1"
Style="{StaticResource PageHeaderTextStyle}"
Text="Basic Data Binding"/>
        </Grid>
        <Border BorderBrush="White" BorderThickness="3" Margin="0"
Grid.Row="1" VerticalAlignment="Center" HorizontalAlignment="Center">
            <Grid HorizontalAlignment="Center" Margin="0"
VerticalAlignment="Center" Width="446">
                <Grid.RowDefinitions>
                    <RowDefinition Height="Auto"/>
                    <RowDefinition Height="Auto"/>
                    <RowDefinition Height="Auto"/>
                    <RowDefinition Height="Auto"/>
                    <RowDefinition Height="Auto"/>
                </Grid.RowDefinitions>
                <Grid.ColumnDefinitions>
                    <ColumnDefinition Width="125*"/>
```

```
                        <ColumnDefinition Width="321*"/>
                    </Grid.ColumnDefinitions>
                    <TextBlock HorizontalAlignment="Right"
Margin="0,30,20,9" TextWrapping="Wrap" Text="First Name:"
VerticalAlignment="Center" FontSize="14"/>
                    <TextBox Margin="0,22,10,2"
Text="{Binding FirstName}" TextWrapping="Wrap"
VerticalAlignment="Center"
Grid.Column="1"
FontSize="14" TextAlignment="Center" Height="32"/>
                    <TextBlock HorizontalAlignment="Right"
Margin="0,20,20,19" Grid.Row="1" TextWrapping="Wrap" Text="Last Name:"
VerticalAlignment="Center" FontSize="14"/>
                    <TextBox Margin="0,12,10,12" Text="{Binding LastName}"
Grid.Row="1" TextWrapping="Wrap" VerticalAlignment="Center"
Grid.Column="1" FontSize="14" TextAlignment="Center" Height="32"/>
                    <TextBlock HorizontalAlignment="Right"
Margin="0,20,20,19" Grid.Row="2" TextWrapping="Wrap" Text="Email"
VerticalAlignment="Center" FontSize="14" Height="17"/>
                    <TextBox Margin="0,12,10,12" Text="{Binding Email}"
Grid.Row="2" TextWrapping="Wrap" VerticalAlignment="Center"
Grid.Column="1"
FontSize="14" TextAlignment="Center" Height="32"/>
                </Grid>
            </Border>

        <VisualStateManager.VisualStateGroups>

            <!-- Visual states reflect the application's view state -->
            <VisualStateGroup x:Name="ApplicationViewStates">
                <VisualState x:Name="FullScreenLandscape"/>
                <VisualState x:Name="Filled"/>

                <!-- The entire page respects the narrower 100-pixel margin
convention for portrait -->
                <VisualState x:Name="FullScreenPortrait">
                    <Storyboard>
                        <ObjectAnimationUsingKeyFrames
Storyboard.TargetName="backButton" Storyboard.TargetProperty="Style">
                            <DiscreteObjectKeyFrame KeyTime="0"
Value="{StaticResource PortraitBackButtonStyle}"/>
                        </ObjectAnimationUsingKeyFrames>
                    </Storyboard>
                </VisualState>

                <!-- The back button and title have different styles
when snapped -->
                <VisualState x:Name="Snapped">
                    <Storyboard>
                        <ObjectAnimationUsingKeyFrames
Storyboard.TargetName="backButton" Storyboard.TargetProperty="Style">
                            <DiscreteObjectKeyFrame KeyTime="0"
Value="{StaticResource SnappedBackButtonStyle}"/>
                        </ObjectAnimationUsingKeyFrames>
                        <ObjectAnimationUsingKeyFrames
```

```
                  Storyboard.TargetName="pageTitle" Storyboard.TargetProperty="Style">
                                                      <DiscreteObjectKeyFrame KeyTime="0"
                  Value="{StaticResource SnappedPageHeaderTextStyle}"/>
                                                  </ObjectAnimationUsingKeyFrames>
                                              </Storyboard>
                                          </VisualState>
                                      </VisualStateGroup>
                              </VisualStateManager.VisualStateGroups>
                      </Grid>
              </common:LayoutAwarePage>
```

As you can see, the magic happens in the setting of the `Text` property for each `TextBox` control. In the following line of code used in the example, the `Text` property of the `TextBox` is set to bind to the `LastName` property of the `Person` object.

```
<TextBox Margin="0,22,10,2" Text="{Binding FirstName}"
TextWrapping="Wrap" VerticalAlignment="Center" Grid.Column="1"
FontSize="14"
TextAlignment="Center" Height="32"/>
```

Now that each `TextBox` is assigned a particular property of the `Person` object, you must assign an actual `Person` object instance to the user interface for the binding to take place. In XAML, every control has a property called the `DataContext`, which can take on almost any valid object, and all children of the control that have an assigned `DataContext` automatically inherit the data from that `DataContext` property. This means that you have choices as to how to make your binding work.

In the following example, the `TextBox` controls are all sitting in a `Grid` control, so you could set the `DataContext` of the `Grid` control as an instance of your `Person` object, and all the data binding would just work. It's that easy. Alternatively, you could even set the `DataContext` on each individual `TextBox` control to be the `Person` object instance; although that wouldn't save you much code. Typically, if a group of controls bind to properties of the same object, you set the `DataContext` of the container that holds them. In this case, you can even go all the way to the top-level container of the `Page`. This example works just fine. In Listing 3-7, you can see that when a user navigates to the page, a `LoadAccount` method is called, and the `DataContext` property of the current `Page` is set to an instance of a `Person` object. Now when you run the app, you see actual data in the `TextBox` controls, as shown in Figure 3-4.

LISTING 3-7: Chapter 3\BasicDataBinding\Home.xaml.cs

```
using BasicDataBinding.Data;
using Windows.UI.Xaml.Navigation;

// The Basic Page item template is documented at
// http://go.microsoft.com/fwlink/?LinkId=234237

namespace BasicDataBinding
{
    /// <summary>
    /// A basic page that provides characteristics common to most applications.
    /// </summary>
```

```
public sealed partial class Home : BasicDataBinding.Common.LayoutAwarePage
{
    public Home()
    {
        this.InitializeComponent();
    }

    protected override void OnNavigatedTo(NavigationEventArgs e)
    {
        base.OnNavigatedTo(e);
        LoadAccount();
    }

    private void LoadAccount()
    {
        this.DataContext = new Person { FirstName = "Nick",
LastName = "Lecrenski", Email = "testuser@testuser.com" };
    }
}
}
```

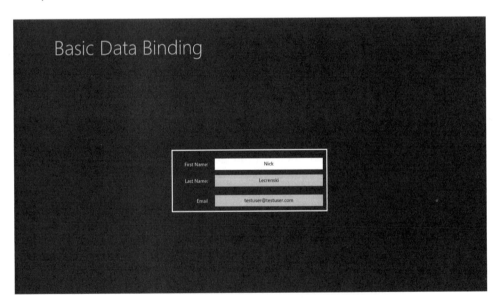

FIGURE 3-4

Data binding almost seems too easy in some ways. Now you don't have any additional code in the code behind to set properties on each individual control. Instead you simply have one line of code to set the `DataContext`, and data binding takes care of the rest.

Updating Data with Two-Way Data Binding

This simple example handles loading data into the user interface, but how can data binding help you retrieve new data entered in the user interface just as easily? All it takes to collect the data in the form is a simple change to the `TextBox` controls. In the following code the `TextBox` declarations in the XAML code have been modified to support *Two-Way* data binding.

```
<TextBlock HorizontalAlignment="Right" Margin="0,30,20,9" TextWrapping="Wrap"
Text="First Name:" VerticalAlignment="Center" FontSize="14"/>
<TextBox Margin="0,22,10,2" Text="{Binding FirstName, Mode=TwoWay}"
TextWrapping="Wrap" VerticalAlignment="Center" Grid.Column="1"
FontSize="14" TextAlignment="Center" Height="32"/>
<TextBlock HorizontalAlignment="Right" Margin="0,20,20,19" Grid.Row="1"
TextWrapping="Wrap" Text="Last Name:" VerticalAlignment="Center"
FontSize="14"/>
<TextBox Margin="0,12,10,12" Text="{Binding LastName, Mode=TwoWay}"
Grid.Row="1" TextWrapping="Wrap" VerticalAlignment="Center"
Grid.Column="1" FontSize="14" TextAlignment="Center" Height="32"/>
<TextBlock HorizontalAlignment="Right" Margin="0,20,20,19"
Grid.Row="2" TextWrapping="Wrap" Text="Email"
VerticalAlignment="Center"
FontSize="14" Height="17"/>
<TextBox Margin="0,12,10,12" Text="{Binding Email, Mode=TwoWay}"
Grid.Row="2" TextWrapping="Wrap" VerticalAlignment="Center"
Grid.Column="1" FontSize="14" TextAlignment="Center" Height="32"/>
```

With the simple addition of Mode=TwoWay, you have now told the user interface to take any user input in those fields and set the appropriate property on the Person instance behind the scenes. This means that when you run the app and make some changes, the same instance of the Person object you used to load the user interface automatically reflects the changes made. Instead of accessing every TextBox control to extract the value and create another Person object, you can simple use the current DataContext to get an updated version of the Person object that reflects any changes. Listing 3-8 shows an updated code-behind file containing a Button click handler that casts the current DataContext back to a Person object and reads the values of the FirstName, LastName, and Email properties, which have been automatically updated to reflect any user changes.

LISTING 3-8: Chapter 3\TwoWayBinding\Home.xaml.cs

```
using TwoWayBinding.Common;
using TwoWayBinding.Data;
using Windows.UI.Xaml;
using Windows.UI.Xaml.Navigation;


namespace TwoWayBinding
{
    /// <summary>
    /// A basic page that provides characteristics common to most applications.
    /// </summary>
    public sealed partial class Home : LayoutAwarePage
    {
        public Home()
        {
            this.InitializeComponent();
        }

        protected override void OnNavigatedTo(NavigationEventArgs e)
        {
            base.OnNavigatedTo(e);
```

```
            LoadAccount();
    }

    private void LoadAccount()
    {
        this.DataContext = new Person();
    }

    private void Submit_Click(object sender, RoutedEventArgs e)
    {
        Person person = this.DataContext as Person;

        string first = person.FirstName;
        string last = person.LastName;
        string email = person.Email;
    }
  }
}
```

Data Binding Summary

Conceptually data binding is a simple thing. You create an instance of a business object and bind it to controls on the user interface. This gives you the ability to auto refresh the user interface when changes are made to the underlying `DataContext`. When you use Two-Way binding, data binding also gives you an easy way to track changes made to the object. With that said, you may wonder what to do if you want to display or manipulate collections of various business objects. Data binding comes in handy here as well — the entire concept becomes even more powerful when you start to look at it with the data controls available in Windows 8. Several controls in the Windows 8 API have been built from the ground up with data binding in mind. When combined with data binding, these controls enable you to manage collections of data with ease.

WINDOWS 8 DATA BINDING CONTROLS

Although you can apply the concept of data binding to any Windows 8 XAML control, several controls were designed to work particularly well when you want to manage and manipulate collections of data. These controls include the `ComboBox`, `ListBox`, `ListView`, and `GridView`. Now take a look at how to use each of these using data binding.

ComboBox

In the previous chapter, you saw how to use the `ComboBox` by hardcoding some individual `ComboBoxItem` objects. You also learned how to capture the selected item using the `SelectionChanged` event handler. In that chapter, you were limited in what kind of data could display in the `ComboBox` control. You were allowed to use only string data, and when a `SelectionChanged` event was handled, you extracted the selected string through the use of the `Content` property of the selected `ComboBoxItem`. With data binding, however, you are free to use a collection of just about any object type to populate the `ComboBox` control. When a `ComboBox` selection is made, instead of working only with string data, you can actually extract the instance of the object that you selected and access any of the properties you require. Now look at some XAML code for a ComboBox that uses data binding instead of hard-coded ComboBoxItem controls. Figure 3-5 shows a basic data entry form along with a ComboBox control for selecting an Account object.

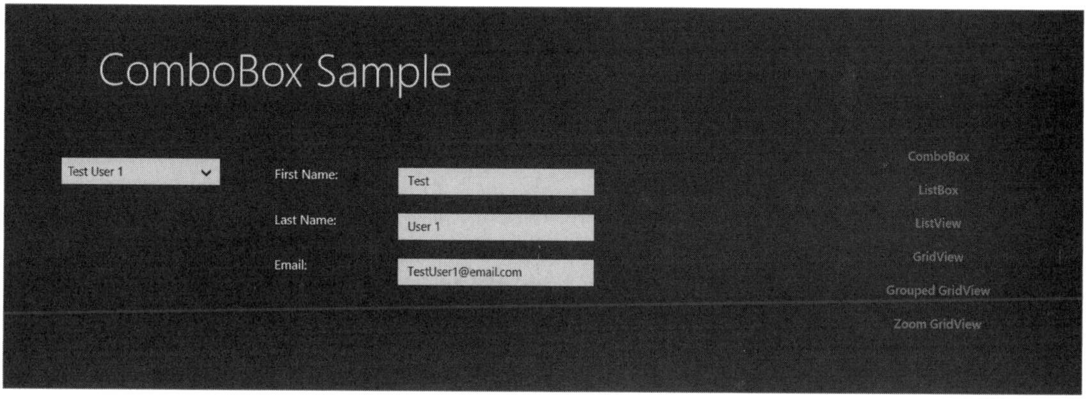

FIGURE 3-5

The purpose of this user interface is to allow the user to select a Person object from the ComboBox and then populate the data entry form to the right. Using Two-Way data binding forces any changes made to the fields in the TextBox controls to propagate to the selected Person instance. The following code shows the XAML required for this data entry form:

```
<ComboBox x:Name="AccountList" SelectionChanged="AccountList_SelectionChanged"
HorizontalAlignment="Left" Margin="73,49,0,0"
Grid.Row="1"
 VerticalAlignment="Top" MinWidth="200" DisplayMemberPath="FullName" />

<Grid x:Name="SelectionGrid" HorizontalAlignment="Left" Margin="332,49,0,0"
Grid.Row="1" VerticalAlignment="Top">
    <TextBlock HorizontalAlignment="Left" Margin="10,10,0,0"
TextWrapping="Wrap" Text="First Name:" VerticalAlignment="Top"
FontSize="16"/>
    <TextBlock HorizontalAlignment="Left" Margin="10,121,0,0"
TextWrapping="Wrap" Text="Email:" VerticalAlignment="Top"
FontSize="16"/>
    <TextBlock HorizontalAlignment="Left" Margin="10,66,0,0"
TextWrapping="Wrap" Text="Last Name:" VerticalAlignment="Top"
FontSize="16"/>
    <TextBox Text="{Binding FirstName, Mode=TwoWay}"
HorizontalAlignment="Left" Margin="166,10,0,0" TextWrapping="Wrap"
VerticalAlignment="Top"
```

```
Width="246"/>
        <TextBox Text="{Binding LastName, Mode=TwoWay}"
HorizontalAlignment="Left" Margin="166,66,0,0" TextWrapping="Wrap"
VerticalAlignment="Top"
Width="246"/>
        <TextBox Text="{Binding Email, Mode=TwoWay}"
HorizontalAlignment="Left" Margin="166,121,0,0" TextWrapping="Wrap"
VerticalAlignment="Top"
Width="246"/>
</Grid>
```

As you can see, each TextBox control uses Two-Way data binding to handle the appropriate property of the Person object. Notice also that in the ComboBox declaration there is an attribute called DisplayMemberPath that's set to "FullName". When binding a collection of Person objects to the ComboBox control, you need to tell the control what property of the Person object it should use to display the selectable text. The FullName property of the Person object, as shown in Listing 3-9, simply concatenates the FirstName and LastName properties of a particular Person instance.

LISTING 3-9: Chapter 3\DataBindingControls\Data\Person.cs

```
using System;

namespace DataBindingControls.Data
{
    public class Person
    {
        public string FirstName { get; set; }
        public string LastName { get; set; }
        public string Email { get; set; }
        public string FullName { get { return String.Format("{0} {1}",
FirstName, LastName); } }
    }
}
```

In the previous example, you set the DataContext of the actual Page to the object against which you wanted to perform data binding. Although the DataContext property is still a valid way to assign objects for data binding against controls such as the ComboBox, ListBox, ListView, and GridView, Windows 8 also offers a property called ItemsSource that is typically used to assign a particular collection of data for binding against. In the following code, the ItemsSource property of the ComboBox is set to a collection of Person objects, and when the program runs, all the binding takes place.

```
Accounts = new List<Person>();

Accounts.Add(new Person { FirstName = "Test", LastName = "User 1", Email =
    "TestUser1@testuser.com" });
Accounts.Add(new Person { FirstName = "Test", LastName = "User 2", Email =
    "TestUser2@testuser.com" });
Accounts.Add(new Person { FirstName = "Test", LastName = "User 3", Email =
    "TestUser3@testuser.com" });
```

```
Accounts.Add(new Person { FirstName = "Test", LastName = "User 4", Email =
"TestUser4@testuser.com" });

AccountList.ItemsSource = Accounts;
```

Because the TextBox controls sit in a Grid control when you make a selection, you can simply set the DataContext to the Person object selected, and the binding populates the TextBox controls with the appropriate properties of the Person object. The following code shows the SelectionChanged event handler for the ComboBox where this takes place:

```
private void AccountList_SelectionChanged(object sender,
SelectionChangedEventArgs e)
{
    SelectionGrid.DataContext = (e.AddedItems[0] as Person);
}
```

You might wonder why sometimes you use the DataContext and other times you use the ItemsSource property. In a way, the ItemsSource property of certain controls is equivalent to the Text property of the TextBox control. It's basically the property responsible to hold the collection of data that you're binding. You can still however set the DataContext at the Page level to the collection of Person objects and set up the ComboBox to make use of it. In that case, simply tell the ItemsSource property to bind to the current DataContext using the following syntax:

```
<ComboBox x:Name="AccountList" SelectionChanged="AccountList_SelectionChanged"
HorizontalAlignment="Left" Margin="73,49,0,0"
Grid.Row="1"
VerticalAlignment="Top" MinWidth="200" DisplayMemberPath="FullName"
ItemsSource="{Bindng}" />
```

Having the ItemsSource property set to just "{Binding}" tells the control to use whatever the currently inherited DataContext is to populate the collection. Of course, this assumes the DataContext is set to an actual collection of objects. If for some reason the DataContext is set to an instance of a business object and the collection you need to display in the ComboBox is a public property of that object, simply change the binding syntax to look for the particular property that represents the collection. The following line of code makes the ComboBox ItemsSource property bind to a property of the DataContext called Accounts.

```
<ComboBox x:Name="AccountList" SelectionChanged="AccountList_SelectionChanged"
HorizontalAlignment="Left" Margin="73,49,0,0" Grid.Row="1"
VerticalAlignment="Top" MinWidth="200" DisplayMemberPath="FullName"
ItemsSource="{Bindng Accounts}" />
```

ListBox

Another Windows 8 control that you can use to present a list of content or data is the ListBox control. It is similar to the ComboBox in many ways, and you can think of it as just a ComboBox control with all its options visible at the same time. Figure 3-6 shows the same data entry form as Figure 3-5, but it makes use of a ListBox control instead of the ComboBox control.

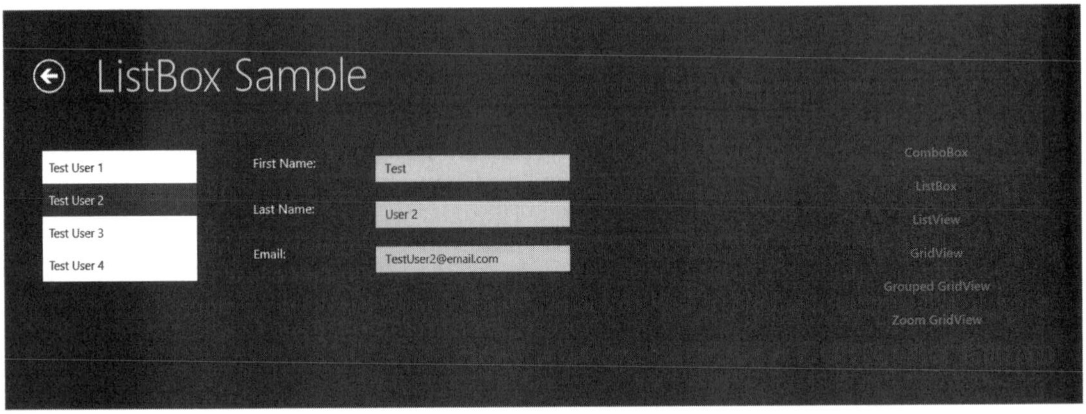

FIGURE 3-6

The XAML code required to use the `ListBox` is similar to the `ComboBox` example. The following code shows the declaration for the `ListBox` control, which again uses the `DisplayMemberPath` property to determine which property of the `Person` object displays content to the user. The `ItemsSource` property is also set to the `Accounts` property of the current `DataContext` containing the actual collection of `Person` objects.

```
<ListBox x:Name="AccountList" SelectionChanged="AccountList_SelectionChanged"
ItemsSource="{Binding Accounts}" DisplayMemberPath="FullName"
HorizontalAlignment="Left" Margin="48,31,0,0" VerticalAlignment="Top"
MinWidth="200" Width="200"/>
```

After you select the `ListBox` control, you handle it the same way as you would with the `ComboBox`. The following code shows the `SelectionChanged` event extracting the selected `Person` object and setting the `DataContext` of the data entry form to that `Person` instance:

```
private void AccountList_SelectionChanged(object sender,
SelectionChangedEventArgs e)
{
    SelectionGrid.DataContext = (e.AddedItems[0] as Person);
}
```

ListView

The `ComboBox` and `ListBox` are solid controls for presenting your users with a basic list of choices in the user interface. For most applications, however, you want more flexibility in presenting content and collections of business objects. This is where the `ListView` and `GridView` come in handy. The `ListView` offers you a way to present customized views of data in a traditional vertical orientation. Figure 3-7 shows a collection of books and thumbnails in a `ListView` control, complete with selection handling.

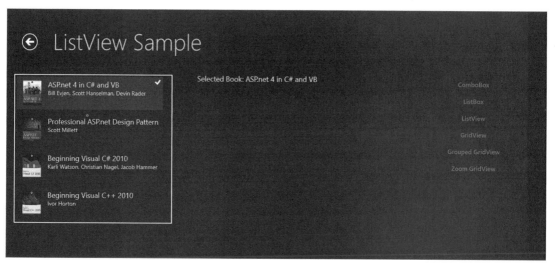

FIGURE 3-7

As you can see, the presentation of the items in a `ListView` are much richer than in the `ComboBox` or `ListBox`. When you make selections, you see a nice check mark in the upper-right corner, and the entire selection changes color to how it's been selected. This is all built into the standard `ListView` control and does not require you to write additional code.

The presentation of each book item shown in the `ListView` control has several pieces to it. Both the `ListView` and `GridView` controls enable you to completely customize the look of each item in the list. You do this using a concept called *data templates*. In this example, you want to display a thumbnail, a title, and author information for each book in the list. To make a `DataTemplate` work, create the user interface to which you want each item in the collection to adhere as well as binding information for the various properties of the object. Then in the `ListView` control, you set the `ItemTemplate` property to use the `DataTemplate` you created for each item in the list. `DataTemplate` declarations are treated as resources and should reside either in App.xaml or in your `Page.Resources` section of the file containing the `ListView` you plan to use it in. For this example, a `DataTemplate` that displays the thumbnail, the title, and author information would look like the following code:

```
<DataTemplate x:Key="BookTemplate">
    <Grid Margin="10">
        <StackPanel Orientation="Horizontal">
            <Image Source="{Binding Thumbnail}" Height="60"
Width="60" Margin="0,0,10,0"/>
            <StackPanel Margin="0,0,0,0" Orientation="Vertical">
                <TextBlock TextWrapping="Wrap"
Style="{StaticResource BookTitleStyle}"
Text="{Binding Title}" />
                <TextBlock TextWrapping="Wrap"
Style="{StaticResource BookAuthorStyle}" Text="{Binding Author}" />
            </StackPanel>
        </StackPanel>
    </Grid>
</DataTemplate>
```

Note the use of the `BookTitleStyle` and `BookAuthorStyle` to handle the formatting of the `TextBlock` controls. Those styles are declared in the same section as the `DataTemplate` using the following code:

```
<Style x:Key="BookTitleStyle" TargetType="TextBlock">
    <Setter Property="FontFamily" Value="Segoe UI Light"/>
    <Setter Property="FontSize" Value="18"/>
</Style>

<Style x:Key="BookAuthorStyle" TargetType="TextBlock">
    <Setter Property="FontFamily" Value="Segoe UI Light"/>
    <Setter Property="FontSize" Value="14"/>
</Style>
```

In this example, it's easiest to just include all this XAML in the `Page.Resources` level. As you can see, an `Image` control is bound to the `Thumbnail` property of the book object. The `TextBlock` controls also use data binding to display the `Title` and `Author` accordingly.

One thing to note about this code is that in Chapter 2 ("What Is XAML?") when you were introduced to the `Image` control, you simply set the `Source` property to the path of the image file you wanted to use. When using it in a data binding scenario (such as this example), you can't simply bind a string based path to the file you want to use. Instead you need to bind to a property that returns the type `ImageSource` for the image to properly display. Listing 3-10 shows the `WroxBook` class along with the `Thumbnail` property that returns an `ImageSource` type.

LISTING 3-10: Chapter 3\DataBindingControls\Data\WroxBook.cs

```
using Windows.UI.Xaml.Media;

namespace DataBindingControls.Data
{
    public class WroxBook
    {
        public string Title { get; set; }
        public string Author { get; set; }
        public string Subject { get; set; }
        public ImageSource Thumbnail { get; set; }
    }
}
```

Now that you have an appropriate `DataTemplate` defined for each item in the `ListView`, you can add some XAML for the `ListView` control. In the following code note how the `ItemTemplate` property is assigned to the `DataTemplate` created previously.

```
<ListView x:Name="MainListView" Margin="20,20,0,0" Grid.Row="1"
VerticalAlignment="Top" MaxWidth="400" HorizontalAlignment="Left"
ItemTemplate="{StaticResource BookTemplate}"
ScrollViewer.VerticalScrollBarVisibility="Auto"
BorderBrush="White"
BorderThickness="2"
ScrollViewer.HorizontalScrollBarVisibility="Disabled" SelectionMode="Single"
SelectionChanged="MainListView_SelectionChanged"/>
```

Another thing to notice about the `ListView` XAML is that the `SelectionMode` property is set to `Single`. This means that a user can select only one item in the list at any given time. You could also set this value to `Multiple`; in that case the `AddedItems` collection you've been using in the `SelectionChanged` event would contain all the selected `WroxBook` instances.

To populate the `ListView` control, you do almost the same thing you've been doing for the `ComboBox` and `ListBox` controls. Just create a collection of `WroxBook` objects and set the `ItemsSource` property as shown in the following code:

```
private ObservableCollection<WroxBook> Books = new ObservableCollection<Wrox
Book>();


protected override void OnNavigatedTo(NavigationEventArgs e)
{
    base.OnNavigatedTo(e);

    Books.Add(new WroxBook
    {
        Title = "ASP.net 4 in C# and VB",
        Author = "Bill Evjen, Scott Hanselman, Devin Rader",
        Thumbnail = new BitmapImage(new Uri("ms-appx:///Assets/aspnet4.jpg",
UriKind.RelativeOrAbsolute))
    });

    Books.Add(new WroxBook
    {
        Title = "Professional ASP.net Design Patterns",
        Author = "Scott Millett",
        Thumbnail = new BitmapImage(new Uri("ms-appx:///Assets/aspnetdesign.jpg",
UriKind.RelativeOrAbsolute))
    });

    Books.Add(new WroxBook
    {
        Title = "Beginning Visual C# 2010",
        Author = "Karli Watson, Christian Nagel, Jacob Hammer
Pedersen, Jon D. Reid,
Morgan Skinner",
        Thumbnail = new BitmapImage(new Uri("ms-appx:///Assets/begincsharp.jpg",
UriKind.RelativeOrAbsolute))
    });

    Books.Add(new WroxBook
    {
        Title = "Beginning Visual C++ 2010",
        Author = "Ivor Horton",
        Thumbnail = new BitmapImage(new Uri("ms-appx:///Assets/visualc2010.jpg",
UriKind.RelativeOrAbsolute))
    });

    MainListView.ItemsSource = Books;
}
```

Note the use of the `ObservableCollection` as opposed to the generic `List` that you have been using. Unlike the `List` class, the `ObservableCollection` class implements the `INotifyPropertyChanged` interface, which has the built in capability to inform the `ListView` when items are added or removed from the collection. By using the `ObservableCollection` here to hold the `WroxBook` items, you can add or remove another book from the collection and the `ListView` automatically updates to reflect the changes without you having to write any code.

GridView

Perhaps the most powerful data control in Windows 8 (and one you will use often) is the `GridView`. The `GridView` works similar to the `ListView` in that it helps you display a collection of content or data. Instead of in a vertical format, the `GridView` typically displays items horizontally and even in groups depending on the configuration you use. The `GridView` is designed to take up much more screen real estate than the `ListView` or any of the other data controls. Just like the `ListView`, the `GridView` control supports data binding and the use of `DataTemplate` definitions for each item that displays in the control.

In its simple form, you can use a `GridView` control just like a `ListView` but with a horizontal display of items. In Figure 3-8 you again see a `GridView` showing a display of book items but in a horizontal layout featuring two book items for each row in the grid.

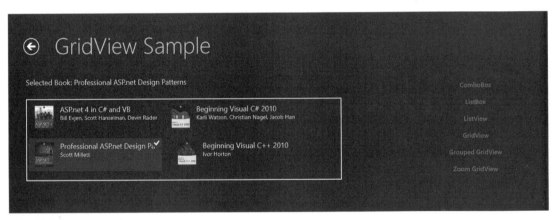

FIGURE 3-8

Just as with the `ListView` when you make a selection, you get a check mark and style applied to the selected item. The XAML required for this particular `GridView` is shown in the following code and looks remarkably similar to what was used for the `ListView`.

```
<GridView x:Name="MainGridView" HorizontalAlignment="Left" Margin="45,70,0,0"
Grid.Row="1" VerticalAlignment="Top"
MinWidth="200"
MinHeight="200"
ItemTemplate="{StaticResource BookTemplate}" ItemsPanel="{StaticResource
GridViewItemsPanel}"
BorderBrush="White" BorderThickness="2"
ScrollViewer.VerticalScrollBarVisibility="Auto"
ScrollViewer.HorizontalScrollBarVisibility="Auto" SelectionMode="Single"
Width="800"
SelectionChanged="MainGridView_SelectionChanged" />
```

Again, you set an `ItemTemplate` so that each `WroxBook` object presents the thumbnail, title, and author information. In addition to the `ItemTemplate`, however, the `ItemsPanel` property is also set to a `StaticResource`. The `ItemsPanel` property enables you to override the actual container that hosts the `GridView` items. In this example, you want to display the items in a table-like presentation containing no more than two rows. By default, the `GridView` does not actually create a table-like presentation, but by overriding the `ItemsPanel` property, you can easily ensure you get the layout you want. In the following code, an `ItemsPanelTemplate` holds a `WrapGrid` control that displays the `GridView` items.

```
<ItemsPanelTemplate x:Key="GridViewItemsPanel">
    <WrapGrid MaximumRowsOrColumns="2" />
</ItemsPanelTemplate>
```

Similar to a `DataTemplate`, the `ItemsPanelTemplate` is another type of XAML template that you can use to manage the container of any data control that displays collections of objects or content. In this case the `MaximumRowsOrColumns` property ensures that only two book items display in any column of the `GridView`. The `WrapGrid` works by hosting child elements in such a way that they are contained within the edge of the parent control. If items do not fit in the available space, they are positioned to the next column or row depending on the value you use for the `MaximumRowsOrColumns` property.

The code for loading the `GridView` works just like the `ListView` in that the `ItemsSource` property is set to a collection of `WroxBook` items such as in the following code:

```
MainGridView.ItemsSource = Books;
```

As was the case with the `ListView`, the `GridView` control can handle either single or multiple item selection. In the `SelectionChanged` event for this example, the `SelectionMode` of the `GridView` is set to `Single`, and the user interface is updated to display the selected book information.

```
private void MainGridView_SelectionChanged(object sender,
SelectionChangedEventArgs e)
{
    SelectedGridItem.Text = String.Format("Selected Book: {0}",
((WroxBook)e.AddedItems[0]).Title);
}
```

Grouped GridView

In addition to simply presenting a collection of content and data in a horizontal display, the `GridView` also supports grouping collection items and presenting the information in a grouped display. Grouping is handled by making use of a few additional `GridView` properties as well as a different type of collection object.

Before getting the `GridView` control ready for grouping, you first need to change the way you set up the collection of data you want to use. Just like most of the examples in this chapter, you build a collection of items using a generic `List<T>` or `ObservableCollection<T>`. When you want to group data for display in the `GridView`, you need to set up your collections differently. Now walk through what it takes to get this example working with a collection of `WroxBook` objects grouped by subject or programming language.

First, you need a basic `List<T>` to hold all your books just as you normally would.

```
private List<WroxBook> AllBooks = new List<WroxBook>();
```

This of course could come from a database or web service, but for this example just hardcode some book objects when the page loads.

```
protected override void OnNavigatedTo(NavigationEventArgs e)
{
    base.OnNavigatedTo(e);

    SetupBookList();
}

private void SetupBookList()
{
    AllBooks.Add(new WroxBook
    {
        Subject = "ASP.NET",
        Title = "Professional ASP.NET MVC 4",
        Author = "Jon Galloway",
        Thumbnail = new BitmapImage(new Uri("ms-appx:///Assets/aspnet4.jpg",
UriKind.RelativeOrAbsolute))
    });

    AllBooks.Add(new WroxBook
    {
        Subject = "ASP.NET",
        Title = "Beginning ASP.NET Web Pages with WebMatrix",
        Author = "Mike Brind, Imar Spaanjaars",
        Thumbnail = new BitmapImage(new Uri("ms-
appx:///Assets/beginaspnetmatrix.jpg", UriKind.RelativeOrAbsolute))
    });

    AllBooks.Add(new WroxBook
    {
        Subject = "ASP.NET",
        Title = "Professional ASP.net Design Patterns",
        Author = "Scott Millett",
```

```
                    Thumbnail = new
BitmapImage(new Uri("ms-
appx:///Assets/aspnetdesign.jpg",
UriKind.RelativeOrAbsolute))
            });


        AllBooks.Add(new WroxBook
        {
            Subject = "C# Development",
            Title = "Beginning Object Oriented Programming with C#",
            Author = "Jack Purdum",
            Thumbnail = new
BitmapImage(new Uri("ms-appx:///Assets/beginoocsharp.jpg",
UriKind.RelativeOrAbsolute))
            });


        AllBooks.Add(new WroxBook
        {
            Subject = "C# Development",
            Title = "Beginning Visual C# 2010",
            Author = "Karli Watson, Christian Nagel,
Jacob Hammer Pedersen, Jon D.
Reid, Morgan Skinner",
            Thumbnail = new
BitmapImage(new Uri("ms-appx:///Assets/begincsharp.jpg",
UriKind.RelativeOrAbsolute))
            });


        AllBooks.Add(new WroxBook
        {
            Subject = "C# Development",
            Title = "Professional Test Driven Development with C#",
            Author = "James Bender, Jeff McWherter",
            Thumbnail = new
BitmapImage(new Uri("ms-appx:///Assets/protestdriven.jpg",
UriKind.RelativeOrAbsolute))
            });


        AllBooks.Add(new WroxBook
        {
            Subject = "C++ Development",
            Title = "Beginning Visual C++ 2010",
            Author = "Ivor Horton",
            Thumbnail = new
BitmapImage(new Uri("ms-appx:///Assets/visualc2010.jpg",
UriKind.RelativeOrAbsolute))
            });


        AllBooks.Add(new WroxBook
        {
            Subject = "C++ Development",
            Title = "Professional C++ 2nd Edition",
            Author = "Marc Gregoire, Nicholas A. Solter, Scott J. Kleper",
            Thumbnail = new
BitmapImage(new Uri("ms-appx:///Assets/procplus.jpg",
```

```
UriKind.RelativeOrAbsolute))
        });

    AllBooks.Add(new WroxBook
    {
        Subject = "SQL Server",
        Title = "Professional SQL Server 2012 Internals
and Troubleshooting",
        Author = "Christian Bolton, James Rowland-Jones, Glenn Berry, Justin
Langford, Gavin Payne, Amit Banerjee",
        Thumbnail = new BitmapImage(new Uri("ms-
appx:///Assets/prosqltroubleshoot.jpg", UriKind.RelativeOrAbsolute))
    });

    AllBooks.Add(new WroxBook
    {
        Subject = "SQL Server",
        Title = "Beginning Microsoft SQL Server 2012 Programming",
        Author = "Paul Atkinson, Robert Vieira",
        Thumbnail = new BitmapImage(new Uri("ms-
appx:///Assets/beginsqlprogramming.jpg", UriKind.RelativeOrAbsolute))
    });

    AllBooks.Add(new WroxBook
    {
        Subject = "SQL Server",
        Title = "Professional Microsoft PowerPivot for Excel and
SharePoint",
        Author = "Sivakumar Harinath, Ron Pihlgren, Denny Guang-Yeu Lee",
        Thumbnail = new
BitmapImage(new Uri("ms-appx:///Assets/propowerpivot.jpg",
 UriKind.RelativeOrAbsolute))
    });
}
```

As you can see, each `WroxBook` object now has an additional `Subject` property by which you can group the items. Because the `GridView` grouping mechanism requires items to be grouped by a particular `Key`, you must create another business object that can hold both the `Key` or `Subject` in this case along with the `WroxBook` instances that belong to that `Key`. The following code shows a `GroupedBookList` class that does the trick. It contains a string property called `Subject`, which works as the `Key` for the `GridView` grouping feature, as well as a `List<WroxBook>` property to hold the books that belong to that subject.

```
using System.Collections.Generic;

namespace DataBindingControls.Data
{
    public class GroupedBookList
    {
        public string Subject { get; set; }
        public List<WroxBook> Books { get; set; }
    }
}
```

Now that you have a class that can hold the grouped books, you need a collection object that can hold a list of these groupings. Windows 8 provides a new class called CollectionViewSource that provides built-in support for sorting, filtering, and grouping and is the perfect candidate for holding the data that is used during the GridView binding operation.

The following code adds a CollectionViewSource instance to the page that is responsible to hold the list of grouped books:

```
private CollectionViewSource BookCollection = new CollectionViewSource {
IsSourceGrouped = true, ItemsPath = new PropertyPath("Books") };
```

In this code, the IsSourceGrouped property is set to true. The CollectionViewSource class uses a Source property to hold the list of items you want to hold in the collection. Because the class supports filtering, sorting, and grouping, it's not required that you place items in a grouped format. But if they are, you need to tell the CollectionViewSource that the items with which you are populating it are grouped. In addition, the ItemsPath property is set to look for a property in your object called Books. This declaration of the CollectionViewSource class expects that all the items in your collection will have a collection of book objects called "Books" and the string property of "Subject".

Because you tell the CollectionViewSource class that its Source property will be set to a collection of items that are already grouped, you need to take care of the grouping code next by utilizing a simple Linq statement to populate the Source property of the CollectionViewSource. In the following code, the current List<WroxBook> collection called AllBooks is grouped according to subject using the GroupBy statement in Linq:

```
protected override void OnNavigatedTo(NavigationEventArgs e)
{
    base.OnNavigatedTo(e);

    SetupBookList();

    var groupedBooks = AllBooks.GroupBy(x => x.Subject).Select(x => new
GroupedBookList { Subject = x.Key, Books = x.ToList() });

    BookCollection.Source = groupedBooks.ToList();
    MainGridView.ItemsSource = BookCollection.View;
}
```

In the last line of this code, the ItemsSource property of the GridView is set to the View property of the CollectionViewSource. The CollectionViewSource also provides different views into the current collection of data without needing to change the user interface. By setting the ItemsSource property to the View property, you can be sure that the GridView control always presents the current view of the data whether that is sorted, filtered, or grouped.

The last thing you need to do is tell the GridView that you want to support grouping so that each item is positioned in the appropriate group with a header displaying the Subject property of the book. The CollectionViewSource object has everything ready to go and arranged in the correct groups, but now you must modify the XAML code for the GridView to take advantage of it. In the following code you can see that the GroupStyle property of the GridView sets up a column header for each group of books.

```
<GridView x:Name="MainGridView" HorizontalAlignment="Left" Margin="45,70,0,0"
Grid.Row="1" VerticalAlignment="Top" MinWidth="200" MinHeight="200"
ItemTemplate="{StaticResource BookTemplate}" ItemsPanel="{StaticResource
GridViewItemsPanel}"
BorderBrush="White" BorderThickness="2"
ScrollViewer.VerticalScrollBarVisibility="Auto"
ScrollViewer.HorizontalScrollBarVisibility="Auto" SelectionMode="Single"
MaxWidth="1000" SelectionChanged="MainGridView_SelectionChanged">
    <GridView.GroupStyle>
        <GroupStyle>
            <GroupStyle.HeaderTemplate>
                <DataTemplate>
                    <TextBlock Text='{Binding Subject}'
Foreground="White" FontSize="25" Margin="5" />
                </DataTemplate>
            </GroupStyle.HeaderTemplate>
        </GroupStyle>
    </GridView.GroupStyle>
</GridView>
```

For this example, the `HeaderTemplate` is bound to the `Subject` property of the underlying `GroupedBookList` object. Because you use a `CollectionViewSource`, the `GridView` automatically looks through the `ItemsSource` for all the `Subject` properties available and creates a header row showing all the subjects in the collection. Then when you run the app, you can see that all the `WroxBook` items sit correctly beneath the appropriate header, as shown in Figure 3-9.

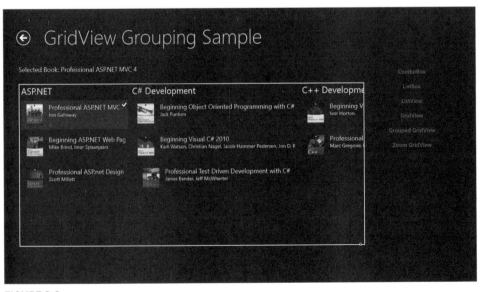

FIGURE 3-9

USING SEMANTICZOOM

The `GridView` gives you a powerful way to display a collection of business objects and content. In addition to grouping items by a particular category, Windows 8 makes it even easier for your users to find what they are looking for when they're presented with a large number of items in your `GridView`. `SemanticZoom`, which supports the pinch gesture and control/mouse wheel, enables you effectively zoom in or out of your `GridView` collection so that users can easily jump around content that has been grouped.

In the previous example, you saw that the `CollectionViewSource` enables you to easily display the list of `WroxBook` objects in a grouped scenario with headers for each programming subject. If you have only a handful of subjects, this setup works fine. If, however, you have a large amount of subjects (as you will in most real-world applications), your users potentially must scroll a long time to reach the end of the list. To help users quickly jump around the various subjects, you can add a small amount of XAML code to create a zoomed out version of the `GridView` that shows only the subject headers. Then when users touch or click a subject, they are automatically taken to the books under the selected subject.

To get this working, simply wrap your `GridView` inside of the new `SemanticZoom` control. The `SemanticZoom` control works by giving you `ZoomedOutView` and `ZoomedInView` properties so that you can include the appropriate view of your collection data. The `ZoomedInView` has the same XAML code you currently use for the `GridView` that supports grouping. However, the `ZoomedOutView` shows only the actual subject headers that exist for each group. The following XAML code shows both zoomed out and zoomed in views of the `GridView` control making use of the `SemanticZoom` control to hold both.

```
<SemanticZoom x:Name="MainZoomControl" HorizontalAlignment="Left"
Margin="45,70,0,0" Grid.Row="1" VerticalAlignment="Top">
    <SemanticZoom.ZoomedOutView>
        <GridView x:Name="ZoomedOutGridView" MinWidth="200" MinHeight="200"
ItemTemplate="{StaticResource ZoomedOutBookTemplate}"
BorderBrush="White" BorderThickness="2"
ScrollViewer.VerticalScrollBarVisibility="Auto"
ScrollViewer.HorizontalScrollBarVisibility="Auto" SelectionMode="Single"
MaxWidth="1000" SelectionChanged="GridView_SelectionChanged">
            <GridView.ItemsPanel>
                <ItemsPanelTemplate>
                    <StackPanel Orientation="Horizontal"
VerticalAlignment="Center" HorizontalAlignment="Center" />
                </ItemsPanelTemplate>
            </GridView.ItemsPanel>
        </GridView>
    </SemanticZoom.ZoomedOutView>
    <SemanticZoom.ZoomedInView>
        <GridView x:Name="ZoomedInGridView" HorizontalAlignment="Left"
Margin="45,70,0,0" Grid.Row="1"
VerticalAlignment="Top" MinWidth="200"
MinHeight="200"ItemTemplate="{StaticResource BookTemplate}"
```

```
            ItemsPanel="{StaticResource GridViewItemsPanel}"
            BorderBrush="White" BorderThickness="2"
            ScrollViewer.VerticalScrollBarVisibility="Auto"
            ScrollViewer.HorizontalScrollBarVisibility="Auto" SelectionMode="Single"
            MaxWidth="1000"
            SelectionChanged="GridView_SelectionChanged"
            ItemsSource="{Binding Source={StaticResource BookCollection}}">
                        <GridView.GroupStyle>
                            <GroupStyle>
                                <GroupStyle.HeaderTemplate>
                                    <DataTemplate>
                                        <TextBlock Text='{Binding Subject}'
            Foreground="White" FontSize="25" Margin="5" />
                                    </DataTemplate>
                                </GroupStyle.HeaderTemplate>
                                <GroupStyle.Panel>
                                    <ItemsPanelTemplate>
                                        <VariableSizedWrapGrid Orientation="Vertical"
            Height="400" />
                                    </ItemsPanelTemplate>
                                </GroupStyle.Panel>
                            </GroupStyle>
                        </GridView.GroupStyle>
                    </GridView>
                </SemanticZoom.ZoomedInView>
            </SemanticZoom>
```

You should already be familiar with the zoomed in version of the GridView, so take a further look at the ZoomedOutView. The ZoomedOutView still contains a GridView, but instead of the standard ItemTemplate that shows the thumbnail, the title, and author information, you use a DataTemplate called ZoomedOutBookTemplate. The following code shows the updated template.

```
<DataTemplate x:Key="ZoomedOutBookTemplate">
    <Border BorderBrush="White" BorderThickness="2" Margin="10" Padding="10">
        <TextBlock Text="{Binding Group.Subject}" FontFamily="Segoe UI Light"
FontSize="25" Foreground="White" />
    </Border>
</DataTemplate>
```

This DataTemplate simply provides a White border surrounding a TextBlock control that is bound to the Group.Subject property. The way that this works is that for each group in the CollectionViewSource instance, there is a Group property. From this property you need to bind to whatever property represents your Key, which in this case is the Subject.

> **NOTE** *In the* GroupedBookList *class that you saw previously, there were two properties: one for* Subject *and one for* Books, *which is the actual collection of* WroxBook *objects. If for some reason you were to use a class containing music information, you may end up grouping by a property called* Genre, *in which case you would set the binding set to* Group.Genre.

The next step for this to work correctly is to bind data to the zoomed-out version of the GridView. Because you don't care about the actual WroxBook items in the zoomed out view, you want to bind only to the list of groups available. The following code sets the ItemsSource of the zoomed-out GridView control to the list of groups available in the CollectionViewSource.

```
ZoomedOutGridView.ItemsSource = BookCollection.View.CollectionGroups;
```

If you were to run the application now, by default you'd still see the same grouped display of books as before (shown in Figure 3-10). In addition, Figure 3-11 shows the zoomed-out view of the GridView control containing only the subjects available to choose from. You can access this view by using Ctrl/Scroll with the mouse wheel, or on a table use the zoom gesture to zoom out.

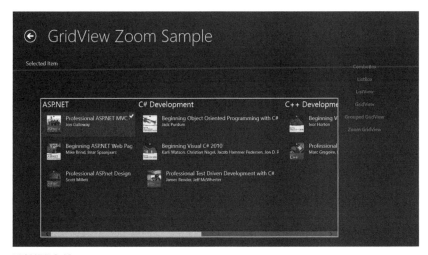

FIGURE 3-10

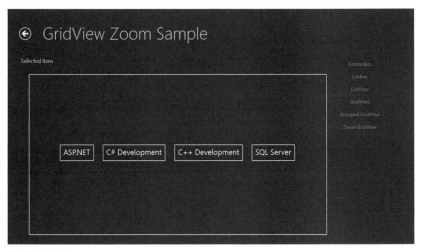

FIGURE 3-11

USING CUSTOM CONTROLS

Now that you are a master at data binding as well as how to use the various data controls to display collections of content and data, you have one remaining helpful topic in this chapter for creating large Windows Store applications. You may have noticed that in all the previous examples, you copied XAML code to display various properties of a `WroxBook` object. These parts included an `Image` control along with a couple `TextBlock` controls. In all cases, these were declared using a `DataTemplate`. If, however, you wanted to reuse this XAML in multiple applications or even to add additional business logic surrounding this visualization of a book, you need to copy/paste that logic into each code behind in which you want to reuse the code. In addition to the standard XAML controls at your disposal for Windows 8, you can also create custom controls that fully support data binding and additional business logic.

Continuing with the previous example to display information about a particular `WroxBook` object, the following example shows how to convert SemanticZoom enabled `GridView` to a custom XAML control, which makes it easier to reuse in other projects or pages in this particular Windows Store app. To create a custom control:

1. Right-click the project node in Solution Explorer, and select Add New Item. From the list of choices, pick the `TemplatedControl` selection.

2. Give the new custom control a name. In Figure 3-12 a custom control called `BookDetails` is created.

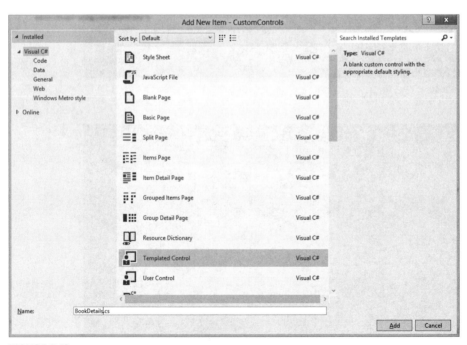

FIGURE 3-12

3. After you click the Add button, a new folder appears in the project called Themes. In this folder you can find a file called Generic.xaml. This is where you place the default XAML for the control you want to create. Because you want to re-create the item display from the previous examples, just copy and paste the XAML code from the `DataTemplate` into this file with a couple of small tweaks.

Listing 3-11 shows the updated Generic.xaml file that holds the XAML code to display the thumbnail, the title, and author.

> **NOTE** *Instead of using a* `DataTemplate`, *this time you actually create a* `Style` *and set the* `TargetType` *to* `BookDetails`, *which is the type of your custom control being created.*

```xml
<ResourceDictionary
    xmlns="http://schemas.microsoft.com/winfx/2006/xaml/presentation"
    xmlns:x="http://schemas.microsoft.com/winfx/2006/xaml"
    xmlns:local="using:CustomControls">

    <Style x:Key="BookTitleStyle" TargetType="TextBlock">
        <Setter Property="FontFamily" Value="Segoe UI Light"/>
        <Setter Property="FontSize" Value="18"/>
    </Style>

    <Style x:Key="BookAuthorStyle" TargetType="TextBlock">
        <Setter Property="FontFamily" Value="Segoe UI Light"/>
        <Setter Property="FontSize" Value="14"/>
    </Style>

    <Style TargetType="local:BookDetails">
        <Setter Property="Template">
            <Setter.Value>
                <ControlTemplate TargetType="local:BookDetails">
                    <Grid Margin="10">
                        <StackPanel Orientation="Horizontal">
                            <Image Source="{TemplateBinding
ThumbnailImage}" Height="60" Width="60" Margin="0,0,10,0"/>
                            <StackPanel Margin="0,0,0,0"
Orientation="Vertical">
                                <TextBlock TextWrapping="Wrap"
Style="{StaticResource BookTitleStyle}"
Text="{TemplateBinding BookTitle}" />
                                <TextBlock TextWrapping="Wrap"
Style="{StaticResource BookAuthorStyle}"
Text="{TemplateBinding BookAuthor}" />
                            </StackPanel>
                        </StackPanel>
                    </Grid>
                </ControlTemplate>
            </Setter.Value>
        </Setter>
    </Style>
</ResourceDictionary>
```

In the previous examples to handle data binding you simply set up the `Image` and `TextBlock` controls to bind to particular properties of a `WroxBook` object. But with custom controls, you want things more flexible, and you don't want to tie anything to one particular object type. Instead you want properties that support data binding from any valid object, not just a `WroxBook` type. You do this by providing data binding specific properties in your custom control. In the previous code the `Image` and `TextBlock` controls were set to use `TemplateBinding`, and instead of the `WroxBook` properties that were used previously, new properties were declared that can actually be part of the `BookDetails` class instead. The following syntax basically means that when this control is used, you take the value of the `BookTitle` property for the `BookDetails` class and use that for the `Text` property of the `TextBlock` being displayed.

```
<TextBlock TextWrapping="Wrap" Style="{StaticResource BookTitleStyle}"
Text="{TemplateBinding BookTitle}" />
```

To support the binding you actually need some properties in the `BookDetails` custom control that match the binding sequence. Because these properties need to support data binding, however, you must use a special syntax when declaring them. Instead of a traditional public property, you must add a *Dependency Property* for the `BookTitle`, `BookAuthor`, and `ThumbnailImage` used in the default style. Listing 3-11 shows the full code for the `BookDetails` class along with the various Dependency Property declarations required to support data binding.

LISTING 3-11: Chapter 3\CustomControls\BookDetails.cs

```
using Windows.UI.Xaml;
using Windows.UI.Xaml.Controls;
using Windows.UI.Xaml.Media;

// The Templated Control item template is documented at
http://go.microsoft.com/fwlink/?LinkId=234235

namespace CustomControls
{
    public sealed class BookDetails : Control
    {
        public BookDetails()
        {
            this.DefaultStyleKey = typeof(BookDetails);
        }

        public ImageSource ThumbnailImage
        {
            get { return (ImageSource)GetValue(ThumbnailImageProperty); }
            set { SetValue(ThumbnailImageProperty, value); }
        }

        public static readonly DependencyProperty ThumbnailImageProperty =
DependencyProperty.Register("ThumbnailImage",
typeof(ImageSource), typeof(BookDetails), new PropertyMetadata(null));
```

```
        public string BookTitle
        {
            get { return (string)GetValue(BookTitleProperty); }
            set { SetValue(BookTitleProperty, value); }
        }

        public static readonly DependencyProperty BookTitleProperty =
    DependencyProperty.Register("BookTitle",
    typeof(string), typeof(BookDetails), new PropertyMetadata(""));

        public string BookAuthor
        {
            get { return (string)GetValue(BookAuthorProperty); }
            set { SetValue(BookAuthorProperty, value); }
        }

        public static readonly DependencyProperty BookAuthorProperty =
    DependencyProperty.Register("BookAuthor",
    typeof(string), typeof(BookDetails), new PropertyMetadata(""));
    }
}
```

As you can see, for each property that you want to make available for data binding in the default `Style`, you must add a `DependencyProperty` line that essentially ties that property to the data binding mechanisms in Windows 8.

At this point you have a new custom control that has properties you can set in XAML and that also supports data binding. This enables you to make use of the control with the following XAML code.

```
<local:BookDetails x:Name="BookDetails" ThumbnailImage="Assets/silverlight.jpg"
BookAuthor="Nick Lecrenski" BookTitle="Silverlight 4 Problem Design Solution" />
```

Or alternatively you can use data binding with these new properties and use the following code to bind to an instance of a `WroxBook` object:

```
<local:BookDetails x:Name="BookDetails" ThumbnailImage="{Binding Thumbnail}"
BookAuthor="{Binding Author}" BookTitle="{Binding Title}" />
```

The more complex the XAML code you try to reuse throughout your app, the better the candidate it is to create a custom XAML control around it.

SUMMARY

This chapter expanded on your already growing knowledge of the XAML user interface language for Windows 8. By now you should have a good grasp of important XAML concepts such as control styling, data binding, and creating custom controls. In addition, you were introduced to new Windows 8 data controls, such as the `ListView` and `GridView`, and saw how to use them to display rich collections of data and content. Combined with grouping and the concept of semantic zoom you now have new ways to present content to users that previously would have required extremely complex user interface code to pull off.

Although some of these examples were simple in nature, they are important to help you fully understand the concepts around them. As you progress through this book, the authors will especially expand on control styles and data binding to include more advanced scenarios, which further reduce code and allow for even richer user interfaces.

Windows 8 User Interface Final Touches

WHAT'S IN THIS CHAPTER?

- ➤ How to support the new Windows Store Application Bar
- ➤ Providing your user with Notifications
- ➤ Configuring and Updating Live Tiles
- ➤ Adding your own custom Splash Screen

WROX.COM CODE DOWNLOADS FOR THIS CHAPTER

You can find the wrox.com code downloads for this chapter in code file 205709 C04.zip at www.wrox.com/remtitle.cgi?isbn=1118205707 on the Download Code tab.

APPLICATION BARS, NOTIFICATIONS, SPLASH SCREENS, AND LIVE TILES

You are now an expert at using XAML to create Windows 8 user interfaces. You have mastered the important techniques of data binding. Your user interfaces now make use of proven Windows 8 styles. What else is left to complete the user interface in a Windows Store Application?

In this chapter you become familiar with several important user interface topics that provide a complete Windows Store App experience to your users. Up next is a discussion about the Windows Store Application Bar and how it replaces the traditional menu system that you may be used to from past WPF/WinForms or even Silverlight development. Notifications are another great new addition to Windows 8, and these give you an easy way to provide toast style notifications in the background while your app runs. Of course, no Windows Store Application would be complete without a customized splash screen, and this chapter shows you how to do just that. Finally, another key component to Windows Store Apps is the Live Tiles. If you want your app to stand out among the soon-to-be hundreds of thousands of apps, you must ensure that your app uses Live Tiles in a unique way; your application tile should give the user a snapshot of information relevant to what the app can do.

WORKING WITH THE APP BAR

In traditional windows applications, the best way to present menu options to your users was to make use of a standard menu control. For more than 20 years, users have become accustomed to a File/Edit/and so on menu at the top of the screen, going there to perform actions in an application. In Windows 8, however, that has changed. Because the primary design goal of a Windows Store Application is to reduce application chrome components and focus more on the actual content of the application, you must think differently when creating menu options for your users. Instead of building a menu with hundreds of different options (many of which won't ever get used) you can focus on exactly what operations are essential for your app.

You should think about what kind of actions users want to perform against the data or content that's presented to them. Because Windows 8 discourages the use of a full-blown menu system, you still need some way to give users the option to take action with the data or content. The answer is the Application Bar. If you have navigated around the new Start Screen in Windows 8, you've already seen the Application Bar in action. Anytime you right-click the screen or swipe from the bottom of a tablet, you are presented with the Application Bar and a neat orderly set of the most important actions you can take with the data or content of the app. For example, right-clicking when the default Weather app runs presents you with a way to set your location for weather updates, as shown in Figure 4-1. As you can see, the App Bar appears at the top and bottom of the screen for this application.

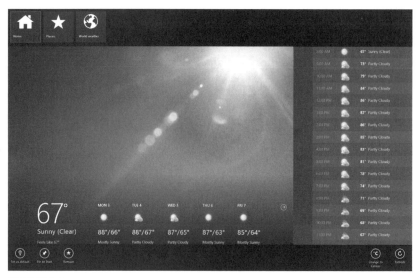

FIGURE 4-1

In Windows Store Apps the rule of thumb is to make use of the top Application Bar for navigation style commands, such as switching to different areas of the app. You then reserve the bottom bar for command type actions that create, edit, sort, filter, or refresh the current view of the data or content. Of course, the best way to gain an understanding of how to use the Application Bar is to just dive right in and add it to your own application.

You can create a sample project that makes use of both Application Bar scenarios.

Creating the Top App Bar Navigation

For this app you enable users to view three categories of Wrox Press books. After users navigate to a particular category, they can perform actions such as sorting and filtering the list of books. In the end, you should have something similar to Figure 4-2. To create this app, follow these steps:

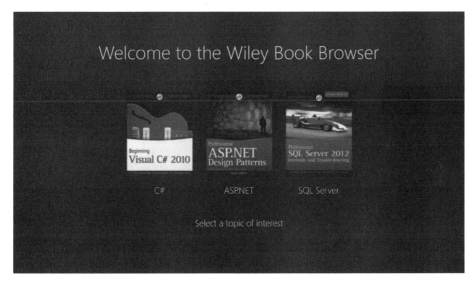

FIGURE 4-2

1. Create a new blank Windows Store project called AppBar in Visual Studio 2012.

2. Add four new pages to the project using the BlankPage item template. Call these Home.xaml, AspBooks.xaml, SqlServerBooks.xaml, and CSharpBooks.xaml, respectively.

3. With the new pages added, you need to set up the main screen, which includes the top and bottom Application Bars.

> **NOTE** *The* `AppBar` *is an object that resides in every* `Page` *object in Windows 8. Every page can essentially have its own* `AppBar` *implementation. However, because the top bar is supposed to assist with navigating through an application, it's best to implement that on the main page of your app and then add an additional Frame to hold the rest of your applications pages. It might sound a little complex, but it's not too difficult. This setup works a lot like Master Pages in the ASP.NET world.*

Now open MainPage.xaml and update it to look like Listing 4-1.

LISTING 4-1: MainPage.xaml

```
<Page
    x:Class="AppBar.MainPage"
    xmlns="http://schemas.microsoft.com/winfx/2006/xaml/presentation"
    xmlns:x="http://schemas.microsoft.com/winfx/2006/xaml"
    xmlns:local="using:AppBar"
    xmlns:d="http://schemas.microsoft.com/expression/blend/2008"
    xmlns:mc="http://schemas.openxmlformats.org/markup-compatibility/2006"
    mc:Ignorable="d">

    <Page.TopAppBar>
        <AppBar>
            <Grid>
                <Grid.ColumnDefinitions>
                    <ColumnDefinition Width="50*" />
                    <ColumnDefinition Width="50*" />
                </Grid.ColumnDefinitions>
                <StackPanel Orientation="Horizontal" Grid.Column="0">
                    <Button Style="{StaticResource
PreviousAppBarButtonStyle}" Click="Previous_Click" />
                    <Button Margin="20,0,0,0" Style="{StaticResource
NextAppBarButtonStyle}" Click="Next_Click" />
                </StackPanel>
            </Grid>
        </AppBar>
    </Page.TopAppBar>

    <Frame x:Name="MainFrame"  />
</Page>
```

Breaking this code down a bit you can see that the Page object has a TopAppBar built in, and all it takes to make use of it is to add a container control and whatever buttons/images or anything else that makes sense to assist with navigation. In this case, you add a couple of navigation buttons for moving back and forward through the app.

4. One cool thing is that the Button Style properties are set to a default Style that is included with Visual Studio 2012. You have many default button styles to choose from, so you don't need to have a designer on retainer to get something to look good. To access these styles, however, you need to include some additional files in your project. The trick is to right-click the project node in Solution Explorer and add a new Page to the project using the BasicPage template. You see an alert message that you need to add several additional files to the project.

5. Simply click OK and then delete the new page that was added. Now you should have a file called StandardStyles.xaml sitting in the Common directory of the project.

6. When in that file search for the PreviousAppBarButton style, and uncomment out the section of code that includes both of the Button styles you use. The following code shows the styles that you need to enable.

```
<Style x:Key="NextAppBarButtonStyle" TargetType="ButtonBase"
BasedOn="{StaticResource AppBarButtonStyle}">
    <Setter Property="AutomationProperties.AutomationId"
Value="NextAppBarButton"/>
    <Setter Property="AutomationProperties.Name" Value="Next"/>
    <Setter Property="Content" Value="&#xE111;"/>
</Style>
<Style x:Key="PreviousAppBarButtonStyle" TargetType="ButtonBase"
BasedOn="{StaticResource AppBarButtonStyle}">
    <Setter Property="AutomationProperties.AutomationId"
Value="PreviousAppBarButton"/>
    <Setter Property="AutomationProperties.Name" Value="Previous"/>
    <Setter Property="Content" Value="&#xE112;"/>
</Style>
```

7. As you look through the StandardStyles.xaml file, you can see a massive amount of styles. If you want to use any of them in your app, simply uncomment them and set them as `StaticResource` in the controls you want.

8. The other addition to the MainPage.xaml is the `Frame` object. By default every Windows Store App has a root `Frame`, but because you want to share the `TopAppBar` across all the pages, you need to force all the additional pages of the application into the sub `Frame` included here. Getting this to work is trivial and becomes a common pattern for you when you create Windows Store Apps that support multiple pages.

9. Now with the MainPage.xaml set, you need to add some logic to set up the sub `Frame` and handle the back/next buttons in the `TopAppBar`. Open the MainPage.xaml.cs file and make the following edits shown in Listing 4-2.

LISTING 4-2: MainPage.xaml.cs

```
using System;
using Windows.UI.Xaml;
using Windows.UI.Xaml.Controls;
using Windows.UI.Xaml.Input;

// The Blank Page item template is documented at
http://go.microsoft.com/fwlink/?LinkId=234238

namespace AppBar
{
    /// <summary>
    /// An empty page that can be used on its own or navigated to within a Frame.
    /// </summary>
    public sealed partial class MainPage : Page
    {
        public MainPage()
        {
            this.InitializeComponent();
        }

        protected override void
```

continues

LISTING 4-2 *(continued)*

```
OnNavigatedTo(Windows.UI.Xaml.Navigation.NavigationEventArgs e)
        {
                base.OnNavigatedTo(e);
                MainFrame.Navigate(typeof(Home));
        }

        private void Previous_Click(object sender, RoutedEventArgs e)
        {
            if (MainFrame.CanGoBack)
                MainFrame.GoBack();
        }

        private void Next_Click(object sender, RoutedEventArgs e)
        {
            if (MainFrame.CanGoForward)
                MainFrame.GoForward();
        }
    }
}
```

Nothing too crazy here, just a couple of `Button` `Click` event handlers that force the sub `Frame` object to move forward and back when clicked.

10. Remember to always check if that action is supported by using the `CanGoForward` and `CanGoBack` properties; otherwise, an `Exception` will be thrown if the user touches the button and there are no pages to navigate to.

11. To set up the first page of the app, use the `MainPage` `Frame` to navigate to the homepage.

12. With the main shell of the app complete, it's time to move onto the additional pages of the app starting with the application homepage. The goal of the homepage is to present three categories of books for the user to choose from. These include CSharp, ASP.NET, and SqlServer. Open the Home.xaml file and replace the existing XAML with that shown in Listing 4-3.

LISTING 4-3: Home.xaml

```
<Page
    x:Class="AppBar.Home"
    xmlns="http://schemas.microsoft.com/winfx/2006/xaml/presentation"
    xmlns:x="http://schemas.microsoft.com/winfx/2006/xaml"
    xmlns:local="using:AppBar"
    xmlns:d="http://schemas.microsoft.com/expression/blend/2008"
    xmlns:mc="http://schemas.openxmlformats.org/markup-compatibility/2006"
    mc:Ignorable="d">

    <Grid Background="{StaticResource ApplicationPageBackgroundThemeBrush}">
```

```
        <TextBlock HorizontalAlignment="Center" Margin="0,100,0,0"
TextWrapping="Wrap" Text="Welcome to the Wiley Book Browser"
VerticalAlignment="Top" Style="{StaticResource PageHeaderTextStyle}"/>
        <StackPanel HorizontalAlignment="Center" Margin="0"
VerticalAlignment="Center" Orientation="Horizontal">
            <StackPanel Margin="0,0,40,0">
                <Image Source="Assets/begincsharp.jpg" Canvas.ZIndex="1"
Stretch="UniformToFill" Width="200" Height="250" Tapped="Image_Tapped"
Tag="CSharpBooks" />
                <TextBlock Text="C#" Margin="0,20,0,0"
HorizontalAlignment="Center" Style="{StaticResource SubheaderTextStyle}" />
            </StackPanel>
            <StackPanel Margin="0,0,40,0">
                <Image Source="Assets/aspnetdesign.jpg" Canvas.ZIndex="1"
Stretch="UniformToFill" Width="200" Height="250" Tapped="Image_Tapped"
Tag="AspBooks" />
                <TextBlock Text="ASP.NET" Margin="0,20,0,0"
HorizontalAlignment="Center" Style="{StaticResource SubheaderTextStyle}" />
            </StackPanel>
            <StackPanel Margin="0">
                <Image Source="Assets/prosqltroubleshoot.jpg" Canvas.ZIndex="1"
Stretch="UniformToFill" Width="200" Height="250" Tapped="Image_Tapped"
Tag="SqlServerBooks" />
                <TextBlock Text="SQL Server" Margin="0,20,0,0"
HorizontalAlignment="Center" Style="{StaticResource SubheaderTextStyle}" />
            </StackPanel>
        </StackPanel>
        <TextBlock HorizontalAlignment="Center" Margin="0,600,0,0"
TextWrapping="Wrap" Text="Select a topic of interest" VerticalAlignment="Top"
Style="{StaticResource PageSubheaderTextStyle}"/>
    </Grid>
</Page>
```

> **NOTE** *This code takes care of displaying the three category images from which users choose as well as adding a* Tapped *event handler so that you can force the navigation to the appropriate page. In the following code the* Image *control uses the* Tag *property to hold onto the destination page it should point to for navigation; in this case it is the CSharpBooks page:*
>
> ```
> <Image Source="Assets/begincsharp.jpg" Canvas.ZIndex="1"
> Stretch="UniformToFill" Width="200" Height="250"
> Tapped="Image_Tapped" Tag="CSharpBooks" />
> ```

13. If you build and run the app using the Simulator at this point, you should see the homepage now. Also if you right-click anywhere on the screen, you should see your `TopAppBar` appear along with the commands to move back/forward, as shown in Figure 4-3.

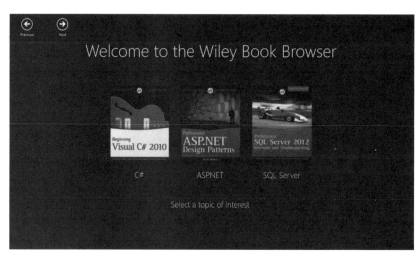

FIGURE 4-3

14. Now you have the main homepage with the required category images. You still need to handle the `Tapped` event for each and tell the `MainFrame` object to navigate to the appropriate pages. Open up Home.xaml.cs and update the code to look like Listing 4-4:

LISTING 4-4: Home.xaml.cs

```
using Windows.UI.Xaml.Controls;
using Windows.UI.Xaml.Input;

// The Blank Page item template is documented at
http://go.microsoft.com/fwlink/?LinkId=234238

namespace AppBar
{
    /// <summary>
    /// An empty page that can be used on its own or navigated to within a Frame.
    /// </summary>
    public sealed partial class Home : Page
    {
        public Home()
        {
            this.InitializeComponent();
        }

        private void Image_Tapped(object sender, TappedRoutedEventArgs e)
        {
```

```
                    string tag = ((Image)sender).Tag.ToString();

                    if (tag == "CSharpBooks")
                        this.Frame.Navigate(typeof(CSharpBooks));
                    else if (tag == "AspBooks")
                        this.Frame.Navigate(typeof(AspBooks));
                    else
                        this.Frame.Navigate(typeof(SqlServerBooks));
            }
        }
    }
```

The cool thing to take away from this code is that normally `this.Frame` refers to the main application frame; however, because the Home.xaml page is actually run from a sub `Frame` object, it correctly is pointed to the `Frame` that is actually hosting the page. This enables you to easily navigate through the subpages without trying to get any special access to the `MainFrame` variable declared in MainPage.xaml.

Wiring Up the App Pages

So now you have the homepage set and ready to navigate to the category pages — time to wire up those pages.

1. Open the AspBooks.xaml file, and replace it with the code in Listing 4-5.

LISTING 4-5: AspBooks.xaml

```
<Page
    x:Class="AppBar.AspBooks"
    xmlns="http://schemas.microsoft.com/winfx/2006/xaml/presentation"
    xmlns:x="http://schemas.microsoft.com/winfx/2006/xaml"
    xmlns:local="using:AppBar"
    xmlns:d="http://schemas.microsoft.com/expression/blend/2008"
    xmlns:mc="http://schemas.openxmlformats.org/markup-compatibility/2006"
    mc:Ignorable="d">

    <Page.BottomAppBar>
        <AppBar>
            <Grid>
                <Grid.ColumnDefinitions>
                    <ColumnDefinition Width="50*" />
                    <ColumnDefinition Width="50*" />
                </Grid.ColumnDefinitions>
                <StackPanel Orientation="Horizontal"
Grid.Column="1" HorizontalAlignment="Right">
                    <Button Style="{StaticResource FilterAppBarButtonStyle}"
Click="FilterBooks_Click" />
                    <Button Margin="20,0,0,0" Style="{StaticResource
SortAppBarButtonStyle}" Click="SortBooks_Click" />
                </StackPanel>
            </Grid>
        </AppBar>
    </Page.BottomAppBar>
```

continues

LISTING 4-5 *(continued)*

```xml
        </Page.BottomAppBar>

    <Grid Background="{StaticResource ApplicationPageBackgroundThemeBrush}">
        <GridView x:Name="BookGridView"
            ItemTemplate="{StaticResource BookTemplate}"
            BorderBrush="White" BorderThickness="2"
            ScrollViewer.VerticalScrollBarVisibility="Auto"
            ScrollViewer.HorizontalScrollBarVisibility="Auto"
            SelectionMode="Single"
            Margin="50">
        </GridView>
    </Grid>
</Page>
```

> **NOTE** *There are a couple things to take away from this code:*
>
> ➤ *You can now add a* BottomAppBar *to the page with a couple* Button *controls. These controls filter and sort the list of books from this category.*
>
> ➤ *A* GridView *displays the list of books, and each book uses a particular* ItemTemplate. *In the previous chapter you saw that by adding an* ItemTemplate *resource to the App.xaml page allows it to be shared across the application so that any control that requires it can have access.*

2. Because you want to reuse this same XAML across all the book list pages, you should put that template in App.xaml. Open App.xaml and replace the existing XAML code with that shown in Listing 4-6.

LISTING 4-6: App.xaml

```xml
<Application
    x:Class="AppBar.App"
    xmlns="http://schemas.microsoft.com/winfx/2006/xaml/presentation"
    xmlns:x="http://schemas.microsoft.com/winfx/2006/xaml"
    xmlns:local="using:AppBar">

    <Application.Resources>
        <ResourceDictionary>
            <ResourceDictionary.MergedDictionaries>

                <!--
                    Styles that define common aspects of the platform look and feel
                    Required by Visual Studio project and item templates
                -->
                <ResourceDictionary Source="Common/StandardStyles.xaml"/>
```

```
                        </ResourceDictionary.MergedDictionaries>

                        <Style x:Key="BookTitleStyle" TargetType="TextBlock">
                            <Setter Property="FontFamily" Value="Segoe UI Light"/>
                            <Setter Property="FontSize" Value="18"/>
                        </Style>

                        <Style x:Key="BookAuthorStyle" TargetType="TextBlock">
                            <Setter Property="FontFamily" Value="Segoe UI Light"/>
                            <Setter Property="FontSize" Value="14"/>
                        </Style>

                        <DataTemplate x:Key="BookTemplate">
                            <Border BorderBrush="White" BorderThickness="2"  Width="700">
                                <Grid Margin="10">
                                    <StackPanel Orientation="Horizontal">
                                        <Image Source="{Binding Thumbnail}" Height="60"
Width="60" Margin="0,0,10,0"/>
                                        <StackPanel Margin="0,0,0,0"
Orientation="Vertical">
                                            <TextBlock Style="{StaticResource
BookTitleStyle}" Text="{Binding Title}" />
                                            <TextBlock Style="{StaticResource
BookAuthorStyle}" Text="{Binding Author}" />
                                        </StackPanel>
                                    </StackPanel>
                                </Grid>
                            </Border>
                        </DataTemplate>

                </ResourceDictionary>
            </Application.Resources>
</Application>
```

3.   Now the GridView is set with the template for each individual book item that will display.
     All you need is some data. Add a new file to the Data folder of the project called WroxBook
     .cs. Replace it with the code in Listing 4-7. This class represents each book object to be
     displayed in the app.

LISTING 4-7: WroxBook.cs

```
using Windows.UI.Xaml.Media;

    namespace AppBar.Data
    {
        public class WroxBook
        {
            public string Title { get; set; }
            public string Author { get; set; }
            public string Subject { get; set; }
            public ImageSource Thumbnail { get; set; }
        }
    }
```

As you can see, each book will have a `Title`, `Author`, `Subject`, and `Thumbnail` image to represent the book cover.

4. You need some sample data, so add that data for the existing ASP.NET books. Open AspBooks.xaml.cs and update it to look like Listing 4-8.

LISTING 4-8: AspBooks.xaml.cs

```
using AppBar.Data;
using System;
using System.Collections.Generic;
using System.Collections.ObjectModel;
using System.Linq;
using Windows.Foundation;
using Windows.UI.Popups;
using Windows.UI.Xaml;
using Windows.UI.Xaml.Controls;
using Windows.UI.Xaml.Media;
using Windows.UI.Xaml.Media.Imaging;
using Windows.UI.Xaml.Navigation;

// The Blank Page item template is documented at
http://go.microsoft.com/fwlink/?LinkId=234238

namespace AppBar
{
    /// <summary>
    /// An empty page that can be used on its own or navigated to within a Frame.
    /// </summary>
    public sealed partial class AspBooks : Page
    {
        public List<WroxBook> Books { get; set; }

        public AspBooks()
        {
            this.InitializeComponent();
            SetupBookList();
        }

        private void SetupBookList()
        {
            Books = new List<WroxBook>();

            Books.Add(new WroxBook
            {
                Subject = "ASP.NET",
                Title = "Professional ASP.NET MVC 4",
                Author = "Jon Galloway",
                Thumbnail = new
BitmapImage(new Uri("ms-appx:///Assets/aspnet4.jpg",
UriKind.RelativeOrAbsolute))
            });

            Books.Add(new WroxBook
            {
```

```
                    Subject = "ASP.NET",
                    Title = "Beginning ASP.NET Web Pages with WebMatrix",
                    Author = "Mike Brind, Imar Spaanjaars",
                    Thumbnail = new BitmapImage(new Uri("ms-
appx:///Assets/beginaspnetmatrix.jpg", UriKind.RelativeOrAbsolute))
                });

            Books.Add(new WroxBook
            {
                    Subject = "ASP.NET",
                    Title = "Professional ASP.net Design Patterns",
                    Author = "Scott Millett",
                    Thumbnail = new BitmapImage(new Uri("ms-
appx:///Assets/aspnetdesign.jpg", UriKind.RelativeOrAbsolute))
                });
        }
    }
}
```

Adding Filtering Capability

So far you have a simple method that adds various books to the main Books collection. With that
complete you can now set the GridView to make use of these. Because you also want to support
filtering and sorting of the Books, it makes sense to point the GridView to a copy of this collection
that can hold the filtered or sorted version of the data. To add this capability, follow these steps:

1. Add the following line of code just below the declaration for the Books collection:

    ```
    public ObservableCollection<WroxBook> FilteredBooks { get; set; }
    ```

2. You can now safely set up the GridView to point to the collection of Book objects. Add the
    following OnNavigatedTo method to the code. This ensures that the GridView is set to dis-
    play the FilteredBooks collection when the page first loads. To start you default to display
    all the Books in the collection unfiltered.

    ```
    protected override void OnNavigatedTo(NavigationEventArgs e)
    {
        base.OnNavigatedTo(e);

        FilteredBooks = new ObservableCollection<WroxBook>(Books);
        BookGridView.ItemsSource = FilteredBooks;
    }
    ```

3. All that is left now is to handle the filter and sort commands that you made available in the
    BottomAppBar. By adding the following code to the file you can create Click event handlers
    for the filter and sort Button controls as well as make use of a new Windows 8 control
    called the PopupMenu.

    ```
    private async void FilterBooks_Click(object sender, RoutedEventArgs e)
    {
        PopupMenu filterMenu = new PopupMenu();

        filterMenu.Commands.Add(new UICommand("Beginner Books", (c) =>
    ```

```
        {
                FilteredBooks = new ObservableCollection<WroxBook>(Books.Where(b =>
        b.Title.IndexOf("Begin") >= 0).ToList());
                BookGridView.ItemsSource = FilteredBooks;
        }));

        filterMenu.Commands.Add(new UICommand("All Books", (c) =>
        {
                FilteredBooks = new ObservableCollection<WroxBook>(Books);
                BookGridView.ItemsSource = FilteredBooks;
        }));

        await filterMenu.ShowForSelectionAsync(GetMenuRectangle
    ((FrameworkElement)sender));
    }

    private async void SortBooks_Click(object sender, RoutedEventArgs e)
    {
        PopupMenu sortMenu = new PopupMenu();

        sortMenu.Commands.Add(new UICommand("Sort By Author", (c) =>
        {
                FilteredBooks = new ObservableCollection<WroxBook>(Books.OrderBy(b =>
        b.Author).ToList());
                BookGridView.ItemsSource = FilteredBooks;
        }));

        sortMenu.Commands.Add(new UICommand("Sort By Title", (c) =>
        {
                FilteredBooks = new ObservableCollection<WroxBook>(Books.OrderBy(b =>
        b.Title).ToList());
                BookGridView.ItemsSource = FilteredBooks;
        }));

        await sortMenu.ShowForSelectionAsync(GetMenuRectangle
    ((FrameworkElement)sender));
    }

    public static Rect GetMenuRectangle(FrameworkElement element)
    {
        GeneralTransform transform = element.TransformToVisual(null);
        Point point = transform.TransformPoint(new Point());
        Rect finalRect = new Rect(point, new Size(element.ActualWidth,
    element.ActualHeight));

        return finalRect;
    }
```

There is a decent amount of information you need to take away from that code, so break it down some so that you understand exactly what happens here.

➤ You want to provide commands to filter and sort the list of books. In Windows 8, when you use the AppBar if you need to provide a list of quick filtering/sorting decisions, the best way is to use the PopupMenu control. This control displays a small rectangle with the available choices to the user. Of course, you want that to display above the `Button` that the user presses, which is a little tricky.

➤ In the `SortBooks_Click` event handler, the first thing you do is create an instance of the `PopupMenu`. Then you add a couple `UICommand` objects to the `Commands` collection of the menu. All the `UICommand` does is to provide you with a way to run code when the option is touched/clicked by the user.

➤ Each command uses a lambda expression to run the appropriate event handling code, which in this case simply adds a filtered or sorted view of the `Books` collection to the `FilteredBooks` collection that the `GridView` uses. After the commands are set up, you then need to actually display the menu.

In Windows 8 the menu display cannot interfere with anything else going on in the app, so it must be done asynchronously. By calling the `ShowForSelectionAsync` method — as shown in the following code — with the `await` keyword, you can be sure that this operation happens asynchronously:

```
await sortMenu.ShowForSelectionAsync(GetMenuRectangle
((FrameworkElement)sender));
```

The only catch to this method is that you must pass in the rectangle of the `Button` that the menu should be displayed above. The `GetMenuRectangle` method is a helper method that simply extracts the bounding `Rectangle` of the `Button` that was clicked so that it can be used to track where the menu should display.

Adding Finishing Touches to the App

Now if you run the app and navigate to the ASP.NET books category page, you should right-click in the Simulator to see the new `BottomAppBar` menu, as shown in Figure 4-4. Try playing around with the filter and sort commands, and you should see the `GridView` refresh with the filtered and sorted data as well.

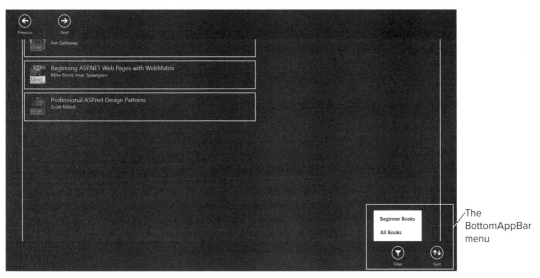

FIGURE 4-4

The only thing left for this sample is to copy all the same XAML code to the remaining category pages and, of course, the code-behind logic as well. The only difference is that you substitute the actual data that you want to display so that both C# and SQL Server books display instead of the ASP.NET book.

ADDING NOTIFICATIONS

A great feature that's been incorporated into many web applications (and some newer thick client apps) is *Toast notifications*, which provide important information, typically in a small rectangular box at the corner of the screen. The notifications usually have some kind of time limit and fade away if the user ignores them. And as a developer these notifications give you a nice way to communicate an important message to the user. Toast notifications are far better than slamming a pop-up window in front of a busy user.

With Silverlight and WPF, you could use some techniques to get something similar to a Toast notification — but nothing easy. The good news is Windows 8 provides notification capabilities in WinRT, which you can easily make use of in your apps. If you've plugged in a USB device while working in desktop mode or running another Windows Store App, you've most likely seen a Windows 8 notification already.

By default, notifications appear in the top-right corner of the primary display and, depending on how you configure them, they also play a short sound. With WinRT, you can create and configure custom notification messages. Users can always disable notifications at the OS level through the Windows 8 settings page, so you are not guaranteed to always be able to send them. You're not restricted to sending notifications from your locally installed Windows Store App either. With the new Windows Push Notification Service, you can remotely send notifications from a cloud-based web service.

In Windows 8, the majority of the Toast messages are standard duration toasts. These messages should actually display only when you need to convey an important message to the user. Standard toast messages display for 7 seconds; during that time the user can touch/click the message, and your app is brought to the forefront for further user interaction. Standard Toast messages also play a brief audio sound as well. The long duration toast message gives you the ability to display a toast notification for 25 seconds. You want to make use of this kind of notification only in limited scenarios in which you must get the attention of the user and get them back into your app.

Understanding Templates

All toast messages that you create and send in your app are done so by creating a simple XML message. The XML message has several properties that you can override to customize the message. Windows 8 provides many different toast message templates that you can choose from. Some of these templates display basic text, whereas others display an image along with text. For an up-to-date list of available toast templates, visit `http://msdn.microsoft.com/en-us/library/windows/apps/hh761494.aspx`. The following is a list of the available templates at the time of this writing.

➤ **ToastText01:** Displays one single line of message text, for example:

```
<toast>
    <visual>
        <binding template="ToastText01">
            <text id="1">message line 1</text>
        </binding>
    </visual>
</toast>
```

➤ **ToastText02:** Displays one line of header text followed by a smaller subtext line, for example:

```
<toast>
    <visual>
        <binding template="ToastText02">
            <text id="1">header message</text>
            <text id="2">message line 1</text>
        </binding>
    </visual>
</toast>
```

➤ **ToastText03:** Same as ToastText02 but enables header text to wrap to the next line:

```
<toast>
    <visual>
        <binding template="ToastText03">
            <text id="1">header message</text>
            <text id="2">message line 1</text>
        </binding>
    </visual>
</toast>
```

➤ **ToastText04:** Displays one header line followed by two additional lines of message text, for example:

```
<toast>
    <visual>
        <binding template="ToastText04">
            <text id="1">header message</text>
            <text id="2">message line 1</text>
            <text id="3">message line 2</text>
        </binding>
    </visual>
</toast>
```

➤ **ToastImageAndText01:** Displays thumbnail image alongside one line of message text, for example:

```
<toast>
    <visual>
        <binding template="ToastImageAndText01">
            <image id="1" src="thumbnail" alt="thumbnail"/>
            <text id="1">message line 1</text>
        </binding>
    </visual>
</toast>
```

➤ **ToastImageAndText02:** Displays a thumbnail image alongside a header message and one additional line of text, for example:

```
<toast>
    <visual>
        <binding template="ToastImageAndText02">
            <image id="1" src="thumbnail" alt="thumbnail"/>
            <text id="1">header message</text>
            <text id="2">message line 1</text>
        </binding>
    </visual>
</toast>
```

➤ **ToastImageAndText03:** Displays a thumbnail image alongside a header message that is allowed to wrap along with an additional line of text. An example follows:

```
<toast>
    <visual>
        <binding template="ToastImageAndText03">
            <image id="1" src="thumbnail" alt="thumbnail"/>
            <text id="1">header message</text>
            <text id="2">message line 1</text>
        </binding>
    </visual>
</toast>
```

➤ **ToastImageAndText04:** Displays a thumbnail image alongside a header message and two additional lines of message text, for example:

```
<toast>
    <visual>
        <binding template="ToastImageAndText04">
            <image id="1" src="thumbnail" alt="thumbnail"/>
            <text id="1">header message</text>
            <text id="2">message line 1</text>
            <text id="3">message line 2</text>
        </binding>
    </visual>
</toast>
```

The most basic template you can choose is the ToastText01 template, which provides you with the following customizable XML:

```
<toast>
    <visual>
        <binding template="ToastText01">
            <text id="1">message goes here</text>
        </binding>
    </visual>
</toast>
```

As you can see this is basic and allows for only one line of message text to display. The following XML shows one of the available templates that supports a thumbnail image alongside the toast message text.

```
<toast>
    <visual>
        <binding template="ToastImageAndText01">
```

```
                <image id="1" src="myimage" alt="myimage"/>
                <text id="1">message goes here</text>
            </binding>
        </visual>
</toast>
```

A Toast Example

Creating Toast messages for your app basically involves replacing the `src` value of the image tag and inserting a message in the text node. You can do this using the standard XML management classes of WinRT. This section looks at how to build a simple toast notification from scratch. All you do here is add a few `Button` controls that when pressed send a few different style toast notifications. One becomes basic text, a second has a thumbnail image, and the last alters the default toast sound that plays.

Creating A Basic Text Based Notification

To create basic text, just follow these steps:

1. Create a new project in Visual Studio 2012 using the BlankApp project template, and call it **Notifications**.

2. With the project created open the MainPage.xaml file, and replace the contents with the XAML shown in Listing 4-9.

LISTING 4-9: MainPage.xaml

```
<Page
    x:Class="Notifications.MainPage"
    xmlns="http://schemas.microsoft.com/winfx/2006/xaml/presentation"
    xmlns:x="http://schemas.microsoft.com/winfx/2006/xaml"
    xmlns:local="using:Notifications"
    xmlns:d="http://schemas.microsoft.com/expression/blend/2008"
    xmlns:mc="http://schemas.openxmlformats.org/markup-compatibility/2006"
    mc:Ignorable="d">

    <Grid Background="{StaticResource ApplicationPageBackgroundThemeBrush}">
        <StackPanel Margin="0" VerticalAlignment="Center"
Orientation="Horizontal" HorizontalAlignment="Center">
            <Button Content="Show Toast Notification"
HorizontalAlignment="Center" Margin="0,0,20,0" VerticalAlignment="Center"
Click="ShowToast_Click"/>
            <Button Content="Show Toast With Image"
HorizontalAlignment="Center" Margin="0" VerticalAlignment="Center"
Click="ShowToastImage_Click" />
            <Button Content="Show Toast With Alternate Sound"
HorizontalAlignment="Center" Margin="20,0,0,0" VerticalAlignment="Center"
Click="ShowToastSound_Click" />
        </StackPanel>
    </Grid>
</Page>
```

3. Open the MainPage.xaml.cs file, and add the following `Click` event handlers:

```
private void ShowToast_Click(object sender, RoutedEventArgs e)
{

}

private void ShowToastImage_Click(object sender, RoutedEventArgs e)
{

}

private void ShowToastSound_Click(object sender, RoutedEventArgs e)
{

}
```

4. Starting with the basic text-based toast message, you need access to the correct toast template. The template is simply an `XmlDocument` object, so you can do this by utilizing the `GetTemplateContent` method of the `ToastNotificationManager` class from WinRT. Add the following code to the `ShowToast_Click` event handler:

```
XmlDocument template = ToastNotificationManager.GetTemplateContent
(ToastTemplateType.ToastText01);
```

5. Now that you have the template, you need to access the `<text>` node so that you can replace the default text with your custom message. Add the following code next to extract the `XmlNodeList` that contains the `<text>` node as well as appending the custom text to that node:

```
XmlNodeList text = template.GetElementsByTagName("text");
text[0].AppendChild(template.CreateTextNode("Welcome To Windows 8"));
```

6. You set your toast message, so all you need to do now is actually send it to the notification system of Windows 8. To do this make use of the `ToastNotificationManager` object and simply create a new `ToastNotification` that contains your customized Toast XML from the template, and call the `Show` method. Add the following code to finish up this method.

```
ToastNotification toast = new ToastNotification(template);
ToastNotificationManager.CreateToastNotifier().Show(toast);
```

7. Now see this in action. Before jumping to debug, toast notifications do not show up when you use the Simulator, so you must run this example as a full-blown Windows Store App on your PC. If you run the app at this point and click the basic toast button, you can see the message appear as it does in Figure 4-5.

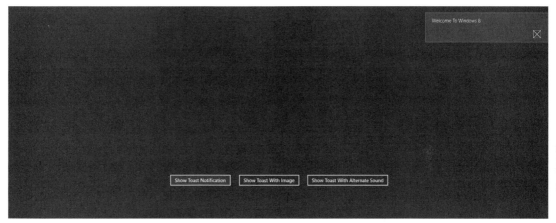

FIGURE 4-5

Adding a Thumbnail Image to the Toast Notification

As you can see it's simple to get a basic toast notification running. Now try getting a toast with a thumbnail image alongside.

1. Modify the ShowToastImage_Click method to look like the following:

```
private void ShowToastImage_Click(object sender, RoutedEventArgs e)
{
    XmlDocument template =
ToastNotificationManager.GetTemplateContent
(ToastTemplateType.ToastImageAndText01);
    XmlNodeList image = template.GetElementsByTagName("image");
    XmlNodeList text = template.GetElementsByTagName("text");

    ((XmlElement)image[0]).SetAttribute("src", "ms-
appx:///Assets/begincsharp.jpg");
    ((XmlElement)text[0]).InnerText = "An image based Toast";

    ToastNotification toast = new ToastNotification(template);
    ToastNotificationManager.CreateToastNotifier().Show(toast);
}
```

> **NOTE** *This code is similar to the previous in that you extract the* XmlNode *objects for the* <text> *and* <image> *tags and swap the content for your own. Again, you make use of the* ToastNotificationManager *to actually display the message.*

2. If you build and run the app now on your PC and click the second toast button, you should see the toast message alongside the thumbnail, as shown in Figure 4-6.

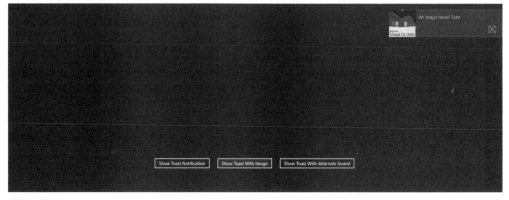

FIGURE 4-6

Changing the Default Audio to Play a Toast Notification Message

The final sample toast message involves changing the default audio that is played when the message appears. There are several different sounds available to choose from when creating Toast messages that are all built into WinRT. You can get the full list along with descriptions of these sounds by visiting http://msdn.microsoft.com/en-us/library/windows/apps/hh761492.aspx. Table 4-1 shows the options available at the time of this writing.

TABLE 4-1: Toast Message Audio Options

CODE	DESCRIPTION
Notification.Default	Default audio played on notifications
Notification.IM	Audio sound reserved for instant messaging
Notification.Mail	Audio played for e-mail arrival notification
Notification.Reminder	Audio for calendar reminder sounds
Notification.Looping.Alarm	Alarm sound

By default none of the toast templates contain an `<audio>` tag, so if you try accessing one and altering the value like you did for the previous `<text>` and `<image>` tags, you won't have much luck. It is, however, included in the official toast message schema, so to support it in this example, you simply just add the new node to the root `<toast>` tag. To do so, follow these steps.

1. Modify the `ShowToastSound_Click` event handler to match the following code, and notice the syntax used to point to the wanted Windows 8 audio file.

```
private void ShowToastSound_Click(object sender, RoutedEventArgs e)
{
    XmlDocument template =
ToastNotificationManager.GetTemplateContent(ToastTemplateType.ToastText01);
    IXmlNode mainNode = template.SelectSingleNode("/toast");
    XmlElement sound = template.CreateElement("audio");

    sound.SetAttribute("src", "ms-winsoundevent:Notification.Reminder");
    mainNode.AppendChild(sound);

    ToastNotification toast = new ToastNotification(template);
    ToastNotificationManager.CreateToastNotifier().Show(toast);
}
```

2. Build and run the app on the PC.

3. Click the third toast button; you should see the toast message and hear a slightly different audio sound being played.

The support for toast message notifications built into Windows 8 and the development methods available in WinRT make it simple to provide important notifications to your users, even when your app is not currently at the forefront of the user. Again, ensure that only important information is used for this feature because you don't want to annoy users or distract them from working on what they are currently involved in.

CREATING LIVE TILES

In previous versions of Windows, when an application was installed a custom icon was placed in the Start Menu or on the Desktop that when clicked, started your app. For the most part little time was spent designing this icon because it didn't serve any function other than to provide users with a way to run the app. In Windows 8, however, this is no longer the case. Windows Store Apps are not installed just with a plain, ordinary icon but rather use a concept called *Live Tiles*. Although you can make these Tiles static images showing your company or app logo, you can also use them to provide the user with real-time information from your app. Dynamic types of tiles are called *Live Tiles*, and when implemented, they can make your app stand out from other apps. Of course, by now you are familiar with Tiles because you're confronted with them as soon as the operating system starts. Figure 4-7 shows the all-important Start Screen that (when filled with properly implemented Live Tiles) can serve as a user dashboard, allowing the user to see what's going on with the various apps installed.

FIGURE 4-7

When considering how to use the Live Tiles feature, consider what kind of information the user would want to see without actually entering the app. Think of a Live Tile as a snapshot of the application state. If you have the type of application that monitors something in the background, it should also update the state of the Tile, so the user can view new information. The default weather app installed with Windows 8 is a great example of this. As the weather changes the Live Tile for the app updates to reflect these changes, and the user can quickly see the current/forecasted weather on the Start Screen without entering the app itself.

Implementing Live Tiles is not unlike sending Toast notifications in your app. The way Live Tiles works is basically the same in that you choose from a set of available tile templates and then send some customized XML back to the WinRT object responsible for updating your applications tile.

Available Tile Templates

As you can imagine, many different templates are available to you. Some are text-based, and others include the ability to add images. One important thing to remember, however, is that no matter what template you choose, your tile customization always starts with a background image and color, both of which you choose using the project properties page in Visual Studio. The templates simply provide a layer of images and text that overlay the background image of your tile when necessary, so it is still important to spend some time designing the background of the static display for your tile.

Again Microsoft provides plenty of guidance around this topic. To get the most up-to-date information about which templates and styles are available for your Live Tiles, visit:
`http://msdn.microsoft.com/en-us/library/windows/apps/hh761491.aspx`.

The following sections present all available Tile templates with sample XML (from at the time of writing).

Live Tiles Example

By now you are probably anxious to start creating your own Live Tiles, and there's no better way than to just jump in and create a sample project that creates a custom tile for your app and sends notifications to the tile, so it can update on the Start screen. To start, follow these steps:

1. Create a new project in Visual Studio 2012 using the BlankApp project template.

2. For this project, use one of the wide tile templates to ensure your tile isn't ignored. Start by giving the wide version of the tile a background image other than the default. Wide versions of tiles are 310x150, so the first thing you should do is add an image of that size to the Assets folder of the project.

3. Open the Package.appmanifest file, and scroll to the Tile section. There, you can set the Logo, Wide logo, and Small logo versions of your tile. For this example set the Wide logo to the image you added in the Assets folder, as shown in Figure 4-8.

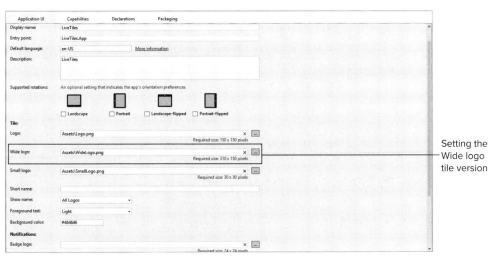

Setting the Wide logo tile version

FIGURE 4-8

4. Depending on the image you choose, you may also want to set the Background color to better match the overall tile if you have any transparency in your image.

5. Now you are ready for some code; you will be surprised at how little code it takes. In this sample, you allow the user to enter some text and click/touch the button, so the text is sent to your application's Live Tile. Open the MainPage.xaml and replace its contents with the code in Listing 4-10. This code provides the user with a simple TextBox and Button control to supply the app with content for updating the Tile.

LISTING 4-10: MainPage.xaml

```
<Page
    x:Class="LiveTiles.MainPage"
    xmlns="http://schemas.microsoft.com/winfx/2006/xaml/presentation"
    xmlns:x="http://schemas.microsoft.com/winfx/2006/xaml"
    xmlns:local="using:LiveTiles"
    xmlns:d="http://schemas.microsoft.com/expression/blend/2008"
    xmlns:mc="http://schemas.openxmlformats.org/markup-compatibility/2006"
    mc:Ignorable="d">

    <Grid Background="{StaticResource ApplicationPageBackgroundThemeBrush}">
        <StackPanel HorizontalAlignment="Center" Margin="0"
VerticalAlignment="Center" Orientation="Horizontal">
            <TextBox x:Name="LiveTileText" HorizontalAlignment="Left"
TextWrapping="Wrap" VerticalAlignment="Top" Width="250" Height="29"/>
            <Button Content="Update Live Tile" HorizontalAlignment="Left"
VerticalAlignment="Top" Margin="20,0,0,0" Click="UpdateTile_Click"/>
        </StackPanel>
    </Grid>
</Page>
```

6.   There's not much to this user interface but it gets the job done. Next, open the MainPage.
xaml.cs file and replace its contents with the code shown in Listing 4-11.

LISTING 4-11: MainPage.xaml.cs

```
using System;
using Windows.Data.Xml.Dom;
using Windows.UI.Notifications;
using Windows.UI.Xaml;
using Windows.UI.Xaml.Controls;

// The Blank Page item template is documented at
http://go.microsoft.com/fwlink/?LinkId=234238

namespace LiveTiles
{
    /// <summary>
    /// An empty page that can be used on its own or navigated to within a Frame.
    /// </summary>
    ///
    public sealed partial class MainPage : Page
    {
        public MainPage()
        {
            this.InitializeComponent();
        }

        private void UpdateTile_Click(object sender, RoutedEventArgs e)
        {
            /*
             * XML For Live Tile to be used
             *
```

```
            *   <tile>
                    <visual>
                        <binding template="TileWideText01">
                            <text id="1">Message Line 1</text>
                            <text id="2">Message Line 2</text>
                            <text id="3">Message Line 3</text>
                            <text id="4">Message Line 4</text>
                            <text id="5">Message Line 5</text>
                        </binding>
                    </visual>
            </tile>
            */

            XmlDocument template =
    TileUpdateManager.GetTemplateContent(TileTemplateType.TileWideText01);
            XmlNodeList nodes = template.GetElementsByTagName("text");

            nodes[0].InnerText = LiveTileText.Text;

            TileNotification notification = new TileNotification(template);
            notification.ExpirationTime = DateTimeOffset.UtcNow.AddSeconds(10);

            TileUpdater tileUpdater =
    TileUpdateManager.CreateTileUpdaterForApplication();
            tileUpdater.Update(notification);
        }
    }
}
```

Breaking down the previous code a little bit; it looks similar to what you did to send toast notifications in the last sample app. Actually, many of the same mechanisms are at work here:

➤ You want to grab the tile template; to do that use the `TileUpdateManager`.

➤ You extract the collection of available `<text>` nodes that are contained in this template. Although the template allows for up to five lines of text, you don't need to use them all. For this example you use only the first line.

7. Now that you have the nodes required for updating text, simply set the `InnerText` property of the first node to the message entered by the user, as shown here.

```
nodes[0].InnerText = LiveTileText.Text;
```

8. With the correct line of text ready to go, just as you did with toast notifications, you now create another type of notification called a `TileNotification`. The following code creates the notification object using the updated tile template and sets the duration to 10 seconds. This ensures that the Tile update stays on the screen for only that duration. You want the Tile to feel dynamic, so setting the duration ensures that the notification goes away, and upon completion the default Tile displays again.

```
TileNotification notification = new TileNotification(template);
notification.ExpirationTime = DateTimeOffset.UtcNow.AddSeconds(10);
```

9. Use the `TileUpdater` class to actually update your application's Tile using the newly created `TileNotification` object. If you want to see this in action, you can build and run the app on your local PC using the Visual Studio 2012 debugger. You need to run locally on the PC, however, because the Simulator does not currently support Live Tiles and Notifications.

10. After the app is running, enter a message and click the button. Then quickly press the Windows key on the keyboard to jump back to the Start Screen. In a second or two your application Tile displays the new notification message. Figure 4-9 shows the static version of your Tile before the update, while Figure 4-10 shows the Live Tile update with the custom message that was entered.

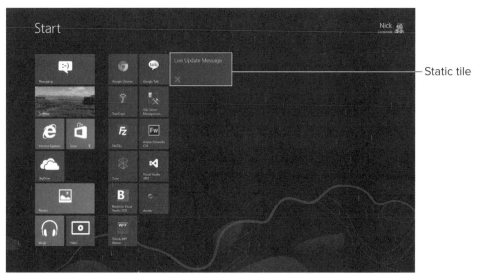

Static tile

FIGURE 4-9

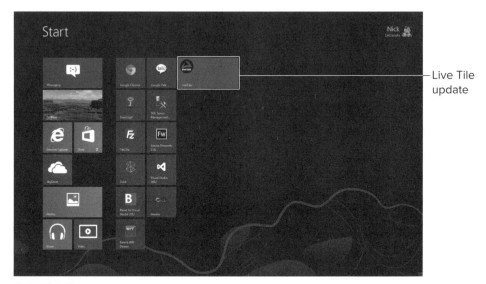

Live Tile update

FIGURE 4-10

Hopefully, you have a good understanding of how to set up Live Tiles and Tile notifications for your app. You learn much more about this topic, including how to use Push Notifications from a web service to update your Tile, in Chapter 12.

SPLASH SCREEN

The final topic to cover in this chapter is a simple but important one — how to create a custom splash screen for your app. When an application starts in Windows 8, your splash screen displays until the app is fully loaded. Figure 4-11 shows what your users are presented with by default.

FIGURE 4-11

Yeah, it's ugly and not impressive — definitely not something that can help promote your brand. So before telling your potential users that you have no design skills whatsoever, you should count on replacing that. Luckily for Windows Store Apps, there is no special code or wizardry needed to show your custom splash screen. All you need to do is simply replace the one currently sitting in the Assets folder of your project. In that folder you can see the following files:

- ➤ Logo.png
- ➤ SmallLogo.png
- ➤ SplashScreen.png
- ➤ StoreLogo.png

Take a guess as to which file you need to replace! The only thing you must worry about is that it conforms to the Windows 8 splash screen specifications. This means that the image you replace it with must be 620x300 in size. When replaced when you start your app, you should see your custom splash screen. Figure 4-12 shows a custom Wrox splash screen that clearly looks better than the default.

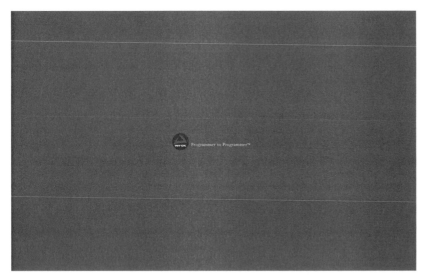

FIGURE 4-12

SUMMARY

In this chapter you learned several important concepts about Windows Store App development. You saw how to best make use of the new `AppBar` and how it replaces the traditional menu system you may find in legacy Windows apps. In the sample app you created, you added an `AppBar` to both the top and bottom of the screen. Per Windows 8 guidance you learned that the bottom bar is the best place to put important action commands, whereas the top bar is best reserved for navigation controls if necessary.

In addition to the `AppBar` feature, you also saw how to create toast notifications that can display when your app runs in the background. You should use toast notifications only to display important information, such as in response to the toast when your users will most likely touch/click the notification message and be brought back into your app. You don't want them to do that unless there is a good reason for doing so.

Next, you learned how to make use of Live Tiles for your app, which give you a great way to interact with your users from the Windows 8 Start Screen. They also give you a way to differentiate your app from others that provide only static tiles with no dynamic update capabilities.

Finally, you saw how easy it is to replace the default splash screen used when your Windows Store App launches. Although it may seem like a trivial component of your app, you must take care in designing the screen because it is always the first thing your users see when the app launches — first impressions of apps count for a lot these days.

5

Application Life Cycle

WHAT'S IN THIS CHAPTER?

➤ Understanding and handling the Windows 8 life cycle

➤ Implementing background operations

WROX.COM CODE DOWNLOADS FOR THIS CHAPTER

You can find the wrox.com code downloads for this chapter at `www.wrox.com/remtitle` `.cgi?isbn=1118205707` on the Download Code tab, in the zip file 205709 C05.zip.

APPLICATIONS REBORN

Microsoft says that Windows 8 is an OS of no compromise. This vision has even led it to rethink how the OS manages applications, resulting in a new way to hook into Windows, which provides a standard interface so that Windows can *understand* the needs of your applications rather than just let them run. This reimagining of how the OS interacts with applications significantly enhances the user experience for the applications and the device running them.

WHAT IS THE WINDOWS 8 LIFE CYCLE?

In traditional desktop applications, the life cycle of an application is cut and dry. An application starts via a shortcut and runs until the user closes it or initiates a shutdown. While it is running, it has unregulated access to the processor, disk, and network resources. This model has worked great since the dawn of PCs, but in the realm of mobile devices, this life cycle breaks down mainly because of battery life and heat concerns. Mobile operating systems, such as Windows Phone, limit when and how long apps have access to system resources.

Windows 8 borrows this app life-cycle model because of the increased mobility of PCs such as laptops, ultrabooks, and tablets.

Much like Windows Phone apps, Windows Store apps suspend when they are no longer used, yet they remain in memory. Keeping them in memory enables a seamless transition when they are reactivated without compromising battery life. However, what if the PC runs low on memory? Luckily, Windows 8 takes care of this situation by terminating apps to free up memory when necessary. You can also close apps by using one of the following methods if you no longer need them:

➤ **Using a gesture with touch or a mouse:** Swipe or drag, respectively, from the top of the screen to the bottom. When using a mouse, the cursor changes to a hand at the top of the screen indicating that you can drag the app. In both cases, the application is visibly picked up and moves along with the gesture.

➤ **A keyboard shortcut:** Keeping in tradition with Windows compatibility, Alt+F4 still closes Windows Store apps when a keyboard is available.

➤ **Task Manager:** Over the years, many users used this method and it continues to be useful for closing applications. Although there are several existing ways to open Task Manager, a new one has been added to Windows 8; Win+X is a quick way to open Task Manager along with many other handy administration tools.

> **NOTE** *To comply with Store certification, your apps cannot include any UI elements that close the app.*

Figure 5-1 shows the new app life cycle. The states an app can be in are in the `ApplicationExecutionState` enumeration.

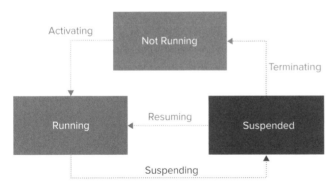

FIGURE 5-1

App Launch

When an app first launches, Windows 8 displays a splash screen such as the one shown in Figure 5-2. This splash screen enables a fast and fluid transition while Windows loads the app. Windows dismisses it after the app is ready for interaction. The screen clearly shows which app is loading and showcases the app's branding. To customize the splash screen, create a transparent

PNG and choose a background color that clearly identifies your app. These are set in the `package.appxmanifest` on the `SplashScreen` element:

FIGURE 5-2

```
<SplashScreen Image="Assets\SplashScreen.png" BackgroundColor="#000000" />
```

> **WARNING** *Although JPEG images are also supported, it is highly recommended that you use a transparent PNG instead, so the background color and image blend together smoothly. JPEG images may introduce unwanted artifacts and color variations.*

The `Image` attribute is a relative path to a file or a resource reference to an image, which must be the required dimensions. When using the Visual Studio project templates, a default image is included under `Assets\SplashScreen.png`. To support additional scaled images for high DPI displays, you must include additional files decorated with scale identifiers as part of their names. The specific sizes for the primary and the various scaled splash screen images are shown in Table 5-1.

TABLE 5-1: SplashScreen Sizes

SCALE	SIZE	FILENAME
Default	620 x 300	SplashScreen.png
100%	620 x 300	SplashScreen.scale-100.png
140%	868 x 420	SplashScreen.scale-140.png
180%	1116 x 540	SplashScreen.scale-180.png

You can add support for accessibility (high contrast) or localized images that match different languages by structuring the images in folders, as shown in Figure 5-3. The `BackgroundColor` attribute can either be a RGB value in hexadecimal preceded by a # or a supported, named color.

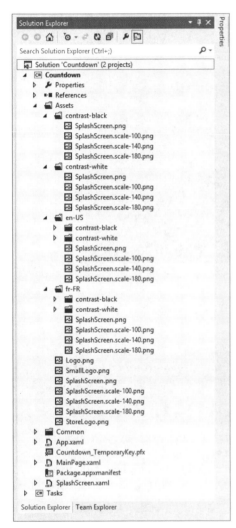

FIGURE 5-3

Extending the Splash Screen

When the splash screen displays, the app should quickly register any event handlers and load custom UI elements and assets it requires. This should happen as quickly as possible. If you require potentially long-running methods, such as reading large amounts of data from a disk or retrieving data from a network connection, you should perform them after activation. In cases where activation requires such methods, you should extend the splash screen with a page that imitates the Windows splash screen, as shown in Figure 5-4. This creates a seamless transition when the app takes control.

FIGURE 5-4

To extend the splash screen, follow these steps:

1. Add a new blank page to the project.

2. Name the page SplashScreen.xaml.

3. Edit this new page to match the look of the Windows 8-provided splash screen by setting its background color and adding an image in the same location, as shown in Listing 5-1.

The code behind for the splash page, which places the image in the correct location and navigates to the main page after the app completes loading, is shown in Listing 5-2.

LISTING 5-1: SplashScreen.xaml

```
<Page
    x:Class="Countdown.SplashScreen"
    IsTabStop="false"
    xmlns="http://schemas.microsoft.com/winfx/2006/xaml/presentation"
    xmlns:x="http://schemas.microsoft.com/winfx/2006/xaml"
    xmlns:local="using:Countdown"
    xmlns:d="http://schemas.microsoft.com/expression/blend/2008"
    xmlns:mc="http://schemas.openxmlformats.org/markup-compatibility/2006"
    mc:Ignorable="d">

    <Grid Background="#000000">
        <Canvas>
            <Image Name="SplashImage"
                Source="Assets/SplashScreen.png"
                Stretch="None" />
        </Canvas>
    </Grid>

</Page>
```

LISTING 5-2: SplashScreen.xaml.cs

```
using System;
using System.Collections.Generic;
using System.IO;
using System.Linq;
using Windows.Foundation;
using Windows.Foundation.Collections;
using Windows.UI.Core;
using Windows.UI.Xaml;
using Windows.UI.Xaml.Controls;
using Windows.UI.Xaml.Controls.Primitives;
using Windows.UI.Xaml.Data;
using Windows.UI.Xaml.Input;
using Windows.UI.Xaml.Media;
using Windows.UI.Xaml.Navigation;

// The Blank Page item template is documented at
// http://go.microsoft.com/fwlink/?LinkId=234238

namespace Countdown
{
    /// <summary>
    /// An empty page that can be used on its own or navigated to within a Frame.
    /// </summary>
    public sealed partial class SplashScreen : Page
    {
        private Windows.ApplicationModel.Activation.SplashScreen _splashScreen;

        public SplashScreen()
        {
            this.InitializeComponent();

            Window.Current.SizeChanged += Current_SizeChanged;
        }


        void Current_SizeChanged(object sender, WindowSizeChangedEventArgs e)
        {
            PositionImage();
        }

        private void PositionImage()
        {
            // Only update the position if the splash screen is set.
            if (_splashScreen != null)
            {
                // Get the location of the splash screen.
                var location = _splashScreen.ImageLocation;

                SplashImage.SetValue(Canvas.TopProperty, location.Top);
                SplashImage.SetValue(Canvas.LeftProperty, location.Left);
                SplashImage.Width = location.Width;
                SplashImage.Height = location.Height;
```

```
            }
        }

        /// <summary>
        /// Invoked when this page is about to be displayed in a Frame.
        /// </summary>
        /// <param name="e">Event data that describes how this page was reached.
        /// The Parameter property is typically used to configure the page.</param>
        protected override void OnNavigatedTo(NavigationEventArgs e)
        {
            // Get the splash screen parameter
            var splash = e.Parameter
                            as Windows.ApplicationModel.Activation.SplashScreen;

            if (splash != null)
            {
                // Register the event handler for when
                // Windows dismisses the splash screen
                splash.Dismissed += splash_Dismissed;

                // Store the splash screen and update the position of the image
                _splashScreen = splash;
                PositionImage();
            }
        }

        async void splash_Dismissed(
                        Windows.ApplicationModel.Activation.SplashScreen sender,
                        object args)
        {
            // Since the dismissal is not on the main thread,
            // dispatch to the main thread to navigate the frame
            await Dispatcher.RunAsync(CoreDispatcherPriority.Normal, () =>
                {
                    Frame.Navigate(typeof(MainPage), this);
                });
        }
    }
}
```

Enabling the extended splash screen is as simple as changing the initial page that is loaded to the extended splash screen page just created in App.xaml.cs, as shown in Listing 5-3. The SplashScreen Windows provided is passed to the page.

LISTING 5-3: App.xaml.cs

```
using System;
using System.Collections.Generic;
using System.IO;
using System.Linq;
using Windows.ApplicationModel;
```

continues

LISTING 5-3 *(continued)*

```csharp
using Windows.ApplicationModel.Activation;
using Windows.Foundation;
using Windows.Foundation.Collections;
using Windows.UI.Xaml;
using Windows.UI.Xaml.Controls;
using Windows.UI.Xaml.Controls.Primitives;
using Windows.UI.Xaml.Data;
using Windows.UI.Xaml.Input;
using Windows.UI.Xaml.Media;
using Windows.UI.Xaml.Navigation;

// The Blank Application template is documented at
// http://go.microsoft.com/fwlink/?LinkId=234227

namespace Countdown
{
    /// <summary>
    /// Provides application-specific behavior to
    /// supplement the default Application class.
    /// </summary>
    sealed partial class App : Application
    {
        /// <summary>
        /// Initializes the singleton application object.  This is the first line
        /// of authored code executed, and as such is the logical equivalent of
        /// main() or WinMain().
        /// </summary>
        public App()
        {
            this.InitializeComponent();
            this.Suspending += OnSuspending;
        }

        /// <summary>
        /// Invoked when the application is launched normally by the end user.
        /// Other entry points will be used when the application is launched to
        /// open a specific file, to display search results, and so forth.
        /// </summary>
        /// <param name="args">Details about the launch request
        ///                    and process.</param>
        protected override void OnLaunched(LaunchActivatedEventArgs args)
        {
            // Do not repeat app initialization when already running,
            // just ensure that the window is active
            if (args.PreviousExecutionState
                    == ApplicationExecutionState.Running)
            {
                Window.Current.Activate();
                return;
            }

            if (args.PreviousExecutionState
```

```
                       == ApplicationExecutionState.Terminated)
               {
                   //TODO: Load state from previously suspended application
               }

               // Create a Frame to act navigation context
               // and navigate to the first page
               var rootFrame = new Frame();
               rootFrame.Navigate(typeof(SplashScreen), args.SplashScreen);

               // Place the frame in the current Window and ensure that it is active
               Window.Current.Content = rootFrame;
               Window.Current.Activate();
           }

           /// <summary>
           /// Invoked when application execution is being suspended.
           /// Application state is saved without knowing whether the application will
           /// be terminated or resumed with the contents of memory still intact.
           /// </summary>
           /// <param name="sender">The source of the suspend request.</param>
           /// <param name="e">Details about the suspend request.</param>
           private void OnSuspending(object sender, SuspendingEventArgs e)
           {
               var deferral = e.SuspendingOperation.GetDeferral();
               //TODO: Save application state and stop any background activity
               deferral.Complete();
           }
       }
   }
```

Enhancing the Splash Screen

Now that you've extended the splash screen, it should also present some status information to the user if loading the app takes more than a few seconds; this lets the user know the app is still loading. This needs to be simple to follow Windows 8 design principals, so it requires only a progress indicator and, optionally, some text explaining the delay. Listing 5-4 shows the additional ProgressRing and Listing 5-5 shows the code to set the size and location based on the splash screen image.

LISTING 5-4: SplashScreen.xaml

```
<Page
    x:Class="Countdown.SplashScreen"
    IsTabStop="false"
    xmlns="http://schemas.microsoft.com/winfx/2006/xaml/presentation"
    xmlns:x="http://schemas.microsoft.com/winfx/2006/xaml"
    xmlns:local="using:Countdown"
    xmlns:d="http://schemas.microsoft.com/expression/blend/2008"
    xmlns:mc="http://schemas.openxmlformats.org/markup-compatibility/2006"
    mc:Ignorable="d">

    <Grid Background="#000000">

        <Canvas>
```

continues

LISTING 5-4 *(continued)*

```xml
            <Image Name="SplashImage"
                Source="Assets/SplashScreen.png"
                Stretch="None" />

            <ProgressRing Name="Progress"
                        IsActive="True"
                        Foreground="White" />
        </Canvas>

    </Grid>

</Page>
```

LISTING 5-5: SplashScreen.xaml.cs

```csharp
using System;
using System.Collections.Generic;
using System.IO;
using System.Linq;
using System.Threading.Tasks;
using Windows.Foundation;
using Windows.Foundation.Collections;
using Windows.UI.Core;
using Windows.UI.Xaml;
using Windows.UI.Xaml.Controls;
using Windows.UI.Xaml.Controls.Primitives;
using Windows.UI.Xaml.Data;
using Windows.UI.Xaml.Input;
using Windows.UI.Xaml.Media;
using Windows.UI.Xaml.Navigation;

// The Blank Page item template is documented at
// http://go.microsoft.com/fwlink/?LinkId=234238

namespace Countdown
{
    /// <summary>
    /// An empty page that can be used on its own or navigated to within a Frame.
    /// </summary>
    public sealed partial class SplashScreen : Page
    {
        private Windows.ApplicationModel.Activation.SplashScreen _splashScreen;

        public SplashScreen()
        {
            this.InitializeComponent();

            Window.Current.SizeChanged += Current_SizeChanged;
        }


        void Current_SizeChanged(object sender, WindowSizeChangedEventArgs e)
```

```csharp
{
    PositionImage();
}

private void PositionImage()
{
    // Only update the position if the splash screen is set.
    if (_splashScreen != null)
    {
        // Get the location of the splash screen.
        var location = _splashScreen.ImageLocation;

        SplashImage.SetValue(Canvas.TopProperty, location.Top);
        SplashImage.SetValue(Canvas.LeftProperty, location.Left);
        SplashImage.Width = location.Width;
        SplashImage.Height = location.Height;

        // Set the size and location based on the splash image.
        var progressScale = 12;
        Progress.Width = location.Width / progressScale;
        Progress.Height = location.Width / progressScale;

        Progress.SetValue(Canvas.TopProperty, location.Top
                                    + location.Height);

        Progress.SetValue(Canvas.LeftProperty, location.Left
                                    + location.Width / 2
                                    - Progress.Width / 2);

    }
}

/// <summary>
/// Invoked when this page is about to be displayed in a Frame.
/// </summary>
/// <param name="e">Event data that describes how this page was reached.
/// The Parameter property is typically used to configure the page.</param>
protected override void OnNavigatedTo(NavigationEventArgs e)
{
    // Get the splash screen parameter
    var splash = e.Parameter
                    as Windows.ApplicationModel.Activation.SplashScreen;

    if (splash != null)
    {
        // Register the event handler for when
        // Windows dismisses the splash screen
        splash.Dismissed += splash_Dismissed;

        // Store the splash screen and update the position of the image
        _splashScreen = splash;
        PositionImage();
    }
}

async void splash_Dismissed(
```

LISTING 5-5 *(continued)*

```
                               Windows.ApplicationModel.Activation.SplashScreen sender,
                               object args)
            {

                // Simulate loading additional content
                await Task.Delay(3000);


                // Since the dismissal is not on the main thread,
                // dispatch to the main thread to navigate the frame
                await Dispatcher.RunAsync(CoreDispatcherPriority.Normal, () =>
                    {
                        Frame.Navigate(typeof(MainPage), this);
                    });
            }


        }
    }
```

You can change the size of the `ProgressRing` by adjusting the the `progressScale` amount. You can add a `TextBlock` below the `ProgressRing` that contains additional information about what the app is doing. This can be as simple as Loading Current News or something more fun for a game such as Reconstructing Alien Genetic Structure.

> **NOTE** *Apps can provide changes over time to encourage repeat usage. Background imagery based on current events or a page's context, or subtle animations that occur rarely, may keep the user's attention or interest.*

App Activation

There are many reasons why an app can be activated beyond the traditional way you are accustom to. Windows 8 adds a new concept of activating apps with specific context using *contracts* or *extensions* (both are explained in more detail in Chapter 7, "Sensors"). They enable apps to provide additional rich functionality in a standard way. A contract is an interface between two apps that neither app is aware of. An extension is an interface with Windows 8 and is the primary way an app can enhance built-in Windows 8 features. In a sense, this is a modern version of command-line parameters but far more capable. To add support for one or more of contracts or extensions, open the app manifest and add the appropriate declarations the app will support. Each type of declaration has additional options. A few of the most common contracts with their additional options are listed here:

➤ **File Open Picker and File Save Picker:** Describes when the app is available for an open or save operation. You should include these if the app provides cloud storage or sharing. These require the file type(s) that are supported, as shown in Figure 5-5.

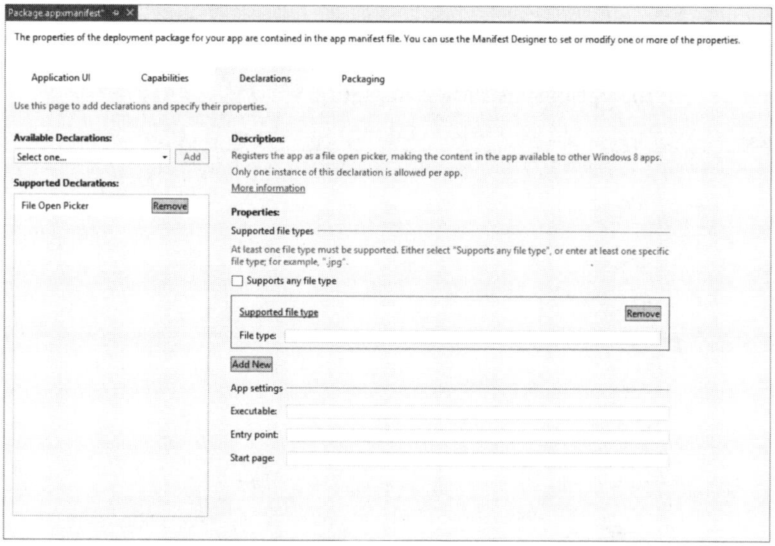

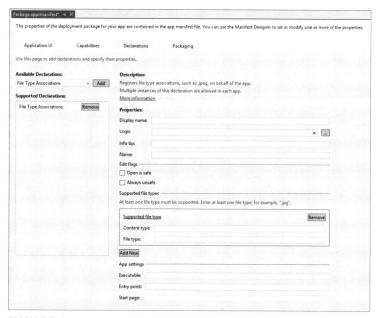

FIGURE 5-5

- **File Type Association:** Enables the app to open file(s) of a particular type. Options, such as the label and logo for the file type, can be set. In addition, flags for the security of files downloaded from the Internet can be set, as shown in Figure 5-6.

FIGURE 5-6

- **Background Tasks:** Enables the app to respond to external trigger events, which is described in more detail in the "App Resume" section.
- **AutoPlay:** Registers the app to receive events when new media is available such as a camera, PMP, or storage device. It can even handle NFC file type of

➤ **Search:** Enables the app to be searched.

➤ **Share Target:** Enables the app to receive shared content. Supported data formats and file type(s) can be set in the options, as shown in Figure 5-7.

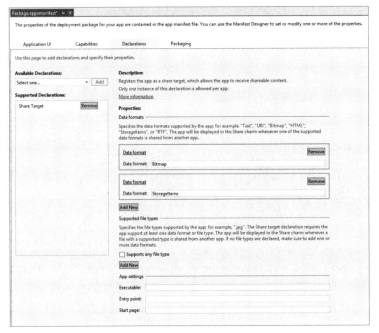

FIGURE 5-7

➤ **Game Explorer:** This enables the app to provide Parental Control support and various ratings standards.

When the app launches, `LaunchActivatedEventArgs` provides an enumeration of what caused the app to launch on the `Kind` property. The `ActivationKind` enumeration shown in Table 5-2 describes what each value means.

TABLE 5-2: ActivationKind Members

MEMBER	DESCRIPTION
CachedFileUpdater	Saves a file in which the app provides content management.
CameraSettings	Captures a photo or video using a camera.
ContactPicker	Picks from a list of contacts.
Device	Provides AutoPlay.
File	A file type the app is registered to handle was opened.
FileOpenPicker	Picks files or folders provided by the app.
FileSavePicker	Saves a file to the app.
Launch	Launches as a normal app.

Protocol	A URL is opened whose protocol is registered to the app.
PrintTaskSettings	Provides printing.
Search	Shows results from a search.
ShareTarget	Shares content.

App Resume

If an app is suspended, it can resume when the user switches to it or Windows 8 resumes from a low-power state. Because the app remains in memory when suspended, the app continues from where it was when suspended. This is generally transparent to the user and to the app. However, because the app could have been suspended for a large amount of time, the app may want to refresh potentially stale data when it resumes. This can be done by registering for the Resuming event, as shown in Listing 5-6.

> **WARNING** *Although the app is suspended, network events are not received, so the current network status should be tested when it resumes.*

LISTING 5-6: App.xaml.cs

```
using System;
using System.Collections.Generic;
using System.IO;
using System.Linq;
using Windows.ApplicationModel;
using Windows.ApplicationModel.Activation;
using Windows.Foundation;
using Windows.Foundation.Collections;
using Windows.UI.Xaml;
using Windows.UI.Xaml.Controls;
using Windows.UI.Xaml.Controls.Primitives;
using Windows.UI.Xaml.Data;
using Windows.UI.Xaml.Input;
using Windows.UI.Xaml.Media;
using Windows.UI.Xaml.Navigation;

// The Blank Application template is documented at
// http://go.microsoft.com/fwlink/?LinkId=234227

namespace Countdown
{
    /// <summary>
    /// Provides application-specific behavior to
    /// supplement the default Application class.
    /// </summary>
```

continues

LISTING 5-6 *(continued)*

```
sealed partial class App : Application
{
    /// <summary>
    /// Initializes the singleton application object.  This is the first line
    /// of authored code executed, and as such is the logical equivalent of
    /// main() or WinMain().
    /// </summary>
    public App()
    {
        this.InitializeComponent();
        this.Suspending += OnSuspending;
        this.Resuming += OnResuming;
    }

    /// <summary>
    /// Invoked when the application is launched normally by the end user.
    /// Other entry points will be used when the application is launched to
    /// open a specific file, to display search results, and so forth.
    /// </summary>
    /// <param name="args">Details about the launch request
    ///                    and process.</param>
    protected override void OnLaunched(LaunchActivatedEventArgs args)
    {
        // Do not repeat app initialization when already running,
        // just ensure that the window is active
        if (args.PreviousExecutionState
            == ApplicationExecutionState.Running)
        {
            Window.Current.Activate();
            return;
        }

        if (args.PreviousExecutionState
            == ApplicationExecutionState.Terminated)
        {
            //TODO: Load state from previously suspended application
        }

        // Create a Frame to act navigation context
        // and navigate to the first page
        var rootFrame = new Frame();
        rootFrame.Navigate(typeof(SplashScreen), args.SplashScreen);

        // Place the frame in the current Window and ensure that it is active
        Window.Current.Content = rootFrame;
        Window.Current.Activate();
    }

    /// <summary>
    /// Invoked when application execution is being suspended.
    /// Application state is saved without knowing whether the application will
    /// be terminated or resumed with the contents of memory still intact.
```

```
    /// </summary>
    /// <param name="sender">The source of the suspend request.</param>
    /// <param name="e">Details about the suspend request.</param>
    private void OnSuspending(object sender, SuspendingEventArgs e)
    {
        var deferral = e.SuspendingOperation.GetDeferral();
        //TODO: Save application state and stop any background activity
        deferral.Complete();
    }

    void OnResuming(object sender, object e)
    {

    }

    }
}
```

App Close

When an app is closed, it is suspended, and then terminated. The app is given the opportunity to save application and user data by handling the Suspending event. However, this should be done quickly because Windows 8 allows only approximately 10 seconds to process this event. The next time the app launches, the Activated event enables the app to determine how it was last terminated using PreviousExecutionState. This is one of the values shown in Table 5-3.

PERSISTING STATE

It is recommended to save state locally when an app is suspending so that it is fast enough to complete in the allotted time. The following list shows the app behavior given the previous execution state:

➤ CloseByUser: A new session opens. Occurs when the app is closed by a user.

➤ NotRunning: A new session opens. Occurs when the app hasn't run in the current session or unexpectedly terminates.

➤ Terminated: The app loads the previous session. Occurs when Windows 8 closes the app due to resource constraints or shutdown.

App Crash

In the rare event that an app crashes, the app should simply return to the Start screen rather than provide any additional UI during the crash experience. This provides a common behavior across all apps and prevents delaying the user with annoying warnings or notifications. Because the app is no longer visible, the user knows that something went awry.

When this occurs or the app stops responding, Windows 8 asks the user for consent to send a problem report, which is visible in the Windows Dev Center under the Quality page, so such issues can be evaluated and fixed.

App Removal

When an app is uninstalled by the user, the app is removed along with all its local data. This does not remove any files created by the app in other locations such as Documents, Pictures, or SkyDrive.

BACKGROUND OPERATIONS

As mentioned earlier, when apps suspend, they no longer can execute code. However, there are a few special cases in which an app can continue to run in the background. Most of these have been directly lifted from the Windows Phone. The four basic background tasks follow:

➤ Playing audio

➤ Transferring files

➤ Updating app data via push notifications

➤ Sharing data with other apps

These background tasks are given a limited amount of system resources; therefore, they should not perform resource intensive or long-running tasks. Each app is given a quota of up to one second of CPU time every two hours unless the app is on the lock screen. These apps are given up to two seconds of CPU time every 15 minutes. Any unused time does not accumulate across intervals. If the app is in the foreground while the background task is triggered, it has no CPU quota applied. Network resources are constrained based on the amount of energy used by the network interface unless the device is on AC power.

> **NOTE** CPU time *is the amount of actual time the CPU is used by the app rather than clock time. For example, if the background task waits for a response from a remote server, it does not use the CPU, so the time spent waiting for the response isn't counted against the CPU quota.*

Background tasks should not rely on user interaction and shouldn't display any UI other than toast notifications, tiles, or badges. A background task has one external trigger that indicates the task should run, and optional conditions, which must be true for the task to run when triggered. To add a background task to a project, follow these steps:

1. Add a new Windows Runtime Component project to the solution.

2. Add a reference to this project in the main app project.

3. Add the background task declaration to the main app project, and allow the supported tasks used by the app, as shown in Figure 5-8.

4. Create a new sealed class for the task, and implement `IBackgroundTask`, as shown in Listing 5-7.

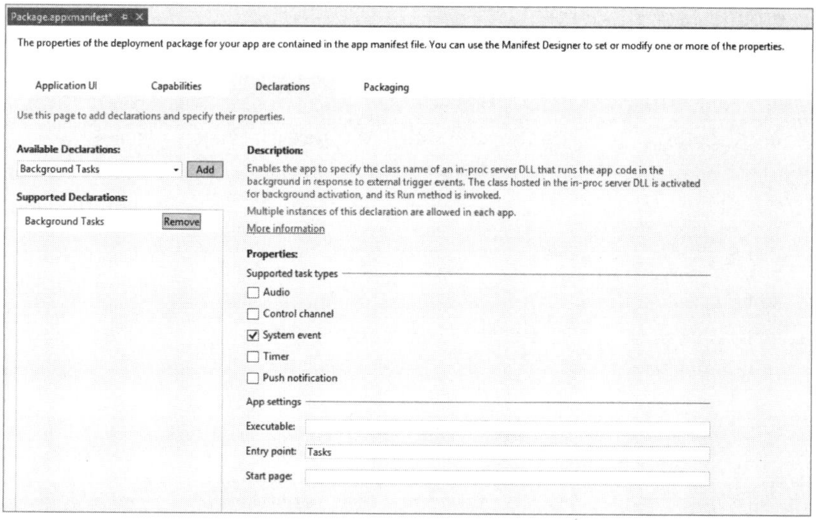

FIGURE 5-8

LISTING 5-7: RefreshDataTask.cs

```
using System;
using System.Collections.Generic;
using System.Linq;
using System.Text;
using System.Threading.Tasks;
using Windows.ApplicationModel.Background;
using Windows.System.Threading;

namespace Tasks
{
    public sealed class RefreshDataTask : IBackgroundTask
    {

        async public void Run(IBackgroundTaskInstance taskInstance)
        {
            var deferral = taskInstance.GetDeferral();

            // Simulate getting data
            await Task.Delay(3000);
            deferral.Complete();
        }

    }
}
```

Triggers and Conditions

An app registers background tasks using the `BackgroundTaskBuilder` class. The class name for the background task is specified in the `TaskEntryPoint` property of `BackgroundTaskBuilder`. Each background task must have exactly one trigger, which is set using the `SetTrigger` method on the `BackgroundTaskBuilder`. Table 5-4 shows all the available triggers.

TABLE 5-4: Background Task Triggers

TRIGGER TYPE	TRIGGER EVENT	WHEN THE TRIGGER OCCURS
ControlChannelTrigger	ControlChannelTrigger	There are incoming messages on the control channel.
MaintenanceTrigger	MaintenanceTrigger	Maintenance tasks should be performed.
PushNotificationTrigger	PushNotificationTrigger	A notification arrives on the WNS channel.
SystemEventTrigger	InternetAvailable	The Internet becomes available.
SystemEventTrigger	LockScreenApplicationAdded	An app tile is added to the lock screen.
SystemEventTrigger	LockScreenApplicationRemoved	An app tile is removed from the lock screen.
SystemEventTrigger	ControlChannelReset	A network channel is reset.
SystemEventTrigger	NetworkStateChange	A network state change such as the type of network.
SystemEventTrigger	OnlineIdConnectedStateChange	Online ID associated with the account changes.
SystemEventTrigger	ServicingComplete	The system has finished updating an app.
SystemEventTrigger	SessionConnected	The session is connected.
SystemEventTrigger	SessionDisconnected	The session is disconnected.
SystemEventTrigger	SmsReceived	A new SMS message is received.
SystemEventTrigger	TimeZoneChange	The time zone changes on the device (or changed because of daylight saving time).

SystemEventTrigger	UserAway	The user becomes absent.
SystemEventTrigger	UserPresent	The user becomes present.
TimeTrigger	TimeTrigger	A time event occurs.

A background task can have conditions that must be true for the task to launch when the trigger occurs. They should filter out trigger events that shouldn't be processed because of the lack of required resources such as the availability of a network connection. You can add these by using the AddCondition method of the BackgroundTaskBuilder. Table 5-5 shows the list of available conditions. When a trigger occurs, each condition is evaluated to see if it is satisfied. If any are not, Windows waits until all conditions are satisfied and then triggers the task. This means if you use a TimeTrigger with any conditions, the task may not run at that specific time. Listing 5-8 shows using the BackgroundTaskBuilder to register a background task.

TABLE 5-5: Background Task Conditions

CONDITION TYPE	THE CONDITION THAT MUST BE SATISFIED
InternetAvailable	The Internet must be available.
InternetNotAvailable	The Internet must be unavailable.
SessionConnected	The session must be connected.
SessionDisconnected	The session must be disconnected.
UserNotPresent	The user must be away.
UserPresent	The user must be present.

LISTING 5-8: App.xaml.cs

```
using System;
using System.Collections.Generic;
using System.IO;
using System.Linq;
using Windows.ApplicationModel;
using Windows.ApplicationModel.Activation;
using Windows.ApplicationModel.Background;
using Windows.Foundation;
using Windows.Foundation.Collections;
using Windows.UI.Xaml;
using Windows.UI.Xaml.Controls;
using Windows.UI.Xaml.Controls.Primitives;
using Windows.UI.Xaml.Data;
using Windows.UI.Xaml.Input;
```

continues

LISTING 5-8 *(continued)*

```csharp
using Windows.UI.Xaml.Media;
using Windows.UI.Xaml.Navigation;

// The Blank Application template is documented at
// http://go.microsoft.com/fwlink/?LinkId=234227

namespace Countdown
{
    /// <summary>
    /// Provides application-specific behavior to
    /// supplement the default Application class.
    /// </summary>
    sealed partial class App : Application
    {
        /// <summary>
        /// Initializes the singleton application object.  This is the first line
        /// of authored code executed, and as such is the logical equivalent of
        /// main() or WinMain().
        /// </summary>
        public App()
        {
            this.InitializeComponent();
            this.Suspending += OnSuspending;
            this.Resuming += OnResuming;

            RegisterBackgroundTasks();

        }

        void RegisterBackgroundTasks()
        {
            if (!BackgroundTaskRegistration.AllTasks.Any())
            {
                var builder = new BackgroundTaskBuilder()
                {
                    Name = "RefreshDataTask",
                    TaskEntryPoint = "Tasks.RefreshDataTask"
                };

                // Run the task every hour if the interweb is available.
                builder.SetTrigger(new TimeTrigger(60, false));
                builder.AddCondition(
                    new SystemCondition(SystemConditionType.InternetAvailable));

                builder.Register();
            }
        }


        /// <summary>
        /// Invoked when the application is launched normally by the end user.
```

```
        /// Other entry points will be used when the application is launched to
        /// open a specific file, to display search results, and so forth.
        /// </summary>
        /// <param name="args">Details about the launch request
        ///                    and process.</param>
        protected override void OnLaunched(LaunchActivatedEventArgs args)
        {
            // Do not repeat app initialization when already running,
            // just ensure that the window is active
            if (args.PreviousExecutionState
                == ApplicationExecutionState.Running)
            {
                Window.Current.Activate();
                return;
            }

            if (args.PreviousExecutionState
                == ApplicationExecutionState.Terminated)
            {
                //TODO: Load state from previously suspended application
            }

            // Create a Frame to act navigation context
            // and navigate to the first page
            var rootFrame = new Frame();
            rootFrame.Navigate(typeof(SplashScreen), args.SplashScreen);

            // Place the frame in the current Window and ensure that it is active
            Window.Current.Content = rootFrame;
            Window.Current.Activate();
        }


        /// <summary>
        /// Invoked when application execution is being suspended.
        /// Application state is saved without knowing whether the application will
        /// be terminated or resumed with the contents of memory still intact.
        /// </summary>
        /// <param name="sender">The source of the suspend request.</param>
        /// <param name="e">Details about the suspend request.</param>
        void OnSuspending(object sender, SuspendingEventArgs e)
        {
            var deferral = e.SuspendingOperation.GetDeferral();
            //TODO: Save application state and stop any background activity
            deferral.Complete();
        }

        void OnResuming(object sender, object e)
        {

        }

    }
}
```

Lock Screen

Apps that provide social media, communication, scheduling, and so on likely should support the lock screen and add background tasks to provide updates even if users aren't actively using their device. Presumably, when user pin an app to the lock screen, they feel that it is important to them to stay up to date. To be notified if an app is pinned or unpinned from the lock screen, register for `LockScreenApplicationAdded` or `LockScreenApplicationRemoved` triggers provided by `SystemTrigger`. An app can also programmatically add itself to the lock screen by using `RequestAccessAsync` in the `BackgroundExecutionManager` class.

Specific types of triggers are restricted only to apps on the lock screen. If an app is not on the lock screen and a restricted trigger is used, the background task will not trigger. Table 5-6 shows the trigger types that require the app to be on the lock screen.

TABLE 5-6: Trigger Types

TRIGGER TYPE	LOCK SCREEN REQUIRED
TimeTrigger	Yes
PushNotificationTrigger	Yes
ControlChannelTrigger	Yes
SystemTrigger	No
MaintenanceTrigger	No

Progress Reporting

When the app is running in the foreground at the time a background task triggers, it may optionally report progress to the app, which can be used to display the UI or a progress bar while the task runs.

When the `Run` method is called, it is given an `IBackgroundTaskInstance` that can communicate to the foreground app by setting the `Progress` property, as shown in Listing 5-9. To receive the progress updates, the app must register the `Progress` event, as shown in Listing 5-10. This listing also registers the `Completed` event as well, which enables the app to refresh the UI when the task finishes.

LISTING 5-9: RefreshDataTask.cs

```
using System;
using System.Collections.Generic;
using System.Linq;
using System.Text;
using System.Threading.Tasks;
using Windows.ApplicationModel.Background;
using Windows.System.Threading;

namespace Tasks
{
```

```csharp
public sealed class RefreshDataTask : IBackgroundTask
{
    ThreadPoolTimer _timer;
    IBackgroundTaskInstance _task;
    bool _cancelRequested;
    BackgroundTaskDeferral _deferral;

    public void Run(IBackgroundTaskInstance taskInstance)
    {
        _task = taskInstance;
        _deferral = taskInstance.GetDeferral();

        taskInstance.Canceled += OnTaskCanceled;

        // Simulate getting data
        _timer = ThreadPoolTimer.CreatePeriodicTimer(OnTimer,
                            TimeSpan.FromMilliseconds(30));
    }

    void OnTaskCanceled(IBackgroundTaskInstance sender,
                        BackgroundTaskCancellationReason reason)
    {
        _cancelRequested = true;
    }

    void OnTimer(ThreadPoolTimer timer)
    {
        if (_cancelRequested || _task.Progress >= 100)
        {
            timer.Cancel();
            _deferral.Complete();
        }
        else
        {
            _task.Progress += 1;
        }
    }
}
}
```

LISTING 5-10: App.xaml.cs

```csharp
using System;
using System.Collections.Generic;
using System.IO;
using System.Linq;
using Windows.ApplicationModel;
using Windows.ApplicationModel.Activation;
using Windows.ApplicationModel.Background;
using Windows.Foundation;
using Windows.Foundation.Collections;
using Windows.UI.Xaml;
using Windows.UI.Xaml.Controls;
using Windows.UI.Xaml.Controls.Primitives;
using Windows.UI.Xaml.Data;
```

LISTING 5-10 *(continued)*

```csharp
using Windows.UI.Xaml.Input;
using Windows.UI.Xaml.Media;
using Windows.UI.Xaml.Navigation;

// The Blank Application template is documented at
// http://go.microsoft.com/fwlink/?LinkId=234227

namespace Countdown
{
    /// <summary>
    /// Provides application-specific behavior to
    /// supplement the default Application class.
    /// </summary>
    sealed partial class App : Application
    {
        /// <summary>
        /// Initializes the singleton application object.  This is the first line
        /// of authored code executed, and as such is the logical equivalent of
        /// main() or WinMain().
        /// </summary>
        public App()
        {
            this.InitializeComponent();
            this.Suspending += OnSuspending;
            this.Resuming += OnResuming;

            foreach (var task in BackgroundTaskRegistration.AllTasks.Values)
            {
                task.Progress += OnTaskProgress;
                task.Completed += OnTaskCompleted;
            }
        }

        void OnTaskCompleted(BackgroundTaskRegistration sender,
                             BackgroundTaskCompletedEventArgs args)
        {
            try
            {
                args.CheckResult();

                // Refresh any UI elements that rely on content from the task
            }
            catch (Exception)
            {
                // Handle and/or report errors that occured in the task
            }
        }

        void OnTaskProgress(BackgroundTaskRegistration sender,
                            BackgroundTaskProgressEventArgs args)
        {
            // Show progress for the task in the app
            var progress = args.Progress;
```

```
        }

        /// <summary>
        /// Invoked when the application is launched normally by the end user.
        /// Other entry points will be used when the application is launched to
        /// open a specific file, to display search results, and so forth.
        /// </summary>
        /// <param name="args">Details about the launch request
        ///                    and process.</param>
        protected override void OnLaunched(LaunchActivatedEventArgs args)
        {
            // Do not repeat app initialization when already running,
            // just ensure that the window is active
            if (args.PreviousExecutionState
                == ApplicationExecutionState.Running)
            {
                Window.Current.Activate();
                return;
            }

            if (args.PreviousExecutionState
                == ApplicationExecutionState.Terminated)
            {
                //TODO: Load state from previously suspended application
            }

            // Create a Frame to act navigation context
            // and navigate to the first page
            var rootFrame = new Frame();
            rootFrame.Navigate(typeof(SplashScreen), args.SplashScreen);

            // Place the frame in the current Window and ensure that it is active
            Window.Current.Content = rootFrame;
            Window.Current.Activate();
        }

        /// <summary>
        /// Invoked when application execution is being suspended.
        /// Application state is saved without knowing whether the application will
        /// be terminated or resumed with the contents of memory still intact.
        /// </summary>
        /// <param name="sender">The source of the suspend request.</param>
        /// <param name="e">Details about the suspend request.</param>
        private void OnSuspending(object sender, SuspendingEventArgs e)
        {
            var deferral = e.SuspendingOperation.GetDeferral();
            //TODO: Save application state and stop any background activity
            deferral.Complete();
        }

        void OnResuming(object sender, object e)
        {

        }
    }
```

Debugging

Visual Studio provides a way to trigger background tasks. Just put a breakpoint in the Run method and trigger the background task using the Suspend drop-down menu on the Debug Location toolbar, as shown in Figure 5-9. It shows the names of the background tasks that can be triggered by Visual Studio.

```
Process: [2828] Countdown.exe           Suspend    Thread:                            Stack Frame:

App.xaml.cs    MainPage.xaml          Suspend
Countdown.App                         Resume
  using System;                       Suspend and shutdown
  using System.Collections.Generic;
  using System.IO;
  using System.Linq;
  using Windows.ApplicationModel;
  using Windows.ApplicationModel.Activation;
  using Windows.ApplicationModel.Background;
  using Windows.Foundation;
  using Windows.Foundation.Collections;
  using Windows.UI.Xaml;
  using Windows.UI.Xaml.Controls;
  using Windows.UI.Xaml.Controls.Primitives;
  using Windows.UI.Xaml.Data;
  using Windows.UI.Xaml.Input;
  using Windows.UI.Xaml.Media;
  using Windows.UI.Xaml.Navigation;

  // The Blank Application template is documented at
  // http://go.microsoft.com/fwlink/?LinkId=234227

  namespace Countdown
  {
      /// <summary>
      /// Provides application-specific behavior to
      /// supplement the default Application class.
      /// </summary>
      sealed partial class App : Application
      {
          /// <summary>
          /// Initializes the singleton application object.  This is the first line
          /// of authored code executed, and as such is the logical equivalent of
          /// main() or WinMain().
          /// </summary>
          public App()
          {
              this.InitializeComponent();
              this.Suspending += OnSuspending;
              this.Resuming += OnResuming;

              RegisterBackgroundTasks();
```

FIGURE 5-9

If the background task does not activate despite a properly set up manifest, correctly registered code, and meeting the lock screen requirements, you can enable debug tracing to allow further debugging. To enable debug tracing, use the following steps:

1. In event viewer, navigate to Application and Services Logs ➪ Microsoft ➪ BackgroundTaskInfrastructure.

2. On the actions pane, select View ➪ Show Analytic and Debug Logs.

3. Select the Diagnostic log and click Enable Log.

4. Try to activate the background tasks again and review the logs for detailed error information, as shown in Figure 5-10.

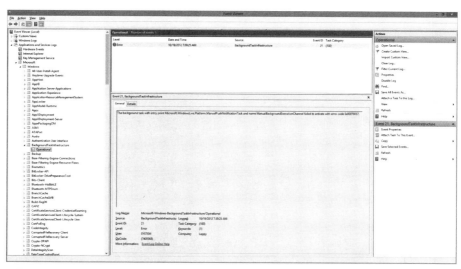

FIGURE 5-10

Deadlock

Yup, the dreaded deadlock. It can actually rear its ugly head with background tasks. How? Well, because background tasks are actually loaded in-process with the app if it is already running *and* because suspended apps have the UI thread blocked, when a background task is triggered in this scenario, it cannot access any object owned by the UI thread or it results in a deadlock. To prevent this deadlock, background tasks should not share data between the app and the background task. An alternative approach is to use persistent storage to share the data.

SUMMARY

This chapter discussed what transpires from an app launch to its untimely termination and how an app can stay refreshed, even when it isn't running. First impressions say a lot, and the first thing a user sees is the splash screen, so it needs to shine and move to content as fast as possible. Make the transition to the app content smoothly, and add subtle animations where needed to give a natural feel to what happens. Refer to existing apps to get a feel for what might work for your apps.

Ultimately, the goal is to keep your apps in the foreground as much as possible for the hundreds of millions of Windows users out there. Using the techniques in this chapter help your apps become fast and fluid when transitioning between life-cycle states, stay current and alive when the app isn't in the foreground, and gracefully recover from errors that invite return visits to your apps, creating an excitement that your app "just works." When users receive that impression, they'll encourage people to try your apps, which can extend your market reach.

6

Handling Data, Files, and Networking

WHAT'S IN THIS CHAPTER?

- ➤ Application data: local, roaming, and temporary
- ➤ File access and permissions
- ➤ Working with data over the network
- ➤ Socket connectivity and WebSockets
- ➤ Proximity and tapping
- ➤ Data serialization and deserialization
- ➤ Data encryption
- ➤ Examples: DataSamples and Leaderboard apps

WROX.COM CODE DOWNLOADS FOR THIS CHAPTER

You can find the wrox.com code downloads for this chapter in code file 205709 C06.zip at www.wrox.com/remtitle.cgi?isbn=1118205707 on the Download Code tab. To illustrate handling data, files, and networking, the code for this chapter includes several app examples located in:

- ➤ DataSamplesCS.zip
- ➤ Leaderboard.zip

In addition, NfcSimulatorDriver.zip contains a proximity device driver simulator for the Proximity section in this chapter.

GETTING STARTED WITH DATA, FILES, AND NETWORKING

As devices become more diverse in features, added sensors, storage, and networking capabilities, apps go beyond simply storing data in files. Windows 8 adds a wealth of new APIs, enabling apps to do tasks they couldn't do before.

In this chapter, you'll explore new and familiar tasks for handling application data, files, access permissions, and networking. You will learn where you can store your data (depending on various factors) and how to access data in various libraries on the user device, such as music, videos, documents, removable storage, and networks. In order to keep user experience fast and fluid, without locking the user interface while lengthy file and networking tasks are performed, developers are encouraged to use the asynchronous programming discussed in this chapter.

This chapter also shows you how to transfer and download data and files, use WebSockets, UDP and TCP connections, serialize and deserialize data, and connect to network services and storage.

HANDLING APPLICATION DATA AND FILES

Windows Store apps can access the app install folder, app data locations, the Downloads folder, and additional locations, such as the Documents library, Music Library, Pictures Library, Videos, home-group libraries, removable devices, and media server devices supporting *Digital Living Network Alliance (DLNA)* protocol.

While some files and folder locations don't require any special access declarations, other locations may need access declaration in an application's manifest. Pictures, music, and videos locations, for example, need to be declared in the manifest. All these declarations and file access permissions are discussed in the following sections.

Getting Started with the Data Samples App

To work with the Data Samples app, you need Windows 8 with Visual Studio 2012. The app is a collection of examples that illustrates application data, file access, networking, and other material from this chapter. Later in this chapter, a standalone Leaderboard example is introduced. Figure 6-1 shows the main screen of the Data Samples app.

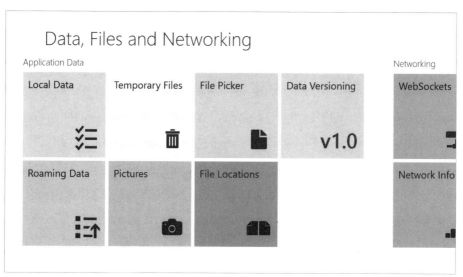

FIGURE 6-1

There's a complete version of the app in the archive, but if you want to start the project from scratch, open Visual Studio and create a new solution based the on C# Grid App (XAML) template:

1. From the File menu, select Add ⇨ New Project.

2. Select Templates ⇨ Visual C# ⇨ Windows Store ⇨ Grid App (XAML).

3. Name the project **DataSamplesAppCS**.

4. Table 6-1 lists the files that were added or modified from the standard template.

TABLE 6-1: Affected Project Files

FILE	TASK
GroupedItemsPage.xaml	A summary of various data samples provided in this chapter. You can click a specific example to see the details.
ItemDetailPage.xaml	An example detail; click the Run It button to run the example.
ItemDetailPage.xaml.cs	The code behind for examples.
DataModel\ExampleDataModel.cs	The data model for the catalog of examples in this chapter.
Examples\AppDataDemo.cs	The application data examples for local, roaming, and temporary files and settings.

continues

TABLE 6-1 *(continued)*

FILE	TASK
`Examples\BackgroundTransferDemo.cs`	The background transfer demo.
`Examples\FilePickerDemo.cs`	The file pickers examples.
`Examples\NetworkDemo.cs`	Various networking examples for this chapter.
`Examples\PictureViewer.xaml`	The sample picture viewer control.
`Examples\PictureViewer.xaml.cs`	The code behind for the Picture Viewer control.
`Examples\SocketExamples.xaml`	The markup file for TCP/UDP sockets example.
`Examples\SocketExamples.xaml.cs`	The code-behind file for TCP/UDP sockets example.
`Examples\WebSocketsClient.xaml`	The markup file for WebSockets.
`Examples\WebSocketsClient.xaml.cs`	The code-behind file for WebSockets.
`Helpers\Helpers.cs`	The various helpers used in the project.
`Helpers\PictureConverter.cs`	A picture converter.

Understanding Windows.Storage API

Windows provides a new `Windows.Storage` namespace, which contains types for storage and data-related operations and accessing data. You use this API any time you want to write or read application settings, store data in files, or access content from user libraries. For example, you use this API for documents, music, pictures, videos, managing cached data, and downloads.

Table 6-2 shows most classes you'll use from the `Windows.Storage` namespace as part of this chapter:

TABLE 6-2: Windows.Storage API

CLASS	DESCRIPTION
`ApplicationData`	Application data access is used throughout most examples in the chapter for local, roaming, and temporary data access.
`ApplicationDataCompositeValue`	Provides access to related app settings handled atomically. See the examples that follow for composite containers.
`ApplicationDataContainer`	Represents a container of app data.

`ApplicationDataContainerSettings`	Provides access to the settings in a settings container.
`CachedFileManager`	For real-time updates to files.
`DownloadsFolder`	Downloads folder access.
`FileIO`	Helper methods for file operations.
`KnownFolders`	Provides access to most common locations.
`PathIO`	Helper methods for path and URIs.
`SetVersionDeferral`	Provides delayed version operations.
`SetVersionRequest`	Provides data when an app sets the version of the application data in its app data store.
`StorageFile`	Represents a file. Provides information about the file and its content and ways to manipulate them.
`StorageFolder`	Manipulates folders and their contents, and it provides information about them.
`StorageStreamTransaction`	Represents a write transaction for a random-access stream.
`StreamedFileDataRequest`	Represents a sequential-access output stream request.

Working with Data and Files Locations

Windows provides three data stores for application data: local, roaming, or temporary. They are accessible from `LocalFolder`, `RoamingFolder`, and `TemporaryFolder` properties of `ApplicationData.Current` object.

As a developer, you decide what data stores to use, mostly by estimating the size of your data, its update frequency, and any usage scenarios. For example, local application data stays on the device. Roaming application data is handy when you need to have a small amount of data to transition to other devices with the same Microsoft account. Later, this chapter discusses in detail the limits imposed on roaming data and recommendations on using it. The best part of it is that while roaming data is stored in the cloud, it's 100 percent free for a developer to use. Windows discards temporary data when it's not in use.

All apps can access the application installation directory by using the `InstalledLocation` property of the `ApplicationModel.Package.Current` object or by using the `ms-appx:///` protocol from the URI, as is discussed in detail in the section "File Access Permissions."

Other file locations are available to Windows Store apps. Table 6-3 shows well-known folders in Windows Store apps:

TABLE 6-3: Known Folders for Windows Store apps

Folder	DESCRIPTION
DocumentsLibrary	Retrieves the Documents library
HomeGroup	Retrieves the `HomeGroup` folder
MediaServerDevices	Retrieves the media server (Digital Living Network Alliance (DLNA)) devices folder
MusicLibrary	Retrieves the Music library
PicturesLibrary	Retrieves the Pictures library
RemovableDevices	Retrieves the removable devices folder
VideosLibrary	Retrieves the Videos library

File Access Permissions

All apps have access to some locations without declaring any extra capabilities. For example, to access settings in the roaming data store, you can simply reference `RoamingSettings` property and assign values to the `Values` collection. If you have other Windows devices trusted from your Microsoft account, these settings will roam to those devices:

```
var roamingSettings = ApplicationData.Current.RoamingSettings;

// Save roaming setting
roamingSettings.Values["HelloWorld"] = "Hello World";
```

Other locations may require an explicit declaration. Declared capabilities show your users that your app may potentially access these locations. Remember that in Windows Store apps, users are in control. For example, to access the Music library, you may need to declare Music capability in Visual Studio. Figure 6-2 shows adding Music capability from Visual Studio:

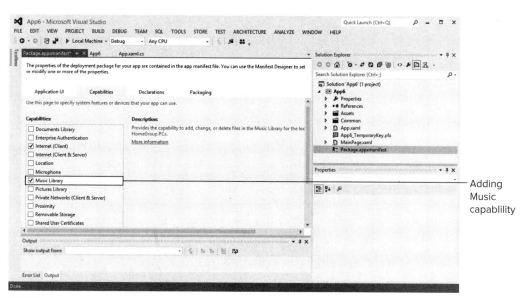

FIGURE 6-2

The following shows the file locations that can be accessed by all apps:

➤ **Application install directory:** This can be accessed programmatically via `Package`
`.Current.InstalledLocation` by using `ms-appx:///` protocol programmatically or from
the markup (HTML or XAML).

➤ **Application data stores, such as local, roaming, or temporary data locations:**
Programmatically, these locations are available from the `ApplicationData.Current`
object as `LocalSettings`, `LocalFolder`, `RoamingSettings`, `RoamingFolder`, and
`TemporaryFolder`. These locations can also be accessed from the markup or programmatically
by using the `ms-appdata:///` protocol, for example:

    ➤ **For local data:** `ms-appdata:///local/`

    ➤ **For roaming data:** `ms-appdata:///roaming/`

    ➤ **For temporary data:** `ms-appdata:///temporary/`

➤ **User Downloads folder:** Programmatically, you can access files in the Downloads folder that
only your app created, but the user can pick files from Downloads not necessarily created by
your app with the File Picker. In the code snippet that follows, a new folder is created in the
Downloads folder and added to `FutureAccessList`, which allows the file pickers to later
access this folder. The snippet that follows shows how to add a folder to a future access list:

```
try
{
    StorageFolder newFolder
        = await DownloadsFolder.CreateFolderAsync("My New Folder");
    if (newFolder != null)
    {
        var listToken =
```

```
        StorageApplicationPermissions.FutureAccessList.Add(newFolder);
        return listToken;
    }
    return String.Empty;
}
catch (Exception)
{
    return "Unable to create folder.";
}
```

Additional file locations can be accessed by apps after they declare additional capabilities in the manifest, by calling file pickers or by declaring an Auto-Play Device extension:

➤ **Documents library:** This can be accessed with the `DocumentsLibrary` capability after adding a file type association. In the following example, a File Save Picker gets access to the Documents library and declares .txt file type association. The snippet shows using a File Picker to access the Documents library:

```
FileSavePicker filePicker = new FileSavePicker
{
    SuggestedStartLocation =
            PickerLocationId.DocumentsLibrary,
    SuggestedFileName = "New Document"
};

filePicker.FileTypeChoices.Add("Text
File", new string[] { ".txt" });

StorageFile file = await filePicker.PickSaveFileAsync();
```

➤ **Music, Pictures, and Videos libraries:** These can be accessed by declaring `MusicLibrary`, `PicturesLibrary`, or `VideosLibrary` capability, respectively.

➤ `Homegroup` **libraries and DLNA (media server devices) access:** These need *at least* one of the following capabilities declared: `MusicLibrary`, `PicturesLibrary`, or `VideosLibrary`.

➤ **Removable devices:** These require `RemovableDevices` capability plus file types association, similar to the previous Documents library example.

➤ **UNC folders:** These require some of the following capabilities (depending on the location): `PrivateNetworkClientServer`, `InternetClient`, `InternetClientServer`, and `EnterpriseAuthentication`.

When you develop your application, pay attention to the locations your app may need to access. The following sections cover various file locations in detail, starting with application data and settings.

Local Settings and Application Data

Local application data store is used for a persistent application state, such as settings and files. Settings are objects of `ApplicationDataContainer` type. Settings names are at most 255 characters in length. Settings can also be 8 K in size. For composite settings, it's 64 K. When you develop an app, you decide when to use specialized settings and when to use files.

`LocalSettings` is an object of `ApplicationDataContainer` type, representing the local data store. Settings can be accessed by a key. If the setting key doesn't exist, it's created dynamically by the dictionary. This approach simplifies the code and error handling.

Simple Settings

The following code snippet creates a Hello World setting and assigns a string to it. You can then retrieve the setting from the `Values` collection and remove the setting from collection using the `Remove` method. This snippet shows basic settings usage:

```
var localSettings = ApplicationData.Current.LocalSettings;

// Save local setting
localSettings.Values["HelloWorld"] = "Hello World";
// Retrieve local setting
var value = localSettings.Values["HelloWorld"];

// Remove local setting
localSettings.Values.Remove("HelloWorld");
```

Composite Settings

If you need more complex data that must be accessed atomically, you can create composite settings. Composite settings are created as an instance of the `ApplicationDataCompositeValue` class. You can store composite settings in local or roaming data stores. The snippet that follows shows how to use composite settings:

```
// Composite Settings

var localSettings = ApplicationData.Current.LocalSettings;
ApplicationDataCompositeValue composite = new ApplicationDataCompositeValue();
composite["MyIntegerValue"] = 1;
composite["MyStringValue"] = "String";
localSettings.Values["MyCompositeSetting"] = composite;
```

Working with Containers

Sometimes you may need to organize your settings hierarchically, similar to folders in the filesystem. Windows Storage provides the `CreateContainer` method to create settings in containers. The enumeration value `ApplicationDataCreateDisposition.Always` is provided as an argument to the method to indicate that the container should be created if it doesn't exist. The snippet shows how to use a container:

```
var localSettings = ApplicationData.Current.LocalSettings;

// Create a container
var container = localSettings.CreateContainer("MyContainer",
                    ApplicationDataCreateDisposition.Always);

// Assign value
container.Values["MyContainer"] = "Hello World";
```

Working with Local Files

You can use local files when you need to save larger amounts of data, binary data, or data with a more complex data structure. You can simply use `ApplicationData.Current.LocalFolder` as the location to local files, and use `FileIO` methods to write and read files.

Remember that because your files may grow large and many API methods have been rewritten to support asynchronous model, you may need to use `async` and `await` keywords for your C# code, or *promises* in JavaScript to keep your user experience fast and fluid. Most file-related operations are explicitly asynchronous.

You use format-specific versions of writing and reading methods to write text, bytes, and buffer data. In the following snippet `WriteTextAsync` is used to write current date and time as a text:

```
var localFolder = ApplicationData.Current.LocalFolder;
StorageFile sampleFile = await localFolder.CreateFileAsync("file.txt",
                    CreationCollisionOption.OpenIfExists);
await FileIO.WriteTextAsync(sampleFile, String.Format("{0}",DateTime.Now));
```

To read a local file, use `FileIO.ReadTextFileAsync` for text files or methods that can read binary files. The snippet that follows shows how to read a text file from the `LocalFolder`:

```
var localFolder = ApplicationData.Current.LocalFolder;

string result = null;

try
{
    StorageFile file = await localFolder.GetFileAsync("file.txt");
    result = await FileIO.ReadTextAsync(file);
}
catch (FileNotFoundException)
{
    // handle errors
}
```

Roaming Settings and Application Data

You may have several devices running Windows. Actually, you may buy a new device, and as soon as you log onto the new device with your Microsoft account, you'll see that apps that use roaming data automatically applied your favorite themes, colors, and wanted settings in the apps. It works like magic!

This happens because of Windows' roaming data store: Roaming provides a great user experience when users have more than one device. As soon as a change is made to data in the roaming store, Windows does all the heavy lifting to synchronize data between devices.

Fortunately, using a roaming data store is also easy from the developer's prospective, and almost no different than using local settings and data! Most important, you need to observe these simple considerations when using a roaming data store from your app:

➤ **Do roam settings, customization data, and small data sets.** This may include user preferences and settings.

➤ **Do roam application state, navigation, and properties.** These help users begin a task on one device and continue on another. This may include user navigation stack, bookmarks in a book reader app, and so on.

➤ **Do not roam data that changes frequently or may cause synchronization conflicts.** It's recommended to roam only slowly changing data. You can always use dedicated data services in the cloud for rapidly changing data.

> **NOTE** *Instead of using a roaming data store for large sets of data, use dedicated cloud services, such as Windows Azure or SkyDrive to exchange large amounts of data. Check the Leaderboard example at the end of this chapter for online storage on Azure. A roaming store is intended for light-weight settings and small objects. You can always check the roaming storage quota by inspecting* `ApplicationData.RoamingStorageQuota`.

Remember that apps can benefit from roaming if the user signed in with the Microsoft account and the device is trusted by the user. Roaming is not instant; before deciding on roaming your data, Windows considers multiple factors, including `RoamingStorageQuota`. Also, because opened files cannot be roamed, it's a good idea to close files when you no longer need them.

When roaming data changes you can handle the `DataChanged` event:

```
ApplicationData.Current.DataChanged += Application_DataChanged;
```

Because data may change on a different thread, you use the `Dispatcher` object to notify the user or the user interface of any changes in the data. The snippet that follows uses a `Dispatcher` in the event handler for `DataChanged` event:

```
async void Application_DataChanged(ApplicationData sender, object args)
{
    // Use Dispatcher, because this may happen on a different thread
    await this.Dispatcher.RunAsync(CoreDispatcherPriority.Normal, () =>
    {
        DisplayResult("Data has changed!", null);
    });
}
```

Setting High Priority for Roaming Data

As stated before, you use roaming data for slowly changing data sets. You can somewhat recommend Windows to consider faster roaming for small sets of data by incrementing a `HighPriority` counter. Although there's no guarantee that this data will be available immediately, it still increases the likelihood of faster data transitioning to other devices. The snippet that follows shows how to use `HighPriority` counter:

```
int counter = Convert.ToInt32(roamingSettings.Values["HighPriority"]);
roamingSettings.Values["HighPriority"] = counter + 1;
```

Temporary Application Data

You use temporary application data to store files that may be deleted when they are not in use. Windows automatically deletes temporary files, by considering disk space and other factors. You access temporary data from the `ApplicationData.TemporaryFolder` or by using the `ms-appdata:///temp/` protocol. For example, in JavaScript apps you can access temporary data as follows:

```
<img src="ms-appdata:///temp/image.png" alt="" />
```

From code, you can access the TemporaryFolder and work with the temporary files just like other stores.

```
var temporaryFolder = ApplicationData.Current.TemporaryFolder;
```

> **NOTE** *Naturally, a temporary data store is not intended for settings, so it doesn't provide settings objects, only file objects.*

Versioning Application Data

When you deal with application data, you often need to deal with changes in the data; for example, after updating your app. When the user updates the app, you may need to convert old application data to a new format. In the snippet that follows, you create a local setting value `VersionExample` and set it to string `"Current Version v0"`. In the subsequent code, you simulate upgrading your data to the next version. Listing 6-1 shows how to use data versioning.

LISTING 6-1: AppDataDemo.cs

```
public async Task<string> DemoVersioning()
{
    ApplicationData appData = ApplicationData.Current;
    var localSettings = appData.LocalSettings;

    // save local setting
    localSettings.Values["VersionExample"] = "Current Version v0";

    // simulate setting version 0
    await appData.SetVersionAsync(0,
        new ApplicationDataSetVersionHandler(OnSetVersion));

    // simulate setting version 1
    await appData.SetVersionAsync(1,
        new ApplicationDataSetVersionHandler(OnSetVersion));

    return localSettings.Values["VersionExample"] as string;
}


void OnSetVersion(SetVersionRequest request)
```

```
        {
            ApplicationData appData = ApplicationData.Current;
            var localSettings = appData.LocalSettings;

            SetVersionDeferral deferral = request.GetDeferral();

            if (request.DesiredVersion > request.CurrentVersion)
            {
                // simulate converting to new version
                localSettings.Values["VersionExample"]
                    = String.Format("Current Version v{0}",
                    request.DesiredVersion);
            }
            else
            {
                // do nothing: our example only converts
                // from lower to higher versions
            }

            deferral.Complete();
        }
```

Then you call the `SetVersionAsync` method twice, first to set application data version to 0, and then to set it to 1. In both cases, you provide a callback `OnSetVersion`, which is called every time a version change occurs in the application data. Because the `SetVersionRequest` argument passed to this method has `DesiredVersion` and `CurrentVersion` properties, you know the old and new versions of data and can apply data conversion rules if necessary.

For this example, you check whether the current version is lower than the wanted version. It is typical for the apps to provide data upgrades (downgrading data is less common) but the decision is up to the developer.

Clearing Application Data

You may need to clear all application data or individual settings, containers, or files. You can use the `ClearAsync` method to clear data in data stores. This may be useful when you debug your app or upgrade data to a new version:

```
    // clear all data, including local, temporary and roaming
    await ApplicationData.Current.ClearAsync();
```

Displaying Pictures Library Content

In this example you learn how to query libraries; for example, the Pictures library — and you can display pictures from the user's Pictures library in a grid. This example is available from the DataSamples app if you click the Pictures button on the main page. Figure 6-3 shows the result of displaying pictures from the Pictures library.

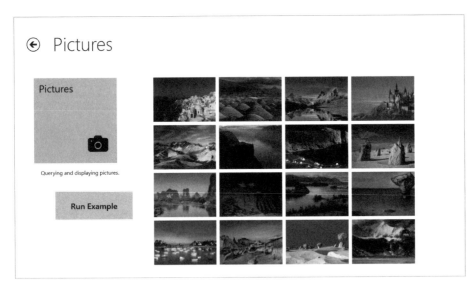

FIGURE 6-3

1. Declare Pictures Library capability by opening the manifest file in Visual Studio, selecting the Capabilities tab, and checking the Pictures Library check box.

2. Create a new user control called `PictureViewer`, and replace the XAML of this control with Listing 6-2.

LISTING 6-2: PictureViewer.xaml

```
<UserControl
    x:Class="DataFilesNetworkingSampleCS.PictureViewer"
    xmlns="http://schemas.microsoft.com/winfx/2006/xaml/presentation"
    xmlns:x="http://schemas.microsoft.com/winfx/2006/xaml"
    xmlns:local="using:DataFilesNetworkingSampleCS"
    xmlns:d="http://schemas.microsoft.com/expression/blend/2008"
    xmlns:mc="http://schemas.openxmlformats.org/markup-compatibility/2006"
    mc:Ignorable="d">

    <UserControl.Resources>
        <local:PictureConverter x:Key="picConverter"/>

        <DataTemplate x:Key="PictureItemTemplate">
            <Grid Width="200" Height="150">
                <Image
                    Source="{Binding Path=Thumbnail,
                            Converter={StaticResource picConverter}}"
                    Stretch="None" Width="200" Height="150"/>
            </Grid>
        </DataTemplate>

        <!-- Collection of items -->
        <CollectionViewSource
```

```
                x:Name="itemsViewSource"/>

        </UserControl.Resources>

        <Grid>
            <!-- grid to show pictures -->
            <GridView Width="1000" Height="600"
                x:Name="itemGridView"
                AutomationProperties.AutomationId="ItemGridView"
                AutomationProperties.Name="Items"
                ItemsSource="{Binding
                        Source={StaticResource itemsViewSource}}"
                ItemTemplate="{StaticResource PictureItemTemplate}"
                SelectionMode="None"/>

        </Grid>
    </UserControl>
```

> **NOTE** *The* `PictureViewer` *control defines an instance of a converter for images called* `PictureConverter` *in the* `Resources` *section. In the same section, you define a* `DataTemplate` *to display pictures. And you use a* `CollectionViewSource` *to bind all your pictures to the Grid.*

3. Add a picture converter helper class to convert images from stream to bitmaps for data binding. You use this converter in the preceding XAML file: `Source="{Binding Path=Thumbnail, Converter={StaticResource picConverter}}"`. Listing 6-3 shows the code behind for the picture converter.

LISTING 6-3: PictureConverter.cs

```csharp
using System;
using Windows.Storage.Streams;
using Windows.UI.Xaml;
using Windows.UI.Xaml.Data;
using Windows.UI.Xaml.Media.Imaging;

namespace DataFilesNetworkingSampleCS
{
    public class PictureConverter : IValueConverter
    {
        public object Convert(object value, Type targetType,
            object parameter, string culture)
        {
            if (value != null)
            {
                var stream = (IRandomAccessStream)value;
                var image = new BitmapImage();
                image.SetSource(stream);
                return image;
            }
```

LISTING 6-3 *(continued)*

```
            return DependencyProperty.UnsetValue;
        }

        public object ConvertBack(object value, Type targetType,
            object parameter, string culture)
        {
            throw new NotImplementedException();
        }
    }
}
```

4. In the code-behind file for the `PictureViewer` control, declare an asynchronous `Display` method used to query `PicturesLibrary`, and bind the result to the Source property of the `itemsViewSource` collection you declared earlier in the markup.

LISTING 6-4: PictureViewer.xaml.cs

```
        public async void Display()
        {
            var pics = KnownFolders.PicturesLibrary;

            var sortEntry = new SortEntry
            {
                PropertyName = "System.FileName",
                AscendingOrder = true
            };

            var queryOptions = new QueryOptions
            {
                FolderDepth = FolderDepth.Deep,
                IndexerOption = IndexerOption.UseIndexerWhenAvailable
            };

            queryOptions.SortOrder.Clear();
            queryOptions.SortOrder.Add(sortEntry);

            // create query
            var query = pics.CreateFileQueryWithOptions(queryOptions);

            var file = new FileInformationFactory(query,
                ThumbnailMode.PicturesView,
                190,
                ThumbnailOptions.UseCurrentScale,
                true);

            // set data source
            itemsViewSource.Source = file.GetVirtualizedFilesVector();
        }
```

You are done! In the `DataSamples` example, the `Display` method is invoked when the Run Example button is pressed. This method creates a query and populates the grid with images from Pictures Library.

Selecting Files: User Experience

In Windows 8 the file pickers are also contracts; they provide services to apps installed on the user's device. File pickers serve three important functions:

➤ Accessing files by user

➤ Saving files

➤ Handling updates for files

The following sections start with a simple example to open a picture file with a file picker and display the name of the opened file to the user. Figure 6-4 shows the result of this example.

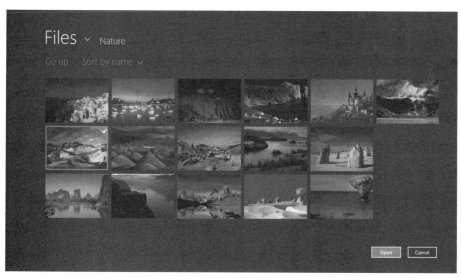

FIGURE 6-4

Opening Files

In the following example, you create a `FileOpenPicker` object in thumbnail mode, with the `SuggestedStartLocation` in the `PicturesLibrary`. You choose the `PickSingleFileAsync` method to select a file. This method returns one file, as opposed to `PickMultipleFilesAsync`, which allows selecting multiple files.

To open files, follow these steps:

1. Open the Data Samples project with Visual Studio, and navigate to the Examples folder. This folder contains the `FilesDemo.cs` file.

2. Examine the `PickFileAsync` method declared in this file. Listing 6-5 shows usage of the file picker.

LISTING 6-5: FilePickerDemo.cs

```csharp
public async Task<string> PickFileAsync()
{
    FileOpenPicker filePicker = new FileOpenPicker{
        ViewMode = PickerViewMode.Thumbnail,
        SuggestedStartLocation = PickerLocationId.PicturesLibrary
    };
    filePicker.FileTypeFilter.Add(".jpg");
    filePicker.FileTypeFilter.Add(".png");
    StorageFile file = await filePicker.PickSingleFileAsync();
    if (file != null)
    {
        return "Picked: " + file.Name;
    }
    else
    {
        return "Cancelled.";
    }
}
```

Saving Files

To save files, you use a different type of picker: `FileSavePicker`. With this picker users can select a location to save a file and save files, including choices of file types. Listing 6-6 shows usage of the file picker for saving files.

LISTING 6-6: FilePickerDemo.cs

```csharp
public async Task<string> SaveFileAsync()
{
    FileSavePicker filePicker = new FileSavePicker
    {
        SuggestedStartLocation =
                    PickerLocationId.DocumentsLibrary,
        SuggestedFileName = "New Document"
    };

    filePicker.FileTypeChoices.Add("Text File", new string[] { ".txt" });

    StorageFile file = await filePicker.PickSaveFileAsync();
    if (file != null)
    {
        CachedFileManager.DeferUpdates(file);
        await FileIO.WriteTextAsync(file, file.Name);
        FileUpdateStatus status
                = await CachedFileManager.CompleteUpdatesAsync(file);
        if (status == FileUpdateStatus.Complete)
        {
            return String.Format("Saved file {0}", file.Name);
        }
        else
        {
```

```
                    return "Unable to save the file.";
                }
            }
            else
            {
                return "Cancelled.";
            }
        }
```

Tracking Files and Folders

Windows provides two lists you can use to maintain access to the files users used recently: `MostRecentlyUsedList` and `FutureAccessList`. The main difference between the two lists is that the *most recently used (MRU)* list is automatically managed by Windows and limited to 25 entries. The *future access list* can hold up to 1,000 items, and you must remove items from your code.

Allocating the Most Recently Used List

You can access the most recently used (MRU) list via the `MostRecentlyUsedList` property of the `StorageApplicationPermissions` object. Windows automatically removes items from this list when the limit is reached.

The MRU list is allocated per app, and you can use it to track objects that implement the `IStorageItem` interface; that is, files and folders. You should consider adding files your user picks to the MRU list because users tend to return to files with which the user is familiar.

In the following example, the user picks a picture from the Pictures library, and when you get back `StorageFile`, you can add it to `MostRecentlyUsedList` by calling the `Add` method. This method simultaneously adds the file to the future access list. This method has an optional meta-data argument that you can use; for example, to give that file a user-defined name. Listing 6-7 shows how to add a recently picked file to an MRU list.

LISTING 6-7: FilesDemo.xaml.cs

```csharp
public async Task<string> PickFileAsync()
{
    var mruList = StorageApplicationPermissions.MostRecentlyUsedList;
    var futureList = StorageApplicationPermissions.FutureAccessList;
    FileOpenPicker filePicker = new FileOpenPicker{
        ViewMode = PickerViewMode.Thumbnail,
        SuggestedStartLocation = PickerLocationId.PicturesLibrary
    };
    filePicker.FileTypeFilter.Add(".jpg");
    filePicker.FileTypeFilter.Add(".png");
    StorageFile file = await filePicker.PickSingleFileAsync();
    if (file != null)
    {
        var mruToken = mruList.Add(file);
        var futureToken = futureList.Add(file);
        return String.Format("Picked {0} MRU Token {1} Future Token {2}",
            file.Name, mruToken, futureToken);
```

continues

LISTING 6-7 *(continued)*

```
        }
        else
        {
            return "Cancelled.";
        }
    }
```

> **NOTE** *You can use the MRU token you get back after adding a file or folder to the MRU list to retrieve a file. Alternatively, you can navigate the Entries collection of the* `MostRecentlyUsedList` *object and retrieve the most recently used entries that interest you.*

Listing 6-8 shows how to retrieve entries from the MRU list.

LISTING 6-8: **FilesDemo.xaml.cs**

```
public async Task<string> GetMostRecentlyUsedEntryAsync()
{
    var MRU = StorageApplicationPermissions.MostRecentlyUsedList;
    if (MRU.Entries.Count > 0)
    {
        var token = MRU.Entries.First().Token;
        try
        {
            var file = await MRU.GetFileAsync(token);
            if (file != null)
            {
                return file.Name;
            }
            else
            {
                return "Couldn't get mruList file";
            }
        }
        catch (Exception)
        {
            // handle exception here
            return "Error";
        }
    }
    else
    {
        return "mruList List Empty";
    }
}
```

Using the Future Access List

A future access list is different from the MRU list in that it has more capacity (up to 1,000 entries), and you must manage it from your code; that is, take care of removing entries when they are no longer needed.

The following example is similar to the GetRecentlyUsedEntryAsync previously shown, but after retrieving the item from the list, it automatically removes it by using the same token. Listing 6-9 shows usage of the future access list.

LISTING 6-9: FilesDemo.xaml.cs

```csharp
public async Task<string> GetFutureAccessEntryAsync()
{
    var FutureList = StorageApplicationPermissions.FutureAccessList;
    if (FutureList.Entries.Count > 0)
    {
        var token = FutureList.Entries.First().Token;
        try
        {
            var file = await FutureList.GetFileAsync(token);
            if (file != null)
            {
                // now, remove the file from list:
                // future access list is managed by you
                FutureList.Remove(token);
                return file.Name;
            }
            else
            {
                return "Couldn't get Future Access List file";
            }
        }
        catch (Exception)
        {
            // handle exception here
            return "Error";
        }
    }
    else
    {
        return "Future Access List Empty";
    }
}
```

Serializing and Deserializing Data

With C# or .NET languages, your typical choice of a serialization/deserialization mechanism for Windows Store apps will be DataContract. JavaScript typically uses JSON. With JavaScript support for Windows Store apps, WinRT adds DataContractJsonSerializer for interoperability with .NET languages.

As an example of `DataContract` serialization, use the `Leaderboard` class defined in the final example of this chapter. This class is used as a Leaderboard score item for an online gaming service and contains a username and a score.

```
[DataContract]
public class LeaderboardItem
{
    [DataMember(Name = "id")]
    public int Id { get; set; }
    [DataMember(Name = "username")]
    public string UserName { get; set; }
    [DataMember(Name = "score")]
    public int Score { get; set; }
}
```

This example creates an object of type `LeaderboardItem` and serializes this object into a file in the roaming folder with the `SerializeIntoRoamingFile` method. Then for the sake of this example, you deserialize this file into an object of `LeaderboardItem` type with a call to `DeserializeFromRoamingFile`.

> **NOTE** *Because the roaming store size is limited to 100 K, one of the ways to save space for serialized XML data is setting the* `DataMember` `Name` *property to optimize names — maybe make them shorter. This may be helpful when dealing with data in a roaming store.*

Listing 6-10 shows how to serialize and deserialize data.

LISTING 6-10: AppDataDemo.cs

```
public async void DemoSerialization()
{
    await SerializeIntoRoamingFile("LeaderBoard",
        new LeaderboardItem { UserName = "test", Score = 100 }
    );
    LeaderboardItem item = await DeserializeFromRoamingFile(
        "LeaderBoard", typeof(LeaderboardItem)) as LeaderboardItem;
}

public async Task SerializeIntoRoamingFile(string key, object obj)
{
    var appData = ApplicationData.Current;
    var roamingFolder = appData.RoamingFolder;

    try
    {               StorageFile file = await roamingFolder.
CreateFileAsync(key,
            CreationCollisionOption.ReplaceExisting);
        using (var writeStream
            = await file.OpenAsync(FileAccessMode.ReadWrite))
        {
            Stream stream = writeStream.AsStreamForWrite();
```

```
                    DataContractSerializer ser
                        = new DataContractSerializer(obj.GetType());
                    ser.WriteObject(stream, obj);
                    await stream.FlushAsync();
                    return;
                }
            }
            catch (Exception)
            {
                // handle exception here
                return;
            }
        }

        public async Task<object> DeserializeFromRoamingFile(string key,
            Type type)
        {
            var appData = ApplicationData.Current;
            var roamingFolder = appData.RoamingFolder;
            object obj = null;
            try
            {
                using (var stream =
                    await roamingFolder.OpenStreamForReadAsync(key))
                {
                    DataContractSerializer ser
                        = new DataContractSerializer(type);
                    return ser.ReadObject(stream);
                }
            }
            catch (Exception)
            {
                // handle exception here
                return null;
            }
        }
    }
```

Data Encryption and Decryption

To encrypt and decrypt data in a Windows Store app, you can use objects from the `Windows` `.Security.Cryptography` namespace. The `EncryptAsync` method in the snippet that follows encrypts a plain text input. The `DecryptAsync` converts an encrypted buffer back to plain text. Listing 6-11 shows a data encryption example.

LISTING 6-11: AppDataDemo.cs

```
        public async Task<IBuffer> EncryptAsync(string stringToEncrypt)
        {
            IBuffer buffer = CryptographicBuffer.ConvertStringToBinary(
                stringToEncrypt,
                BinaryStringEncoding.Utf8);

            // create data protection provider
```

continues

LISTING 6-11 *(continued)*

```
        DataProtectionProvider crypt =
            new DataProtectionProvider("LOCAL=user");
        // return encrypted buffer
        return await crypt.ProtectAsync(buffer);
    }

    public async Task<string> DecryptAsync(IBuffer buffer)
    {
        // create protection data provider
        DataProtectionProvider crypt = new DataProtectionProvider();

        // decrypt the input
        IBuffer bufferDecrypted = await crypt.UnprotectAsync(buffer);

        // return clear text back
        return CryptographicBuffer.ConvertBinaryToString(
            BinaryStringEncoding.Utf8,
            bufferDecrypted);
    }
```

> **NOTE** *The authors recommend that before you submit your app through the Windows Store certification, you should review policies related to the use of cryptography in apps.*

NETWORKING

For modern day apps, connectivity and networking is more a rule than an extra feature. You have many ways to connect your apps to the world: from a web service connection, using accounts for other services, local area networks for enterprise and home groups, near-field communication, and proximity.

In this section you learn about networking and connectivity for Windows Store apps, including how to add networking capabilities, transfer data, and access network information and connection profiles. You see examples for using WebSockets and TCP and UDP socket connections, and connecting your app to services, such as Windows Azure.

Establishing Socket Connectivity

When you need to connect to services that use protocols such as SMTP, POP, IMAP, or MAPI, protocols not supported by higher level APIs or protocols that connect to another computer, you can rely on TCP and UDP socket connectivity provided by the `Windows.Networking.Sockets` and `Windows.Networking` namespace. For servers that implement HTTP, WebSockets is a standard that you can use for transporting messages and binary data with web servers.

Testing WebSockets

WebSocket protocol (RFC 6455) is layered over TCP and provides a mechanism for two-way communication between the client and the server. The protocol implements an HTTP handshake, which makes it suitable for web servers and browser clients or clients such as Windows Store apps. Unlike the full HTTP, WebSocket is intended mostly for server/application communication.

Windows 8 provides two types of WebSockets. The main distinction is that one type of socket supports large binary-only messages (`StreamWebSocket`), and another supports UTF-8 and binary messages of smaller size (`MessageWebSocket`), as Table 6-4 illustrates.

TABLE 6-4: WebSockets

CLASS	DESCRIPTION
`MessageWebSocket`	These regular-sized messages enable acknowledgments that the message was received. They resemble UDP sockets (UTF8 and binary).
`StreamWebSocket`	Binary only. These work for large messages, such as media, including partial messages. They resemble TCP sockets.

Figure 6-5 shows the WebSockets sample Windows app connecting to the echo WebSocket service.

FIGURE 6-5

To test WebSocket you can use the `ws://echo.websocket.org` echo service or the sample `WebSocketServer` included with the project. The `WebSocketServer` project implements a small echo service as an HTTP handler. The service checks whether the incoming request is a WebSocket request and processes it by echoing the message that was sent back to the client.

To start this example, in Visual Studio open the Data Samples solution.

1. From Solution Explorer, right-click WebSocketServer ➪ Set as StartUp Project.

2. Select the default.html file; right-click and select Set as Start Page.

3. With the WebSocketServer selected, click Ctrl-F5 to start the project without debugging.

4. You should see the web browser opening with http://localhost:28383/default.html in the address field.

The sample project is set up to use port 28383, but you can change if there's a port conflict by opening project properties, selecting Web tab, and updating the project URL. Listing 6-12 shows the EchoWebSocket.ashx handler that accepts WebSocket requests and replies with an echo.

LISTING 6-12: EchoWebSocket.ashx

```csharp
<%@ WebHandler Language="C#" Class="EchoWebSocket" %>

#define TRACE

using System;
using System.Web;
using System.Net.WebSockets;
using System.Web.WebSockets;
using System.Runtime.InteropServices;
using System.Text;
using System.Threading;
using System.Threading.Tasks;

public class EchoWebSocket : IHttpHandler {

    public void ProcessRequest(HttpContext context)
    {
        try{
            if (context.IsWebSocketRequest)
            {
                context.AcceptWebSocketRequest(EchoRequest);
            }
            else
            {
                context.Response.StatusCode = 400;
            }
        }
        catch (Exception ex)
        {
            System.Diagnostics.Trace.WriteLine(ex);
            context.Response.StatusCode = 500;
            context.Response.StatusDescription = ex.Message;
            context.Response.End();
        }

    }

    private const int MaxBufferSize = 65536;

    private async Task EchoRequest(WebSocketContext wsContext)
```

```
{
    const int maxMessageSize = 1024;
    byte[] receiveBuffer = new byte[maxMessageSize];
    WebSocket socket = wsContext.WebSocket;

    while (socket.State == WebSocketState.Open)
    {
        WebSocketReceiveResult receiveResult = await socket.ReceiveAsync(
            new ArraySegment<byte>(receiveBuffer),
            CancellationToken.None);

        if (receiveResult.MessageType == WebSocketMessageType.Close)
        {
            // Close the socket
            await socket.CloseAsync(WebSocketCloseStatus.NormalClosure,
                string.Empty,
                CancellationToken.None);
            return;
        }
        else if (receiveResult.MessageType == WebSocketMessageType.Binary)
        {
            // Binary data, close the socket
            await socket.CloseAsync(WebSocketCloseStatus.InvalidMessageType,
                "Binary not accepted ",
                CancellationToken.None);
            return;
        }

        int count = receiveResult.Count;

        while (receiveResult.EndOfMessage == false)
        {
            if (count >= maxMessageSize)
            {
                string closeMessage =
                    string.Format("Exceed max size: {0} bytes.",
                                        maxMessageSize);
                await socket.CloseAsync(WebSocketCloseStatus.MessageTooBig,
                    closeMessage, CancellationToken.None);
                return;
            }

            receiveResult = await socket.ReceiveAsync(
                new ArraySegment<byte>(receiveBuffer,
                    count,
                        maxMessageSize - count),
                CancellationToken.None);
            count += receiveResult.Count;
        }

        var receivedString = Encoding.UTF8.GetString(receiveBuffer, 0, count);
        var echoString = "ECHO " + receivedString;
        ArraySegment<byte> outputBuffer =
            new ArraySegment<byte>(Encoding.UTF8.GetBytes(echoString));

        await socket.SendAsync(outputBuffer,
```

LISTING 6-12 *(continued)*

```
                    WebSocketMessageType.Text, true, CancellationToken.None);
            }
        }

        public bool IsReusable
        {
            get
            {
                return false;
            }
        }
    }
```

The client-side WebSocket code is implemented in the `WebSocketsClient` control in the Examples folder of the `DataSamplesCS` project. You can launch it by starting the app and selecting WebSockets on the main page.

To initiate a `MessageWebSocket` connection, you create an instance of the object, set message type to UTF-8, and register an event handler for `MessageReceived` and `Closed` events. Then you open the socket connection by calling `ConnectAsync` and writing to the socket output stream using `DataWriter`, as shown in the snippet that follows:

```
var socket = new MessageWebSocket();
socket.Control.MessageType = SocketMessageType.Utf8;
socket.MessageReceived += MessageReceived;

// use Dispatcher to avoid synchronizatio issues on UI thread
socket.Closed += async (senderSocket, args) =>
{
    await Window.Current.Dispatcher.RunAsync(
            CoreDispatcherPriority.Normal,
            () => Closed(senderSocket, args));
};

await socket.ConnectAsync(server);
writer = new DataWriter(socket.OutputStream);
```

Connecting TCP and UDP Sockets

For TCP and UDP connections, you can use `StreamSocket` for TCP connections, `DatagramSocket` for UDP connections, and `StreamSocketListener` for listening on incoming TCP connections.

> **NOTE** *When you use TCP or UDP socket objects, your app needs to declare Private Client/Server network capabilities in the manifest. You open the manifest file in Visual Studio and make sure this capability is checked.*

The Stream sockets example is available in the `SocketExamples` control. You can invoke it by clicking the TCP Socket button on the sample app main page. The example in this section creates two objects, `StreamSocketListener` and `StreamSocket` for client connections, connects them, and starts sending messages until you press the Stop button. To start, follow these steps:

1. Declare the state variables to hold the number of bytes received, hostname, and port, and to listen to the client socket objects. The following snippet shows initial declarations from the sockets example:

```
int totalReceived = 0;
string port = "24551";
string host = "localhost";

StreamSocketListener listener;
StreamSocket clientSocket;
```

2. When the user presses the Start button, you start listening on the listener socket, and when data is received, you increase the counter for the number of bytes received. Listing 6-13 shows methods added to handle socket connections:

LISTING 6-13: SocketExamples.xaml.cs

```
private async void StartListener()
{
    listener = new StreamSocketListener();
    listener.ConnectionReceived += OnListenerConnectionReceived;

    // start listening...
    try
    {
        await listener.BindServiceNameAsync(port);
    }
    catch (Exception exception)
    {
        listener = null;
        // fatal error
        if (SocketError.GetStatus(exception.HResult)
            == SocketErrorStatus.Unknown)
        {
            throw;
        }
    }
}

private async void OnListenerConnectionReceived(
    StreamSocketListener sender,
    StreamSocketListenerConnectionReceivedEventArgs args)
{
    DataReader reader = new DataReader(args.Socket.InputStream);
    try
    {
        while (true)
        {
            // read the lenth of the string (first bytes)
            uint length = await reader.LoadAsync(sizeof(uint));
            if (length != sizeof(uint))
```

continues

LISTING 6-13 *(continued)*

```
                            {
                                // clientSocket couldn't read data
                                return;
                            }

                            totalReceived += (int)length;

                            Dispatcher.RunAsync(CoreDispatcherPriority.Normal, () => {
                                receivedBytes.Text=String.Format("{0}",totalReceived);
                            });
                        }
                    }
                    catch (Exception exception)
                    {
                        // fail
                        if (SocketError.GetStatus(exception.HResult)
                            == SocketErrorStatus.Unknown)
                        {
                            throw;
                        }

                        Dispatcher.RunAsync(CoreDispatcherPriority.Normal, () => {
                                resultText.Text=exception.Message;
                            });

                    }
            }
```

3.   Now that the listening socket is ready, you can connect to it and send data. In the
     `StartSending` method you create the `StreamSocket` object, connect to it with
     `ConnectAsync`, and pass the hostname and port. After the connection to the listening socket
     is established, you can start sending the data packets with a simple format. The data packet
     begins with a `uint` length followed by the string. Listing 6-14 shows the code that sends
     data with sockets.

LISTING 6-14: SocketExamples.xaml.cs

```
            private async void StartSending()
            {

                clientSocket = new StreamSocket();

                try
                {
                    // connect...
                    await clientSocket.ConnectAsync(host, port);
                    resultText.Text = String.Format("Connected {0}:{1}",
                                                    host.RawName,port);
                }
```

```
        catch (Exception exception)
        {
            // fail...
            resultText.Text = "Unable to connect.";
            if (SocketError.GetStatus(exception.HResult)
                == SocketErrorStatus.Unknown)
            {
                throw;
            }
        }

        // create data writer...
        DataWriter writer = new DataWriter(clientSocket.OutputStream);

        while(!IsStopped)
        {
            // write data to the network
            string data = "Hello World!";
            writer.WriteUInt32(writer.MeasureString(data));
            writer.WriteString(data);

            try
            {
                await writer.StoreAsync();
            }
            catch (Exception exception)
            {
                // fatal error
                if (SocketError.GetStatus(exception.HResult)
                    == SocketErrorStatus.Unknown)
                {
                    throw;
                }
            }

            await Task.Delay(2000);
        }
    }
```

Data Transfers

Most networking apps need data transfers to get additional assets and content from network resources. This section combines a data transfer example with a background transfer.

For long-term data transfers, Windows provides an API defined in `Windows.Networking.BackgroundTransfer`. If your app needs to download images of files, but there's no guarantee that the user will keep the app active during the download, you can take advantage of the background transfer upload or download features. Figure 6-6 shows a background transfer sample from the DataSamples app.

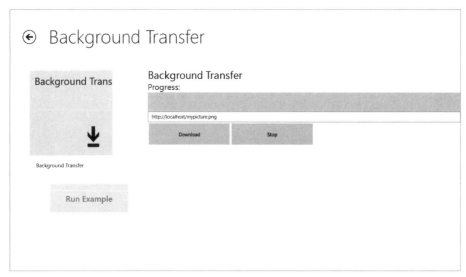

FIGURE 6-6

The code-behind example for the background transfer is in Listing 6-15. In this example, when the user clicks the Download button, you check for the download URI and begin the download to the Pictures library.

LISTING 6-15: BackgroundTransferDemo.xaml.cs

```
using System;
using System.IO;
using System.Threading;
using System.Threading.Tasks;
using Windows.Networking.BackgroundTransfer;
using Windows.Storage;
using Windows.UI.Core;
using Windows.UI.Xaml;
using Windows.UI.Xaml.Controls;
using Windows.Web;

namespace DataFilesNetworkingSampleCS.Examples
{
    public sealed partial class BackgroundTransferDemo : UserControl
    {
        private CancellationTokenSource cancellationToken;

        public BackgroundTransferDemo()
        {
            this.InitializeComponent();
            cancellationToken = new CancellationTokenSource();
        }

        private async void download_Click(object sender, RoutedEventArgs e)
```

```
{
    progress.Value = 0;

    Uri source;
    if (!Uri.TryCreate(address.Text.Trim(), UriKind.Absolute, out source))
    {
        resultText.Text = "This location is invalid!";
        return;
    }

    var ext = Path.GetExtension(source.ToString());

    if (ext == null)
    {
        resultText.Text = "Only .jpg, .png and .jpeg!";
        return;
    }

    ext = ext.ToLower();

    if(ext != ".jpg" || ext != ".png" || ext != ".jpeg"){
        resultText.Text = "Only .jpg, .png and .jpeg!";
        return;
    }

    StorageFile destination;
    try
    {
        var picturesLibrary = KnownFolders.PicturesLibrary;
        destination = await picturesLibrary.CreateFileAsync(
            String.Format("SampleImage{0}",
            Path.GetExtension(source.ToString())),
            CreationCollisionOption.GenerateUniqueName);
    }
    catch (FileNotFoundException ex)
    {
        resultText.Text = String.Format("ERROR: {0}", ex.Message);
        return;
    }

    BackgroundDownloader downloader = new BackgroundDownloader();
    DownloadOperation download =
        downloader.CreateDownload(source, destination);

    resultText.Text = String.Format(
        "Downloading {0}", source.AbsoluteUri);

    await HandleDownloadAsync(download, true);
}

private void stop_Click(object sender, RoutedEventArgs e)
{
    cancellationToken.Cancel();
```

continues

LISTING 6-15 *(continued)*

```
            cancellationToken.Dispose();
            cancellationToken = new CancellationTokenSource();
            resultText.Text = "Cancelled Download";
        }

        private async Task HandleDownloadAsync(DownloadOperation download,
            bool isNew)
        {
            try
            {
                Progress<DownloadOperation> progressCallback =
                    new Progress<DownloadOperation>
                        (ReportDownloadProgress);
                if (isNew)
                {
                    // new download, start it
                    await download.StartAsync().AsTask(
                        cancellationToken.Token,
                        progressCallback);
                }
                else
                {
                    // attach download that's already running
                    await download.AttachAsync().AsTask(
                        cancellationToken.Token,
                        progressCallback);
                }

                ResponseInformation response
                    = download.GetResponseInformation();

                resultText.Text =
                    String.Format("Completed: {0}, Status Code: {1}",
                        download.Guid,
                        response.StatusCode);
            }
            catch (TaskCanceledException)
            {
                resultText.Text = "Canceled: " + download.Guid;
            }
            catch (Exception ex)
            {
                WebErrorStatus error
                    = BackgroundTransferError.GetStatus(ex.HResult);
                if (error != WebErrorStatus.Unknown)
                {

                    Dispatcher.RunAsync(CoreDispatcherPriority.Normal, () =>
                    {
                        resultText.Text = String.Format("Error: {0}: {1}",
```

```
                    title, error);
            });

        }
    }
}

private void ReportDownloadProgress(DownloadOperation download)
{
    double percent = 100;
    if (download.Progress.TotalBytesToReceive > 0)
    {
        percent = download.Progress.BytesReceived * 100
            / download.Progress.TotalBytesToReceive;
    }

    Dispatcher.RunAsync(CoreDispatcherPriority.Normal, () =>
    {
        progress.Value = percent;
    });
}

    }
}
```

The `BackgroundDownloader` object receives two arguments: the source and the destination, created earlier in the code.

```
BackgroundDownloader downloader = new BackgroundDownloader();
DownloadOperation download =
    downloader.CreateDownload(source, destination);
```

You want to track download progress to show the progress bar updating, so you pass the `progressCallback` to the background transfer object you instantiated. In addition, it's important to cancel the download gracefully. Thanks to the asynchronous nature of the calls, you can pass a `CancellationToken` to the background transfer, which takes care of the cancellations. Finally, you call the `StartAsync` method to initiate the download:

```
// new download, start it
await download.StartAsync().AsTask(cancellationToken.Token,
                                    progressCallback);
```

Activating Proximity and Tapping

Exploring new ideas in computing is always exciting. Proximity, near-field communication (NFC), and Wi-Fi Direct support in Windows 8 opens doors for new types of apps that can connect and communicate via a simple user tap gesture. To support these features, your device needs to have a proximity device, such as an NFC device. For Wi-Fi Direct, your computer must have a wireless device that supports peer browsing.

If you don't have a proximity device, we'll show you how to use a Microsoft driver that simulates such as device.

Proximity Overview

Proximity classes are defined in the `Windows.Networking.Proximity` namespace. You can use proximity classes to communicate with peer apps in the range of three to four centimeters. You can exchange a small amount of data between closely located devices during a tap gesture with a `ProximityDevice` object or establish a long-term connection with a `PeerFinder` class.

These operations are enabled only when your app runs in the foreground. When you use `PeerFinder` on one device, and the device is tapped, the device in proximity raises the `Activated` event in the peer app running in the foreground, or notifies the user to activate the app if it's not running.

Table 6-5 shows proximity classes you can use in Windows Store apps:

> **NOTE** *You must enable Proximity capability in the manifest to use proximity in your apps.*

TABLE 6-5: Proximity Classes

CLASS	DESCRIPTION
`ProximityDevice`	With this class, you can subscribe or publish messages on proximity devices. This class has two major events: `DeviceArrived` and `DeviceDeparted`. You can use them to track proximity devices. `PublishMessage` and `SubscribeForMessage` methods (including binary and URI-specific methods). You can also publish or subscribe for messages.
`PeerFinder`	Discovers another instance of your app on another device and creates a socket connection between devices.

INSTALLING NEAR FIELD SIMULATOR DRIVER

If your device does not support near field communications (NFC) and Wi-Fi Direct, you can use the NetNfpProvider driver provided by Microsoft to simulate near field capabilities. Only use the following procedure if your device doesn't support NFC. You can check Windows Device Manager if it has any devices listed in the Proximity Devices category, or run the proximity examples to check if it's supported. To build and install the driver:

1. Locate the latest version of Windows Device Driver Kit (WDK) on the Microsoft website. At the time of this writing the latest version was WDK 8.0 available at the following location: http://msdn.microsoft.com/en-us/windows/hardware/gg487463

2. Download and install the kit, following the instructions. After installing the WDK, install co-installers when prompted.

3. Extract and copy binary files from `NfcSimulatorDriver.zip` from `\bin` directory (x86 or x64, depending on your architecture) to a new directory on your hard drive; for example `c:\nfc`:

4. Double-click package.cer located in that directory; click Install certificate.

5. Select Local Machine, and click Next.

6. Select the Place All Certificate in the Following Store option, and click Browse.

7 Select the Trusted Root Certificate Authorities options.

8. Start the Command Prompt in Administrator Mode.

9. Run the following command to install the driver (in Administrator mode):

```
devcon.exe install NetNfpProvider.inf WUDF\NetNfpProvider
```

10. Create an inbound firewall rule for the Proximity driver on port 9299 by launching wf.exe.

You can now see the Network Near-Field Proximity Provider under the Proximity Devices in the Device Manager. You can now simulate proximity with the examples.

Initiating Proximity and Registering for Events

To start with proximity, you need two PCs with proximity devices or NetNfpProvider drivers installed. Then, follow these steps:

1. If you use the simulator driver, run the following command, substituting `MyOtherPC` with the name or IP of the device where you'll be running DataSamples:

```
NetNfpControl.exe  MyOtherPC /k
```

If you have a proximity device, simply tap both devices to connect. (There's no need to run the preceding command.)

2. Start the Data Samples app, and click Proximity on the main page. (Scroll to the right to see all examples.)

3. Click Run Example, and you should see a message that a proximity device is found, followed by the device id. If the example cannot find the proximity device, check your simulator driver installation or confirm that your PC has NFC devices.

4. If you run the simulator, press Ctrl+F1 on the PC running NetNfpControl.exe, or tap devices, and you'll see that the sample code registers `DeviceDeparted` **and** `DeviceArrived` proximity device events. Figure 6-7 shows a screenshot of the Data Samples app after a proximity was initiated from another PC. Note that your app must be running in the foreground for proximity to work.

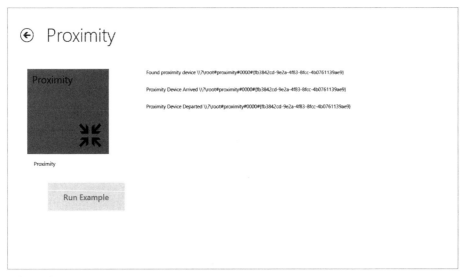

FIGURE 6-7

5.   NetNfpControl uses a proximity duration of one second, so after the device arrives, it departs shortly after. Listing 6-16 shows how to check for a proximity device and register for `DeviceDeparted` **and** `DeviceArrived` events.

LISTING 6-16: ProximityDemo.xaml.cs

```
using System;
using Windows.Networking.Proximity;
using Windows.UI.Core;
using Windows.UI.Xaml.Controls;

namespace DataFilesNetworkingSampleCS.Examples
{
    public sealed partial class ProximityDemo
        : UserControl
    {
        ProximityDevice _proximityDevice;

        public ProximityDemo()
        {
            this.InitializeComponent();
            _proximityDevice = ProximityDevice.GetDefault();
            if (_proximityDevice != null)
            {
                log.Items.Add(String.Format(
                    "Found proximity device {0}",
                    _proximityDevice.DeviceId));

                _proximityDevice.DeviceArrived +=
                    _proximityDevice_DeviceArrived;
```

```
            _proximityDevice.DeviceDeparted +=
                _proximityDevice_DeviceDeparted;
        }
        else
        {
            log.Items.Add(
                "Unable to find proximity devices");
        }
    }

    void _proximityDevice_DeviceDeparted(
        ProximityDevice sender)
    {
        Dispatcher.RunAsync(CoreDispatcherPriority.Normal,
            () =>
        {
            log.Items.Add(
                String.Format(
                "Proximity Device Departed {0}",
                sender.DeviceId)
                );
        });
    }

    void _proximityDevice_DeviceArrived(
        ProximityDevice sender)
    {
        Dispatcher.RunAsync(CoreDispatcherPriority.Normal, () =>
        {
            log.Items.Add(
                String.Format(
                "Proximity Device Arrived {0}",
                sender.DeviceId)
                );
        });
    }

    }
}
```

Subscribing and Publishing Messages

In this section, you subscribe for proximity messages on one PC and send a proximity message from another. To do so, follow these steps:

1. If you run the NetNfpProvider simulator driver, you need to run the following command (substitute MyOtherPC with the name or IP of your second PC; remember what was discussed earlier about firewall, ports, and driver configuration):

```
NetNfpControl.exe  MyOtherPC
```

This establishes proximity with MyOtherPC until you press a key to terminate it.

2. Launch the Data Samples on both PCs with proximity initiated, and bring the apps to the foreground.

3. Click the Proximity example on both PCs, select the Subscribe for Messages option on one, and the Publish Message option on another, and you should publish and receive a message. Figure 6-8 shows the screen of the receiving PC with a Hello World message transmitted and received via proximity.

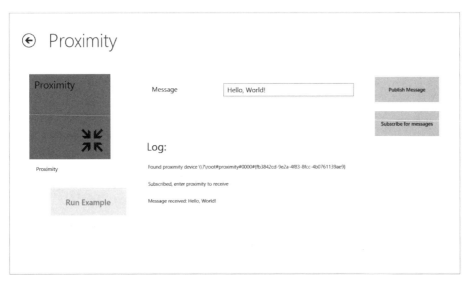

FIGURE 6-8

Listing 6-17 shows the `ProximityDemo.xaml.cs` code-behind file with publishing and receiving messages via `PublishMessage` and `SubscribeForMessage` methods of `ProximityDevice` type.

LISTING 6-17: ProximityDemo.xaml.cs

```
        private void send_Click(object sender,
            Windows.UI.Xaml.RoutedEventArgs e)
        {
            if (Message.Text.Length > 0)
            {
                _publishedMessage = _proximityDevice
                    .PublishMessage("Windows.SampleMessageType", Message.Text);
                log.Items.Add("Published, tap another device to transmit.");
            }
            else
            {
                Message.Text = "Type a message";
            }
        }

        private void subscribe_Click(object sender,
            Windows.UI.Xaml.RoutedEventArgs e)
        {

            _receivedMessage = _proximityDevice
```

```
        .SubscribeForMessage("Windows.SampleMessageType",
        OnMessageReceived);
    log.Items.Add(
        "Subscribed, enter proximity to receive"
        );
}

void OnMessageReceived(ProximityDevice proximityDevice,
    ProximityMessage message)
{
    Dispatcher.RunAsync(CoreDispatcherPriority.Normal, () =>
    {
        log.Items.Add(
            String.Format("Message received: {0}",
            message.DataAsString));
    });
}
```

Syndicated Content

Web syndication refers to websites making content available via standard formats, such as RSS or Atom. Sites that expose syndicated content benefit from additional traffic, and consuming apps benefit from content made available by the websites and app-specific presentation. Accessing syndicated content in Windows is accomplished with Windows.Web.Syndication types.

In the Syndication example available in the Data Samples app shipped with this example, you can see how to access a web feed using the SyndicationFeed class. First, you retrieve the feed with RetrieveFeedAsync, and then somewhat shape that feed by creating an anonymous feed item type with LINQ's new operator, which is used as a DataContext for the ListView control. Listing 6-18 shows a method that retrieves, shapes, and associates the feed with the data context.

LISTING 6-18: SyndicationDemo.xaml.cs

```
public async Task DisplayFeedAsync()
{
    string feedUriString
        = "http://windowsteamblog.com/windows/b/bloggingwindows/rss.aspx";
    SyndicationClient client = new SyndicationClient();
    Uri feedUri = new Uri(feedUriString);

    try
    {
        SyndicationFeed feed =
            await client.RetrieveFeedAsync(feedUri);

        var feedSource = from post in feed.Items
            select new
            {
                Title = post.Title.Text,
                Author = post.Authors[0].Name,
                PubDate = post.PublishedDate.DateTime
```

continues

LISTING 6-18 *(continued)*

```
                    };

            this.DataContext = feedSource.Take(5);
        }
        catch (Exception ex)
        {
            // handle errors
            resultText.Text = ex.Message;
        }
    }
}
```

Finally, the ListView control uses a DataTemplate and data binding to bind it to the feed. Listing 6-19 shows DataTemplate for the syndication example.

LISTING 6-19: SyndicationDemo.xaml

```xml
<DataTemplate>
  <StackPanel Orientation="Horizontal">
    <Grid Background="#FF14AFF7" Width="200">
      <TextBlock Margin="5"
          x:Name="pubdate"
          Text="{Binding PubDate}"
          FontSize="40"
          Foreground="White"/>
    </Grid>
    <StackPanel Margin="5,0,0,0" >
     <TextBlock x:Name="title"
      Text="{Binding Title}"
      FontSize="22"/>
      <TextBlock x:Name="author"
        Text="{Binding Author}"
        FontSize="22"/>
    </StackPanel>
  </StackPanel>
</DataTemplate>
```

Accessing Network Information

In the Windows Store apps, you may need to access network information from objects in Windows. Network.Connectivity namespace, for example, to retrieve data plan information from network providers, connection usage, and so on. The ConnectionProfile object specifies a single connection and may be accessed by calling the GetInternetConnectionProfile method. Listing 6-20 shows how to get network information.

LISTING 6-20: NetworkDemo.cs

```csharp
using System;
using Windows.Networking.Connectivity;

namespace DataFilesNetworkingSampleCS.Examples
```

```
{
    public class NetworkDemo
    {
        public string GetNetworkInfo()
        {
            string connectionProfileInfo = string.Empty;
            try
            {
                var conn = NetworkInformation.GetInternetConnectionProfile();
                string report = conn.GetNetworkConnectivityLevel().ToString();
                var networks = conn.GetNetworkNames();
                foreach (var network in networks)
                    report += "\n" + network;
                return report;
            }
            catch (Exception)
            {
                return "Unexpected exception occured:";
            }
        }

    }
}
```

You can also retrieve all connection profiles by using the static `GetConnectionProfiles` method of `NetworkInformation` type:

```
var profiles = NetworkInformation.GetConnectionProfiles();
```

When a connection changes, you can report that change back to the application by registering for a `NetworkStatusChanged` event. This event may indicate that the connection cost or other connectivity options have changed, and in more advanced scenarios, you can use this to adapt your application to network connection changes. To register for this event, simply add a handler to it, as follows:

```
NetworkInformation.NetworkStatusChanged += NetworkInformation_NetworkStatusChanged;
```

> **NOTE** *Events signaling network information change may be delivered on threads other than the UI thread, and you may need to use a* `Dispatcher` *object to properly update your user interface.*

EXAMPLE: LEADERBOARD APP

This section shows a higher level networking example that connects to an online game Leaderboard service, which you can create for this example. Azure Mobile Services is a super-fast way to add Azure backend to your existing app, or create a brand new app with preconfigured, cloud-based services. You can also quickly add authentication and push notifications to your app. If you want a prebuilt version, use the `Leaderboard.zip` file from the code examples to this chapter. Figure 6-9 shows a Leaderboard app in action:

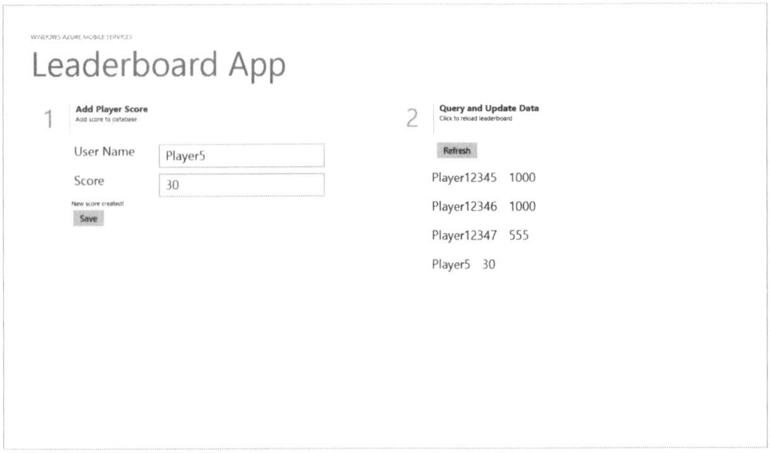

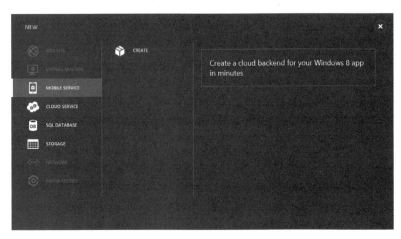

FIGURE 6-9

To perform the steps in this example, you must login into your Windows Azure account or create one if it doesn't exist yet. Microsoft often offers trials and great deals on the Azure website, so check for the latest information at `http://www.windowsazure.com`.

1. In an Azure dashboard click New; then select Mobile Service ⇨ Create. Figure 6-10 shows how to create a new mobile service in Azure Web console:

FIGURE 6-10

2. Follow the prompts to create or choose an existing SQL database for your app.

3. Select a language to generate the app: JavaScript or C#.

4. Download and install Azure Mobile Services SDK from the link provided on the page where you select the language for your app. Apps generated by Azure reference this SDK, so you need to have it to compile the app.

5. Choose between creating a new Windows Store app or select an existing app. For a new app, Azure generates all app code automatically. For an existing app, you add the following code to `App.xaml.cs` or default.js for a JavaScript app. Azure automatically places your secret key and app name instead of YOURAPPNAME and YOUR-SECRET-KEY.

MobileServiceClient in JavaScript in default.js

```javascript
var client = new Microsoft.WindowsAzure.MobileServices.MobileServiceClient(
    "https://YOURAPPNAME.azure-mobile.net/",
    "YOUR-SECRET-KEY"
);
```

MobileServiceClient in C# in App.xaml.cs

```csharp
public static MobileServiceClient MobileService = new MobileServiceClient(
    "https:// YOURAPPNAME.azure-mobile.net/",
    " YOUR-SECRET-KEY"
);
```

6. If you decide to create a new app, download the app generated by Azure by clicking the Download button. You need to make a few changes to it to make the Leaderboard app work.

> **NOTE** *Behind the scenes, Azure generates an entire application skeleton for you. The application* `App.xaml.cs` *file instantiates the* `MobileService` *object from Windows Azure Mobile Service managed client, which is preconfigured to communicate with your Azure app and includes the URL to the app and secret key.*
>
> *In the* `MainPage.xaml` *file you have two fields to input a username and a score. The Save button saves or updates score changes to the Azure hosted database:*
>
> ```xml
> <StackPanel  Margin="72,0,0,0">
>         <StackPanel Orientation="Horizontal" Margin="5">
>                 <TextBlock MinWidth="150" Text="User Name"
>     FontSize="22"/>
>                 <TextBox Name="UserName" MinWidth="300"
>     Text="Player12345"
>                         FontSize="22"/>
>         </StackPanel>
>         <StackPanel Orientation="Horizontal" Margin="5">
>                 <TextBlock MinWidth="150" Text="Score"
>     FontSize="22"/>
>                 <TextBox Name="Score" MinWidth="300" Text="1000"
>                         FontSize="22"/>
>         </StackPanel>
>                 <TextBlock x:Name="resultText" />
>                 <Button Name="ButtonSave"
>                         Click="ButtonSave_Click">Save</Button>
>         </StackPanel>
> ```

7. To show `UserName` and `Score` fields in your app, you can update the data template as follows:

```
<DataTemplate>
    <StackPanel Orientation="Horizontal" >
        <TextBlock Text="{Binding UserName}" FontSize="22" />
        <TextBlock Text="{Binding Score}" FontSize="22" Margin="20,0,0,0" />
    </StackPanel>
</DataTemplate>
```

8. In the code behind for `MainPage.xaml.cs`, you defined `LeaderboardItem` as a data model for the Azure table.

> **NOTE** *To simplify your coding, you don't need to create columns in an Azure Mobile Services SQL table. Azure Mobile Services SDK picks your data model from the app code automatically when you run it! All you need to do is define your model in code and create a* `LeaderboardItem` *table in Azure.*

Listing 6-21 shows code behind for the main page of the Leaderboard app.

LISTING 6-21: MainPage.xaml.cs

```
using Microsoft.WindowsAzure.MobileServices;
using System;
using System.Linq;
using System.Runtime.Serialization;
using Windows.UI.Xaml;
using Windows.UI.Xaml.Controls;
using Windows.UI.Xaml.Navigation;

namespace leaderboard
{
    public class LeaderboardItem
    {
        public int Id { get; set; }
        [DataMember(Name = "username")]
        public string UserName { get; set; }
        [DataMember(Name = "score")]
        public int Score { get; set; }
    }

    public sealed partial class MainPage : Page
    {
        // MobileServiceCollectionView implements ICollectionView
        // (useful for databinding to lists) and is integrated with
        // your Mobile Service to make it easy to bind your data
        private MobileServiceCollectionView<LeaderboardItem> items;

        private IMobileServiceTable<LeaderboardItem> leaderboardTable
            = App.MobileService.GetTable<LeaderboardItem>();

        public MainPage()
```

```csharp
{
    this.InitializeComponent();
}

private async void InsertLeaderboardItem(LeaderboardItem item)
{
    // This code inserts a new item into the database.
    // When the operation completes and Mobile Services
    // has assigned an Id, the item is added to the view
    await leaderboardTable.InsertAsync(item);
    items.Add(item);
}

private void RefreshLeaderboardItems()
{
    // This code refreshes the entries in the list view
    items = leaderboardTable.ToCollectionView();
    ListItems.ItemsSource = items;
}

private async void UpdateLeaderboardItem(LeaderboardItem item)
{
    // This code takes a freshly completed item and updates the database.
    // When the MobileService responds, the item is removed from the list
    await leaderboardTable.UpdateAsync(item);
    items.Remove(item);
}

private void ButtonRefresh_Click(object sender, RoutedEventArgs e)
{
    RefreshLeaderboardItems();
}

private async void ButtonSave_Click(object sender, RoutedEventArgs e)
{

    var list = await leaderboardTable
        .Where(s => s.UserName == UserName.Text).ToListAsync();

    bool userExists = (list != null && list.Count > 0);

    LeaderboardItem currentScore;

    if (userExists)
    {
        currentScore = list.First();
    }
    else
    {
        currentScore = new LeaderboardItem();
        if (String.IsNullOrWhiteSpace(UserName.Text))
        {
            resultText.Text = "Please enter a user name";
            return;
        }
```

continues

LISTING 6-21 *(continued)*

```
            currentScore.UserName = UserName.Text;
        }

        int score;
        if (!int.TryParse(Score.Text, out score))
        {
            resultText.Text = "Please enter an integer score";
            return;
        }
        currentScore.Score = score;

        if (userExists)
        {
            UpdateLeaderboardItem(currentScore);
            resultText.Text = "Score updated!";
        }
        else
        {
            InsertLeaderboardItem(currentScore);
            resultText.Text = "New score created!";
        }
    }

    protected override void OnNavigatedTo(NavigationEventArgs e)
    {
        RefreshLeaderboardItems();
    }
  }
}
```

In the `ButtonSave_Click` event, you should check if the score already exists in the database for a user with the name specified on the `UserName` text box on the page:

```
var list = await leaderboardTable
    .Where(s => s.UserName == UserName.Text).ToListAsync();
```

In a more advanced scenario, you may need to identify your users by their e-mail or other type of id, but for the purpose of this example, you use a username as a user id. If the user exists, simply update the score; otherwise create a new `LeaderboardItem` with a new username defined in the `UserName` text box.

SUMMARY

In this chapter you learned about managing you application data and data stores available to Windows Store apps, including local, roaming, and temporary. You learned differences between these stores and best practices on using each of them. You learned how Windows Store apps work with files, including more advanced topics to use most recently used and other lists to track files. In the networking section you covered WebSockets, TCP and UDP sockets, data transfers, accessing network information, and proximity, and provided a Leaderboard example for accessing network services.

Sensors

WROX.COM CODE DOWNLOAD FOR THIS CHAPTER

You can find the wrox.com code downloads for this chapter in code file 205709 C07.zip at `www.wrox.com/remtitle.cgi?isbn=9781118205709`. The code for this chapter is conveniently contained within a single Visual Studio 2012 solution with seven sample projects.

Our devices change every year, adding new capabilities, becoming thinner, lighter, and are also becoming "smarter" with sensors. There are thousands of practical scenarios, as well as real-life examples, of how sensors impact computing experiences every day. This chapter navigates the developer through a wealth of new APIs and features available within Windows 8 that enable your apps to become "smarter" with sensors.

WINDOWS SENSOR PLATFORM

As humans, we are equipped with biological sensors needed to perceive changes in the real world. The devices mankind has developed are just starting to catch up with those biological sensors. In the last few years, the industry has experienced an enormous growth in sensor technology, giving such devices the ability to sense touch, orientation, position changes and proximity, with more sensors being developed every day!

With the Windows Sensor Platform your apps are able to become "smarter", reacting to changes in acceleration, orientation, and ambient light levels, etc. Given the vast range of devices upon which your apps will run the sensor platform provides abstractions for the various hardware sensors.

Hardware for the Sensor Platform

When designing the Windows Runtime, the architects and developers at Microsoft built a run-time as re-imagined as the Windows 8 operating system. As with the core operating system, the run-time embraced several disruptions, or strategic inflection points.

➤   **The expanded hardware ecosystem:** Windows 8 Pro systems run on Intel x86 and x64 processors, such the Intel Core i3, Core i5, and Core i7 processors. However, Windows RT devices, such as Microsoft Surface, use ARM-based processors from manufacturers, such as NVIDIA, Qualcomm, and Texas Instruments.

➤   **Windows 8 Pro and Windows RT-based devices also embrace** *System-on-a-Chip (SoC)* **architectures.** SoC architectures have numerous benefits to hardware designers that ultimately provide more responsive experiences to users and increased battery life.

➤   **Windows embraces mobility like never before.** Mobile systems are increasingly providing sensors that enable exciting new scenarios for application developers.

Windows Sensor Platform Overview

With Windows 8 Pro and Windows RT, the Windows Sensor Platform provides developers with access to multiple sensors, through a unified set of APIs. Within this chapter you will learn how to use Windows Sensors APIs and the sensor types, shown in Table 7-1, from the Windows.Devices .Sensors namespace:

TABLE 7-1: Some Classes from the Windows.Devices.Sensors Namespace

CLASS	DESCRIPTION
Accelerometer	3-D accelerometer sensor
Compass	3-D compass sensor
Gyrometer	3-D gyrometer sensor
Inclinometer	3-D inclinometer sensor
LightSensor	3-D ambient-light sensor
OrientationSensor	Represents an orientation sensor
SimpleOrientationSensor	Represents a simple orientation sensor

Windows expanded some of the requirements for hardware manufacturers. The *Windows Certification Program* (previously known as the *Windows Logo Program*) requires that hardware manufacturers provide an integrated 3-D accelerometer, 3-D gyrometer, and 3-D magnetometer in all tablet and convertible-tablet form factors. If the system is equipped with mobile broadband, an integrated GPS receiver is also required.

Windows also provides the Hardware Certification Kit and tools to support hardware and sensor development. The kit provides development and debugging tools for driver developers and testers.

When you look at the variety of sensors and devices the Windows Sensor Platform supports, you'll notice many similarities in the way a developer works with them. Many types are instantiated similarly, and have similar data structures, making it easier to develop for multiple sensors. The Windows Sensor Platform also employs a technique called *sensor fusion*: the process of using data from multiple sensors to enhance existing sensor data, or to synthesize new sensor data types from raw sensor data. Figure 7-1 shows that the accelerometer, gyrometer, and magnetometer provide data that synthesizes virtual compass, inclinometer, and device-orientation sensors.

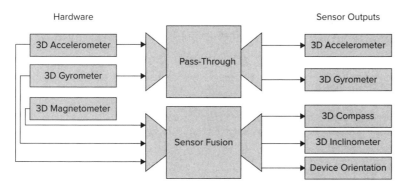

FIGURE 7-1

Given that the Windows Certification Program does not require all sensors on all form factors, you must ensure that your application can account for the presence, or absence, of given sensors. It is for this reason that the types in the `Windows.Devices.Sensors` namespace representing sensors do not provide parameterless constructors. They instead provide a static `GetDefault` method that returns the default sensor instance if that sensor has been integrated into the computer by the manufacturer; otherwise, it returns `null`. You could therefore write the following statements to get the default `Accelerometer` and then determine if the `GetDefault` method returned `null` before using it.

```
Accelerometer accelerometer = Accelerometer.GetDefault();

if (accelerometer == null)
{
    ...
}
else
{
    ...
}
```

The rest of this chapter explores each of the sensors beginning with the `Accelerometer` class.

USING THE 3-D ACCELEROMETER

An accelerometer is a device designed to measure acceleration forces. Windows automatically uses the accelerometer to adjust the screen orientation as the user rotates the device.

As mentioned previously, the Windows Certification Program requires an accelerometer, and this accelerometer provides measurements of acceleration forces across three axes, and the data rate of the accelerometer must be >= 50 Hz.

As you can see in the class diagram shown in Figure 7-2, the `Accelerometer` class provides two events enabling your app to respond to changes in acceleration forces.

`ReadingChanged` occurs each time the accelerometer has a new reading containing values for g-force acceleration along the x, y, and z axes. `Shaken` occurs each time the PC has been shaken. To see this in action, follow these steps:

1. Open Visual Studio 2012, and create a new project using the Blank App (XAML) project template.

2. Open the `MainPage.xaml` file, and add the `TextBlock` as defined in the code that follows to the `Grid` element within the page.

    ```
    <Grid Background="{StaticResource ApplicationPageBackgroundThemeBrush}">
        <TextBlock x:Name="AccelerometerReadingTextBlock"
                FontSize="48"
                VerticalAlignment="Center"
                HorizontalAlignment="Center"/>
    </Grid>
    ```

3. With the page defined in XAML, turn your attention to the code in the `MainPage` `.xaml.cs` file. Start by adding the `using` directive for the `Windows.Devices.Sensors` namespace and then add a field to the class of type `Accelerometer` naming the field `accelerometer`.

    ```
    public sealed partial class MainPage : Page
    {
        private Accelerometer accelerometer;


    }
    ```

4. Initialize the accelerometer in the class constructor and then ensure that an instance of the `Accelerometer` class is returned. If the PC upon which you test this code doesn't have an integrated accelerometer and appropriate device drivers installed, `GetDefault`, of course, returns `null`. If the `GetDefault` method does return `null`, at least you have an excellent excuse for a new tablet or convertible tablet PC with Windows 8 Pro or Windows RT!

```
public MainPage()
{
    this.InitializeComponent();

    this.accelerometer = Accelerometer.GetDefault();

    if (this.accelerometer != null)
    {
        this.accelerometer.ReadingChanged
            += this.AccelerometerReadingChanged;

        this.accelerometer.Shaken += this.AccelerometerShaken;
    }
    else
    {
        this.AccelerometerReadingTextBlock.Text =
                "Unable to initialize default Accelerometer instance";
    }
}
```

5. In the event handler for the ReadingChanged event, display the values for g-force acceleration along the x, y, and z-axes. Referring to the class diagram in Figure 7-2, you can see that the AccelerometerReadingChangedEventArgs contains a single property of type AccelerometerReading. AccelerometerReading providing properties for the acceleration along each axis as well as the Timestamp property that gets the time at which the accelerometer reported the reading.

```
async private void AccelerometerReadingChanged
    (Accelerometer sender, AccelerometerReadingChangedEventArgs e)
{
    await Dispatcher.RunAsync(CoreDispatcherPriority.Normal,() =>
    {
        this.AccelerometerReadingTextBlock.Text = string.Format
            ("Accelerometer Reading: X: {0:0.000} Y: {1:0.000} Z: {2:0.000}",
                        e.Reading.AccelerationX,
                        e.Reading.AccelerationY,
                        e.Reading.AccelerationZ);
    });
}
```

6. In the event handler for the Shaken event, indicate that the PC is shaken. You can see that the AccelerometerShakenEventArgs class also provides the Timestamp property that gets the time at which the accelerometer reports the PC is shaken.

```
async private void AccelerometerShaken
    (Accelerometer sender, AccelerometerShakenEventArgs e)
{
        await Dispatcher.RunAsync(CoreDispatcherPriority.Normal,() =>
        {
            this.AccelerometerReadingTextBlock.Text =
                "Shaken, But Not Stirred!";
        });
}
```

Figure 7-2 shows the class diagram of the accelerometer example:

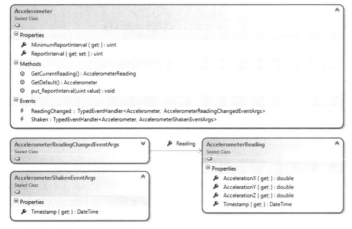

FIGURE 7-2

7. If you run the accelerometer sample application, you see readings for g-force acceleration along the x, y, and z-axes. In case you do not have an integrated accelerometer on your PC, these are some example readings for g-force acceleration:

```
Accelerometer Reading: X: -0.066 Y: 0.183 Z: -1.010
```

Shaking the PC, of course, results instead in the following message:

```
Shaken, But Not Stirred!
```

USING THE 3-D COMPASS

A *compass* is a navigational device designed to measure directional headings. You can use the compass sensor in your apps to detect directional headings and there are numerous scenarios where this would prove useful such as navigational apps. Within the Windows Sensor Platform, the compass sensor is synthesized using sensor fusion.

Using the Compass Class

The Compass class provides a single ReadingChanged event that occurs each time the 3-D compass sensor has new readings for the headings using magnetic north and true north.

Figure 7-3 shows that the CompassReadingChangedEventArgs class contains a single property of type CompassReading. The CompassReading class provides properties for both the magnetic north and true north headings along with the Timestamp property recording the time at which the compass reported the reading. To use the Compass class, follow these steps:

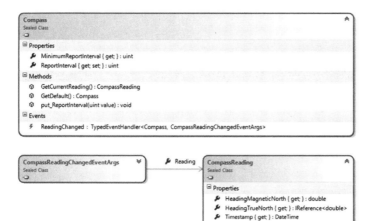

FIGURE 7-3

1. Open Visual Studio 2012, and create a new project using the Blank App (XAML) project template.

2. Open the `MainPage.xaml` file, and add the `TextBlock` as defined in the following markup to the `Grid` element in the page.

```
<Grid Background="{StaticResource ApplicationPageBackgroundThemeBrush}">
    <TextBlock x:Name="CompassReadingTextBlock"
               FontSize="22"
               VerticalAlignment="Center"
               HorizontalAlignment="Center"/>
</Grid>
```

3. With the page markup defined, edit the `MainPage.xaml.cs` file, again adding the `using` directive for the `Windows.Devices.Sensors` namespace.

4. Add a field to the class of type `Compass` naming the field `compass`.

```
public sealed partial class MainPage : Page
{
    private Compass compass;



}
```

5. Initialize the compass in the class constructor, and then ensure that the required 3-D accelerometer, gyrometer, and magnetometer are present to enable sensor fusion. If these components are not present on the PC, the `GetDefault` method returns `null`.

```
public MainPage()
{
    this.InitializeComponent();
```

```
        this.compass = Compass.GetDefault();

        if(this.compass != null)
        {
            this.compass.ReadingChanged += this.CompassReadingChanged;
        }
        else
        {
            this.CompassReadingTextBlock.Text =
                "Unable to initialize default Compass instance";
        }
    }
```

6. In the event handler for the `ReadingChanged` event, display the values for the magnetic north and true north headings.

```
    async private void CompassReadingChanged
        (Compass sender, CompassReadingChangedEventArgs e)
    {
        await Dispatcher.RunAsync(CoreDispatcherPriority.Normal,() =>
        {
            this.CompassReadingTextBlock.Text =
                string.Format
                    ("Compass Reading: {0}° Magnetic North {1}° True North",
                    e.Reading.HeadingMagneticNorth,
                    e.Reading.HeadingTrueNorth);
        });
    }
```

7. If you run the compass sample application, you can see readings for the magnetic north and true north headings.

In case you do not have the integrated 3-D accelerometer, gyrometer, and magnetometer on your PC required for sensor fusion, following is an example reading for the magnetic and true north headings.

```
    Compass Reading: 241° Magnetic North 226° True North
```

Calculating True North Headings

As a practical example of using the 3-D Compass API, this section considers a task solved by pilots every day. Pilots use sectional charts to navigate in the United States. These charts show isogonic lines for every one degree of magnetic variation. An isogonic line is a line drawn through points of equal magnetic variation.

Figure 7-4 shows an isogonic line for 15° E from the San Francisco sectional chart. If you want to calculate the true north heading given a magnetic heading of 241°, you would subtract the 15° magnetic variance giving you the true north heading of 226°.

FIGURE 7-4

For example, when flying in the eastern United States, the isogonic line would instead be 15°W, and the true north heading would then need to be calculated by adding the magnetic variance. If you fly a heading of 241° magnetic, the resulting true north heading would be 256°.

It is obviously critical for pilots to know when to add or subtract the magnetic variance; therefore, during flight school student pilots are taught the mnemonic "East is least and West is best." Using the mnemomic its easy to remember that if the isogonic is 15°E you would subtract the magnetic variance, and if it is 15°W you would add the magnetic variance.

USING THE 3-D GYROMETER

Gyrometers often complement accelerometers as controllers for games. The accelerometer can measure linear motion while the gyrometer measures angular velocity (or rotational motion). As with the 3-D accelerometer and magnetometer, the Windows Certification Program also requires an integrated 3-D gyrometer on tablet and convertible tablet form factors.

The `Gyrometer` class provides a single `ReadingChanged` event that occurs each time the 3-D gyrometer sensor has new readings for angular velocity along the x, y, and z-axes.

Figure 7-5 shows that the `GyrometerReadingChangedEventArgs` class contains a single property of type `GyrometerReading`. The `GyrometerReading` class provides three properties that get the angular velocity along the x, y, and z-axes along with the `Timestamp` property that records the time at which the gyrometer reported the reading. To see this in action, follow these steps:

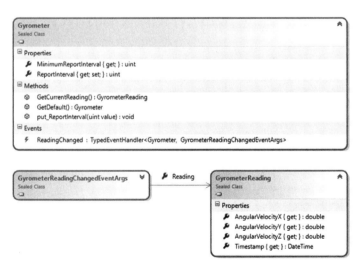

FIGURE 7-5

1. Open Visual Studio 2012, and create a new project using the Blank App (XAML) project template.

2. Open the `MainPage.xaml` file, and add the `TextBlock` as defined in the following code to the `Grid` element in the page.

```xml
<Grid Background="{StaticResource ApplicationPageBackgroundThemeBrush}">
    <TextBlock x:Name="GyrometerReadingTextBlock"
            FontSize="48"
            VerticalAlignment="Center"
            HorizontalAlignment="Center"/>
</Grid>
```

3. With the page markup defined, you then need to edit the `MainPage.xaml.cs` file, again adding the `using` directive for the `Windows.Devices.Sensors` namespace. Then add a field to the class of type `Gyrometer` naming the field `gyrometer`.

```csharp
public sealed partial class MainPage : Page
{
    private Gyrometer gyrometer;

    ...
}
```

4. Initialize the gyrometer in the class constructor, and then ensure that the integrated 3-D gyrometer is present. If the gyrometer is not present the `GetDefault` method returns `null`. It's worth noting that when a system is in Connected Standby mode, a call to the `GetDefault` method returns immediately with `null`.

```csharp
public MainPage()
{
    this.InitializeComponent();

    this.gyrometer = Gyrometer.GetDefault();

    if(this.gyrometer != null)
    {
        this.gyrometer.ReadingChanged += this.GyrometerReadingChanged;
    }
    else
    {
        this.GyrometerReadingTextBlock.Text =
            "Unable to initialize default Gyrometer instance";
    }
}
```

5. Within the event handler for the `ReadingChanged` event, display the values for angular velocity along the x, y, and z-axes.

```csharp
async private void GyrometerReadingChanged
    (Gyrometer sender, GyrometerReadingChangedEventArgs e)
{
    await Dispatcher.RunAsync(CoreDispatcherPriority.Normal, () =>
    {
        this.GyrometerReadingTextBlock.Text =
            string.Format
```

```
                    ("Gyrometer Reading: X: {0:0.000} Y: {1:0.000} Z: {2:0.000}",
                        e.Reading.AngularVelocityX,
                        e.Reading.AngularVelocityY,
                        e.Reading.AngularVelocityZ);
            });
        }
```

6. If you run the gyrometer sample application, you see readings for angular velocity along the x, y, and z-axes.

In case you do not have an integrated 3-D gyrometer on your PC, the following is an example reading for angular velocity:

```
Gyrometer Reading: X: -1.610 Y: 0.980 Z: -3.080
```

USING THE INCLINOMETER

If your app requires the ability to determine relative angles of pitch, roll, and yaw you would use the inclinometer sensor. An inclinometer is a device designed to measure angles of slope (or tilt) from an artificial horizon and would therefore be very useful when developing flight simulators. On the Windows Sensor Platform an inclinometer is synthesized using sensor fusion.

The `Inclinometer` class provides a single `ReadingChanged` event that occurs each time the 3-D inclinometer sensor has new readings for angles of pitch, roll, and yaw.

Figure 7-6 shows that the `InclinometerReadingChangedEventArgs` class contains a single property of type `InclinometerReading`. The `InclinometerReading` class provides three properties that get the angles of pitch, roll, and yaw along with the `Timestamp` property recording the time at which the inclinometer reported the reading. To use this in your app, follow these steps:

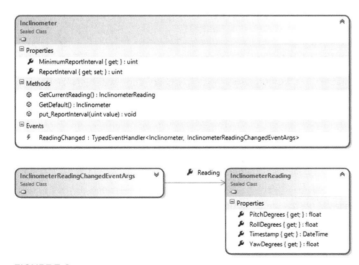

FIGURE 7-6

1. Open Visual Studio 2012, and create a new project using the Blank App (XAML) project template.

2. Open the `MainPage.xaml` file, and add the `TextBlock` as defined in the following code to the `Grid` element in the page.

```
Background="{StaticResource ApplicationPageBackgroundThemeBrush}">
    <TextBlock x:Name="InclimometerReadingTextBlock"
               FontSize="48"
               VerticalAlignment="Center"
               HorizontalAlignment="Center"/>
</Grid>
```

3. With the page markup defined, edit the `MainPage.xaml.cs` file, again adding the `using` directive for the `Windows.Devices.Sensors` namespace.

4. Add a local variable `inclinometer` to the `MainPage` class of type `Inclinometer`.

```
public sealed partial class MainPage : Page
{
    private Inclinometer inclinometer;

    ...
}
```

5. Initialize the inclinometer in the class constructor, and then ensure that the inclinometer is synthesized using sensor fusion. If the synthesized inclinometer is not available, the `GetDefault` method returns `null`.

```
public MainPage()
{
    this.InitializeComponent();

    this.inclinometer = Inclinometer.GetDefault();

    if(this.inclinometer!= null)
    {
        this.inclinometer.ReadingChanged += this.InclinometerReadingChanged;
    }
    else
    {
        this.InclinometerReadingTextBlock.Text =
            "Unable to initialize default Inclinometer instance";
    }
}
```

6. In the event handler for the `ReadingChanged` event, display the angles of pitch, roll, and yaw.

```
async private void InclinometerReadingChanged
    (Inclinometer sender, InclinometerReadingChangedEventArgs e)
{
```

```
await Dispatcher.RunAsync(CoreDispatcherPriority.Normal,() =>
{
    this.InclinometerReadingTextBlock.Text = string.Format
            ("Inclinometer Reading: Pitch: {0}° Roll: {1}° Yaw: {2}°",
                e.Reading.Pitch,
                e.Reading.Roll,
                e.Reading.Yaw);
});
}
```

USING THE AMBIENT LIGHT SENSOR

Imagine that you're creating a photo app, and you need to measure light conditions for your picture. An ambient light sensor is a device designed to measure luminance, a photometric measure of the luminous intensity, in a given area.

The LightSensor class provides a single ReadingChanged event that occurs each time the ambient light sensor has new readings for luminance measured in lux (symbol: lx).

Figure 7-7 shows that the LightSensorReadingChangedEventArgs class contains a single property of type LightSensorReading. The LightSensorReading class provides the IlluminanceInLux property that gets luminance along with the Timestamp property that gets the time at which the ambient light sensor reported the reading. You can incorporate this in your app by following these steps:

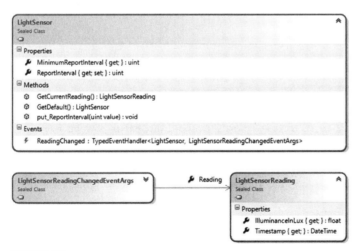

FIGURE 7-7

1. Open Visual Studio 2012, and create a new project using the Blank App (XAML) project template.

2. Open the MainPage.xaml file, and add the TextBlock as defined in the following code to the Grid element in the page.

```
<Grid Background="{StaticResource ApplicationPageBackgroundThemeBrush}">
    <TextBlock x:Name="LightSensorReadingTextBlock"
            FontSize="48"
            VerticalAlignment="Center"
            HorizontalAlignment="Center"/>
</Grid>
```

3. With the page markup defined, edit the `MainPage.xaml.cs` file, again adding the required `using` directive for the `Windows.Devices.Sensors` namespace. Then add a field to the class of type `LightSensor` naming the field `sensor`.

```
public sealed partial class MainPage : Page
{
    private LightSensor sensor;

    ...
}
```

4. Initialize the light sensor in the class constructor and then ensure that an appropriate light sensor is integrated in the system. If the light sensor is not integrated, the `GetDefault` method returns `null`.

```
public MainPage()
{
    this.InitializeComponent();

    this.sensor = LightSensor.GetDefault();

    if(this.sensor != null)
    {
        this.sensor.ReadingChanged += this.LightSensorReadingChanged;
    }
    else
    {
        this.LightSensorReadingTextBlock.Text =
                "Unable to initialize default LightSensor insatnce";
    }
}
```

5. In the event handler for the `ReadingChanged` event, display readings for luminance.

```
async private void LightSensorReadingChanged
    (LightSensor sender, LightSensorReadingChangedEventArgs e)
{
    await Dispatcher.RunAsync(CoreDispatcherPriority.Normal,() =>
    {
        this. LightSensorReadingTextBlock.Text =
            string.Format("Light Sensor Reading: {0:0.000} lx",
                e.Reading.IlluminanceInLux.ToString());
    });
}
```

If you run the light sensor sample application, you see readings for luminance. In case you do not have an integrated ambient light sensor within your PC, the following is an example of reading for luminance:

```
Light Sensor Reading: 51.250 lx
```

USING THE ORIENTATION SENSORS

You can use orientation sensor data in a game app to adjust a user's prospective in a game. Orientation sensor objects are used similarly to other sensors in Windows but your code should first check if the device is supported. `OrientationSensor` returns a rotation matrix and a Quaternion that can be used to adjust the user's perspective in a game application.

Using the OrientationSensor Class

The `OrientationSensor` class provides a single `ReadingChanged` event that occurs each time the device orientation sensor has new readings.

Figure 7-8 shows that the `OrientationSensor ReadingChangedEventArgs` class contains two properties that provide the rotation matrix and the sensor Quaternion along with the `Timestamp` property that records the time at which the device orientation sensor reported the reading. Follow these steps to try out the `OrientationSensor` class:

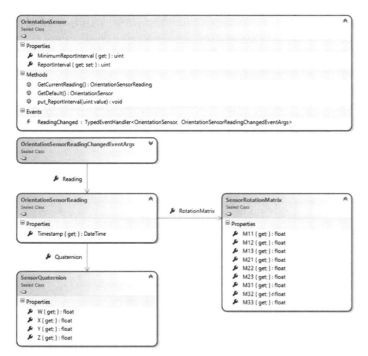

FIGURE 7-8

1. Open Visual Studio 2012, and create a new project using the Blank App (XAML) project template.

2. Open the `MainPage.xaml` file, and add the `TextBlock` as defined in the code that follows to the `Grid` element in the page.

```
<Grid Background="{StaticResource ApplicationPageBackgroundThemeBrush}">
    <TextBlock x:Name="OrientationSensorReadingTextBlock"
            FontSize="22"
            VerticalAlignment="Center"
            HorizontalAlignment="Center"/>
</Grid>
```

3. With the page markup defined, edit the `MainPage.xaml.cs` file, again adding the `using` directive for the `Windows.Devices.Sensors` namespace.

4. In the following code segment, add a variable to `MainPage` with the type `OrientationSensor`, naming this variable `sensor`.

```
public sealed partial class MainPage : Page
{
    private OrientationSensor sensor;



}
```

5. Initialize the orientation sensor in the class constructor, and then ensure that the orientation sensor is synthesized using sensor fusion. If the synthesized orientation sensor is not available, the `GetDefault` method returns `null`.

```
public MainPage()
{
    this.InitializeComponent();

    this.sensor = OrientationSensor.GetDefault();

    if(this.sensor != null)
    {
        this.sensor.ReadingChanged += this.OrientationSensorReadingChanged;
    }
    else
    {
        this.OrientationSensorReadingTextBlock.Text =
            "Unable to initialize default OrientationSensor instance";
    }
}
```

6. In the event handler for the `ReadingChanged` event, display the values for the Quaternion and rotation matrix.

```
async private void OrientationSensorReadingChanged
    (OrientationSensor sender, OrientationSensorReadingChangedEventArgs e)
{
    await Dispatcher.RunAsync(CoreDispatcherPriority.Normal,() =>
    {
        this.OrientationSensorReadingTextBlock.Text = string.Format
            ("OrientationSensor Reading: W: {0} X: {1} Y: {2} Z: {3} RM: {4}",
                e.Reading.Quaternion.W,
                e.Reading.Quaternion.X,
                e.Reading.Quaternion.Y,
                e.Reading.Quaternion.Z,
                e.Reading.RotationMatrix.ToString());
    });
}
```

Using the SimpleOrientationSensor Class

Instead of the `OrientationSensor` class, you can instead use the `SimpleOrientationSensor`. This sensor detects the current quadrant orientation of the specified device as well as its face-up or face-down status, which may be easier than using Quaternion data. The `SimpleOrientationSensor` class provides a single `ReadingChanged` event that occurs each time the device orientation sensor has new readings.

Figure 7-9 shows that the `SimpleOrientationSensor ReadingChangedEventArgs` class contains the `Orientation` property that provides the orientation of the device as a value from the `SimpleOrientation` enumeration. As with the other sensors discussed in this chapter, the `Timestamp` property records the time at which the device orientation sensor reported the reading. To see this in action, follow these steps:

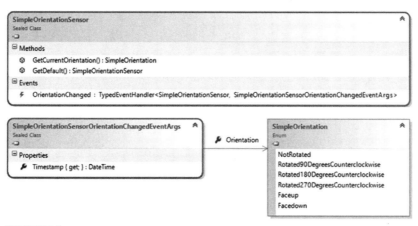

FIGURE 7-9

1. Open Visual Studio 2012, and create a new project using the Blank App (XAML) project template.

2. Open the `MainPage.xaml` file, and add the `TextBlock` as defined in the code that follows to the `Grid` element within the page.

```
<Grid Background="{StaticResource ApplicationPageBackgroundThemeBrush}">
    <TextBlock x:Name="SimpleOrientationSensorReadingTextBlock"
            FontSize="22"
            VerticalAlignment="Center"
            HorizontalAlignment="Center"/>
</Grid>
```

3. With the page markup defined, edit the `MainPage.xaml.cs` file, again adding the required `using` directive for the `Windows.Devices.Sensors` namespace.

4. Add a field to the class of type `SimpleOrientationSensor` naming the field `sensor`.

```
public sealed partial class MainPage : Page
{
    private SimpleOrientationSensor sensor;

    ...
}
```

5. Initialize the simple orientation sensor in the class constructor, and then ensure that the simple orientation sensor is synthesized using sensor fusion. If the simple orientation sensor is not synthesized, the `GetDefault` method returns `null`.

```
public MainPage()
{
    this.InitializeComponent();

    this.sensor = SimpleOrientationSensor.GetDefault();

    if(this.sensor != null)
    {
        this.sensor.ReadingChanged +=
            this.SimpleOrientationSensorReadingChanged;
    }
    else
    {
        this.OrientationSensorReadingTextBlock.Text =
            "Unable to initialize default SimpleOrientationSensor instance";
    }
}
```

6. In the event handler for the `ReadingChanged` event, display the device orientation.

```
async private void SimpleOrientationSensorReadingChanged
(OrientationSensor sender, SimpleOrientationSensorReadingChangedEventArgs e)
{
    await Dispatcher.RunAsync(CoreDispatcherPriority.Normal,() =>
    {
        this.SimpleOrientationSensorReadingTextBlock.Text =
            string.Format("SimpleOrientationSensor Reading: {0}",
                e.Orientation.ToString());
    });
}
```

SUMMARY

In this chapter you learned how to use various sensors within your apps; either directly provided by hardware or synthesized using sensor fusion. You are now able to design apps that are capable of reacting to changes in acceleration, orientation, and ambient light levels, etc. As Windows devices become "smarter", through the addition of more sensors, more and more scenarios are enabled by "smarter" apps that are aware of their environment. It will certainly be exciting to see these "smarter" apps within the Windows Store.

Geolocation

WROX.COM CODE DOWNLOADS FOR THIS CHAPTER

You can find the wrox.com code downloads for this chapter at www.wrox.com/remtitle
.cgi?isbn=1118205707 on the Download Code tab in the 311813 C08.zip download.

WHAT IS GEOLOCATION?

In the last few years, some of the most popular and impactful apps on mobile platforms have
implemented location awareness. These apps have subsequently provided their users with abilities
to determine the exact location of the user — or more accurately the device — on the Earth.

Foursquare, as an example, enables users to share their location with others via Facebook,
Twitter, and other social networks. Using foursquare, users can determine what is nearby to
see or do, abilities that would not be possible without location awareness.

Geolocation is the identification of the real-world geographic location of an object. Although
it is often considered as merely the positioning of an object, the greater emphasis is on
determining a meaningful location such as a street address.

The Windows Store has numerous apps that use location awareness, and you can explore
some of the scenarios in which developers have used *geolocation* by searching the store for
geolocation using the Windows 8 search charm.

Consider for a moment the Windows 8 Maps app (as shown in Figure 8-1), which indicates the user's location on the map, in this case the Orlando International Airport (KMCO). The Windows 8 Maps app enables users to get directions from one location on the Earth to another. Figure 8-2 shows the directions from the Orange County Convention Center to the Orlando International Airport.

FIGURE 8-1

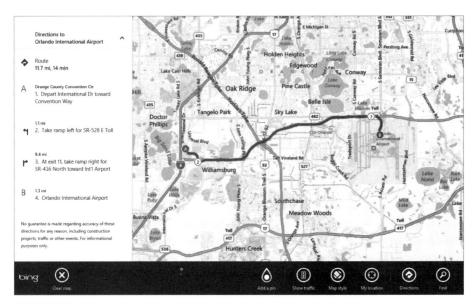

FIGURE 8-2

This chapter works through several examples, showing you how to develop your own app so that users have some of the abilities that the Windows 8 Maps app provides.

GEOLOCATION IN WINDOWS 8

In Windows 8, the `Geolocator` class is the type that enables location awareness for Windows 8 store apps. This section shows how you can use the `Geolocator` class to determine the latitude and longitude of the user (or rather the device) upon the Earth.

You might be asking: What about devices without a GPS sensor? Can those devices determine their location? The `Geolocator` class certainly uses a GPS sensor, if one is present, to determine the location of the PC on the Earth; although, the `Geolocator` can use the network information to determine your location.

> **NOTE** *Latitude and longitude are angles that uniquely define points on a sphere such as the planet Earth. Together, the angles define a coordinate system that can precisely identity geographic positions.*

Using the Geolocator Class

In this section, you use Visual Studio 2012 to create a new Windows Store app to demonstrate the use of the `Geolocator` class:

1. Open Visual Studio 2012, and create a new project using the Blank App (XAML) project template.

2. Open the MainPage.xaml file, and add the two `TextBlock` controls as defined in the markup below that follows the `Grid` element within the page.

    ```
    <Grid Background="{StaticResource ApplicationPageBackgroundThemeBrush}">
        <TextBlock x:Name="GeolocatorStatusTextBlock"
            FontSize="48"
            Text="Unknown"
            VerticalAlignment="Center"
            HorizontalAlignment="Center"
            Margin="50,38,1115,672"/>

        <TextBlock x:Name="GeolocatorPositionTextBlock"
            FontSize="48"
            Text="Unknown"
            VerticalAlignment="Center"
            HorizontalAlignment="Center"/>
    </Grid>
    ```

3. With the page defined in XAML, turn your attention to the code in the `MainPage.xaml.cs` file. Start by adding the `using` directive for the `Windows.Devices.Geolocation` namespace and then add a field to the class of type `Geolocator` naming the field `locator`.

```
public sealed partial class MainPage : Page
{
    private Geolocator locator;



}
```

4. Initialize the `Geolocator` in the class constructor, determine the `DesiredAccuracy`, and define event handlers for the `StatusChanged` and `PositionChanged` events.

```
public MainPage()
{
    this.InitializeComponent();

    this.locator = new Geolocator();

    this.locator.DesiredAccuracy = PositionAccuracy.Default;

    this.locator.StatusChanged += this.GeolocatorStatusChanged;

    this.locator.PositionChanged += this.GeolocatorPositionChanged;
}
```

The `PositionAccuracy` enumeration enables you to specify the accuracy level for the location data that the application requires. With this option, you choose either `Default` or `High` accuracy; for the purpose of this example use `Default` accuracy.

5. In Figure 8-3 you can see that the `Geolocator` class defines two events, `StatusChanged` and `PositionChanged`. Following the definition of the constructor, add the following asynchronous event handlers.

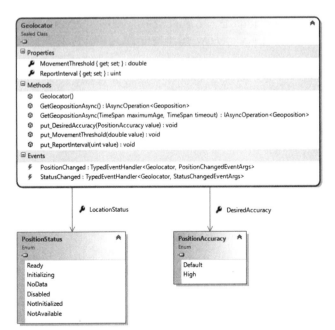

FIGURE 8-3

```
async private void GeolocatorStatusChanged
    (Geolocator sender, StatusChangedEventArgs e)
{
    await Dispatcher.RunAsync(CoreDispatcherPriority.Normal,() =>
    {
        this.GeolocatorStatusTextBlock.Text = e.Status.ToString();
    });
}

async private void GeolocatorPositionChanged
    (Geolocator sender, PositionChangedEventArgs e)
{
    await Dispatcher.RunAsync(CoreDispatcherPriority.Normal,() =>
    {
        this.GeolocatorPositionTextBlock.Text = string.Format("{0}, {1}",
            e.Position.Coordinate.Longitude.ToString(),
            e.Position.Coordinate.Latitude.ToString());
    });
}
```

You might wonder why you are using the CoreDispatcher in the event handlers for the PositionChanged and StatusChanged events. You use the CoreDispatcher because the asynchronous event handlers do not operate upon the UI thread, and only the UI thread can update the state of UI controls.

The GeolocatorStatusChanged event handler receives the current status of the Geolocator as a PositionStatus enumeration contained within the StatusChangedEventArgs class. The Text property of the GeolocatorStatusTextBlock is then set to the status received within the StatusChangedEventArgs instance.

The GeolocatorPositionChanged event handler is where the application becomes location-aware, and it does this through the PositionChangedEventArgs instance that it receives. The PositionChangedEventArgs class provides you the current position as an instance of the Geoposition class. As you'll see in Figure 8-4, the Geoposition class defines two properties: One that provides you with the Geocoordinate representing the current position upon the Earth and the other representing the CivicAddress associated with the current position.

Understanding the CivicAddress Class

You may recognize the CivicAddress class if you've written any location-aware applications on Windows Phone. Compared to its counterpart on Windows Phone, the Windows Runtime version is on a diet and is much leaner. In Windows 8, the CivicAddress associated with a given Geoposition is populated by a specialized device driver that must be present on the user's PC. The specialized device driver populates the CivicAddress information from a third-party provider based on the latitude and longitude that the Geolocator determines.

> **NOTE** *The Windows team recommended that developers requiring accurate civic address information should instead use an appropriate Web API to determine the corresponding civic address for a given latitude and longitude.*

If you run the app now, you may be surprised to see that the PositionStatus is disabled, and therefore the latitude and longitude is unknown. You first need to declare that the app uses the location capability, which asks users whether they want to allow the app to access their location. To do this, follow these steps:

1. Open the Package.appxmanifest file in the Visual Studio 2012 project created above, and click the Capabilities tab.

2. Select the Location capability check box within the list of capabilities.

3. With the Location capability declared, run the application. You will see that Windows 8 asks the user *Can GeoPositionSample Use Your Location?* The user can either allow or block the app's ability to access location information.

If you allow the app to access your location, you see PositionStatus is set to Initializing momentarily and then to Ready. As soon as the PositionStatus is set to Ready, you'll see a display of your current position's latitude and longitude. For example, if you were at the Orlando International Airport (KMCO) you'd see values for latitude near to 28° 25' 45.81" N and longitude of 81° 18' 32.37" W. How cool is that?

Figure 8-4 shows a Visual Studio class diagram illustrating the static class structure for types within the Windows.Devices.Geolocation namespace discussed in the previous example.

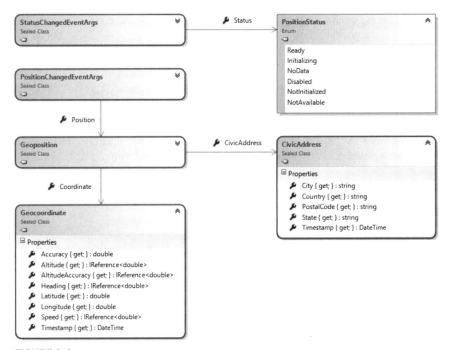

FIGURE 8-4

Recall that the Windows team recommends that developers requiring accurate civic address information should use an appropriate Web API to determine the corresponding civic address for a given latitude and longitude. As an example, the Virtual Earth Locations Web API does exactly that in the following code.

> **NOTE** *The following example requires a Bing Maps key, and you must sign up for a free key to use Bing Maps and Virtual Earth Web APIs in your apps. You can do this easily at the Bing Maps Developer Portal at* https://www .bingmapsportal.com. *You then place the key in the* BingMapsKey *read-only string that follows. You'll use this key in several examples in this chapter, so keep it handy, but remember that you can always access your keys at any time on the Bing Maps Developer Portal.*

```csharp
private readonly string BingMapsKey =
    "TODO: insert your Bing Maps License Key here";

private readonly XNamespace BingMapsNamespace =
    "http://schemas.microsoft.com/search/local/ws/rest/v1";

async private void GetCivicAddress(Location location)
{
    HttpClient client = new HttpClient();

    StringBuilder builder =
        new StringBuilder("http://dev.virtualearth.net/REST/v1/Locations/");

    builder.Append(location.Latitude.ToString());

    builder.Append(",");

    builder.Append(location.Longitude.ToString());

    builder.Append("?o=xml&key=");

    builder.Append(this.BingMapsKey);

    HttpResponseMessage response = await client.GetAsync(builder.ToString());

    response.EnsureSuccessStatusCode();

    Stream stream = await response.Content.ReadAsStreamAsync();

    XDocument document = XDocument.Load(stream);

    string addressLine =
        (from l in document.Descendants(this.BingMapsNamespace + "AddressLine")
        select l).First().Value;

    string city =
        (from l in document.Descendants(this.BingMapsNamespace + "Locality")
        select l).First().Value;

    string stateProvince =
```

```
            (from l in document.Descendants
                (this.BingMapsNamespace + "AdminDistrict")
                    select l).First().Value;

    string postalCode =
            (from l in document.Descendants
                (this.BingMapsNamespace + "PostalCode")
                    select l).First().Value;

    string countryRegion =
            (from l in document.Descendants
                (this.BingMapsNamespace + "CountryRegion")
                    select l).First().Value;
}
```

USING THE BING MAPS SDK

When you have your user's latitude and longitude, or more accurately that of the device, you can now use the Bing Maps SDK for Windows 8 to give users a map showing their current location. This section explores some of the features of the Bing Maps SDK that you can use in your Windows 8 Store apps.

Referencing the Bing Maps SDK

When building Windows Store apps that will use the Bing Maps SDK, you must add references to the following Windows extensions:

➤ Bing Maps for C#, C++, and Visual Basic

➤ Microsoft Visual C++ Runtime Package

> **NOTE** *You can install the Bing Maps SDK for Windows Store apps from Visual Studio 2012 Extensions and Updates available in Visual Studio from the Tools menu. You can also find the Bing Maps SDK for Windows Store apps online by searching the Visual Studio Gallery:* http://visualstudiogallery.msdn .microsoft.com/

To reference the Bing Maps SDK, follow these steps:

1. Open another instance of Visual Studio 2012.

2. Create a new Windows 8-style application using the Blank App (XAML) template, and name the project BingMapsLocation. Notice the small warning symbols overlaid on the newly added extensions because the current target configuration for the project is Any CPU.

3. In the Visual Studio 2012, open the Configuration Manager by clicking Build ⇨ Configuration Manager.

4. Change the target platform from Any CPU to x86, x64, or ARM. Choosing either x64 or ARM can result in an error when you open any XAML file in design view, so you may want to consider targeting x86 initially, even if you ultimately plan to target processors supporting the x64 or ARM instruction sets.

Using the Bing.Maps.Map Class

With the Bing Maps SDK for Windows Store apps referenced within the project you can now add the Map control to the page and then configure the information displayed on the map.

1. With the required changes to the solution made, open the MainPage.xaml file and update the user interface by adding a <Map/> control to the <Grid/> as well as ensuring that the required XML namespace is also defined, as shown in the following code.

```
<Page
    x:Class="BingMapsLocation.MainPage"
    IsTabStop="false"
    xmlns="http://schemas.microsoft.com/winfx/2006/xaml/presentation"
    xmlns:x="http://schemas.microsoft.com/winfx/2006/xaml"
    xmlns:local="using:BingMapsLocation"
    xmlns:d="http://schemas.microsoft.com/expression/blend/2008"
    xmlns:mc="http://schemas.openxmlformats.org/markup-compatibility/2006"
    xmlns:bing="using:Bing.Maps"
    mc:Ignorable="d">

    <Grid Background="{StaticResource ApplicationPageBackgroundThemeBrush}">
        <bing:Map x:Name="Map"
            ZoomLevel="8"
            Credentials="TODO: insert your Bing Maps License Key here "/>
    </Grid>
</Page>
```

2. With the user interface defined in XAML, open the MainPage.xaml.cs file, and add another Geolocator instance above the constructor. You again use the default accuracy for the Geolocator; although, you use only the PositionChanged event this time.

3. In the GeolocatorPositionChanged event handler, create an instance of the Bing.Maps .Location class based on the latitude and longitude that the Geolocator determines. You then use the Location instance to center the map on the user's location using the SetView method of the Map class.

```
public sealed partial class MainPage : Page
{
    private Geolocator locator;

    public MainPage()
    {
        this.InitializeComponent();

        this.locator = new Geolocator();

        this.locator.DesiredAccuracy = PositionAccuracy.Default;

        this.locator.PositionChanged += this.GeolocatorPositionChanged;
    }

    async private void GeolocatorPositionChanged
        (Geolocator sender, PositionChangedEventArgs e)
    {
```

```
await Dispatcher.RunAsync(CoreDispatcherPriority.Normal,() =>
{
    Location location =
        new Location(e.Position.Coordinate.Latitude,

                     e.Position.Coordinate.Longitude);

            this.Map.SetView(location);
});
}

}
```

Figure 8-5 shows that the Geolocator has determined that the author is at the Orlando International Airport where he's awaiting a flight to return home from the Microsoft TechEd North America 2012 conference. You'll notice that while the map is centered on the airport, the lack of a pushpin on the map makes it difficult to determine the location. You'll now explore how to easily add pushpins to the map using the `Bing.Maps.Pushpin` class.

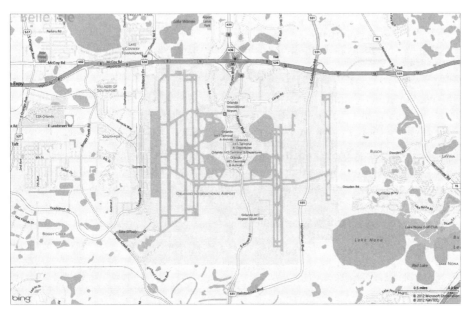

FIGURE 8-5

Using Pushpins on the Map

Using the Bing Maps SDK, you can add pushpins to the map to highlight given locations simply using the `Bing.Maps.Pushpin` class. The advantage of using pushpins is that it makes it easier for you to convey information to the user such as where the nearest Starbucks Coffee stores are located.

You'll now explore how to add pushpins wherever the user taps on the map, assuming a touch-enabled screen, or clicks with the mouse:

1. Open the `MainPage.xaml` file in the `BingMapsLocation` project, and add the `Tapped` event handler, as shown in the following code.

```
<Grid Background="{StaticResource ApplicationPageBackgroundThemeBrush}">
    <bing:Map x:Name="Map"
              ZoomLevel="8"
              Credentials="TODO: insert your Bing Maps License Key here "
              Tapped="MapTapped"/>
</Grid>
```

2. In the `MainPage.xaml.cs` file, add a field to store the count of pushpins you want to place on the map. Use this count in a few moments to set the text displayed in the Pushpin.

```
public sealed partial class MainPage : Page
{
    private Geolocator locator;

    private uint count;

}
```

3. When the user taps the map, you want a pushpin to appear at that location, so you must translate the pixel location on the screen to the appropriate latitude and longitude. The `Bing.Maps.Map` class provides the `TryPixelToLocation` method, which returns true if it can successfully resolve the latitude and longitude for a given pixel on the display. With the latitude and longitude, you can create an instance of the `Bing.Maps.Pushpin` class and then set its position on the map using the `MapLayer.SetPosition` method.

```
private void MapTapped(object sender, TappedRoutedEventArgs e)
{
    var position = e.GetPosition(this.Map);

    Location location;

    if(this.Map.TryPixelToLocation(position, out location))
    {
        Pushpin pin = new Pushpin();

        MapLayer.SetPosition(pin, location);

        pin.Text = (++count).ToString();

        this.Map.Children.Add(pin);

        this.Map.SetView(location);
    }
}
```

Figure 8-6 shows several pushpins displayed on the map after the user taps (or clicks) it.

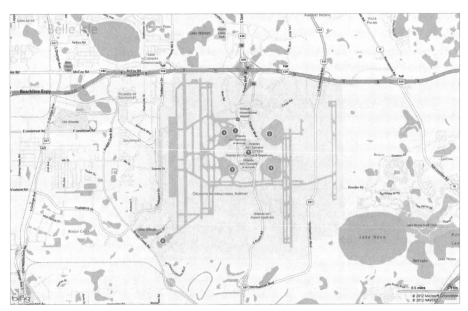

FIGURE 8-6

Adding Traffic Information

Almost anyone who drives these days has used a mapping service such as Bing Maps to explore current traffic conditions and how those traffic conditions might affect their journey. Using the Bing Maps SDK, you can overlay traffic information on your map by setting the `Map.ShowTraffic` property to true, as shown in the following code:

```
public MainPage()
{
    this.InitializeComponent();

    this.locator = new Geolocator();

    this.locator.DesiredAccuracy = PositionAccuracy.Default;

    this.locator.PositionChanged += this.GeolocatorPositionChanged;

    this.Map.ShowTraffic = true;
}
```

In Figure 8-7, you can see the result of showing traffic in the `BingMapsLocation` project. Severe traffic would appear as a red overlay, whereas moderate traffic appears as a yellow overlay. A green overlay indicates no significant traffic.

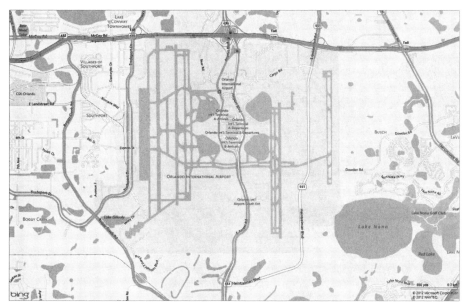

FIGURE 8-7

It wasn't that long ago that satellite imagery was something only intelligence agencies and the armed forces had access to. Today, access to such imagery is almost ubiquitous.

Using the `Bing.Maps.MapType` enumeration, you can display your map using the default road imagery using `MapType.Road`, an aerial view — such as what's shown in Figure 8-8 using `MapType.Aerial` — or a bird's eye view, as shown in Figure 8-9 using `MapType.BirdsEye`.

```
public MainPage()
{
    this.InitializeComponent();

    this.locator = new Geolocator();

    this.locator.DesiredAccuracy = PositionAccuracy.Default;

    this.locator.PositionChanged += this.GeolocatorPositionChanged;

    this.Map.MapType = MapType.Aerial;
}
```

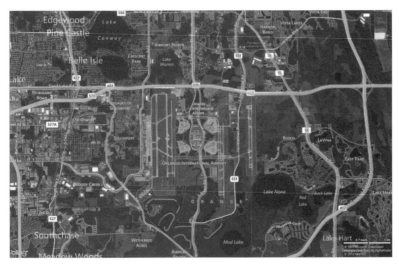

FIGURE 8-8

FIGURE 8-9

GETTING DIRECTIONS

Another common scenario for location-aware applications, especially upon mobile platforms, is to provide directions for the user between two locations. Although the Bing Maps SDK for Windows Store apps does not provide this capability, you can use another Web API to determine directions for walking, driving, or even using public transit.

> **NOTE** *You can find more information on the Routes Web API on MSDN:*
> `http://msdn.microsoft.com/en-us/library/ff701705.`

Enabling Directions with Pushpins

To enable users to get directions, follow these steps:

1. Open Visual Studio 2012 and create a new Windows 8-style application using the Blank App (XAML) template and name the project `BingMapsDirections`.

2. Open the `MainPage.xaml` file in the `BingMapsDirections` project, and add the following markup:

```
<Grid Background="{StaticResource ApplicationPageBackgroundThemeBrush}">
    <bing:Map x:Name="Map"
            ZoomLevel="8"
            Credentials="TODO: insert your Bing Maps License Key here "
            Tapped="MapTapped"/>
    <Grid Background="Black"
        Width="300" Height="100"
        Margin="10,658,1056,10"
        Opacity="0.85">
        <TextBlock x:Name="DistanceTextBlock"
                VerticalAlignment="Center"
                HorizontalAlignment="Center"
                FontSize="36"
                Foreground="White"
                Text="0.0 miles"/>
    </Grid>
</Grid>
```

3. Open the `MainPage.xaml.cs` file in the `BingMapsDirections` project and add the following fields:

```
private readonly string BingMapsKey =
"TODO: insert your Bing Maps License Key here";

private readonly XNamespace BingMapsNamespace =
    "http://schemas.microsoft.com/search/local/ws/rest/v1";

private Geolocator locator;

private uint count;
```

4. In the constructor, initialize an instance of the `Geolocator` class as well as a new collection for the way-points along the route.

```
public MainPage()
{
    this.InitializeComponent();

    this.way-points = new List<string>();

    this.locator = new Geolocator();

    this.locator.DesiredAccuracy = PositionAccuracy.Default;

    this.locator.PositionChanged += this.GeolocatorPositionChanged;
}
```

5. Define a property called `WayPoints` of type `List<string>` to contain the list of way-points along the route.

```
public List<string> WayPoints
{
    get;
    set;
}
```

6. Add the event handler for the `PositionChanged` event that will center the map to the current position.

```
async private void GeolocatorPositionChanged
    (Geolocator sender, PositionChangedEventArgs e)
{
    await Dispatcher.RunAsync(CoreDispatcherPriority.Normal,() =>
    {
        Location location = new Location(e.Position.Coordinate.Latitude,
                             e.Position.Coordinate.Longitude);

        this.Map.SetView(location);
    });
}
```

7. Add the event handler for the `MapTapped` event that will determine the `Location` on the map that was tapped (or clicked) and then call the `GetDirections` method to update the directions.

```
private void MapTapped(object sender, TappedRoutedEventArgs e)
{
    var position = e.GetPosition(this.Map);

    Location location;

    if(this.Map.TryPixelToLocation(position, out location))
    {
        Pushpin pin = new Pushpin();

        MapLayer.SetPosition(pin, location);

        pin.Text = (++count).ToString();

        this.Map.Children.Add(pin);

        this.Map.SetView(location);

        this.GetDirections(location);
    }
}
```

8. Add the asynchronous `GetDirections` method to call the Routes Web API to get the directions. The `MapPolyline` class is then used to draw the route of travel upon the map.

```
async private void GetDirections(Location location)
{
    this.WayPoints.Add(string.Format("{0}, {1}",
```

```
    location.Latitude, location.Longitude));

    if(this.WayPoints.Count < 2) return;

    HttpClient client = new HttpClient();

    StringBuilder builder = new StringBuilder
        ("http://dev.virtualearth.net/REST/V1/Routes/Driving?o=xml&");

    for (int index = 0; index < this.WayPoints.Count; index++)
    {
        builder.Append(
            string.Format("wp.{0}={1}&", index, this.WayPoints[index]));
    }

    builder.Append("avoid=minimizeTolls&key=");

    builder.Append(this.BingMapsKey);

    HttpResponseMessage response = await client.GetAsync(builder.ToString());

    response.EnsureSuccessStatusCode();
    Stream stream = await response.Content.ReadAsStreamAsync();

    XDocument document = XDocument.Load(stream);

    var query = from p
        in document.Descendants(this.BingMapsNamespace + "ManeuverPoint")
            select new
        {
            Latitude = p.Element(this.BingMapsNamespace + "Latitude").Value,
            Longitude = p.Element(this.BingMapsNamespace + "Longitude").Value
            };

    MapShapeLayer layer = new MapShapeLayer();

    MapPolyline polyline = new MapPolyline();

    foreach (var point in query)
    {
        double latitude, longitude;

        double.TryParse(point.Latitude, out latitude);
        double.TryParse(point.Longitude, out longitude);

        polyline.Locations.Add(new Location(latitude, longitude));
    }

    polyline.Color = Colors.Red;

    polyline.Width = 5;

    layer.Shapes.Add(polyline);

    this.Map.ShapeLayers.Add(layer);
```

```
        in document.Descendants
            (this.BingMapsNamespace + "TravelDistance")
        select d).First().Value;

    this.DistanceTextBlock.Text =
        string.Format("{0} miles", distance.ToString());
}
```

If you run the application now, you can calculate a route from Jacksonville, FL to Miami, FL via Tampa, FL (see Figure 8-10). Using the Routes Web API, you can see that the distance is approximately 785 miles.

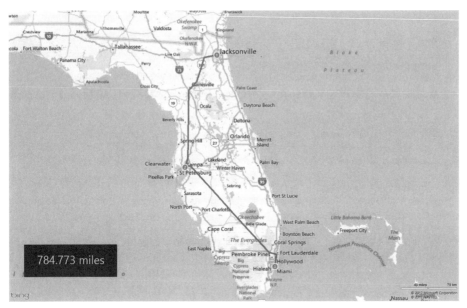

FIGURE 8-10

You can also see that the `MapPolyLines` have also been added to the map; they show each of the maneuvering points along the route. Note that the lines aren't following the highways accurately along the route because the maneuvering points do not provide enough precision but are instead describing points along the route where the driver must maneuver, such as Take Ramp Left and Follow Signs for I-95 South.

When you call the Routes Web API, you can specify that you want more precision. In response, the API then returns more points to generate a more accurate route of travel. You must specify that you want these additional points, however, noting that because they increase the length of the response from the service. You can specify that you want these additional points using the `routePathOutput` parameter, which you can make either `None`, the default if omitted, or `Points`. If you specify `Points` you'll be provided a list of point values for the route's path.

```
builder.Append("routePathOutput=Points&avoid=minimizeTolls&key=");
```

You must then change the LINQ query by simply changing `ManeuverPoint` to `Point`.

```
var query = from p
            in document.Descendants(this.BingMapsNamespace + "ManeuverPoint")
            select new
            {
                Latitude = p.Element(this.BingMapsNamespace + "Latitude").Value,
                Longitude = p.Element(this.BingMapsNamespace + "Longitude").Value
            };
```

When you calculate the route of travel after these code changes; you will see a route of travel on the map that more accurately follows the route of travel such as in Figure 8-11.

FIGURE 8-11

Another important optional parameter is the tolerances parameter, which you can specify whenever you set the `routePathOutput` parameter to `Points`. Using this parameter, you specify tolerances that reduce the number of points needed to display a route on a map but still maintain the route shape. Consider using this parameter to ensure adequate performance. For example, if you calculate the route of travel between Seattle, WA and Washington, DC, you can see the performance impact that a large number of points can impose on an application; without specifying tolerances for this 4,644-mile trip, your route contains almost 10,000 points!

SUMMARY

In this chapter you learned about geolocation and how to enable location awareness within your Windows Store apps. You also explored the Locations and Routes Web APIs to determine the civic address associated with given locations on the Earth and then calculate routes between different locations. Using the Bing Maps SDK, you saw how you can easily display information on a map and display routes of travel.

Application Contracts and Extensions

WROX.COM CODE DOWNLOAD FOR THIS CHAPTER

You can find the wrox.com code downloads for this chapter in code file 205709 C09.zip at `www.wrox.com/remtitle.cgi?isbn=1118205707` on the Download Code tab. The code for this chapter is conveniently contained in a single Visual Studio 2012 solution with eight sample projects.

APP CONTRACTS AND EXTENSIONS

Windows Store apps use contracts and extensions to declare interactions that are supported with Windows and other Windows Store apps. You can think of an *Application Contract* as an agreement between one or more Windows Store apps. It defines requirements that each app must satisfy for them to participate in the given interaction. An *Extension* is an agreement between an app and the Windows operating system. Using extensions, developers can extend the capabilities of Windows features primarily within their own Windows Store apps and potentially within other Windows Store apps.

In this chapter, you explore each of the Application Contracts and extensions to gain an appreciation for how apps you write can benefit from them. Although you'll gain an appreciation for each of the contracts and extensions, this chapter is intended to provide you with an overview of them and does not provide an exhaustive description of each.

Windows 8 provides support for the following Application Contracts:

- ➤ File Picker
- ➤ Cached File Updater
- ➤ Play To
- ➤ Search
- ➤ Settings
- ➤ Share

Windows 8 provides support for the following extensions:

- ➤ Account Picture Provider
- ➤ AutoPlay
- ➤ Background Tasks
- ➤ Camera Settings
- ➤ Contact Picker
- ➤ File Activation
- ➤ Game Explorer
- ➤ Print Task Settings
- ➤ Protocol Activation
- ➤ SSL/Certificates

USING THE FILE PICKER CONTRACT

Windows Store apps use the File Picker Contract to enable users to select files, chose a save location, or update existing files.

Using the `FileOpenPicker` class your app can enable the user to select and open one or more files. For example, in the Visual Studio 2012 solution for this chapter, you'll find the PhotoChooser app, which uses the `FileOpenPicker` class, so users can select either a single photo or multiple photos and then display the images within a FlipView control.

Selecting a Single File

In the `SelectSinglePhotoButton_Click` event handler, a new `FileOpenPicker` instance is created and configured to initially open in the user's Pictures Library. It is then configured, so users can select files with .png, .jpg, or .jpeg extensions. Then the asynchronous `PickSingleFileAsync` method is called and returns a `StorageFile` instance representing the file the user chooses. Assuming that the `StorageFile` is not `null`, the file is read asynchronously using the `OpenReadAsync` method and the resulting stream is used to set the source of the image:

```
private async void SelectSinglePhotoButton_Click(object sender, RoutedEventArgs e)
{
    FileOpenPicker picker = new FileOpenPicker();

    picker.ViewMode = PickerViewMode.Thumbnail;

    picker.SuggestedStartLocation = PickerLocationId.PicturesLibrary;

    picker.FileTypeFilter.Add(".png");

    picker.FileTypeFilter.Add(".jpg");

    picker.FileTypeFilter.Add(".jpeg");

    StorageFile file = await picker.PickSingleFileAsync();

    var photos = new ObservableCollection<PhotoViewModel>;

    if (file != null)
    {
        IRandomAccessStream stream = await file.OpenReadAsync();

        BitmapImage image = new BitmapImage();

        image.SetSource(stream);

        photos.Add(new PhotoViewModel()
        {
            Image = image
        });
    }

    this.SelectedPhotoFlipView.ItemsSource = photos;
}
```

Selecting Multiple Files

Essentially, the `SelectMultiplePhotosButton_Click` event handler, shown in the following code, is similar; although, the asynchronous `PickMultipleFilesAsync` method retrieves an `IReadOnlyList<StorageFile>` representing the photos the user chooses.

```
private async void SelectMultiplePhotosButton_Click
    (object sender, RoutedEventArgs e)
{
    FileOpenPicker picker = new FileOpenPicker();

    picker.ViewMode = PickerViewMode.Thumbnail;

    picker.SuggestedStartLocation = PickerLocationId.PicturesLibrary;
```

```
picker.FileTypeFilter.Add(".png");

picker.FileTypeFilter.Add(".jpg");

picker.FileTypeFilter.Add(".jpeg");

IReadOnlyList<StorageFile> files = await picker.PickMultipleFilesAsync();

if (files != null)
{
    var photos = new ObservableCollection<PhotoViewModel>;

    for (int index = 0; index < files.Count; index++)
    {
        IRandomAccessStream stream = await file.OpenReadAsync();

        BitmapImage image = new BitmapImage();

        image.SetSource(stream);

        photos.Add(new PhotoViewModel()
        {
            Image = image
        });
    }
}

    this.SelectedPhotoFlipView.ItemsSource = photos;
}
```

If you run the PhotoChooser sample and click the button to select a single photo or multiple photos, you'll see a file picker similar to that shown in Figure 9-1. You may have noticed in the previous code, the `SuggestedStartLocation` property sets the initial start location as the user's Pictures Library. The user can then click the chevron next to *Files* for a drop-down list of other locations from which you can select files. The drop-down list not only includes common locations such as libraries but also other Windows Store apps that implement the File Open Picker Contract! In Figure 9-2 you can see several such apps listed.

FIGURE 9-1

Selecting Files from Windows Store Apps

To illustrate the ability to select files directly from other Windows Store apps, right-click the SkyDrive Photos sample app in the Visual Studio 2012 Solution Explorer and select Deploy. If you then use the PhotoChooser sample to select one or more photos, you'll see the SkyDrive Photos app appears in the list when the chevron is clicked. In Figure 9-2 you can see several apps that support the File Open Picker Contract such as the Box, Camera, Photos, SkyDrive, and of course the SkyDrive Photos app.

> **NOTE** *The SkyDrive Photos sample is used extensively in this chapter to illustrate various Application Contracts and extensions, so you'll gradually become very familiar with the code in that project.*

The following steps help you explore the SkyDrive Photos app and how it enables users of other apps to select photos from SkyDrive:

1. Open the Application Contracts and Extensions solution, from the books sample code in Visual Studio 2012. You can find the project for the SkyDrive Photos in the Application Contracts\File Picker Contract solution folder.

2. Open the App.xaml.cs file in the SkyDrivePhotos project and find the following asynchronous method, which is responsible for displaying the file picker shown in Figure 9-2.

FIGURE 9-2

```
protected async override void OnFileOpenPickerActivated
    (FileOpenPickerActivatedEventArgs e)
{
    await this.GetLiveConnectSession();

    var picker = new FileOpenPickerPage();

    picker.Activate(e);
}
```

This code first establishes a connection to SkyDrive using the Windows LIVE SDK and then creates and activates a new instance of the `FileOpenPickerPage` class.

> **NOTE** *The SkyDrive Photos app requires you to install the Windows LIVE SDK, which you can downloaded from:* http://go.microsoft.com/fwlink/?LinkID=242807

In Figure 9-3, you can see that three photos are selected. When the user clicks the Open button, the asynchronous `PickMultipleFilesAsync` method returns the list of selected files in an `IReadOnlyList<StorageFile>`.

Selected photos

FIGURE 9-3

In the `SelectMultiplePhotosButton_Click` event handler, the asynchronous `OpenReadAsync` method reads each of these files and adds them to a view model collection that the `FlipView` control is then bound to. Figure 9-4 shows the photos selected within the SkyDrive Photos app displayed within the `FlipView` control within the Photo Chooser app.

FIGURE 9-4

Debugging File Picker Activation

As developers, we often need to debug our apps to isolate and resolve issues with the code we've written. When Windows Store apps are activated using File Picker Activation (as well as other methods of activation explored in this chapter) you must indicate to Visual Studio that instead of launching the app it should debug your code when it starts. To do so, follow these simple steps:

1. Open the Debug tab in the project properties Window for the SkyDrive Photos app.

2. Select the "Do not launch, but debug my code when it starts" check box under the Start Action heading as shown in Figure 9-5. Using this option, Visual Studio allows you to place, and subsequently hit, breakpoints in the overridden `OnFileOpenPickerActivated` method.

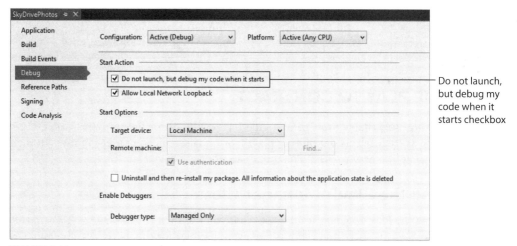

FIGURE 9-5

3. With Visual Studio configured to debug file picker activation, open the PhotoChooser app, and then click one of the two buttons to either select a single photo or multiple photos.

4. Select the SkyDrive Photos app as the location from which you want to select the photos. Any breakpoints in the SkyDrive Photos app will be hit.

> **NOTE** *You can insert breakpoints in Visual Studio by placing the cursor on the given line of code and pressing F9. Pressing F9 again removes the breakpoint. Breakpoints can be disabled by pressing Ctrl+F9.*

5. With the option "Do not launch, but debug my code when it starts" selected within the project properties, you can now start debugging by pressing F5. The app does not launch; but rather the debugger prepares to debug the app when it is activated.

USING THE CACHED FILE UPDATER CONTRACT

Windows Store apps that use the File Picker Contract can also utilize the Cached File Updater Contract to enable real-time file synchronization if the files are stored in a cloud-based repository, such as Microsoft SkyDrive. The official SkyDrive app on Windows 8 uses this contract so that files either picked from, or saved to, SkyDrive can seamlessly update or refresh. If the SkyDrive Photos app you explored in the section "Selecting Files from Windows Store Apps" were to implement the Cached File Updater Contract, you could open photos from SkyDrive, edit them in an image editing app, and automatically replicate those edits to the original photos in the SkyDrive album.

> **NOTE** *The Cached File Updater Contract is designed for apps that provide storage, typically cloud-based, from which users access or save files. It is likely that your app will not require you to implement this contract; although, if it is necessary, you can use the following Quickstart on MSDN.* http://msdn .microsoft.com/en-us/library/windows/apps/hh465192.aspx.

USING THE PLAY TO CONTRACT

Windows Store apps enable users to play video, view photos, or listen to music on DNLA-certified devices, such as their television, Blu-ray player, or touchscreen computer monitor. In the following example you explore how to play video on an appropriate device.

Introducing the PlayToManager Class

Implementing the Play To Contract requires that you use the `PlayToManager` class in the `Windows .Media.PlayTo` namespace and establish an event handler for the `SourceRequested` event. The `SourceRequested` event occurs when a user requests media to stream to an appropriate device.

```
PlayToManager manager = new PlayToManager();

manager.SourceRequested += this.PlayToManager_SourceRequested;

manager.SourceSelected += this.PlayToManager_SourceSelected;
```

Another event that the `PlayToManager` class provides is the `SourceSelected` event, which occurs when an appropriate source element is selected. Using an event handler for this event, an app can discover the name of the selected device and its capabilities, such as whether it can play audio and video or display images.

In the following markup, a `MediaElement` is declared that plays an MP4 format video.

```
<Grid Background="{StaticResource ApplicationPageBackgroundThemeBrush}">
    <MediaElement x:Name="MediaElement"
                  AutoPlay="True"
                  IsLooping="True"
                  Source="Media/iStock_000020635487BigWeb.mp4"/>

    <Grid x:Name="DeviceInformationGrid" Background="Black"
          Width="300" Height="100"
```

```
            Margin="10,658,1056,10"
            Opacity="0.85"
            Visibility="Collapsed">
        <TextBlock x:Name="DeviceInformationTextBlock"
                   VerticalAlignment="Center" HorizontalAlignment="Center"
                   FontSize="36" Foreground="White" Text="Disconnected"/>
    </Grid>
</Grid>
```

When the user selects the Devices charm, the event handler for the `SourceRequested` event assigns an appropriate source provided by the `MediaElement` class. You can use a deferral if you want to retrieve the media element to stream using an asynchronous call. When using the deferral, Play To waits until the deferral is marked as complete before continuing.

```
private async void PlayToManager_SourceRequested
    (PlayToManager sender, PlayToSourceRequestedEventArgs e)
{
    var deferral = e.SourceRequest.GetDeferral();

    await Dispatcher.RunAsync(CoreDispatcherPriority.Normal, () =>
    {
        e.SourceRequest.SetSource(this.VideoPlayerMediaElement.PlayToSource);

        deferral.Complete();
    });
}
```

The `Windows.UI.Xaml.Controls.Image` class also provides the `PlayToSource` property to enable images to display on an appropriate device. Using an event handler for the `SourceSelected` event, an app can determine the friendly name of the device the user has chosen as the target device as well as the capabilities of the device. The `PlayToSourceSelectedEventArgs` class provides properties indicating whether the device supports audio, video, or the display of images.

```
private void PlayToManager_SourceSelected
    (PlayToManager sender, PlayToSourceSelectedEventArgs e)
{
    await Dispatcher.RunAsync(CoreDispatcherPriority.Normal, () =>
    {
        this.DeviceInformationTextBlock.Text = e.FriendlyName;

        if (this.DeviceInformationTextBlock.Visibility == Visibility.Collapsed)
        {
            this.DeviceInformationTextBlock.Visibility = Visibility.Visible;
        }
    });
}
```

You can also access an icon representing the selected device. The following event handler illustrates how the icon image can display.

```
private void PlayToManager_SourceSelected
    (PlayToManager sender, PlayToSourceSelectedEventArgs e)
{
    await Dispatcher.RunAsync(CoreDispatcherPriority.Normal, () =>
    {
```

```
            BitmapImage image = new BitmapImage();

            image.SetSource(e.Icon);

            this.DeviceIconImage.Source = image;
        });
    }
```

Testing PlayTo Scenarios

With the Video Player app, you are now ready to test video playback using the Play To Contract and an appropriate DNLA device. While writing this chapter, the author tested the Video Player app against a Samsung UN46D6500 LED television. You should see supported devices that are connected to your network in the Devices and Printers control panel, as shown in Figure 9-6. If you do not see your devices, you must ensure they are appropriately connected to the network and then select the *Add a Device* option. To test the PlayTo scenario, follow these steps:

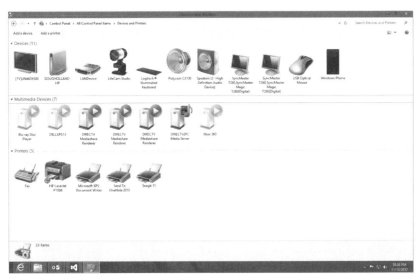

FIGURE 9-6

1. Open the Application Contracts and Extensions solution in Visual Studio 2012.

2. Ensure that the Video Player project is set as the Startup project.

3. Build and run the Video Player project.

4. Select the Devices charm. You see a list of devices that can receive content from the Video Player app. In Figure 9-7, the Samsung UN46D6500 television is listed as such a device.

FIGURE 9-7

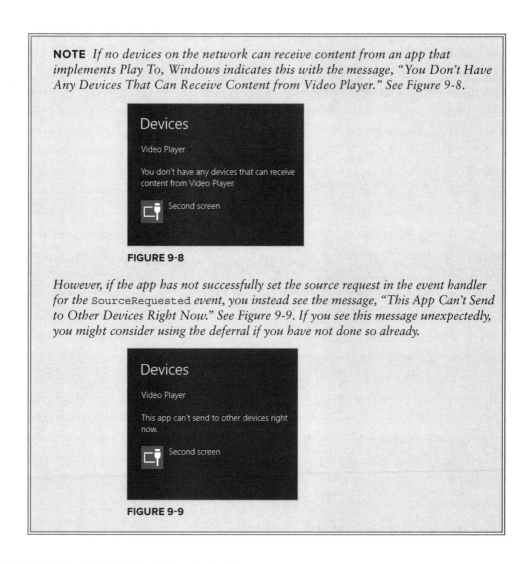

NOTE *If no devices on the network can receive content from an app that implements Play To, Windows indicates this with the message, "You Don't Have Any Devices That Can Receive Content from Video Player." See Figure 9-8.*

FIGURE 9-8

However, if the app has not successfully set the source request in the event handler for the `SourceRequested` *event, you instead see the message, "This App Can't Send to Other Devices Right Now." See Figure 9-9. If you see this message unexpectedly, you might consider using the deferral if you have not done so already.*

FIGURE 9-9

USING THE SEARCH CONTRACT

With the Search charm, the concept of search has been elevated from individual Windows Store apps to the Windows operating system. Search is one of the pivotal contracts from which almost all apps can benefit.

In most cases, an app that implements the Search Contract will do so consistently throughout the app, which means that the search experience is exactly the same regardless of where in the app the user is. Therefore, the `Windows.UI.Xaml.Application` class contains a virtual method that is called whenever the app is activated using the Search charm.

If you open the Visual Studio 2012 solution accompanying this chapter, you can find the Netflix Search sample app in the Application Contracts\Search Contract solution folder. Netflix Search uses the OData feed that Netflix provides. The App.xaml.cs file has the App class, which overrides the OnSearchActivated method from the base Application class.

In the overridden OnSearchActivated method, the app establishes the search query entered in the Search flyout, which is provided by the SearchActivatedEventArgs class. It then navigates to the SearchResultsPage passing the query text as the navigation parameter.

```
protected async override void OnSearchActivated(SearchActivatedEventArgs e)
{
    var previousContent = Window.Current.Content;

    var frame = previousContent as Frame;

    if (frame == null)
    {
        frame = new Frame();

        SuspensionManager.RegisterFrame(frame, "AppFrame");

        if (e.PreviousExecutionState == ApplicationExecutionState.Terminated)
        {
            try
            {
            }
            catch(SuspensionManagerException)
            {
            }
        }
    }

    frame.Navigate(typeof(SearchResultsPage), e.QueryText);

    Window.Current.Content = frame;

    Window.Current.Activate();
}
```

In cases where you want a contextual search experience, the active page can use the SearchPane class and establish an event handler for the QuerySubmitted event.

```
public GroupedItemsPage()
{
    SearchPane.GetForCurrentView().QuerySubmitted += this.OnQuerySubmitted;
}
```

If you were to write an app that provided e-mail and a calendar, you could use the Tuple class to pass an enumeration describing the search type as well as the query text. In the SearchResultsPage, the search could then be performed in the context of the calendar.

```
private void OnQuerySubmitted
    (SearchPane sender, SearchPaneQuerySubmittedEventArgs e)
{
    var previousContent = Window.Current.Content;

    var frame = previousContent as Frame;

    if (frame == null)
```

```
        {
            frame = new Frame();
        }

        frame.Navigate(typeof(SearchResultsPage),
            new Tuple<SearchType, string>(SearchType.Calendar, e.QueryText));

        Window.Current.Content = frame;

        Window.Current.Activate();
    }
```

Visual Studio 2012 provides a template for the Search Contract, which you can add to a Windows Store app project by following these steps:

1. Right-click the project, select Add New Item, and then select Search Contract.

2. Complete the implementation of the `OnSearchActivated` method, which the template adds.

3. Complete the implementation of the `SearchResultsPage` class, which the template adds.

The updated `Package.appxmanifest` with the Search declaration is shown in Figure 9-10.

> **NOTE** *The Netflix Search sample depends on the WCF Data Services Tools for Windows Store apps, which you can download from* `http://www.microsoft` `.com/en-us/download/details.aspx?id=30714.`

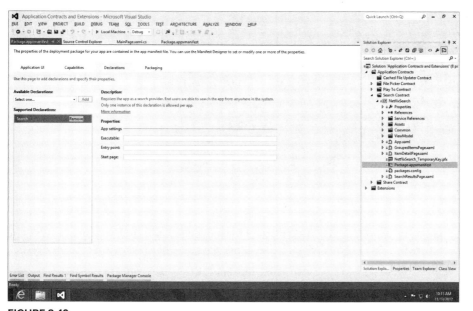

FIGURE 9-10

In `NetflixViewModel`, the movies for a given release year are retrieved using the LINQ query in the code segment that follows. Figure 9-11 shows the results.

```
private async Task<IEnumerable<Title>> GetTitles()
{
    if (this.context == null)
    {
        this.context =
            new NetflixCatalog(new Uri(@http://odata.netflix.com/v2/Catalog,
                UriKind.RelativeOrAbsolute));
    }

    IEnumerable<Title> titles
        = await ((DataServiceQuery<Title>)
            this.context.Titles
            .Where(title => title.ReleaseYear == this.ReleaseYear &&
                    title.Rating == "PG" &&
                    (title.BoxArt.HighDefinitionUrl != null ||
                     Title.BoxArt.HighDefinitionUrl == string.Empty))
            .OrderByDescending(title => title.AverageRating)
            .Take(12)).ExecuteAsync()'

    return titles;
}
```

FIGURE 9-11

The `NetflixViewModel` class provides a static method for implementing search that uses a LINQ query to return movies where the query text is contained in either the name of the movie or the synopsis.

```
private async static Task<ObservableCollection<Title>> Search(string queryText)
{
    NetflixCatalog context =
            new NetflixCatalog(new Uri(@http://odata.netflix.com/v2/Catalog,
                UriKind.RelativeOrAbsolute));

    IEnumerable<Title> titles
```

```
        = await ((DataServiceQuery<Title>)
            context.Titles
            .Where(title => title.Name.Contains(queryText) ||
                            title.Synopsis.Contains(queryText) &&
                    (title.BoxArt.HighDefinitionUrl != null ||
                        Title.BoxArt.HighDefinitionUrl == string.Empty))
            .OrderByDescending(title => title.AverageRating)
            .Take(12)).ExecuteAsync()'

    return new ObservableCollection<Title>(titles);
}
```

The Search method is called from the SearchResultsPage in the following LoadState method. Figure 9-12 shows the results.

```
protected async override void LoadState
    (object navigationalParameter, Dictionary<string, object> pageState)
{
    var queryText = navigationParameter as string;

    this.DefaultViewModel["QueryText"] = '\u201c' + queryText + '\u201d';

    var results = await NetflixViewModel.Search(queryText);

    this.DefaultViewModel["Results"] = results;

    var filterList = new List<Filter>();

    filterList.Add(new Filter("All", 0, true));

    this.DefaultViewModel["Filters"] = filterList;

    this.DefaultViewModel["ShowFilters"] = filterList.Count > 1;
}
```

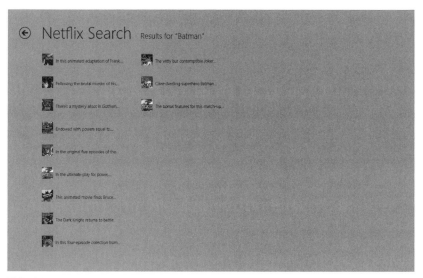

FIGURE 9-12

USING THE SETTINGS CONTRACT

The Windows 8 Settings charm gives users a consistent way to access settings for Windows and Windows Store apps.

In the SkyDrive Photos sample app, the constructor for the `GroupedItemsPage` establishes an event handler for the `SettingsPage.CommandsRequested` event.

```
SettingsPane.GetForCurrentView().CommandsRequested += this.OnCommandsRequested;
```

`SettingsPage.CommandsRequested` occurs when the user opens the Settings pane using the Settings charm. In the event handler, you then create `SettingsCommand` instances to represent each command you want to be listed in the Settings pane.

The SkyDrive Photos app uses Callisto, a control library written by Tim Heuer, available via NuGet or the Visual Studio Gallery. You can install Callisto using the following command in the Visual Studio Package Manager Console.

```
PM> Install-Package Callisto
```

Callisto has several controls for Windows Store app developers using C# and XAML, including the `Flyout` and `SettingsFlyout` classes. If you've also explored writing Windows Store apps using HTML5 and JavaScript, you might be aware that WinJS provides developers with a `Flyout` control commonly used to implement app settings. Unfortunately, no such control exists natively for C# developers.

The `SettingsFlyout` class, found in the `Callisto.Controls` namespace, represents a customizable flyout window. You can then use a user control to define the settings or information on the flyout. You add this to the flyout using the `Content` property of the `SettingsFlyout` class.

```
private void OnCommandsRequested(SettingsPane sender,
    SettingsPaneCommandsRequestedEventArgs e)
{
    SettingsCommand about = new SettingsCommand("AboutSettingsCommandId",
                                                "About",
                                                (handler) =>
    {
        SettingsFlyout settings = new SettingsFlyout();

        settings.HeaderBrush = new SolidColorBrush(Color.FromArgb(255, 50, 50, 50);

        settings.Background = new SolidColorBrush(Colors.White);

        AboutSettingUserControl content = new AboutSettingUserControl;

        settings.Content = content;

        settings.HeaderText = "About";

        settings.IsOpen = true;
    });

    e.Request.ApplicationCommands.Add(about);
}
```

Windows configures Windows Store apps with the Permissions command as shown in Figure 9-13. Any apps installed with Windows, or via the Windows Store, will additionally provide the Rate and Review command. You are not required to write a single line of code for these commands. In Figure 9-14 you can see the About flyout in the SkyDrive Photos app.

FIGURE 9-13

The About flyout

FIGURE 9-14

USING THE SHARE CONTRACT

With Windows Store apps, you have the potential to create truly global apps, and with the Share Contract, you no longer need to write custom code for specific social networks. Although Facebook and Twitter are the most prevalent social networks in the United States today, different social networks are more prevalent in other countries. Without the Share Contract app, developers would need to write custom code so users could share to a variety of social networks and have a great global experience. With the Share Contract, however, the concept of sharing has been elevated from Windows Store apps to the Windows operating system. Using the Share charm, users have a consistent share experience whereby they elect the information they want to share as well as the apps with which they want to share that information.

Introducing the DataTransferManager Class

Implementing the Share Contract requires that you use the `DataTransferManager` class and establish an event handler for the `DataRequested` event. The `DataTransferManager` class also offers you the opportunity to discover the name of the application the user chooses to receive the information shared by using the `TargetApplicationChosen` event.

```
DataTransferManager manager = new DataTransferManager();

manager.DataRequested += this.DataTransferManager_DataRequested;

manager.TargetApplicationChosen +=
    this.DataTransferManager_TargetApplicationChosen;
```

DataTransferManager.DataRequested

The `DataRequested` event occurs when either the user selects the Share charm or an app initiates the sharing operation programmatically.

The SkyDrive Photos app uses the Share Contract to allow users to send photos to friends and family. The event handler for the `DataRequested` event initially establishes the photo that is currently selected and then sets the title and description. The `StringBuilder` class then constructs HTML that displays the photo and a link to open the photo in the SkyDrive Photos app if the user is running Windows 8.

```
private void DataTransferManager_DataRequested
    (DataTransferManager sender, DataRequestedEventArgs e)
{
    SkyDrivePhoto photo = SkyDrivePhotoFlipView.SelectedItem as SkyDrivePhoto;

    e.Request.Data.Properties.Title = "SkyDrive Photos";

    e.Request.Data.Properties.Description = "Shares this photo";

    StringBuilder builder = new StringBuilder("<img src=\"");

    builder.Append(photo.Source);

    builder.Append("\"><br/><b>If you have Windows 8, <a href=\"");
    builder.Append("skydrivephotos://?id=");

    builder.Append(photo.Id);

    builder.Append("\">");

    builder.Append("open this in SkyDrive Photos.</a></b>");

    e.Request.Data.SetHtmlFormat
    (HtmlFormatHelper.CreateHtmlFormat(builder.ToString()));
}
```

DataTransferManager.TargetApplicationChosen

The `TargetApplicationChosen` event occurs when users select the target application for the sharing operation. The `TargetApplicationChosenEventArgs` class provides the `ApplicationName` property.

```
private void DataTransferManager_TargetApplicationChosen
    (DataTransferManager sender, TargetApplicationChosenEventArgs e)
{
    string target = e.ApplicationName;
}
```

Share Contract Scenarios

Windows Store app developers should consider using the Share Contract for any scenario where information is shared from one app to another. You might think of the Share Contract as an enhanced cut-and-paste capability.

Imagine you are a developer for a major online retailer and you've been asked to design and develop an app to enable users to perform comparative shopping. The Share Contract enables such an app to receive product information, as a share target, and then provides pricing for the same product from your company.

The Share Contract enables many innovative solutions to common tasks users perform each day, so consider how your app can both provide and receive information using the Share Contract.

USING THE ACCOUNT PICTURE PROVIDER EXTENSION

Users can decide to change their account picture either using an existing picture or using an appropriate app from the Windows Store. If your app can take pictures, you can use the Account Picture Provider extension and Windows lists your app in the Account Picture Settings control panel, as shown in Figure 9-15. By default on Windows 8 the only app that implements this extension is the Camera app. If you build and deploy the AccountPictureProvider sample app from this chapter, you will see it listed alongside the Camera app and any other such apps.

FIGURE 9-15

In the following code segment, the OnNavigatedTo method uses the UserInformation class to access the small account picture, large account picture, and account video. You can find the UserInformation class in the Windows.System.UserProfile namespace.

```
protected async override void OnNavigatedTo(NavigationEventArgs e)
{
    StorageFile smallAccountPicture =
        UserInformation.GetAccountPicture(AccountPictureKind.SmallImage)
            as StorageFile;

    if (smallAccountPicture != null)
    {
        IRandomAccessStream stream = await smallAccountPicture.OpenReadAsync();

        BitmapImage image = new BitmapImage();
```

```
        image.SetSource(stream);

        this.SmallAccountPictureImage.Height = image.PixelHeight;

        this.SmallAccountPictureImage.Width = image.PixelWidth;

        this.SmallAccountPictureImage.Source = image;
    }

    StorageFile largeAccountPicture =
        UserInformation.GetAccountPicture(AccountPictureKind.LargeImage)
            as StorageFile;

    if (largeAccountPicture != null)
    {
        IRandomAccessStream stream = await largeAccountPicture.OpenReadAsync();

        BitmapImage image = new BitmapImage();

        image.SetSource(stream);

        this.LargeAccountPictureImage.Height = image.PixelHeight;

        this.LargeAccountPictureImage.Width = image.PixelWidth;

        this.LargeAccountPictureImage.Source = image;
    }

    StorageFile accountVideo =
        UserInformation.GetAccountPicture(AccountPictureKind.Video)
            as StorageFile;

    if (accountVideo != null)
    {
        IRandomAccessStream stream = await accountVideo.OpenReadAsync();

        this.AccountVideo.SetSource(stream, "video/mp4");
    }
}
```

In the following code segments, an instance of the CameraCaptureUI class is created and configured using the CameraCaptureUIMode enumeration for either photo or video. The resulting photo or video then sets the account picture or video using the asynchronous SetAccountPictureAsync and SetAccountVideoAsync methods.

```
private async void SetAccountPictureButton_Click(object sender,
RoutedEventArgs e)

{
    CameraCaptureUI cameraCaptureUI = new CameraCaptureUI();

    cameraCaptureUI.PhotoSettings.CroppedSizeInPixels = new Size(448, 448);

    StorageFile picture =
        await cameraCaptureUI.CaptureFileAsyc(CameraCaptureUIMode.Photo);
```

```
        {
            SetAccountPictureResult result =
                await UserInformation.SetAccountPictureAsync(picture);
        }
    }
```

If your app uses the `SetAccountPictureAsync` method, the Webcam capability must be declared in the `Package.appxmanifest`. The Webcam and Microphone capabilities must be declared by apps intending to use the `SetAccountVideoAsync` method.

```
    private async void SetAccountVideoButton_Click(object sender, RoutedEventArgs e)
    {
        CameraCaptureUI cameraCaptureUI = new CameraCaptureUI();

        cameraCaptureUI.VideoSettings.Format = CameraCaptureUIVideoFormat.Mp4;

        StorageFile video =
            await cameraCaptureUI.CaptureFileAsyc(CameraCaptureUIMode.Video);

        if (video != null)
        {
            SetAccountPictureResult result =
                await UserInformation.SetAccountVideoAsync(null, null, video);
        }
    }
```

In Figure 9-16 you can see the package.appxmanifest file declaring that the `AccountPictureProvider` requires the Microphone and Webcam capabilities. While the Webcam capability allows an app to capture and set an account picture, the Microphone capability is also required to capture and set an account video.

FIGURE 9-16

USING THE AUTOPLAY EXTENSION

Windows Store apps can use the AutoPlay Extension to allow them to respond to AutoPlay events that Windows raises. AutoPlay events are raised by Windows when users connect devices to their PC such as cameras, cell phones, or USB storage.

In Figure 9-17 the Video Player app, introduced earlier during the "Using the Play To Contract" discussion, is listed among the apps that can respond to the AutoPlay event. Windows is asking the user to choose what to do with removable drives such as the USB drive that was connected to the PC.

You can also see the `Package.appxmanifest` file for the Video Player app in Figure 9-17. When you declare the AutoPlay Content declaration, you must specify the verb (such as *play, open,* and so on), the action display name, and finally the content event.

FIGURE 9-17

In the `App.xaml.cs` file it is then necessary to override the `OnFileActivated` method as in the following example and then navigate to the appropriate page in the app. In this example, the app then navigates to the page defined in the `MainPage.xaml` file passing the `Files` collection from the `FileActivatedEventArgs` class.

```
protected override void OnFileActivated(FileActivatedEventArgs e)
{
    if (e.Verb == "play" || e.Verb == "open")
    {
        var rootFrame = new Frame();

        rootFrame.Navigate(typeof(MainPage), e.Files);

        Window.Current.Content = rootFrame;

        Window.Current.Activate();
    }

    base.OnFileActivated(e);
}
```

In the `MainPage` class, the overridden `OnNavigatedTo` method casts the `Parameter` property from the `NavigationEventArgs` class to an `IReadOnlyList<IStorageItem>`. If the cast succeeds, the list is searched for the first file with either an .mp4 or .wmv file extension. The `StorageFile` for the given video is then opened asynchronously, and the stream is passed to the `MediaElement.SetSource`

```
protected async override void OnNavigatedTo(NavigationEventArgs e)
{
    IReadOnlyList<IStorageItem> files = e.Parameter as IReadOnlyList<IStorageItem>;

    if (files != null)
    {
        for (int index = 0; index < files.Count; index++)
        {
            if (files[index].Name.EndsWith(".mp4") ||
                files[index].Name.EndsWith(".wmv"))
            {
                StorageFile file = files[index] as StorageFile;

                var stream = await file.OpenAsync(FileAccessMode.Read);

                this.VideoSource.SetSource(stream, file.ContentType);

                break;
            }
        }
    }

    this.VideoSource.Play();
}
```

USING THE BACKGROUND TASKS EXTENSION

Windows Store apps are intended to be full screen and users typically give their full attention to the app in the foreground. You should, therefore, design your apps to suspend when users navigate away and to resume again when users navigate back to the app. In most cases, an app can deliver on its intended purpose while suspending and resuming. However, sometimes an app must continue to run even when users navigate away from the app. Several mechanisms are available to developers to have some code to continue to run while an app is suspended.

It is said that every privilege implies a responsibility, so developers should always consider the implications of using background tasks before implementing them within their apps. Given that so many devices upon which your apps will run are mobile and therefore depend on battery power, it is imperative you consider this before allowing code to continue to execute in the background. To that end, Windows 8 provides developers with several capabilities that enable apps to perform limited tasks in the background without requiring the background tasks extension.

Using Push Notifications

You can use Windows Push Notifications to ensure that the app's primary and secondary tiles update with useful information even when the app is suspended. If the app you are writing plays audio, you can use the Playback Manager to allow audio to continue playing when the app isn't in the foreground and is suspended. Windows Store apps can use the Background Transfer API to download or upload files while the app is suspended, and File Share Contracts enable users to open and save files between apps, as discussed earlier in this chapter.

If these capabilities do not adequately address your given scenario and your app must continue to run code in the background, background tasks may be the answer.

Using Background Tasks

Background tasks are designed for real-time apps, such as e-mail, VOIP, or social media clients. Using background tasks, an app receives a limited amount of the system resources to enable a small amount of work to occur that requires no interaction with the user.

Windows Store apps register a background task using the `BackgroundTaskBuilder` class defined in the `Windows.ApplicationModel.Background` namespace. You define Background tasks in a type that implements the `IBackgroundTask` interface and that you can host in the app itself, in an in-proc server DLL, or in a host-executable provided by Windows.

When you create a background task, you must determine when the task will trigger. You can then allocate system resources to run the task. Table 9-1 details the trigger types that you can use to trigger background tasks to run.

TABLE 9-1: Background Task Events

BACKGROUND TASK TRIGGER TYPE	TRIGGER EVENT	WHEN THE BACKGROUND TASK IS TRIGGERED
`ControlChannelTrigger`	`ControlChannelTrigger`	On incoming messages on the control channel.
`MaintenanceTrigger`	`MaintenanceTrigger`	When it's time for maintenance background tasks.
`PushNotificationTrigger`	`PushNotificationTrigger`	A raw notification arrives on the WNS channel.
`SystemEventTrigger`	`InternetAvailable`	The Internet becomes available.
`SystemEventTrigger`	`LockScreenApplicationAdded`	An app tile is added to the lock screen.
`SystemEventTrigger`	`LockScreenApplicationRemoved`	An app tile is removed from the lock screen.
`SystemEventTrigger`	`ControlChannelReset`	A network channel is reset.
`SystemEventTrigger`	`NetworkStateChange`	A network change such as a change in cost or connectivity occurs.
`SystemEventTrigger`	`OnlineIdConnectedStateChange`	Online ID associated with the account changes.
`SystemEventTrigger`	`ServicingComplete`	The system has finished updating an application.
`SystemEventTrigger`	`SessionConnected`	The session is connected.

SystemEventTrigger	SessionDisconnected	The session is disconnected.
SystemEventTrigger	SmsReceived	A new SMS message is received by an installed mobile broadband device.
SystemEventTrigger	TimeZoneChange	The time zone changes on the device (for example, when the system adjusts the clock for daylight saving time).
SystemEventTrigger	UserAway	The user becomes absent.
SystemEventTrigger	UserPresent	The user becomes present.
TimeTrigger	TimeTrigger	A time event occurs.

Table 9-1 is an excerpt from *Introduction to Background Tasks* available from MSDN.

You must also determine whether there are any conditions that must be true for the task to be triggered. The `SystemTriggerType` enumeration specifies the system events that trigger a background task, such as `InternetAvailable`. You add conditions to background tasks using the `BackrgoundTaskBuilder` class, which provides the `AddCondition` method for this purpose.

> **NOTE** *If you intend to use background tasks in your app, it is highly recommended that you read* Introduction to Background Tasks. *You should also always be mindful how each background task impacts system resources, such as battery life. You can find* Introduction to Background Tasks, *which gives more information on using the Background Tasks Extension, at* `http://www.microsoft.com/en-us/download/details.aspx?id=27411`.

USING THE CAMERA SETTINGS EXTENSION

Using the Camera Settings extension, camera manufacturers can develop companion Windows Store apps for their cameras that automatically install when the user connects the device to their PC.

> **NOTE** *If you are interested in exploring the capabilities of the Camera Settings extension further, you should read the article "Developing Windows Store Device Apps for Cameras" on MSDN at* `http://msdn.microsoft.com/library/windows/hardware/hh454870`.

USING THE CONTACT PICKER EXTENSION

Windows Store apps use the Contact Picker extension to select one or more contacts. Implementing the extension begins with creating and configuring an instance of the `ContactPicker` class.

```
using Windows.ApplicationModel.Contacts;

...

var picker = new ContactPicker();
```

It is then necessary to specify the text that you want to display on the Commit button, which users click to indicate they have chosen the required contact or contacts.

```
picker.CommitButtonText = "Select";
```

The `ContactPicker` class enables you to either select one or more contacts or simply select a particular field, such as an e-mail address. The `ContactSelectionMode` enumeration is used to specify the type of selection that is required.

```
picker.SelectionMode = ContactSelectionMode.Contacts;
```

Using the `PickSingleContactAsync` method, a single contact is selected asynchronously and returns an instance of the `ContactInformation` class that encapsulates information about the selected contact. The `PickMultipleContactsAsync` method enables multiple contacts to be selected and returns an `IReadOnlyList<ContactInformation>`.

The `GetThumbnailAsync` method returns an instance of a class implementing the `IRandomAccessStreamWithContentType` interface allowing you to retrieve the thumbnail image associated with the given contact.

```
ContactInformation contact = await picker.PickSingleContactAsync();

if (contact != null)
{
    this.NameTextBlock.Text = contact.Name;

    if (contact.Emails.Count > 0)
    {
        this.EmailTextBlock.Text = contact.Emails[0].Value;
    }
    else
    {
        this.EmailTextBlock.Text = string.Empty;
    }

    var stream = await contact.GetThumbnailAsync();

    if (stream != null && stream.Size > 0)
    {
        BitmapImage image = new BitmapImage();

        image.SetSource(stream);

        this.ContactImage.Height = image.PixelHeight;

        this.ContactImage.Width = image.PixelWidth;
```

```
            this.ContactImage.Source = image;
        }
        else
        {
            this.ContactImage.Source = null;
        }
    }
}
```

USING THE FILE ACTIVATION EXTENSION

Windows Store apps can use the File Activation Extension to enable the apps to activate whenever the user attempts to open a file with a given file extension. Windows Store apps can register to handle one or more file extensions by declaring the File Type Associations within the `Package.appxmanifest` file and overriding the `OnFileActivated` method in the App.xaml.cs file.

Implementing the File Activation Extension

To see this in action, follow these steps:

1. Open the Visual Studio 2012 solution for this chapter, and then find the Notes project within the Extensions\File Activation solution folder. The Notes app opens text files with the .note file extension.

2. In the Notes project, open the `App.xaml.cs` file and you see that the `OnFileActivated` method is overridden to navigate directly to the MainPage.xaml and provide the list of files as an optional parameter to the `Frame.Navigate` method.

```
protected override void OnFileActivated(FileActivatedEventArgs e)
{
    var rootFrame = new Frame();

    rootFrame.Navigate(typeof(MainPage), e.Files);

    Window.Current.Content = rootFrame;

    Window.Current.Activate();
}
```

3. Open the MainPage.xaml.cs file, and you see that the `OnNavigatedTo` method is also overridden. The optional parameter passed to the `Frame.Navigate` method can then be accessed from the `Parameter` property of the `NavigationEventArgs` class.

4. The parameter is cast as an `IReadOnlyList<StorageItem>`, and then the first entry in the list is cast as an instance of the `StorageFile` class. Using the `StorageFile` instance, the contents of the file can be read asynchronously using the `FileIO.ReadTextAsync` method.

```
protected async override void OnNavigatedTo(NavigationEventArgs e)
{
    if (e.Parameter != null)
    {
        IReadOnlyList<IStorageItem> files
            = e.Parameter as IReadOnlyList<IStorageItem>;

        if (files != null)
        {
```

```
            StorageFile file = files[0] as StorageFile;

            if (file != null)
            {
                string contents = await FileIO.ReadTextAsync(file);

                this.NotesTextBlock.Text = contents;
            }
        }
    }
}
```

5. Open the Declarations tab of the `Package.appxmanifest` file, and you see the list of available declarations. Select the File Type Association declaration, and then click the Add button.

6. You must specify the name of the File Type Association and the file extension. Figure 9-18 shows that the name of the File Type Association is specified as *note* and the file extension as *.note*.

7. If you click the Add New button, you can specify additional file types, and Windows Store apps can also declare multiple instances of this declaration.

FIGURE 9-18

Debugging File Activation

To successfully debug an app that uses the File Activation extension, you must instruct Visual Studio to debug your code when it starts instead of launching the app. To do so, follow these steps:

1. In the project properties Window, open the Debug tab as shown in Figure 9-19.

2. Under the Start Action heading, select the "Do not launch, but debug my code when it starts" check box. This configures Visual Studio to allow the debugger to begin debugging as soon as the app starts as a result of a file type activation. You are then able to place and subsequently hit breakpoints in the overridden `OnFileActivated` method.

3. With Visual Studio configured to debug file activation, you simply need to double-click a file with the supported file extension to launch the Notes app and hit breakpoints defined in the project.

4. In the Documents folder, create a test file by running the following code in the command prompt. Visual Studio 2012 creates a command prompt called Developer Command Prompt for VS 2012 on the Windows 8 Start Screen.

5. With Notepad open, simply write some text in the file, and then save the file.

6. Launch the Notes app by double-clicking the newly created file and observe that any breakpoints previously defined are subsequently hit.

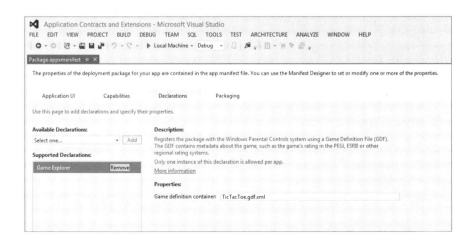

FIGURE 9-19

USING THE GAME EXPLORER EXTENSION

Windows Store games must use the Games Explorer Extension to define metadata about the game, such as the associated ratings.

In the installation folder of the Windows 8.0 SDK, you'll find the Game Definition File Editor.

```
C:\Program Files (x86)\Windows Kits\8.0\bin\x86\gdfmaker.exe
```

Using the Game Definition File Editor, you can provide metadata about the game, and the tool generates the required Game Definition File. In the `Package.appxmanifest` file shown in Figure 9-20, the Game Explorer declaration is declared and the associated Game Definition File is specified.

USING THE PRINT TASK SETTINGS EXTENSION

The Print Task Settings Extension enables printer manufacturers to develop companion Windows Store apps for their printers so that the app automatically installs when the user connects the device to their PC.

> **NOTE** *If you are interested in exploring the capabilities of the Print Task Settings Extension further, you should read the "Developing a Windows Store Device App for Printers" article on MSDN At* `http://msdn.microsoft.com/library/windows/hardware/br259129`.

USING THE PROTOCOL ACTIVATION EXTENSION

You can register a Windows Store app to become the default handler for a given URI scheme name. When registered as the default handler for a given URI scheme, your app activates every time that type of URI launches. As an example of where protocol activation can be useful, consider the use of the Share Contract. In Figure 9-21, the Maps app enables users to share maps using the Share Contract. The Maps app then enables recipients of the e-mail to open the map in the browser or if they use Windows 8 or Windows RT, to open the Map directly in the Maps app.

FIGURE 9-21

Activating the Maps App

The following URI activates the Maps app, and the URI provides the necessary latitude and longitude to enable the app to center the map to the specified coordinates. It also provides the pushpin on the map identifying the location.

```
bingmaps:///?cp=38.53114~-121.79038&lvl=11&sty=r&trfc=0&where=University%20Airport
```

Making the Required Declarations

Windows Store developers should seriously consider the implications of the Protocol Activation Extension and register for only URI schemes in which the app is intended to handle all URI launches for that type of URI scheme. After you make this decision, you must make the required declarations in the `Package.appxmanifest` file. To do so, on the Declarations tab of the `Package.appxmanifest` file, as shown in Figure 9-22, you see the list of available declarations. Select the Protocol declaration and click the Add button.

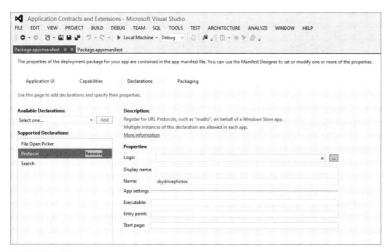

FIGURE 9-22

Windows Store apps can declare multiple instances of this declaration; although, the SkyDrive Photos app uses just one to declare the following URI scheme.

```
skydrivephotos:///?id=file.20abc2386c9f7426.34GHS6725D2B2647!932
```

When activated using the URI scheme, the entry point for the app is the `OnActivated` method in the `App.xaml.cs` file. The `OnActivated` method from the SkyDrive Photos app is listed here.

The `OnActivated` method receives the event data as an instance of an object implementing the `IActivatedEventArgs` interface. `IActivatedEventArgs.Kind` enables you to determine how the app was activated and then cast the object accordingly to the appropriate class given the activation type. When activated using Protocol activation, that class is the `ProtocolActivatedEventArgs` class. Using the `ProtocolActivatedEventArgs` class, you can then access the URI that activates the app and, therefore, any parameters — such as longitude and latitude in the case of the Maps app — or the unique identifier for the item stored within SkyDrive.

After accessing the item identifier from the URI, the `Navigate` method of the `Frame` class is called to navigate to the `ItemDetailPage`, and the item identifier is passed as a parameter.

```
protected override void OnActivated(IActivatedEventArgs e)
{
    if (e.Kind == ActivationKind.Protocol)
    {
        ProtocolActivatedEventArgs args = e as ProtocolActivatedEventArgs;
```

```
        Frame rootFrame = new Frame();

        string id = args.Uri.OriginalString.TrimStart(
            "skydrivephotos://?id=".ToCharArray());

        rootFrame.Navigate(typeof(ItemDetailPage), id);

        Window.Current.Content = rootFrame;
    }

    Window.Current.Activate();
}
```

Upon navigating to the `ItemDetailPage`, the `LoadState` method provides access to the navigation parameter, which then accesses the photo and album in SkyDrive.

```
protected async override void LoadState(object navigationParameter,
    Dictionary<string, object> pageState)
{
    if (pageState != null && pageState.ContainsKey("SelectedItem"))
    {
        navigationParameter = pageState["SelectedItem"];
    }

    string id = navigationParameter as string;

    SkyDrivePhoto photo = await SkyDrivePhoto.GetSkyDrivePhotoByIdAsync(id);

    SkyDriveAlbum album =
        await SkyDriveAlbum.GetSkyDriveAlbumByIdAsync(photo.ParentId);

    this.DefaultViewModel["Group"] = album;

    this.DefaultViewModel["Items"] = album.Photos;

    this.SkyDrivePhotoFlipView.SelectedItem = photo;
}
```

Debugging Protocol Activation

To successfully debug the Protocol Activation Extension that you use in an app, you must instruct Visual Studio to debug your code when the app starts instead of launching the app. To do so, follow these steps:

1. In the project properties Window, open the Debug tab as shown in Figure 9-23.

2. Under the Start Action heading, select the "Do not launch, but debug my code when it starts" check box. This configures Visual Studio to allow the debugger to begin debugging as soon as the app starts as a result of a file type activation. You are then able to place and subsequently hit breakpoints in the overridden `OnActivated` method.

3. With Visual Studio configured to debug Protocol activation, you can launch the SkyDrive Photos app by clicking on the link provided in an e-mail sent from the SkyDrive Photos app when using the Share Contract to share an individual photo.

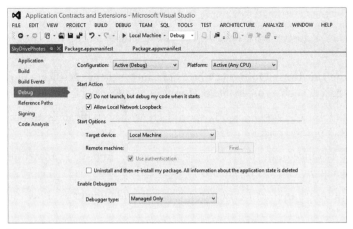

FIGURE 9-23

USING SSL/CERTIFICATES EXTENSION

Windows Store apps can use digital certificates to enable authentication to web services and secure communication over the Secure Sockets Layer (SSL). Using the SSL/certificates extension, you can install digital certificates with your app.

Just as with many of the other Application Contracts and extensions you have explored in this chapter, configuring the extension requires that the extension is declared in the `Package.appxmanifest` file. Follow these steps:

1. In Visual Studio 2012, open the `Package.appxmanifest` file and select the Declarations tab. You can find the Certificates declaration listed in the Available Declarations, as shown in Figure 9-24.

FIGURE 9-24

2. Select the Certificates declaration and click the Add button.

3. In the properties for the Certificates declaration, you see three check boxes:

➤ Selecting the Exclusive Trust check box indicates that the app does not inherit from the system trust.

➤ Selecting the Hardware Only check box indicates that the certificate must be hardware-based, such as a certificate stored in a smartcard.

➤ Selecting the Auto Select check box specifies that the certificate is automatically selected from in the app container.

4. Although only one instance of the declaration is allowed per app, you can define one or more certificates using the Add New button.

5. Each certificate requires that you specify the store name and content as shown in Figure 9-25.

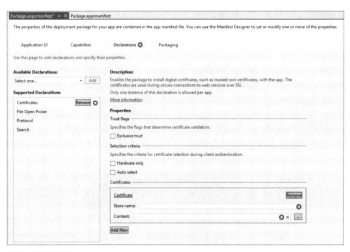

FIGURE 9-25

SUMMARY

The intent of this chapter was to provide you with an awareness of each of the contracts and extensions available to Windows Store app developers.

In this chapter you explored how Application Contracts and extensions allow an app to enter into agreements that enable interaction scenarios with Windows as well as other Windows Store apps.

You explored code samples that illustrated how to implement the more pivotal contracts and extensions such as the Search and Share Contracts. Where contracts and extensions are specialized, such as the camera settings or Print Task Settings Extensions, you gained an appreciation for their intended use as well as a reference to further information should you need to further explore and possibly implement those contracts and extensions.

10

Windows Store Application Architecture

WHAT'S IN THIS CHAPTER?

- ➤ The importance of MVVM
- ➤ Finding ViewModels
- ➤ Using models in the Artist Browser example from Chapter 1
- ➤ How commands can handle input
- ➤ Understanding and utilizing the MVVM Frameworks

WROX.COM CODE DOWNLOADS FOR THIS CHAPTER

You can find the wrox.com code downloads for this chapter at www.wrox.com/remtitle
.cgi?isbn=1182205707 on the Download Code tab in zip file. 205709 C10.zip.

BEST PRACTICES FOR YOUR APPS

Because the framework for building Windows Store apps is based on XAML, many existing techniques and design patterns for solving problems are also applicable on the new platform. Just as architects use different tools and techniques depending on what they're designing, each software project may require a different design to meet the known requirements and constraints. Although there isn't a single solution to every challenge, sometimes, best practices provide guidance to make solving the challenge easier. This chapter outlines best practices to reduce complexity and increase flexibility of your apps.

UNDERSTANDING MVVM

Model-View-ViewModel (*MVVM*) is a design pattern primarily used with XAML-based applications, such as Windows Presentation Foundation (WPF), Silverlight, and Windows Phone applications. It has strong similarities with Model-View-Controller (MVC) and Model-View-Presenter (MVP), but it's designed specifically for XAML applications. It consists of three elements:

➤ **Model:** This is the representation of persistent or external data and is usually entities, such as a row in a table for database apps or a deserialized JSON object from the web.

➤ **View:** This is the user interface presented to the user.

➤ **ViewModel:** This is the model *for* the view, meaning an abstraction of the view, which provides a view-oriented representation of the model. It becomes the link between the view and the model and provides conversion from model content for the view to consume. This is exposed as properties and commands from the view model, which the binder uses in the framework.

It all starts with the View. When the View loads, either it acquires a reference to its associated ViewModel using a locator described in the following section or an existing instance of a ViewModel passed to it. The View binds to properties and actions (commands) that the ViewModel provides. These bindings enable the creator of the View to focus on the *user experience* (*UX*) rather than the code behind it. This enables UX and graphics designers to help build the user interface along with the developer while the developer works on the guts of the app.

The big player out of the three is the ViewModel, which can have one or more classes for each View. The binder (`BindingMarkupExtension`) is the glue that connects the ViewModel to the View. Although the View has a reference to the ViewModel, the ViewModel has no reference or information about the View. This enables multiple Views to share the same ViewModel and enables you to easily unit test the ViewModel because it has no dependency on the UI. This decoupling of the UI from the logic behind it is one of the main benefits of MVVM.

ViewModels generally share a common base class that provides an implementation of `INotifyPropertyChanged` along with additional helper methods. Listing 10-1 shows a simple `ViewModelBase` class that ViewModels can inherit. It provides methods that set the value of a backing field and raise the `PropertyChanged` event.

LISTING 10-1: ViewModelBase.cs

```
using System;
using System.Collections.Generic;
using System.ComponentModel;
using System.Linq;
using System.Runtime.CompilerServices;
using System.Text;
using System.Threading.Tasks;

namespace ArtistBrowser.ViewModels
```

```
{
    /// <summary>
    /// Provides the base implementation of a ViewModel.
    /// </summary>
    Public abstract class ViewModelBase : INotifyPropertyChanged
    {
        /// <summary>
        /// Multicast event for property change notifications.
        /// </summary>
        public event PropertyChangedEventHandler PropertyChanged;

        /// <summary>
        /// Checks if a property already matches a desired value.
        /// Sets the property and notifies listeners only when necessary.
        /// </summary>
        /// <typeparam name="T">Type of the property.</typeparam>
        /// <param name="storage">Reference to a property
        /// with both getter and setter.</param>
        /// <param name="value">Desired value for the property.</param>
        /// <param name="propertyName">Name of the property used to notify
        /// listeners.  This value is optional and can be provided automatically
        /// when invoked from compilers that support CallerMemberName.</param>
        /// <returns>True if the value was changed, false if the existing value
        /// matched the desired value.</returns>
        protected bool Set<T>(ref T storage,
                              T value,
                              [CallerMemberName]
                              string propertyName = null)
        {
            if (object.Equals(storage, value)) return false;

            storage = value;
            this.OnPropertyChanged(propertyName);
            return true;
        }

        /// <summary>
        /// Notifies listeners that a property value has changed.
        /// </summary>
        /// <param name="propertyName">Name of the property used to notify
        /// listeners.  This value is optional and can be provided automatically
        /// when invoked from compilers that support
        /// <see cref="CallerMemberNameAttribute"/>.</param>
        protected void OnPropertyChanged([CallerMemberName]
                                         string propertyName = null)
        {
            var eventHandler = this.PropertyChanged;
            if (eventHandler != null)
            {
                eventHandler(this, new PropertyChangedEventArgs(propertyName));
            }
        }

        public bool IsInDesignMode
        {
```

continues

LISTING 10-1 *(continued)*

```
        get
        {
            return Windows.ApplicationModel.DesignMode.DesignModeEnabled;
        }
    }
}
}
```

LOCATING VIEWMODELS

A `ViewModelLocator` provides the concrete instance of a given ViewModel and is roughly based off the *service locator* design pattern, which provides an abstract way of obtaining a service. `ViewModelLocator` can be as simple as a class, as shown in Listing 10-2, which has properties for all the ViewModels that need to be accessible, or it can be a more flexible approach using an *inversion of control (IoC)* container that dynamically loads the ViewModels.

> **NOTE** *An IoC is a design pattern where an object is requested from a container at run time. The container returns a concrete type that is not known at compile time. This decouples the implementation from the caller.*

LISTING 10-2: ViewModelLocator.cs

```
using ArtistBrowser.Common;
using System;
using System.Collections.Generic;
using System.Linq;
using System.Text;
using System.Threading.Tasks;

namespace ArtistBrowser.ViewModels
{
    public sealed class ViewModelLocator
    {
        public ViewModelLocator()
        { }

        public GroupedItemsViewModel GroupedItems
        {
            get
            {
                return Singleton<GroupedItemsViewModel>.Instance;
            }
        }

    }
}
```

Listing 10-3 shows a simple locator, where a single ViewModel is exposed as a singleton using the following helper class.

> **NOTE** *A singleton is a class that enables only a single instance to be created. This instance is returned when subsequent requests for the class occur.*

LISTING 10-3: Singleton.cs

```
using System;
using System.Collections.Generic;
using System.Linq;
using System.Text;
using System.Threading.Tasks;

namespace ArtistBrowser.Common
{
    public sealed class Singleton<T> where T : new()
    {
        private Singleton()
        { }

        public static T Instance
        {
            get
            {
                return LazyInitializer.Instance;
            }
        }

        private class LazyInitializer
        {
            static LazyInitializer()

            {
            }

            internal static readonly T Instance = new T();
        }
    }
}
```

REFACTORING THE ARTIST BROWSER

Chapter 1, "A Glimpse into the Future," built a small app that shows musicians grouped by genres using a Visual Studio template. Although the template has some aspects of MVVM, this chapter refactors it using additional techniques. We will use a locator to bind to the main page's ViewModel, change the bindings to the ViewModels, and clean up the models.

Instantiating a ViewModelLocator

To provide access to the `ViewModelLocator` from anywhere in the app's markup, an instance is created in `App.xaml`, as shown in Listing 10-4.

LISTING 10-4: App.xaml

```xml
<Application
    x:Class="ArtistBrowser.App"
    xmlns="http://schemas.microsoft.com/winfx/2006/xaml/presentation"
    xmlns:x="http://schemas.microsoft.com/winfx/2006/xaml"
    xmlns:viewModels="using:ArtistBrowser.ViewModels">

    <Application.Resources>
        <ResourceDictionary>
            <ResourceDictionary.MergedDictionaries>

                <!--
                    Styles that define common aspects of the platform look and feel
                    Required by Visual Studio project and item templates
                -->
                <ResourceDictionary Source="Common/StandardStyles.xaml"/>
            </ResourceDictionary.MergedDictionaries>

            <!-- Application-specific resources -->

            <x:String x:Key="AppName">Artist Browser</x:String>

            <viewModels:ViewModelLocator x:Key="locator" />
        </ResourceDictionary>
    </Application.Resources>
</Application>
```

On the landing page, `GroupedItemsPage.xaml`, you can change the binding to use the locator (as shown in Listing 10-5) with the property that returns the ViewModel for this page.

LISTING 10-5: GroupedItemsPage.xaml

```xml
<common:LayoutAwarePage
    x:Name="pageRoot"
    x:Class="ArtistBrowser.GroupedItemsPage"
    xmlns="http://schemas.microsoft.com/winfx/2006/xaml/presentation"
    xmlns:x="http://schemas.microsoft.com/winfx/2006/xaml"
    xmlns:common="using:ArtistBrowser.Common"
    xmlns:viewModels="using:ArtistBrowser.ViewModels"
    xmlns:d="http://schemas.microsoft.com/expression/blend/2008"
    xmlns:mc="http://schemas.openxmlformats.org/markup-compatibility/2006"
    mc:Ignorable="d"
    DataContext="{Binding GroupedItems, Source={StaticResource locator}}"
    d:DataContext="{Binding GroupedItems,
                Source={d:DesignInstance Type=viewModels:ViewModelLocator,
```

```
                    IsDesignTimeCreatable=True}}">

<UserControl.Resources>

    <!-- Collection of grouped items displayed by this page -->
    <CollectionViewSource
        x:Name="groupedItemsViewSource"
        Source="{Binding Groups}"
        IsSourceGrouped="true"
        ItemsPath="Items"
        d:Source="{Binding Groups}"/>

</UserControl.Resources>

<!--
    This grid acts as a root panel for the page that defines two rows:
    * Row 0 contains the back button and page title
    * Row 1 contains the rest of the page layout
-->
<Grid Background="{StaticResource ApplicationPageBackgroundThemeBrush}">
    <Grid.RowDefinitions>
        <RowDefinition Height="140"/>
        <RowDefinition Height="*"/>
    </Grid.RowDefinitions>

    <!-- Back button and page title -->
    <Grid>
        <Grid.ColumnDefinitions>
            <ColumnDefinition Width="Auto"/>
            <ColumnDefinition Width="*"/>
        </Grid.ColumnDefinitions>
        <Button x:Name="backButton" Click="GoBack"
                IsEnabled="{Binding Frame.CanGoBack, ElementName=pageRoot}"
                Style="{StaticResource BackButtonStyle}"/>
        <TextBlock x:Name="pageTitle" Text="{StaticResource AppName}"
                   Grid.Column="1"
                   Style="{StaticResource PageHeaderTextStyle}"/>
    </Grid>

    <!-- Horizontal scrolling grid used in most view states -->
    <ScrollViewer
        x:Name="itemGridScrollViewer"
        AutomationProperties.AutomationId="ItemGridScrollViewer"
        Grid.Row="1"
        Margin="0,-3,0,0"
        Style="{StaticResource HorizontalScrollViewerStyle}">

        <GridView
            x:Name="itemGridView"
            AutomationProperties.AutomationId="ItemGridView"
            AutomationProperties.Name="Grouped Items"
            ItemsSource="{Binding
                Source={StaticResource groupedItemsViewSource}}"
            ItemTemplate="{StaticResource Standard250x250ItemTemplate}"
            SelectionMode="None"
            IsItemClickEnabled="True"
```

LISTING 10-5 *(continued)*

```
            ItemClick="ItemView_ItemClick" Margin="120,0,0,0">

            <GridView.ItemsPanel>
                <ItemsPanelTemplate>
                    <VirtualizingStackPanel Orientation="Horizontal"/>
                </ItemsPanelTemplate>
            </GridView.ItemsPanel>
            <GridView.GroupStyle>
                <GroupStyle>
                    <GroupStyle.HeaderTemplate>
                        <DataTemplate>
                            <Grid Margin="1,0,0,6">
                                <Button
                                    AutomationProperties.Name="Group Title"
                                    Content="{Binding Title}"
                                    Click="Header_Click"
                                    Style="{StaticResource TextButtonStyle}"/>
                            </Grid>
                        </DataTemplate>
                    </GroupStyle.HeaderTemplate>
                    <GroupStyle.Panel>
                        <ItemsPanelTemplate>
                            <VariableSizedWrapGrid Orientation="Vertical"
                                                   Margin="0,0,80,0"/>
                        </ItemsPanelTemplate>
                    </GroupStyle.Panel>
                </GroupStyle>
            </GridView.GroupStyle>
        </GridView>
    </ScrollViewer>

    <!-- Vertical scrolling list only used when snapped -->
    <ScrollViewer
        x:Name="itemListScrollViewer"
        AutomationProperties.AutomationId="ItemListScrollViewer"
        Grid.Row="1"
        Visibility="Collapsed"
        Style="{StaticResource VerticalScrollViewerStyle}">

        <ListView
            x:Name="itemListView"
            AutomationProperties.AutomationId="ItemListView"
            AutomationProperties.Name="Grouped Items"
            Margin="10,-10,0,60"
            ItemsSource="{Binding
                Source={StaticResource groupedItemsViewSource}}"
            ItemTemplate="{StaticResource Standard80ItemTemplate}"
            SelectionMode="None"
            IsItemClickEnabled="True"
            ItemClick="ItemView_ItemClick">

            <ListView.GroupStyle>
                <GroupStyle>
                    <GroupStyle.HeaderTemplate
```

```
                    <DataTemplate>
                        <Grid Margin="7,7,0,0">
                            <Button
                                AutomationProperties.Name="Group Title"
                                Content="{Binding Title}"
                                Click="Header_Click"
                                Style="{StaticResource TextButtonStyle}"/>
                        </Grid>
                    </DataTemplate>
                </GroupStyle.HeaderTemplate>
            </GroupStyle>
        </ListView.GroupStyle>
    </ListView>
</ScrollViewer>

<VisualStateManager.VisualStateGroups>

    <!-- Visual states reflect the application's view state -->
    <VisualStateGroup>
        <VisualState x:Name="FullScreenLandscape"/>
        <VisualState x:Name="Filled"/>

        <!-- The entire page respects the narrower 100-pixel
             margin convention for portrait -->
        <VisualState x:Name="FullScreenPortrait">
            <Storyboard>
                <ObjectAnimationUsingKeyFrames
                        Storyboard.TargetName="backButton"
                        Storyboard.TargetProperty="Style">
                    <DiscreteObjectKeyFrame KeyTime="0"
                      Value="{StaticResource PortraitBackButtonStyle}"/>
                </ObjectAnimationUsingKeyFrames>

                <ObjectAnimationUsingKeyFrames
                        Storyboard.TargetName="itemGridView"
                        Storyboard.TargetProperty="Margin">
                    <DiscreteObjectKeyFrame KeyTime="0"
                                            Value="96,0,10,56"/>
                </ObjectAnimationUsingKeyFrames>
            </Storyboard>
        </VisualState>

        <!--
            The back button and title have different styles when snapped,
            and the list representation is substituted
            for the grid displayed in all other view states
        -->
        <VisualState x:Name="Snapped">
            <Storyboard>
                <ObjectAnimationUsingKeyFrames
                        Storyboard.TargetName="backButton"
                        Storyboard.TargetProperty="Style">
                    <DiscreteObjectKeyFrame KeyTime="0"
                        Value="{StaticResource SnappedBackButtonStyle}"/>
                </ObjectAnimationUsingKeyFrames>
                <ObjectAnimationUsingKeyFrames
                        Storyboard.TargetName="pageTitle"
```

LISTING 10-5 *(continued)*

```
                            Storyboard.TargetProperty="Style">
                    <DiscreteObjectKeyFrame KeyTime="0"
                        Value="{StaticResource SnappedPageHeaderTextStyle}"/>
                </ObjectAnimationUsingKeyFrames>

                <ObjectAnimationUsingKeyFrames
                    Storyboard.TargetName="itemListScrollViewer"
                    Storyboard.TargetProperty="Visibility">
                        <DiscreteObjectKeyFrame KeyTime="0" Value="Visible"/>
                </ObjectAnimationUsingKeyFrames>
                <ObjectAnimationUsingKeyFrames
                    Storyboard.TargetName="itemGridScrollViewer"
                    Storyboard.TargetProperty="Visibility">
                        <DiscreteObjectKeyFrame KeyTime="0" Value="Collapsed"/>
                </ObjectAnimationUsingKeyFrames>
            </Storyboard>
        </VisualState>
    </VisualStateGroup>
</VisualStateManager.VisualStateGroups>
    </Grid>
</common:LayoutAwarePage>
```

Listing 10-6 shows the `GroupedItemsViewModel` that the page binds to and is followed with the underlying `GroupViewModel` and `ItemViewModel` in Listing 10-7 and Listing 10-8, respectively.

LISTING 10-6: GroupedItemsViewModel.cs

```
using ArtistBrowser.Model;
using System;
using System.Collections.Generic;
using System.Collections.ObjectModel;
using System.Linq;
using System.Text;
using System.Threading.Tasks;

namespace ArtistBrowser.ViewModels
{
    public class GroupedItemsViewModel : ViewModelBase
    {
        private readonly ObservableCollection<GroupViewModel> _groups;

        public GroupedItemsViewModel()
        {
            _groups = new ObservableCollection<GroupViewModel>();

            LoadGroups();
        }

        private void LoadGroups()
        {
            var data = new SampleData();
```

```
            {
                _groups.Add(new GroupViewModel(group));
            }
        }

        public IList<GroupViewModel> Groups
        {
            get { return this._groups; }
        }
    }
}
```

LISTING 10-7: GroupViewModel.cs

```
using ArtistBrowser.Model;
using System;
using System.Collections.Generic;
using System.Collections.ObjectModel;
using System.Linq;
using System.Text;
using System.Threading.Tasks;
using Windows.UI.Xaml.Media;
using Windows.UI.Xaml.Media.Imaging;

namespace ArtistBrowser.ViewModels
{
    public class GroupViewModel
    {
        private readonly Group _group;
        private readonly ObservableCollection<ItemViewModel> _items;

        public GroupViewModel(Group group)
        {
            _items = new ObservableCollection<ItemViewModel>(group.Items
                            .Select(i => new ItemViewModel(i, this)));
            _group = group;
        }

        public string Title { get { return _group.Title; } }
        public string Subtitle { get { return _group.Subtitle; } }
        public ImageSource Image
        {
            get
            {
                return new BitmapImage(new Uri("ms-appx:///" + _group.ImagePath));
            }
        }

        public IEnumerable<ItemViewModel> Items { get { return _items; } }

    }
}
```

LISTING 10-8: ItemViewModel.cs

```
using ArtistBrowser.Model;
using System;
using System.Collections.Generic;
using System.Linq;
using System.Text;
using System.Threading.Tasks;
using Windows.UI.Xaml.Media;
using Windows.UI.Xaml.Media.Imaging;

namespace ArtistBrowser.ViewModels
{
    public class ItemViewModel
    {
        private readonly Item _item;

        public ItemViewModel(Item item, GroupViewModel group)
        {
            _item = item;
            Group = group;
        }

        public string Title { get { return _item.Title; } }
        public string Subtitle { get { return _item.Subtitle; } }
        public ImageSource Image
        {
            get
            {
                return new BitmapImage(new Uri("ms-appx:///" + _item.ImagePath));
            }
        }

        public GroupViewModel Group { get; private set; }
    }
}
```

Removing DefaultViewModel

In the Chapter 1, each page in the app had a DefaultViewModel property inherited from LayoutAwarePage. You no longer need this property, and you can remove it along with its backing field. After doing so, you must change the bindings and code that handles parameters when navigating to the page in OnNavigatedTo. Listings 10-9 and 10-10 show the modified GroupDetailPage and Listings 10-11 and 10-12 show the modified ItemDetailPage.

LISTING 10-9: GroupDetail.xaml

```
<common:LayoutAwarePage
    x:Name="pageRoot"
    x:Class="ArtistBrowser.GroupDetailPage"
    xmlns="http://schemas.microsoft.com/winfx/2006/xaml/presentation"
```

```
xmlns:x="http://schemas.microsoft.com/winfx/2006/xaml"
xmlns:common="using:ArtistBrowser.Common"
xmlns:viewModels="using:ArtistBrowser.ViewModels"
xmlns:d="http://schemas.microsoft.com/expression/blend/2008"
xmlns:mc="http://schemas.openxmlformats.org/markup-compatibility/2006"
mc:Ignorable="d">

<UserControl.Resources>

    <!-- Collection of items displayed by this page -->
    <CollectionViewSource
        x:Name="itemsViewSource"
        Source="{Binding Items}"
        d:Source="{Binding GroupedItems.Groups[0].Items,
        Source={d:DesignInstance Type=viewModels:ViewModelLocator,
        IsDesignTimeCreatable=True}}"/>
</UserControl.Resources>

<!--
    This grid acts as a root panel for the page that defines two rows:
    * Row 0 contains the back button and page title
    * Row 1 contains the rest of the page layout
-->
<Grid Background="{StaticResource ApplicationPageBackgroundThemeBrush}"
    d:DataContext="{Binding GroupedItems.Groups[0],
    Source={d:DesignInstance Type=viewModels:ViewModelLocator,
    IsDesignTimeCreatable=True}}">

    <Grid.RowDefinitions>
        <RowDefinition Height="140"/>
        <RowDefinition Height="*"/>
    </Grid.RowDefinitions>

    <!-- Back button and page title -->
    <Grid>
        <Grid.ColumnDefinitions>
            <ColumnDefinition Width="Auto"/>
            <ColumnDefinition Width="*"/>
        </Grid.ColumnDefinitions>
        <Button x:Name="backButton" Click="GoBack"
                IsEnabled="{Binding Frame.CanGoBack, ElementName=pageRoot}"
                Style="{StaticResource BackButtonStyle}"/>
        <TextBlock x:Name="pageTitle" Text="{Binding Title}"
                Style="{StaticResource PageHeaderTextStyle}" Grid.Column="1"/>
    </Grid>

    <!-- Horizontal scrolling grid used in most view states -->
    <ScrollViewer
        x:Name="gridScrollViewer"
        AutomationProperties.AutomationId="DetailsScrollViewer"
        Grid.Row="1"
        Padding="0,-14,0,50"
        Style="{StaticResource HorizontalScrollViewerStyle}">

        <StackPanel x:Name="gridLayoutPanel" Margin="120,0,120,0"
```

continues

LISTING 10-9 *(continued)*

```xml
                            Orientation="Horizontal">
                <StackPanel Width="480" Margin="0,4,14,0">
                    <TextBlock Text="{Binding Subtitle}" Margin="0,0,18,20"
                               Style="{StaticResource SubheaderTextStyle}"
                               MaxHeight="60"/>
                    <Image Source="{Binding Image}" Height="400" Margin="0,0,18,20"
                           Stretch="UniformToFill"/>
                    <TextBlock Text="{Binding Description}" Margin="0,0,18,0"
                               Style="{StaticResource BodyTextStyle}"/>
                </StackPanel>
                <GridView
                    AutomationProperties.AutomationId="ItemGridView"
                    AutomationProperties.Name="Items In Group"
                    ItemsSource="{Binding Source={StaticResource itemsViewSource}}"
                    ItemTemplate="{StaticResource Standard500x130ItemTemplate}"
                    SelectionMode="None"
                    IsItemClickEnabled="True"
                    ItemClick="ItemView_ItemClick">

                    <GridView.ItemContainerStyle>
                        <Style TargetType="GridViewItem">
                            <Setter Property="Margin" Value="52,0,0,10"/>
                        </Style>
                    </GridView.ItemContainerStyle>
                </GridView>
            </StackPanel>
        </ScrollViewer>

        <!-- Vertical scrolling list only used when snapped -->
        <ScrollViewer
            x:Name="snappedScrollViewer"
            AutomationProperties.AutomationId="SnappedDetailsScrollViewer"
            Grid.Row="1"
            Visibility="Collapsed"
            Style="{StaticResource VerticalScrollViewerStyle}">

            <StackPanel>
                <TextBlock Text="{Binding Subtitle}" Margin="20,0,18,20"
                           Style="{StaticResource TitleTextStyle}" MaxHeight="60"/>
                <Image Source="{Binding Image}" Margin="20,0,18,0" MaxHeight="160"
                       Stretch="UniformToFill"/>
                <TextBlock Margin="20,20,18,30" Text="{Binding Description}"
                           Style="{StaticResource BodyTextStyle}"/>
                <ListView
                    AutomationProperties.AutomationId="ItemListView"
                    AutomationProperties.Name="Items In Group"
                    Margin="10,0,0,60"
                    ItemsSource="{Binding Source={StaticResource itemsViewSource}}"
                    ItemTemplate="{StaticResource Standard80ItemTemplate}"
                    SelectionMode="None"
                    IsItemClickEnabled="True"
                    ItemClick="ItemView_ItemClick"/>
```

```xml
            </StackPanel>
    </ScrollViewer>

    <VisualStateManager.VisualStateGroups>

        <!-- Visual states reflect the application's view state -->
        <VisualStateGroup>
            <VisualState x:Name="FullScreenLandscape"/>
            <VisualState x:Name="Filled"/>

            <!-- The entire page respects the narrower
                 100-pixel margin convention for portrait -->
            <VisualState x:Name="FullScreenPortrait">
                <Storyboard>
                    <ObjectAnimationUsingKeyFrames
                        Storyboard.TargetName="backButton"
                        Storyboard.TargetProperty="Style">
                        <DiscreteObjectKeyFrame KeyTime="0"
                            Value="{StaticResource PortraitBackButtonStyle}"/>
                    </ObjectAnimationUsingKeyFrames>

                    <ObjectAnimationUsingKeyFrames
                        Storyboard.TargetName="gridLayoutPanel"
                        Storyboard.TargetProperty="Margin">
                        <DiscreteObjectKeyFrame KeyTime="0"
                            Value="100,0,90,0"/>
                    </ObjectAnimationUsingKeyFrames>
                </Storyboard>
            </VisualState>

            <!--
                The back button and title have different styles when snapped,
                and the list representation is substituted
                for the grid displayed in all other view states
            -->
            <VisualState x:Name="Snapped">
                <Storyboard>
                    <ObjectAnimationUsingKeyFrames
                        Storyboard.TargetName="backButton"
                        Storyboard.TargetProperty="Style">
                        <DiscreteObjectKeyFrame KeyTime="0"
                            Value="{StaticResource SnappedBackButtonStyle}"/>
                    </ObjectAnimationUsingKeyFrames>
                    <ObjectAnimationUsingKeyFrames
                        Storyboard.TargetName="pageTitle"
                        Storyboard.TargetProperty="Style">
                        <DiscreteObjectKeyFrame KeyTime="0"
                            Value="{StaticResource SnappedPageHeaderTextStyle}"/>
                    </ObjectAnimationUsingKeyFrames>

                    <ObjectAnimationUsingKeyFrames
                        Storyboard.TargetName="gridScrollViewer"
                        Storyboard.TargetProperty="Visibility">
                        <DiscreteObjectKeyFrame KeyTime="0" Value="Collapsed"/>
                    </ObjectAnimationUsingKeyFrames>
```

continues

LISTING 10-9 *(continued)*

```
                    <ObjectAnimationUsingKeyFrames
                        Storyboard.TargetName="snappedScrollViewer"
                        Storyboard.TargetProperty="Visibility">
                        <DiscreteObjectKeyFrame KeyTime="0" Value="Visible"/>
                    </ObjectAnimationUsingKeyFrames>
                </Storyboard>
            </VisualState>
        </VisualStateGroup>
    </VisualStateManager.VisualStateGroups>
    </Grid>
</common:LayoutAwarePage>
```

LISTING 10-10: GroupDetail.xaml.cs

```csharp
using ArtistBrowser.ViewModels;
using System;
using System.Collections.Generic;
using System.IO;
using System.Linq;
using Windows.Foundation;
using Windows.Foundation.Collections;
using Windows.UI.Xaml;
using Windows.UI.Xaml.Controls;
using Windows.UI.Xaml.Controls.Primitives;
using Windows.UI.Xaml.Data;
using Windows.UI.Xaml.Input;
using Windows.UI.Xaml.Media;
using Windows.UI.Xaml.Navigation;

// The Group Detail Page item template is documented
// at http://go.microsoft.com/fwlink/?LinkId=234229

namespace ArtistBrowser
{
    /// <summary>
    /// A page that displays an overview of a single group,
    /// including a preview of the items within the group.
    /// </summary>
    public sealed partial class GroupDetailPage :
                            ArtistBrowser.Common.LayoutAwarePage
    {
        public GroupDetailPage()
        {
            this.InitializeComponent();
        }

        /// <summary>
        /// Invoked when this page is about to be displayed in a Frame.
        /// </summary>
        /// <param name="e">Event data that describes how this page was reached.
```

```
        /// The Parameter property provides the group to be displayed.</param>
        protected override void OnNavigatedTo(NavigationEventArgs e)
        {
            var group = (GroupViewModel)e.Parameter;
            DataContext = group;
        }

        /// <summary>
        /// Invoked when an item is clicked.
        /// </summary>
        /// <param name="sender">The GridView (or ListView when the application
        /// is snapped) displaying the item clicked.</param>
        /// <param name="e">Event data that describes the item clicked.</param>
        void ItemView_ItemClick(object sender, ItemClickEventArgs e)
        {
            // Navigate to the appropriate destination page,
            // configuring the new page by passing required
            // information as a navigation parameter
            this.Frame.Navigate(typeof(ItemDetailPage), e.ClickedItem);
        }
    }
}
```

LISTING 10-11: ItemDetail.xaml

```xml
<common:LayoutAwarePage
    x:Name="pageRoot"
    x:Class="ArtistBrowser.ItemDetailPage"
    xmlns="http://schemas.microsoft.com/winfx/2006/xaml/presentation"
    xmlns:x="http://schemas.microsoft.com/winfx/2006/xaml"
    xmlns:common="using:ArtistBrowser.Common"
    xmlns:viewModels="using:ArtistBrowser.ViewModels"
    xmlns:d="http://schemas.microsoft.com/expression/blend/2008"
    xmlns:mc="http://schemas.openxmlformats.org/markup-compatibility/2006"
    mc:Ignorable="d">

    <UserControl.Resources>

        <!-- Collection of items displayed by this page -->
        <CollectionViewSource
            x:Name="itemsViewSource"
            Source="{Binding Group.Items}"
            d:Source="{Binding GroupedItems.Groups[0].Items,
                        Source={d:DesignInstance Type=viewModels:ViewModelLocator,
                        IsDesignTimeCreatable=True}}"/>
    </UserControl.Resources>

    <!--
        This grid acts as a root panel for the page that defines two rows:
        * Row 0 contains the back button and page title
        * Row 1 contains the rest of the page layout
    -->
    <Grid
```

continues

LISTING 10-11 *(continued)*

```xml
Background="{StaticResource ApplicationPageBackgroundThemeBrush}"
d:DataContext="{Binding GroupedItems.Groups[0],
Source={d:DesignInstance Type=viewModels:ViewModelLocator,
IsDesignTimeCreatable=True}}">

<Grid.RowDefinitions>
    <RowDefinition Height="140"/>
    <RowDefinition Height="*"/>
</Grid.RowDefinitions>

<!-- Back button and page title -->
<Grid>
    <Grid.ColumnDefinitions>
        <ColumnDefinition Width="Auto"/>
        <ColumnDefinition Width="*"/>
    </Grid.ColumnDefinitions>
    <Button x:Name="backButton" Click="GoBack"
            IsEnabled="{Binding Frame.CanGoBack, ElementName=pageRoot}"
            Style="{StaticResource BackButtonStyle}"/>
    <TextBlock x:Name="pageTitle" Text="{Binding Title}"
               Style="{StaticResource PageHeaderTextStyle}"
               Grid.Column="1"/>
</Grid>

<!--
    The remainder of the page is one large FlipView that
    displays details for one item at a time, allowing the user
    to flip through all items in the chosen group
-->
<FlipView
    x:Name="flipView"
    AutomationProperties.AutomationId="ItemsFlipView"
    AutomationProperties.Name="Item Details"
    Grid.Row="1"
    Margin="0,-3,0,0"
    ItemsSource="{Binding Source={StaticResource itemsViewSource}}">

    <FlipView.ItemTemplate>
        <DataTemplate>

            <!--
                UserControl chosen as the templated item because it
                supports visual state management Loaded/unloaded events
                explicitly subscribe to view state updates from the page
            -->
            <UserControl Loaded="StartLayoutUpdates"
                         Unloaded="StopLayoutUpdates">
                <ScrollViewer x:Name="scrollViewer"
                    Style="{StaticResource HorizontalScrollViewerStyle}"
                    Grid.Row="1">

                    <!-- Content is allowed to flow across as
```

```
                    many columns as needed -->
<common:RichTextColumns x:Name="richTextColumns"
                    Margin="117,0,117,47">
    <RichTextBlock x:Name="richTextBlock" Width="560"
            Style="{StaticResource ItemRichTextStyle}">
        <Paragraph>
            <Run FontSize="26.667" FontWeight="Light"
                Text="{Binding Title}"/>
            <LineBreak/>
            <LineBreak/>
            <Run FontWeight="SemiBold"
                Text="{Binding Subtitle}"/>
        </Paragraph>
        <Paragraph LineStackingStrategy="MaxHeight">
            <InlineUIContainer>
                <Image x:Name="image" MaxHeight="480"
                        Margin="0,20,0,10"
                        Stretch="Uniform"
                        Source="{Binding Image}"/>
            </InlineUIContainer>
        </Paragraph>
        <Paragraph>
            <Run FontWeight="SemiLight"
                Text="{Binding Content}"/>
        </Paragraph>
    </RichTextBlock>

    <!-- Additional columns are created
        from this template -->
    <common:RichTextColumns.ColumnTemplate>
        <DataTemplate>
            <RichTextBlockOverflow Width="560"
                                Margin="80,0,0,0">
                <RichTextBlockOverflow.RenderTransform>
                    <TranslateTransform X="-1" Y="4"/>
                </RichTextBlockOverflow.RenderTransform>
            </RichTextBlockOverflow>
        </DataTemplate>
    </common:RichTextColumns.ColumnTemplate>
</common:RichTextColumns>

<VisualStateManager.VisualStateGroups>

    <!-- Visual states reflect the application's
        view state inside the FlipView -->
    <VisualStateGroup>
        <VisualState x:Name="FullScreenLandscape"/>
        <VisualState x:Name="Filled"/>

        <!-- Respect the narrower 100-pixel
            margin convention for portrait -->
        <VisualState x:Name="FullScreenPortrait">
            <Storyboard>
                <ObjectAnimationUsingKeyFrames
                    Storyboard.TargetName="richTextColumns"
```

continues

LISTING 10-11 *(continued)*

```
                                           Storyboard.TargetProperty="Margin">
                                             <DiscreteObjectKeyFrame KeyTime="0"
                                               Value="97,0,87,57"/>
                                           </ObjectAnimationUsingKeyFrames>
                                           <ObjectAnimationUsingKeyFrames
                                            Storyboard.TargetName="image"
                                            Storyboard.TargetProperty="MaxHeight">
                                               <DiscreteObjectKeyFrame KeyTime="0"
                                                 Value="400"/>
                                           </ObjectAnimationUsingKeyFrames>
                                       </Storyboard>
                                   </VisualState>

                                   <!-- When snapped, the content is reformatted
                                        and scrolls vertically -->
                                   <VisualState x:Name="Snapped">
                                       <Storyboard>
                                         <ObjectAnimationUsingKeyFrames
                                            Storyboard.TargetName="richTextColumns"
                                            Storyboard.TargetProperty="Margin">
                                               <DiscreteObjectKeyFrame KeyTime="0"
                                                   Value="17,0,17,57"/>
                                           </ObjectAnimationUsingKeyFrames>
                                           <ObjectAnimationUsingKeyFrames
                                            Storyboard.TargetName="scrollViewer"
                                            Storyboard.TargetProperty="Style">
                                               <DiscreteObjectKeyFrame KeyTime="0"
                          Value="{StaticResource VerticalScrollViewerStyle}"/>
                                           </ObjectAnimationUsingKeyFrames>
                                           <ObjectAnimationUsingKeyFrames
                                            Storyboard.TargetName="richTextBlock"
                                            Storyboard.TargetProperty="Width">
                                               <DiscreteObjectKeyFrame KeyTime="0"
                                                   Value="280"/>
                                           </ObjectAnimationUsingKeyFrames>
                                           <ObjectAnimationUsingKeyFrames
                                            Storyboard.TargetName="image"
                                            Storyboard.TargetProperty="MaxHeight">
                                               <DiscreteObjectKeyFrame KeyTime="0"
                                                   Value="160"/>
                                           </ObjectAnimationUsingKeyFrames>
                                       </Storyboard>
                                   </VisualState>
                               </VisualStateGroup>
                           </VisualStateManager.VisualStateGroups>
                       </ScrollViewer>
                   </UserControl>
               </DataTemplate>
           </FlipView.ItemTemplate>
       </FlipView>

       <VisualStateManager.VisualStateGroups>
```

```xml
            <!-- Visual states reflect the application's view state -->
            <VisualStateGroup>
                <VisualState x:Name="FullScreenLandscape"/>
                <VisualState x:Name="Filled"/>

                <!-- The back button respects the narrower
                     100-pixel margin convention for portrait -->
                <VisualState x:Name="FullScreenPortrait">
                    <Storyboard>
                        <ObjectAnimationUsingKeyFrames
                            Storyboard.TargetName="backButton"
                            Storyboard.TargetProperty="Style">
                            <DiscreteObjectKeyFrame KeyTime="0"
                                Value="{StaticResource PortraitBackButtonStyle}"/>
                        </ObjectAnimationUsingKeyFrames>
                    </Storyboard>
                </VisualState>

                <!-- The back button and title have
                     different styles when snapped -->
                <VisualState x:Name="Snapped">
                    <Storyboard>
                        <ObjectAnimationUsingKeyFrames
                            Storyboard.TargetName="backButton"
                            Storyboard.TargetProperty="Style">
                            <DiscreteObjectKeyFrame KeyTime="0"
                                Value="{StaticResource SnappedBackButtonStyle}"/>
                        </ObjectAnimationUsingKeyFrames>
                        <ObjectAnimationUsingKeyFrames
                            Storyboard.TargetName="pageTitle"
                            Storyboard.TargetProperty="Style">
                            <DiscreteObjectKeyFrame KeyTime="0"
                                Value="{StaticResource SnappedPageHeaderTextStyle}"/>
                        </ObjectAnimationUsingKeyFrames>
                    </Storyboard>
                </VisualState>
            </VisualStateGroup>
        </VisualStateManager.VisualStateGroups>
    </Grid>
</common:LayoutAwarePage>
```

LISTING 10-12: ItemDetail.xaml.cs

```csharp
using ArtistBrowser.ViewModels;
using System;
using System.Collections.Generic;
using System.IO;
using System.Linq;
using Windows.Foundation;
using Windows.Foundation.Collections;
using Windows.UI.Xaml;
using Windows.UI.Xaml.Controls;
```

continues

LISTING 10-12 *(continued)*

```
using Windows.UI.Xaml.Controls.Primitives;
using Windows.UI.Xaml.Data;
using Windows.UI.Xaml.Input;
using Windows.UI.Xaml.Media;
using Windows.UI.Xaml.Navigation;

// The Item Detail Page item template is documented
   at http://go.microsoft.com/fwlink/?LinkId=234232

namespace ArtistBrowser
{
    /// <summary>
    /// A page that displays details for a single item within a group
    /// while allowing gestures to flip through other items
    /// belonging to the same group.
    /// </summary>
    public sealed partial class ItemDetailPage :
                            ArtistBrowser.Common.LayoutAwarePage
    {
        public ItemDetailPage()
        {
            this.InitializeComponent();
        }

        /// <summary>
        /// Invoked when this page is about to be displayed in a Frame.
        /// </summary>
        /// <param name="e">Event data that describes how
        /// this page was reached. The Parameter property provides
        /// the initial item to be displayed.</param>
        protected override void OnNavigatedTo(NavigationEventArgs e)
        {
            var item = (ItemViewModel)e.Parameter;
            DataContext = item;
            this.flipView.SelectedItem = item;
        }
    }
}
```

Simplifying the Models

In a scenario in which the UI is binding directly to the model, the model ends up being significantly beyond the scope of representing data. This is poor separation of concerns and leads to complicated classes and ones that reference UI-oriented assemblies rather than sticking with just being representations of data. Listings 10-13 and 10-14 show a simpler version of the `Group` and `Item` models. These can now easily live outside the UI project and expose only simple types in its members. This enables you to share the classes across assemblies or even across tiers.

> **NOTE** *Because these simple models do not require inheriting base implementation, you can derive them from other frameworks that do require inheritance.*

LISTING 10-13: Group.cs

```
using System;
using System.Collections.Generic;
using System.Linq;
using System.Text;
using System.Threading.Tasks;

namespace ArtistBrowser.Model
{
    public sealed class Group
    {
        private readonly List<Item> _items;

        public Group(string uniqueId, string title, string subtitle,
                    string imagePath, string description)
        {
            _items = new List<Item>();
            Title = title;
            Subtitle = subtitle;
            ImagePath = imagePath;
        }


        public string Title { get; private set; }
        public string Subtitle { get; private set; }
        public string ImagePath { get; private set; }

        public IList<Item> Items { get { return _items; } }
    }
}
```

LISTING 10-14: Item.cs

```
using System;
using System.Collections.Generic;
using System.Linq;
using System.Text;
using System.Threading.Tasks;

namespace ArtistBrowser.Model
{
    public sealed class Item
    {
        public Item(string uniqueId, string title, string subtitle,
```

continues

LISTING 10-14 *(continued)*

```
                            string imagePath, string description, string content)
            {
                Title = title;
                Subtitle = subtitle;
                ImagePath = imagePath;
            }

            public string Title { get; private set; }
            public string Subtitle { get; private set; }
            public string ImagePath { get; private set; }
        }
    }
```

USING COMMANDS TO HANDLE INPUT

Commands are a means to pass input from the View to the ViewModel. The View interprets the device input as a semantic action and executes the appropriate command in the ViewModel using binding. These commands are an implementation of the ICommand interface, which at its core, has an action it must perform and optionally specifies if the command can be executed given its current state.

Commands help separate the object that interprets the semantics of an action from the implementation of the logic that executes as a result of the action. The implementation is in the Execute method. This enables several objects to use the same command logic and enables the command logic to be substituted and unit tested easily. A good example of reusing the command logic is editing operations, such as Cut, Copy, and Paste. Usually, multiple user actions, such as a menu item, a button, or a keyboard shortcut, perform these operations. With commands, each user action can bind to the same logic.

Commands also can indicate whether an action is available given the current state. You do this by implementing the CanExecute method. As in the example in the previous paragraph, a cut operation is only available when something is selected. In turn, the UI element can use the result of the method to determine if the element should be enabled or disabled. The controls that support commanding already support this behavior. Listing 10-15 creates a simple command, which marks an artist as a favorite.

> **NOTE** *When the result of* CanExecute *changes, be sure to raise the* PropertyChanged *event with the name of the property for the command so the UI will reflect the new state.*

LISTING 10-15: FavoriteCommand.cs

```csharp
using System;
using System.Collections.Generic;
using System.Linq;
using System.Text;
using System.Threading.Tasks;
using System.Windows.Input;

namespace ArtistBrowser.ViewModels
{
    public class FavoriteCommand : ICommand
    {
        public bool CanExecute(object parameter)
        {
            var item = (ItemViewModel)parameter;
            return item == null || !item.IsFavorite;
        }

        public event EventHandler CanExecuteChanged;

        public void Execute(object parameter)
        {
            var item = (ItemViewModel)parameter;
            item.IsFavorite = true;

            if (CanExecuteChanged != null)
                CanExecuteChanged(this, EventArgs.Empty);
        }
    }
}
```

To determine which item should be marked as a favorite, the `ItemViewModel` is passed in `parameter`. This is the command parameter set on the binding for the command. In addition, this code enables selections on the `GridView`; when a user selects an item, the `AppBar` displays and has a `Button` that binds to the new command (as shown in Listing 10-16).

LISTING 10-16: GroupedItemsPage.xaml

```xml
<common:LayoutAwarePage
    x:Name="pageRoot"
    x:Class="ArtistBrowser.GroupedItemsPage"
    xmlns="http://schemas.microsoft.com/winfx/2006/xaml/presentation"
    xmlns:x="http://schemas.microsoft.com/winfx/2006/xaml"
    xmlns:common="using:ArtistBrowser.Common"
    xmlns:viewModels="using:ArtistBrowser.ViewModels"
    xmlns:d="http://schemas.microsoft.com/expression/blend/2008"
    xmlns:mc="http://schemas.openxmlformats.org/markup-compatibility/2006"
    mc:Ignorable="d"
    DataContext="{Binding GroupedItems, Source={StaticResource locator}}"
    d:DataContext="{Binding GroupedItems,
                        Source={d:DesignInstance Type=viewModels:ViewModelLocator,
```

continues

LISTING 10-16 *(continued)*

```xml
                            IsDesignTimeCreatable=True}}">

    <UserControl.Resources>

        <!-- Collection of grouped items displayed by this page -->
        <CollectionViewSource
            x:Name="groupedItemsViewSource"
            Source="{Binding Groups}"
            IsSourceGrouped="true"
            ItemsPath="Items"
            d:Source="{Binding Groups}"/>

    </UserControl.Resources>

    <!--
        This grid acts as a root panel for the page that defines two rows:
        * Row 0 contains the back button and page title
        * Row 1 contains the rest of the page layout
    -->
    <Grid Background="{StaticResource ApplicationPageBackgroundThemeBrush}">
        <Grid.RowDefinitions>
            <RowDefinition Height="140"/>
            <RowDefinition Height="*"/>
        </Grid.RowDefinitions>

        <!-- Back button and page title -->
        <Grid>
            <Grid.ColumnDefinitions>
                <ColumnDefinition Width="Auto"/>
                <ColumnDefinition Width="*"/>
            </Grid.ColumnDefinitions>
            <Button x:Name="backButton" Click="GoBack"
                    IsEnabled="{Binding Frame.CanGoBack, ElementName=pageRoot}"
                    Style="{StaticResource BackButtonStyle}"/>
            <TextBlock x:Name="pageTitle" Text="{StaticResource AppName}"
                       Grid.Column="1"
                       Style="{StaticResource PageHeaderTextStyle}"/>
        </Grid>

        <!-- Horizontal scrolling grid used in most view states -->
        <ScrollViewer
            x:Name="itemGridScrollViewer"
            AutomationProperties.AutomationId="ItemGridScrollViewer"
            Grid.Row="1"
            Margin="0,-3,0,0"
            Style="{StaticResource HorizontalScrollViewerStyle}">

            <GridView
                x:Name="itemGridView"
                AutomationProperties.AutomationId="ItemGridView"
                AutomationProperties.Name="Grouped Items"
                ItemsSource="{Binding
```

```xml
                    Source={StaticResource groupedItemsViewSource}}"
            ItemTemplate="{StaticResource Standard250x250ItemTemplate}"
            SelectionMode="Single"
            SelectedIndex="-1"
            IsItemClickEnabled="True"
            SelectionChanged="itemGridView_SelectionChanged"
            ItemClick="ItemView_ItemClick" Margin="120,0,0,0">

            <GridView.ItemsPanel>
                <ItemsPanelTemplate>
                    <VirtualizingStackPanel Orientation="Horizontal"/>
                </ItemsPanelTemplate>
            </GridView.ItemsPanel>
            <GridView.GroupStyle>
                <GroupStyle>
                    <GroupStyle.HeaderTemplate>
                        <DataTemplate>
                            <Grid Margin="1,0,0,6">
                                <Button
                                    AutomationProperties.Name="Group Title"
                                    Content="{Binding Title}"
                                    Click="Header_Click"
                                    Style="{StaticResource TextButtonStyle}"/>
                            </Grid>
                        </DataTemplate>
                    </GroupStyle.HeaderTemplate>
                    <GroupStyle.Panel>
                        <ItemsPanelTemplate>
                            <VariableSizedWrapGrid Orientation="Vertical"
                                                  Margin="0,0,80,0"/>
                        </ItemsPanelTemplate>
                    </GroupStyle.Panel>
                </GroupStyle>
            </GridView.GroupStyle>
        </GridView>
</ScrollViewer>

<!-- Vertical scrolling list only used when snapped -->
<ScrollViewer
    x:Name="itemListScrollViewer"
    AutomationProperties.AutomationId="ItemListScrollViewer"
    Grid.Row="1"
    Visibility="Collapsed"
    Style="{StaticResource VerticalScrollViewerStyle}">

    <ListView
        x:Name="itemListView"
        AutomationProperties.AutomationId="ItemListView"
        AutomationProperties.Name="Grouped Items"
        Margin="10,-10,0,60"
        ItemsSource="{Binding
            Source={StaticResource groupedItemsViewSource}}"
        ItemTemplate="{StaticResource Standard80ItemTemplate}"
        SelectionMode="None"
        IsItemClickEnabled="True"
```

continues

LISTING 10-16 *(continued)*

```xml
                    ItemClick="ItemView_ItemClick">

                <ListView.GroupStyle>
                    <GroupStyle>
                        <GroupStyle.HeaderTemplate>
                            <DataTemplate>
                                <Grid Margin="7,7,0,0">
                                    <Button
                                        AutomationProperties.Name="Group Title"
                                        Content="{Binding Title}"
                                        Click="Header_Click"
                                        Style="{StaticResource TextButtonStyle}"/>
                                </Grid>
                            </DataTemplate>
                        </GroupStyle.HeaderTemplate>
                    </GroupStyle>
                </ListView.GroupStyle>
            </ListView>
        </ScrollViewer>

        <AppBar x:Name="appBar" Grid.Row="1"
                VerticalAlignment="Bottom" Height="88">
            <StackPanel Orientation="Horizontal">
                <Button Content="Favorite" Command="{Binding MarkFavorite}"
                        CommandParameter="{Binding SelectedItem,
                                        ElementName=itemGridView}" />
            </StackPanel>
        </AppBar>

        <VisualStateManager.VisualStateGroups>

            <!-- Visual states reflect the application's view state -->
            <VisualStateGroup>
                <VisualState x:Name="FullScreenLandscape"/>
                <VisualState x:Name="Filled"/>

                <!-- The entire page respects the narrower
                    100-pixel margin convention for portrait -->
                <VisualState x:Name="FullScreenPortrait">
                    <Storyboard>
                        <ObjectAnimationUsingKeyFrames
                          Storyboard.TargetName="backButton"
                          Storyboard.TargetProperty="Style">
                            <DiscreteObjectKeyFrame KeyTime="0"
                              Value="{StaticResource PortraitBackButtonStyle}"/>
                        </ObjectAnimationUsingKeyFrames>

                        <ObjectAnimationUsingKeyFrames
                          Storyboard.TargetName="itemGridView"
                          Storyboard.TargetProperty="Margin">
                            <DiscreteObjectKeyFrame KeyTime="0"
                                                Value="96,0,10,56"/>
                        </ObjectAnimationUsingKeyFrames>
```

```
                    </Storyboard>
                </VisualState>

                <!--
                    The back button and title have different styles when snapped,
                    and the list representation is substituted
                    for the grid displayed in all other view states
                -->
                <VisualState x:Name="Snapped">
                    <Storyboard>
                        <ObjectAnimationUsingKeyFrames
                          Storyboard.TargetName="backButton"
                          Storyboard.TargetProperty="Style">
                            <DiscreteObjectKeyFrame KeyTime="0"
                              Value="{StaticResource SnappedBackButtonStyle}"/>
                        </ObjectAnimationUsingKeyFrames>
                        <ObjectAnimationUsingKeyFrames
                          Storyboard.TargetName="pageTitle"
                          Storyboard.TargetProperty="Style">
                            <DiscreteObjectKeyFrame KeyTime="0"
                                Value="{StaticResource SnappedPageHeaderTextStyle}"/>
                        </ObjectAnimationUsingKeyFrames>

                        <ObjectAnimationUsingKeyFrames
                          Storyboard.TargetName="itemListScrollViewer"
                          Storyboard.TargetProperty="Visibility">
                            <DiscreteObjectKeyFrame KeyTime="0" Value="Visible"/>
                        </ObjectAnimationUsingKeyFrames>
                        <ObjectAnimationUsingKeyFrames
                          Storyboard.TargetName="itemGridScrollViewer"
                          Storyboard.TargetProperty="Visibility">
                            <DiscreteObjectKeyFrame KeyTime="0" Value="Collapsed"/>
                        </ObjectAnimationUsingKeyFrames>
                    </Storyboard>
                </VisualState>
            </VisualStateGroup>
        </VisualStateManager.VisualStateGroups>
    </Grid>
</common:LayoutAwarePage>
```

The page's `DataContext` is already bound to an instance of `GroupedItemsViewModel`. The property to which the `Button` on the `AppBar` is binding simply returns an instance of `FavoriteCommand` shown in Listing 10-15. This property is shown in Listing 10-17.

LISTING 10-17: GroupedItemsViewModel.cs

```
using ArtistBrowser.Model;
using GalaSoft.MvvmLight;
using System;
using System.Collections.Generic;
using System.Collections.ObjectModel;
using System.Linq;
using System.Text;
```

continues

LISTING 10-17 *(continued)*

```
using System.Threading.Tasks;
using System.Windows.Input;

namespace ArtistBrowser.ViewModels
{
    public class GroupedItemsViewModel : ViewModelBase
    {
        private readonly ObservableCollection<GroupViewModel> _groups;

        public GroupedItemsViewModel()
        {
            _groups = new ObservableCollection<GroupViewModel>();

            LoadGroups();
        }

        private void LoadGroups()
        {
            var data = new SampleData();

            foreach (var group in data.Groups)
            {
                _groups.Add(new GroupViewModel(group));
            }
        }

        public IList<GroupViewModel> Groups
        {
            get { return this._groups; }
        }

        public ICommand MarkFavorite { get { return new FavoriteCommand(); } }
    }
}
```

USING MVVM FRAMEWORKS

Several frameworks provide implementations of the MVVM design pattern with varying degrees of scope. One of the smaller, yet quite powerful frameworks is MVVM Light. You can add it to a project using NuGet in Visual Studio, as shown in Figure 10-1.

Understanding MVVM Light

MVVM Light has been around for quite a while and is fully supported in Windows 8. It provides several common MVVM foundational classes such as:

➤ **ViewModelBase:** A solid base class for implementing ViewModels.

➤ **RelayCommand:** This is a simple implementation of ICommand and can optionally include a typed parameter.

➤   `SimpleIoC`: An easy-to-use IoC container.

➤   `MessageBase`: You use this to send loosely coupled messages with optional content. You can use some subclasses, such as `NotificationMessage`, `DialogMessage`, and `PropertyChangedMessage`, for common behaviors.

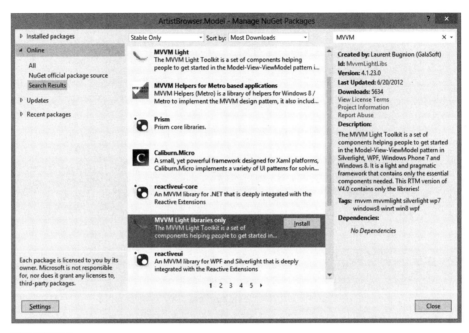

FIGURE 10-1

Because MVVM Light has an implementation of `ViewModelBase`, you can remove the one in your project, and the `ViewModel` classes in the project will need a `using` statement with the `GalaSoft.MvvmLight` namespace. In addition, you can change the `MarkFavorite` property in `GroupedItemsViewModel` to use MVVM Light's `RelayCommand` class, rather than the `ICommand` interface. The class implements `ICommand` and calls the `Action` (or `Action<T>` if a command parameter is used) passed in its constructor when the `Execute` method is invoked on the interface. Optionally, a `Func<T, bool>` can be passed to the constructor as well, which is called when `CanExecute` is invoked on the interface. This results in the creation of fewer classes and moves the implementation to the call site leading to more readable code. An example of this is shown in Listing 10-18.

LISTING 10-18: GroupedItemsViewModel.cs

```
using ArtistBrowser.Model;
using GalaSoft.MvvmLight;
using GalaSoft.MvvmLight.Command;
using System;
using System.Collections.Generic;
using System.Collections.ObjectModel;
```

continues

LISTING 10-18 *(continued)*

```csharp
using System.Linq;
using System.Text;
using System.Threading.Tasks;
using System.Windows.Input;

namespace ArtistBrowser.ViewModels
{
    public class GroupedItemsViewModel : ViewModelBase
    {
        private readonly ObservableCollection<GroupViewModel> _groups;

        public GroupedItemsViewModel()
        {
            _groups = new ObservableCollection<GroupViewModel>();

            LoadGroups();
        }

        private void LoadGroups()
        {
            var data = new SampleData();

            foreach (var group in data.Groups)
            {
                _groups.Add(new GroupViewModel(group));
            }
        }

        public IList<GroupViewModel> Groups
        {
            get { return this._groups; }
        }

        //public ICommand MarkFavorite { get { return new FavoriteCommand(); } }
        public ICommand MarkFavorite
        {
            get
            {
                return new RelayCommand<ItemViewModel>(item =>
                {
                    item.IsFavorite = true;
                    RaisePropertyChanged("MarkFavorite");
                },
                item =>
                {
                    return !item.IsFavorite;
                });
            }
        }
    }
}
```

Messaging in MVVM Light

One issue with apps with lots of models and ViewModels is the tight coupling of events and bindings used to notify of property changes and to invoke actions. To help loosen this tight coupling, you can use a lightweight messaging service to send messages to other classes that have no knowledge or reference to the class that sent the message. In the following example, an artist is marked as a favorite in its ViewModel. If you want to allow only one artist to be the favorite at any given time, without messaging, you must handle the PropertyChanged event on each instance, which requires wiring each one you create to an event handler creating circular references. However, using messaging, you can broadcast a message that can be handled anywhere in the app. In Listing 10-19, you Broadcast a PropertyChangedMessage so that GroupViewModel can remove any existing favorites.

LISTING 10-19: ItemViewModel.cs

```
using ArtistBrowser.Model;
using GalaSoft.MvvmLight;
using System;
using System.Collections.Generic;
using System.Linq;
using System.Text;
using System.Threading.Tasks;
using Windows.UI.Xaml.Media;
using Windows.UI.Xaml.Media.Imaging;

namespace ArtistBrowser.ViewModels
{
    public class ItemViewModel : ViewModelBase
    {
        private readonly Item _item;

        public ItemViewModel(Item item, GroupViewModel group)
        {
            _item = item;
            Group = group;
            _title = _item.Title;
        }

        private bool _isFavorite;
        public bool IsFavorite
        {
            get { return _isFavorite; }
            set
            {
                Broadcast(_isFavorite, value, "IsFavorite");
                Set("IsFavorite", ref _isFavorite, value);
                Set("Title", ref _title, _isFavorite ? _item.Title + " (favorite)"
                                                      : _item.Title);
            }
        }

        private string _title;
```

continues

LISTING 10-19 *(continued)*

```
        public string Title { get { return _title; } }
        public string Subtitle { get { return _item.Subtitle; } }
        public ImageSource Image
        {
            get
            {
                return new BitmapImage(new Uri("ms-appx:///" + _item.ImagePath));
            }
        }

        public GroupViewModel Group { get; private set; }
    }
}
```

This message is broadcast to the entire application. If you want to be notified about this or any other broadcast message, simply `Register` the message, as shown in Listing 10-20.

LISTING 10-20: GroupViewModel.cs

```csharp
using ArtistBrowser.Model;
using GalaSoft.MvvmLight;
using GalaSoft.MvvmLight.Messaging;
using System;
using System.Collections.Generic;
using System.Collections.ObjectModel;
using System.Linq;
using System.Text;
using System.Threading.Tasks;
using Windows.UI.Xaml.Media;
using Windows.UI.Xaml.Media.Imaging;

namespace ArtistBrowser.ViewModels
{
    public class GroupViewModel : ViewModelBase
    {
        private readonly Group _group;
        private readonly ObservableCollection<ItemViewModel> _items;

        public GroupViewModel(Group group)
        {
            _items = new ObservableCollection<ItemViewModel>(group.Items
                                .Select(i => new ItemViewModel(i, this)));
            _group = group;

            MessengerInstance.Register<PropertyChangedMessage<bool>>(this,
                changed =>
                {
                    if (changed.NewValue)
                    {
                        foreach (var item in Items.Where(i => i.IsFavorite))
```

```
                                    item.IsFavorite = false;
                            }
                     });
              }

              public string Title { get { return _group.Title; } }
              public string Subtitle { get { return _group.Subtitle; } }
              public ImageSource Image
              {
                  get
                  {
                      return new BitmapImage(new Uri("ms-appx:///" + _group.ImagePath));
                  }
              }

              public IEnumerable<ItemViewModel> Items { get { return _items; } }

          }
      }
```

The `PropertyChangedMessage<T>` type is registered. This is one of several built-in message types that MVVM Light provides. In addition, `NotificationMessage<T>` enables a text message along with a typed payload to broadcast as does `NotificationMessageAction<TCall backParameter>`, which adds the ability for the recipient to notify the sender that it has processed the message by calling its `Execute` method. If these do not suit your needs, you can extend `MessageBase` or `GenericMessage<T>` and provide any additional properties or methods the message requires. You send these other message types using `Send` on the `IMessenger` interface, located on `ViewModelBase.MessagerInstance` or the static property `Messenger.Default`.

SUMMARY

This chapter shows how to enhance an app with a more robust and maintainable architecture. At a glance, this architecture may appear to take more effort to implement, but it actually requires less effort. As you have seen, it is a fundamental part of the design of XAML. Binding and Commanding are commonplace among the many controls and libraries available. The gains from using MVVM become readily apparent when bug fixes and subsequent maintenance and features are implemented.

Fortunately, this is not a new technique so a lot has been written about this design pattern. As stated at the beginning of this chapter, you have many ways to solve a problem and this chapter shows just one way of implementing MVVM. Choose your own flavor of MVVM that fits your needs for the apps you build. In the end, using MVVM in your design can help you focus on the more creative aspects of your apps rather than getting stuck filling in UI elements and their event handlers.

11

Windows Store and Monetization

WHAT'S IN THIS CHAPTER?

- ➤ Windows Store for developers
- ➤ How to sell and promote apps in the Windows Store
- ➤ Developing trial, in-app purchase and ad-supported apps
- ➤ Application packaging and deployment
- ➤ Windows Application Certification Kit
- ➤ Deploying enterprise (LOB) apps
- ➤ Understanding the Windows Store policies
- ➤ Example: Color Shopping app

WROX.COM CODE DOWNLOADS FOR THIS CHAPTER

You can find the wrox.com code downloads for this chapter in the code file 205709 C11.zip at www.wrox.com/remtitle.cgi?isbn=1118205707 on the Download Code tab. To illustrate Windows Store monetization methods, in-app purchase, advertisements and trial conversions, I included a Color Shopping app example:

- ➤ ColorShoppingAppCS.zip

WINDOWS STORE OVERVIEW

The Windows Store opens a new global market on the largest software platform in the world. It's unmatched in terms of opportunity, scale, and global reach. There're billions of Windows users in the world, and as an app publisher, you can now show your craft and sell and distribute your products.

Planning ahead is always a good idea, and understanding how the Windows Store works can help you build your app to maximize its reach and potential, which is why this chapter is so important.

If you plan to sell your app, which is what most developers want, Windows Store offers flexible business models and pricing tiers. With the Windows Store you can choose between free, paid, in-app purchase, trials, third-party, ad-supported and multiple combinations to sell your apps, which this chapter discusses in detail.

If you develop for an enterprise, a public organization, or a government organization, and plan to distribute your apps, this chapter shows you application deployment options for your organization.

The Windows Store supports transparent terms and fair business, and enables developers to control price and revenue.

A LITTLE BACKGROUND

Being one of the first apps in the Windows Store involves a lot of responsibility. As a publisher of *Card Games Chest*, one of the first top apps released with the Windows Store preview, the author would like to thank all the reviewers, testers, and contributors, who relentlessly played the games, and provided suggestions, ideas, and motivation. You can download this app from the Games section of the Store, or from the Card games category.

I learned a lot from this experience, and in this chapter I'm happy to share this information with you. Many tips in the chapter came with the real-life experience of publishing this and other apps in the Windows Store, going through the app certification process, and making the app successful.

I also would like to thank Microsoft for this opportunity and once-in-a-lifetime experience to bring the app with preview versions of the Windows Store and for helping me with the design guidance.

> **NOTE** *You can use the Color Shopping app, which is referenced to illustrate application packaging, monetization, and other store decisions.*

HOW CONSUMERS SEE YOUR APP

From the customer point of view, the Windows Store is another app, deeply integrated with Windows 8, presented by the Store tile on your Start screen. Customers can also access the Windows Store from the browser (see Figure 11-1).

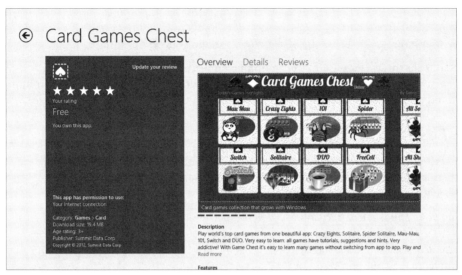

FIGURE 11-1

App Discovery

There are a myriad of ways your users can discover your apps, even if the app is not installed: From a Bing search query in the browser, browse through the Store app, from the Search charm, and of course from third-party sites and apps. Figure 11-2 shows how a Search charm invoked on the right sidebar returns suggestions of card games from Card Games Chest app, in this case a Solitaire game suggestion.

FIGURE 11-2

Investing in how your app looks in the Store and in search results is important: The app background, store logo, promotional images, description, and keywords are a part of your app submission and user impression. These are all keys to your app's success or failure.

With contracts and charms, Windows 8 offers a unique opportunity to you as a developer, which doesn't exist on other platforms. Investing in adding contracts to your app helps your app discoverability and overall user experience.

Making the First Good Impression

Before users install your app, they look at your app's listing. This first impression is often based on your app's listing page, which includes screenshots, app description, a logo, and reviews. The following are things you can do to optimize your app's first impression:

➤ **Naming your app is a key decision every developer makes.** The Windows Store enables you to reserve a 256-character name of your app as the first step in the submission process. You can also reserve names in other languages in addition to your primary app name. Tip: be creative; make your app stand out!

➤ **Consider the Store logo that displays your app's listing in the listing page and search results. These are important to the discoverability of your app.** Try to minimize graphical detail; the size of this image is small (50×50 pixels at 100 percent resolution) and seeing detailed graphics and even text may be hard.

➤ **At least one screenshot is required.** Your app can have up to eight. Each screenshot must be a .png file 1366×768 pixels in landscape or portrait. Tip: Use screenshots to highlight the most important features of your app. The first screenshot makes the best impression, but it's important to follow Windows Store policies regarding screenshots. They must be actual screenshots of the running app, without major enhancements.

➤ **Promotional images are used when your app is featured in the Windows Store.** These come in several sizes, and you must include them if you want your app to be considered for feature promotions. Tip: while promotional images are optional, we recommend submitting them to be considered for store promotional featuring. These images come in several large sizes (414×180, 414×468, 558×756, 846×468 pixels). Spend some time on them, or hire a graphics artist to make an attractive promotion.

➤ **Consider your use of Logo, Small Logo, and Splash Screen:** These are important when your app is installed and launched.

➤ **A description of your app is located right next to your app's screenshot in the detailed store listing.** The current limit is 10,000 characters, but the first paragraph of the description is what people coming to your app store page will read first. Try to capture their attention.

➤ **Features of your app are placed in a separate description section of your Windows Store app listing.** You can list up to 20 features in 200 characters or less.

> **NOTE** *You can make a decision on whether your app listing performs well by checking the Conversion report. (From your Windows Store developer account, select Dashboard ➪ Adoption ➪ Conversion). This report shows how often users looked at your app listing and how often it was downloaded and purchased.*

Promoting Your App

Promoting your app helps your app's visibility and discovery beyond the Windows Store. Bing search can help users find your app if you have a website supporting your app, even if it's a one-page site. Referencing your site from your app's Windows Store page, as well as including correct links, and especially links that follow the Windows Store protocol in your site help users navigate the Web and discover your application.

By adding Windows Store protocol links to your web page, you can provide a seamless connection for your Windows 8 users to the apps in the Windows Store. When users browse the Web with Internet Explorer 10 on Windows 8, Windows Store protocol informs users that there's an app available for the page they're viewing.

For your users who use Windows 8 and IE10, you can add Windows Store protocol links to your web pages by following this URL format: `ms-windows-store:PDP?PFN=`. You can always identify these users by the user agent string of their web browsers: `Windows NT 6.2`.

You can enable direct linking from your web page to your Windows Store app by adding the following meta tags to the `<head>` section of your web pages:

```
<meta name="msApplication-ID" content="MyApp.App"/>
<meta name="msApplication-PackageFamilyName" content="MyApp_h94ms93aemmt"/>
```

You can get your `msApplication-ID` and `msApplication-PackageFamilyName` from the Visual Studio by opening your `package.appxmanifest` manifest file in the Visual Studio and navigating to the Packaging tab. These tags are called `PackageName` and `PackageFamilyName`.

You can use `msApplication-ID` and `msApplication-PackageFamilyName` meta tags to provide a Get App for This Site button for your Windows 8 users.

SELLING YOUR APPS

The Windows Store provides many ways for you to get paid for your apps. Your revenue share starts at 70 percent for new apps and jumps to 80 percent after your app makes $25,000. Compared with other application stores, this model makes a big difference after your app begins to scale: In most other stores if your app makes $1M, you take home $700K, but in the Windows Store, your revenue share will be $97.5K + $700K — almost 13 percent, or $97.5K higher. Given that the size of the market is 700+ million Windows users, this can make a significant difference as your business grows. Table 11-1 shows the advantage of using the Windows Store for each platform.

TABLE 11-1: Windows Store Business Advantages

	WINDOWS	IOS	ANDROID
Your revenue share per $1,000,000	$797.5K	$700K	700K

Windows Store Economics

Compared with other platforms, the bigger size of the Windows market and its lower commission above $25K in revenues means that the Microsoft Windows Store enables you to reach your economic target much faster. Windows Store is designed for scale: if your app makes more than $25K in revenues, you'll be taking home a significantly larger percentage of revenues than that of the competing stores — 80 percent instead of 70 percent.

The Windows Store enables you to use any of the following monetization models, including third-party commerce:

➤ **One-time purchase:** With the one-time purchase model, your customer is charged only once, either full price ahead, or with a time limited or a feature differentiated trial.

➤ **Multiple purchases over time:** You can set a time limit on any of the products the customer buys within your app, for example renting a video over time. Alternatively, you can have purchases that never expire.

➤ **Ad Supported model:** You can have a trial version of your app supported by ads, and after the user buys the app, the ads are disabled. The ad supported model may be based on the Microsoft Advertising SDK or on your own ad system.

➤ **Existing commerce:** Alternatively, you can use your existing commerce, taking advantage of existing relationships, subscription systems and purchases.

> **NOTE** *Trials make a difference. From lessons I learned with my apps for Windows Phone, trials significantly drive downloads and revenue. My average conversion rate is 10 percent. With trials, you may get a significant increase in the number of downloads and revenue. The actual results may vary for your app.*

Windows Store API Overview

All types you need to interact with the Windows Store are defined in the `ApplicationModel.Store` namespace. This namespace also includes a simulator object, `CurrentAppSimulator`, which enables you to develop your apps without adding real products or interacting with the actual store.

> **NOTE** CurrentApp *won't work in your code until you submit the app to the store.*
> *You need to use* CurrentAppSimulator *to develop and test your licensing. After*
> *you finish development and testing, but before you submit your app to the store,*
> *you need to replace* CurrentAppSimulator *with* CurrentApp, *or your app will*
> *fail certification. When using the* CurrentAppSimulator, *the initial licensing is*
> *described in the XML file you can load with the* ReloadSimulatorAsync *method.*

If you don't want to manually search and replace CurrentAppSimulator with the CurrentApp, you can always use conditional directives, such as #if #else #endif. For example:

```
#if !RELEASE
using CurrentAppStore = Windows.ApplicationModel.Store.CurrentAppSimulator;
#else
using CurrentAppStore = Windows.ApplicationModel.Store.CurrentApp;
#endif
```

Table 11-2 shows main classes in the Windows Store API.

TABLE 11-2: ApplicationModel.Store Namespace

FILE	TASK
CurrentApp	Gets license and listing information for the current app and in-app purchases.
CurrentAppSimulator	Provides simulated, development, and testing types for the Windows Store. This includes loading simulated licenses from XML files.
LicenseInformation	Provides access to the app's license.
ListingInformation	Provides access to listing information in the store.
ProductLicense	In-app offer license.
ProductListing	In-app offer listing information.

Getting Started with the Color Shopping App

The Color Shopping app demonstrates how to use Windows Store API to unlock trials, handle in-app purchases and test the app by using a Windows Store proxy file. It also introduces a handy licensing data model you can reuse in your apps.

To begin with the Color Shopping app, you need Windows 8 with Visual Studio 2012. The app illustrates some of the important and advanced concepts of building apps for the Windows Store API. Figure 11-3 shows a screenshot of the Color Shopping app.

FIGURE 11-3

There's a complete version of the app in the archive, but if you want to start the project from scratch, open Visual Studio and create a new solution based on the C# Grid App (XAML) template.

1. Click File ⇨ Add ⇨ New Project.

2. Select a Templates ⇨ Visual C# ⇨ Windows Store ⇨ Grid App (XAML).

3. Name the project **CatalogShoppingAppCS**.

4. Table 11-3 lists the files that were added or modified from the standard template.

TABLE 11-3: Affected Project Files

FILE	TASK
App.xaml.cs	This file contains global event handlers and initialization code for data models.
LicenseControl.xaml	License Control flyout; this also contains a button to purchase application and convert from trial.
LicenseControl.xaml.cs	License Control flyout code-behind file.
License\TrialLicense.xml	Trial license definition file for testing and development. This license file is needed only when you test or develop. You don't need to deploy it to the store.
License\ InAppPurchaseLicense.xml	In-App purchase license definition file for testing and development. This license file is needed only when you test or develop. You don't need to deploy it to the store.

FILE	TASK
`DataModel\` `AppLicenseDataModel.cs`	App license data model for trials and app purchases.
`DataModel\` `CatalogDataModel.cs`	Data model for the shopping catalog.

`DataModel\`
`ProductsLicenseData`
`Model.cs`
	In-App purchase license data model for products associated with the app.

`DataModel\Helpers.cs`	Various helpers used in the project.
`GroupedItemsPage.xaml`	Main catalog page.
`GroupedItemsPage.xaml.cs`	Code behind for the main catalog page.

Application Walkthrough

The goal of this app is to demonstrate how to use the Windows Store API for trial conversions, in-app purchases, and ads. It's assumed that the app is trial-enabled in the beginning, and shows ads to monetize before it's purchased. You can open the Color Shopping example in Visual Studio and build and run the project by clicking F5.

After the app is purchased, it's converted from a trial to a paid version and the ads stop showing. For an in-app purchase, the app enables you to purchase color products. Figure 11-4 shows a flyout with the button that unlocks the trial.

FIGURE 11-4

App Overview

Because your app is not deployed to the store yet, when you run it from Visual Studio, it initializes with a proxy license file, instead of the actual license that comes with the Windows Store. You can check how initialization works in detail in the next few sections. Initialization is important because it enables you create and load license data models and present your products in the shopping app.

The application object also includes the code to initialize the Settings pane, which you can use to purchase the license for the app and convert it from a trial to a paid app.

After the application object and data models are initialized, the app loads GroupedItemsPage, which shows a grid bound to CatalogDataModel. This model includes product ids that match products in the proxy license file, product descriptions, colors, and other information.

> **NOTE** *Restarting the app in Visual Studio reloads the license proxy. Any purchases you make while the app is running in debug mode are only valid until the app is terminated.*

Trial Conversion Experience

You need to convert from the trial by purchasing a license to your app. Open the Settings charm by swiping from the right, or pointing your mouse at the bottom-right corner, and select the Settings charm, then click License menu item.

Click the button with the price of the app. A debug dialog opens, asking you to simulate the response for the Color Shopping app. Click OK. This concludes the trial conversion. Your app is now purchased.

Color Shopping app allows users purchase color products: "Green", "Pink", "Tomato" and others. When the user starts the trial app, the "Tomato" product is hidden, and on top of it we show the ad. When the trial is unlocked, all products show without ads.

> **NOTE** *It's a good practice to disable ads after the app is purchased. Advertisements disappear from the main page of the app after you complete the trial conversion, and you can now see the "Tomato" product.*

In-App Purchasing Experience

After you convert from a trial to a paid version, you can purchase products by following these steps:

1. Clicking "Pink" product, which takes you to the product details.

2. Click the button that shows the product price, and a dialog opens asking you to simulate purchasing. (Remember, your app is not in the store, so it uses CurrentAppSimulator instead of real-store transactions).

3. Click OK. The Pink product is now purchased.

4. Go back to the main app page.

5. Click "Blue" product; you see that in the product details it says PURCHASED. Your proxy license file intentionally includes a purchased product to demonstrate that when the actual app is deployed to the store some products may already be purchased earlier.

```
<!-- simulate purchased product -->
<Product ProductId="Blue">
      <IsActive>true</IsActive>
</Product>
```

App Summary

You know how the trial conversion and purchasing experience works in the app, and you can now dive into the implementation. You can look at three scenarios: supporting trials, in-app purchases, and ads.

Supporting Trials

When you publish your app in the Windows Store, you can specify if your app supports trials. In your app you want to detect whether your app is in trial mode to lock or unlock features, or to detect any license changes for time-limited trial.

You can show license information to the user, when the user invokes the Settings charm, for example in a License or About flyouts, or somewhere on the application canvas. You can also enable or disable some functionality in your app depending on the state of the license.

Throughout this chapter trial conversion and purchasing the app are synonymous events. When the app is purchased, its application license `IsTrial` property is set to false.

> **NOTE** *Typical trial conversion rate is 10 percent but may vary depending on the nature and quality of your app.*

Initializing Your App

In your `App.xaml.cs` you need to add a call to load trial license information and an event handler to support the settings contract to display your license information. A good place to add this event handler is the `OnLaunched` event.

You keep your product and application licensing data in the application-level properties `AppLicenseData` and `ProductLicenseData`. In the example you refer to these properties often when you implement your trial conversion and in-app purchase experience, as shown in Listing 11-1 for `App.xaml.cs` file.

LISTING 11-1: App.xaml.cs

```csharp
using CatalogShoppingAppCS.Common;
using CatalogShoppingAppCS.Common;
using System;
using System.Linq;
using System.Threading.Tasks;
using Windows.ApplicationModel;
using Windows.ApplicationModel.Activation;
using Windows.ApplicationModel.Store;
using Windows.Storage;
using Windows.UI.ApplicationSettings;
using Windows.UI.Xaml;
using Windows.UI.Xaml.Controls;
using Windows.UI.Xaml.Controls.Primitives;

namespace CatalogShoppingAppCS
{
    /// <summary>
    /// Provides application-specific behavior
    /// </summary>
    sealed partial class App : Application
    {
        private AppLicenseDataModel _appLicense = null;

        public AppLicenseDataModel AppLicenseData
        {
            get { return _appLicense; }
            set { _appLicense = value; }
        }

        private ProductLicenseDataModel _productLicenseData = null;

        public ProductLicenseDataModel ProductLicenseData
        {
            get { return _productLicenseData; }
            set { _productLicenseData = value; }
        }


        /// <summary>
        /// Initializes the singleton Application object.
        /// </summary>
        public App()
        {
            this.InitializeComponent();
            this.Suspending += OnSuspending;
        }

        /// <summary>
        /// Invoked when application execution is being suspended.
        /// </summary>
        private async void OnSuspending(object sender, SuspendingEventArgs e)
        {
            var deferral = e.SuspendingOperation.GetDeferral();
```

```csharp
        await SuspensionManager.SaveAsync();
        deferral.Complete();
}


/// <summary>
/// Invoked when the application is launched normally by the end user.
/// </summary>
protected override async void OnLaunched(LaunchActivatedEventArgs args)
{
        // Do not repeat app initialization when already running
        if (args.PreviousExecutionState
            == ApplicationExecutionState.Running)
        {
            Window.Current.Activate();
            return;
        }

        var rootFrame = new Frame();
        SuspensionManager.RegisterFrame(rootFrame, "AppFrame");

        if (args.PreviousExecutionState
            == ApplicationExecutionState.Terminated)
        {
            // Restore the saved session state only when appropriate
            await SuspensionManager.RestoreAsync();
        }

        if (rootFrame.Content == null)
        {
            if (!rootFrame.Navigate(
                typeof(GroupedItemsPage), "AllGroups")
                )
            {
                throw new Exception("Failed to create initial page");
            }
        }

        // Place the frame in the current Window
        // and ensure that it is active
        Window.Current.Content = rootFrame;
        Window.Current.Activate();

        // 1. load license proxy file (for development only)
#if DEBUG
        await LoadAppSimulatorProxyFileAsync("InAppPurchaseLicense.xml");
#endif

        // 2. load data models
        _appLicense = new AppLicenseDataModel();
        _productLicenseData = new ProductLicenseDataModel();

        // 3. update catalog with license data
        await ProductLicenseData.LoadAsync();

        // Register handler for CommandsRequested events
        SettingsPane.GetForCurrentView().CommandsRequested
```

LISTING 11-1 *(continued)*

```
                += OnCommandsRequested;
        }

        void OnCommandsRequested(SettingsPane sender,
            SettingsPaneCommandsRequestedEventArgs args)
        {
            var app = args.Request.ApplicationCommands;
            var license = app.FirstOrDefault(c =>
                (string)c.Id == "Command.License");
            if (license != null)
            {
                app.Remove(license);
            }

            app.Add(new SettingsCommand("Command.License", "License",
                (x) =>
                {
                    var settingsPopup = new Popup();
                    settingsPopup.IsLightDismissEnabled = true;
                    var licenseControl = new LicenseControl();
                    settingsPopup.Child = licenseControl;
                    settingsPopup.SetValue(Canvas.LeftProperty,
                        Window.Current.Bounds.Width - licenseControl.Width);
                    settingsPopup.SetValue(Canvas.TopProperty, 0);
                    settingsPopup.IsOpen = true;
                }));
        }

        public static async Task LoadAppSimulatorProxyFileAsync(string file)
        {
            StorageFolder proxyDataFolder
                = await Package.Current.InstalledLocation.
GetFolderAsync("License");
            StorageFile proxyFile = await proxyDataFolder.GetFileAsync(file);
            await CurrentAppSimulator.ReloadSimulatorAsync(proxyFile);
        }
    }
}
```

Towards the end of the OnLaunched event handler, you load your application license and product license data models. Let's examine these statements closely.

```
// 1. load license proxy file (for development only)
#if DEBUG
  // load license proxy file (for development only)
  await LoadAppSimulatorProxyFileAsync("InAppPurchaseLicense.xml");
#endif

// 2. load data models
_appLicense = new AppLicenseDataModel();
_productLicenseData = new ProductLicenseDataModel();

// 3. update catalog with license data
await ProductLicenseData.LoadAsync();
```

1. You need this step only at development time, and it asynchronously calls a method to load a license proxy file for CurrentAppSimulator. This method call is not needed when the app is deployed to the store.

```
public static async Task LoadAppSimulatorProxyFileAsync(string file)
{
    StorageFolder proxyDataFolder = await
        Package.Current.InstalledLocation.GetFolderAsync("License");
    StorageFile proxyFile = await proxyDataFolder.GetFileAsync(file);
    await CurrentAppSimulator.ReloadSimulatorAsync(proxyFile);
}
```

2. This step creates two data models included with the sample app:

   ➤ AppLicenseDataModel supports trial/paid scenarios for the app. If you need a simple data model without an in-app purchase, you can use this model and the corresponding TrialLicense.xml file for a proxy license.

   ➤ ProductLicenseDataModel supports trial/paid scenarios and also an in-app purchase. Use this model for more sophisticated in-app purchasing scenarios. The corresponding proxy file for this model is InAppPurchaseLicense.xml.

3. This step loads the product data model with store pricing and other product listing information.

```
// 3. update catalog with license data
 await ProductLicenseData.LoadAsync();
```

The actual method implementation for this call connects catalog data model with live product listing information, in the snippet that follows:

```
/// <summary>
/// Loads products with
/// </summary>
/// <returns></returns>
public async Task LoadAsync()
{
    var groups = CatalogDataModel.GetGroups("AllGroups");

    var listing = await
        CurrentAppSimulator.LoadListingInformationAsync();
    if (listing != null)
    {
        foreach (var productListing in listing.ProductListings)
        {
            var product = new ProductLicense
            {
                ProductId = productListing.Key,
                Listing = productListing.Value
            };
            Items.Add(product);
```

```
                    UpdateCatalogWithProductListings(groups, product);
                }
            }
        }
```

In the `OnCommandRequested` event handler, you need to add the `LicenseControl` object, which is simply a `UserControl` with bindings in `LicenseDataModel`, the license data model class. The `LoadTrialModeProxyFileAsync` method is a helper to load your development time license and product data into the `CurrentAppSimulator`. Remember that this code needs to be replaced with `CurrentApp` when you deploy it to the store, so you may want to enclose all `CurrentAppSimulator` references in `#if… #endif` conditional blocks.

```
        void OnCommandsRequested(SettingsPane sender,
            SettingsPaneCommandsRequestedEventArgs args)
        {
            var app = args.Request.ApplicationCommands;
            var license = app.FirstOrDefault(c =>
                (string)c.Id == "Command.License");
            if (license != null)
            {
                app.Remove(license);
            }

            app.Add(new SettingsCommand("Command.License",
    "License",
                (x) =>
            {
                var settingsPopup = new Popup();
                settingsPopup.IsLightDismissEnabled = true;
                var licenseControl = new LicenseControl();
                settingsPopup.Child = licenseControl;
                settingsPopup.SetValue(Canvas.LeftProperty,
                 Window.Current.Bounds.Width - licenseControl.Width);
                settingsPopup.SetValue(Canvas.TopProperty, 0);
                settingsPopup.IsOpen = true;
            }));

        }
```

Testing with Trial License Proxy File

The proxy trial license information file is simply an XML file with the schema defined by the Windows Store. You can change the proxy listing information to fit your development goals. Typical changes include modifying `<IsActive>`,`<IsTrial>` and `<ExpirationDate>` to test various scenarios and responses for your app. Listing 11-2 shows an example of a trial license simulator file.

LISTING 11-2: TrialLicense.xml

```
<?xml version="1.0" encoding="utf-16" ?>
<CurrentApp>
  <ListingInformation>
```

```
    <App>
      <AppId>CatalogShoppingAppCS</AppId>
      <LinkUri>http://apps.microsoft.com/app/2B14D306-D8F8-4066-A45B-0FB3464C67F2
      </LinkUri>
      <CurrentMarket>en-US</CurrentMarket>
      <AgeRating>3</AgeRating>
      <MarketData xml:lang="en-us">
        <Name>Trial license</Name>
        <Description>Sample app trial license</Description>
        <Price>4.99</Price>
        <CurrencySymbol>$</CurrencySymbol>
      </MarketData>
    </App>
  </ListingInformation>
  <LicenseInformation>
    <App>
      <IsActive>true</IsActive>
      <IsTrial>true</IsTrial>
      <ExpirationDate>2013-01-01T00:00:00.00Z</ExpirationDate>
    </App>
  </LicenseInformation>
</CurrentApp>
```

App License Data Model

Because you need to present license information in your pages and controls, adding a data model is always a good idea. This example includes a class for a basic license data model: AppLicenseDataModel. The class implements the INotifyPropertyChanged interface and can be used in data-bound scenarios. Listing 11-3 shows the app license data model.

LISTING 11-3: AppLicenseDataModel.cs

```
using CatalogShoppingAppCS.Data;
using System;
using System.ComponentModel;
using Windows.ApplicationModel.Core;
using Windows.ApplicationModel.Store;
using Windows.UI.Core;

namespace CatalogShoppingAppCS
{
    public class AppLicenseDataModel : INotifyPropertyChanged
    {
        public event PropertyChangedEventHandler PropertyChanged;

        private bool _licensed = false;
        private string _price;

        public AppLicenseDataModel()
        {
            if (CurrentAppSimulator.LicenseInformation.IsTrial)
            {
```

continues

LISTING 11-3 *(continued)*

```csharp
            CurrentAppSimulator.LicenseInformation.LicenseChanged
                += OnLicenseChanged;
            GetListingInformationAsync();
        }
        else
            _licensed = true;
    }

    private async void GetListingInformationAsync()
    {
        var listing =
            await CurrentAppSimulator.LoadListingInformationAsync();
        _price = listing.FormattedPrice;
    }

    private async void OnLicenseChanged()
    {
        if (!CurrentAppSimulator.LicenseInformation.IsTrial)
        {
            _licensed = true;
            CurrentAppSimulator.LicenseInformation.LicenseChanged
                -= OnLicenseChanged;

            // need this if the license change occurs on a different
            // thread to update UI bound elements from the data model
            CoreApplication.MainView.CoreWindow.Dispatcher.RunAsync(
                CoreDispatcherPriority.Normal, () =>
            {
                if (IsLicensed)
                {
                    var groups = CatalogDataModel.GetGroups("AllGroups");
                    foreach (var group in groups)
                    {
                        foreach (var item in group.Items)
                        {
                            item.IsAdDisplayed = false;
                        }
                    }
                }

                if (PropertyChanged != null)
                {
                    PropertyChanged(this,
                        new PropertyChangedEventArgs(String.Empty));
                }
            });
        }
    }

    public bool IsLicensed
    {
        get { return _licensed; }
    }
```

```
public bool IsTrial
{
    get { return !_licensed; }
}

public string LicenseInfo
{
    get
    {
        var expiration =
        CurrentAppSimulator.LicenseInformation.ExpirationDate;
        if (!_licensed)
        {
            return "Trial Version";
        }
        else
        {
            return ("Valid until "
                + expiration.LocalDateTime.ToString("dddd, MMMM d, yyyy"));
        }
    }
}

public string FormattedPrice
{
    get
    {
        if (!String.IsNullOrEmpty(_price))
        {
            return
                "Upgrade to the full version for "
                + _price;
        }
        else
        {
            return "Upgrade to the full Version";
        }
    }
}
}
}
```

And finally, to complete this example, you need to add a LicenseControl, based on a UserControl. This control opens when the user invokes a Settings charm and selects License. The content of your purchase Button binds to the FormattedPrice property of your data model.

You'll need to make your LicenseControl bind to your license data model in the control's constructor:

```
this.DataContext = App.LicenseData;
```

Listing 11-4 shows License Control flyout XAML.

LISTING 11-4: LicenseControl.xaml

```xml
<UserControl
    x:Class="CatalogShoppingAppCS.LicenseControl"
    xmlns="http://schemas.microsoft.com/winfx/2006/xaml/presentation"
    xmlns:x="http://schemas.microsoft.com/winfx/2006/xaml"
    xmlns:local="using:CatalogShoppingAppCS"
    xmlns:common="using:CatalogShoppingAppCS.Common"
    xmlns:d="http://schemas.microsoft.com/expression/blend/2008"
    xmlns:mc="http://schemas.openxmlformats.org/markup-compatibility/2006"
    mc:Ignorable="d"
    Width="346"
    Height="768"
    Background="#FF77DE3D"
    d:DesignHeight="346"
    d:DesignWidth="768">

    <UserControl.Resources>
        <common:BooleanToVisibilityConverter x:Key="BooleanToVisibilityConverter"/>
    </UserControl.Resources>

<Grid Background="#FF77DE3D">
        <StackPanel Margin="20,20,0,0">
            <TextBlock Text="License Sample" FontFamily="Segoe UI"
              FontWeight="SemiLight" FontSize="26" />
            <TextBlock Text="{Binding LicenseInfo}" FontFamily="Segoe UI"
              FontWeight="SemiLight" FontSize="18" TextWrapping="Wrap" />
            <Button x:Name="purchase" Background="White" Width="225" Height="120"
             Margin="0,24,0,0"
              Visibility="{Binding IsTrial, Converter={StaticResource
              BooleanToVisibilityConverter}}"
              Click="purchase_Click">
                <Button.Content>
                    <TextBlock Text="{Binding FormattedPrice}"
                     TextWrapping="Wrap"
                     TextAlignment="Center" />
                </Button.Content>
            </Button>
        </StackPanel>
    </Grid>
</UserControl>
```

Trial Conversions

Now when the user invokes your License control from the Settings charm, you can show them the state of your license, and offer an opportunity to purchase the app and unlock or convert the trial version.

```
/// <summary>
/// App purchase (Trial Conversion)
/// </summary>
```

```
/// <param name="sender"></param>
/// <param name="e"></param>
private async void purchase_Click(object sender, RoutedEventArgs e)
{
  try
  {
    // purchase the app
    await CurrentAppSimulator.RequestAppPurchaseAsync(false);
  }
  catch (Exception)
  {
    // handle this exception if something goes wrong
    // with the purchase
  }
}
```

The purchase_Click event handler calls the
CurrentAppSimulator RequestAppPurchaseAsync
method, which presents you with an option to choose
whether you want to simulate purchasing the app or
return any of the error codes back to the app. When you
deploy your app, you'll need to replace this with a call to
CurrentApp. Figure 11-5 shows a dialog that
simulates the purchase.

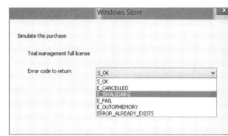

FIGURE 11-5

When license changes, for example if it expires, or the app gets purchased, the store calls the
LicenseChanged event handler defined in your license data model:

```
public AppLicenseDataModel()
{
   if (CurrentAppSimulator.LicenseInformation.IsTrial)
   {
     CurrentAppSimulator.LicenseInformation.LicenseChanged +=
         OnLicenseChanged;
     GetListingInformationAsync();
   }
   else
     _licensed = true;
}
```

The License Data Model uses this to fire PropertyChanged events, from the INotifyProperty
changed interface, which updates any data bound controls in your user interface, so your user
interface will be up to date with the state of the license.

```
private async void OnLicenseChanged()
{
    if (!CurrentAppSimulator.LicenseInformation.IsTrial)
    {
        _licensed = true;
        CurrentAppSimulator.LicenseInformation.LicenseChanged -=
            OnLicenseChanged;

        // need this to the license change occurs on a different thread
        // to update UI bound elements from the data model
```

```
CoreApplication.MainView.CoreWindow.Dispatcher.RunAsync(
  CoreDispatcherPriority.Normal,
  () =>
  {
    if (IsLicensed)
    {
        var groups = CatalogDataModel.GetGroups("AllGroups");
        foreach (var group in groups)
            foreach (var item in group.Items)
                item.IsAdDisplayed = false;
    }

    if (PropertyChanged != null)
    {
        PropertyChanged(this, new
            PropertyChangedEventArgs(String.Empty));
    }
  });
}
}
```

In-App Purchases

The in-app purchase model offers the most flexibility for developers. With trials users can either purchase the whole app or keep it as a trial. With in-app purchases you can offer products or features from within your app. Before you implement an in-app purchase, think about your business model:

➤ **Individual features:** Are there any features you want to sell separately in your app?

➤ **Product expiration:** Will your products be a one-time purchase, or you want them to expire so that users can renew them?

➤ **Think about the competition:** Do they offer the same features free of charge?

From the API prospective, the in-app purchases model adds another object tier for the store associated with your app: products. You can add as many products as you want to any of your apps; after you add them to the production store, you cannot delete them, so it's a good idea to play with the `CurrentAppSimulator` and XML licenses.

Product Data Model

Just like you did with the app license data model, let's add a data model for products. This can help you display license information in the application and handle license-specific events. Listing 11-5 shows a file with licenses for in-app purchase products.

LISTING 11-5: ProductLicenseDataModel.cs

```
using CatalogShoppingAppCS.Data;
using System;
using System.Collections.Generic;
using System.Collections.ObjectModel;
```

```csharp
using System.ComponentModel;
using System.Linq;
using System.Threading.Tasks;
using Windows.ApplicationModel.Core;
using Windows.ApplicationModel.Store;
using Windows.UI.Core;

namespace CatalogShoppingAppCS
{
    public class ProductLicense : INotifyPropertyChanged
    {
        #region Properties

        private string _productId;
        public string ProductId
        {
            get
            {
                return _productId;
            }
            set
            {
                _productId = value;
                var licenseInfo = CurrentAppSimulator.LicenseInformation;
                var license = licenseInfo.ProductLicenses[_productId];
                if (license.IsActive)
                {
                    _licensed = true;
                }
                else
                {
                    licenseInfo.LicenseChanged += OnLicenseChanged;
                    GetListingInformationAsync();
                }

            }
        }

        private ProductListing _listing;

        public ProductListing Listing
        {
            get { return _listing; }
            set { _listing = value; }
        }

        private bool _licensed = false;

        public bool IsLicensed
        {
            get { return _licensed; }
        }

        public bool IsTrial
        {
```

continues

LISTING 11-5 *(continued)*

```
            get { return !_licensed; }
        }

        public string OwnerStatus
        {
            get {
                if (_licensed)
                {
                    return "PURCHASED";
                }
                else
                {
                    return "";
                }
            }
        }

        public string VerbosePrice
        {
            get
            {
                if (_listing != null &&
                    !String.IsNullOrEmpty(_listing.FormattedPrice))
                    return "Purchase product for " + _listing.FormattedPrice;
                else
                    return "Purchase this product";
            }
        }

        #endregion

        #region Events

        // Event for INotifyPropertyChanged interface
        public event PropertyChangedEventHandler PropertyChanged;

        private void OnLicenseChanged()
        {
            var licenseInfo = CurrentAppSimulator.LicenseInformation;
            if (licenseInfo.ProductLicenses[_productId].IsActive)
            {
                _licensed = true;
                licenseInfo.LicenseChanged -= OnLicenseChanged;

                // need this to the license change occurs on a different thread
                // to update UI bound elements from the data model
                CoreApplication.MainView.CoreWindow.Dispatcher.RunAsync(
                    CoreDispatcherPriority.Normal, () =>
                {
                    if (PropertyChanged != null)
                    {
                        PropertyChanged(this,
                            new PropertyChangedEventArgs(String.Empty));
```

```
                        }

                });

            }

        }

        #endregion

        /// <summary>
        /// Loads listing information asynchronously
        /// </summary>
        private async void GetListingInformationAsync()
        {
            var listing = await CurrentAppSimulator.LoadListingInformationAsync();
            _listing = listing.ProductListings[_productId];
            if (PropertyChanged != null)
            {
                PropertyChanged(this,
                    new PropertyChangedEventArgs(String.Empty));
            }
        }


    }

    public class ProductLicenseDataModel : INotifyPropertyChanged
    {
        public ObservableCollection<ProductLicense> Items { get; set; }

        public ProductLicenseDataModel()
        {
            Items = new ObservableCollection<ProductLicense>();
        }

        /// <summary>
        /// Loads products with
        /// </summary>
        /// <returns></returns>
        public async Task LoadAsync()
        {
            var groups = CatalogDataModel.GetGroups("AllGroups");

            var listing = await CurrentAppSimulator.LoadListingInformationAsync();
            if (listing != null)
            {
                foreach (var productListing in listing.ProductListings)
                {
                    var product = new ProductLicense
                    {
                        ProductId = productListing.Key,
                        Listing = productListing.Value
```

continues

LISTING 11-5 *(continued)*

```
                };
                Items.Add(product);
                UpdateCatalogWithProductListings(groups, product);
            }


        }
    }

    private void UpdateCatalogWithProductListings(
            IEnumerable<CatalogDataGroup> groups,
            ProductLicense product)
    {
        foreach (var group in groups)
        {
            var item = group.Items.FirstOrDefault(i => i.Title ==
              product.ProductId);
            if (item != null)
            {
                item.Product = product;
                break;
            }
        }
    }

    void OnPropertyChanged(object sender, PropertyChangedEventArgs e)
    {
        NotifyPropertyChanged(String.Empty);
    }


    public event PropertyChangedEventHandler PropertyChanged;
    private void NotifyPropertyChanged(String propertyName)
    {
        PropertyChangedEventHandler handler = PropertyChanged;
        if (null != handler)
        {
            handler(this, new PropertyChangedEventArgs(propertyName));
        }
    }
    }
    }
}
```

Testing with License Proxy File

You need a test license proxy located in the License folder of the Color Shopping app. In a real app this license is associated with the app installation and provided by the Windows Store. In the following example it comes from the proxy XML file. To test your in-app purchase app, you also need to load `CurrentAppSimulator` with an in-app purchase license file. You can notice in Listing 12-6 that the file looks similar to your TrialLicense.xml but adds `<Product>` tags to the `<ListingInformation>` and `<LicenseInformation>`. Listing 11-6 shows listing information for in-app purchases.

LISTING 11-6: InAppPurchaseLicense.xml for the "Pink" product

```xml
<?xml version="1.0" encoding="utf-16" ?>
<CurrentApp>
  <ListingInformation>
    <App>
      <AppId>a8695030-29b8-45c4-8a5b-a1647a1bb104</AppId>
      <LinkUri>
         http://apps.microsoft.com/app/a8695030-29b8-45c4-8a5b-a1647a1bb104
      </LinkUri>
      <CurrentMarket>en-US</CurrentMarket>
      <AgeRating>3</AgeRating>
      <MarketData xml:lang="en-us">
        <Name>Color Shopping</Name>
        <Description>Color Shopping Sample App</Description>
        <Price>4.99</Price>
        <CurrencySymbol>$</CurrencySymbol>
      </MarketData>
    </App>
    <Product ProductId="Pink">
      <MarketData xml:lang="en-us">
        <Name>Pink</Name>
        <Price>1.99</Price>
        <CurrencySymbol>$</CurrencySymbol>
      </MarketData>
    </Product>
  </ListingInformation>
  <LicenseInformation>
    <App>
      <IsActive>true</IsActive>
      <IsTrial>true</IsTrial>
      <ExpirationDate>2013-01-01T00:00:00.00Z</ExpirationDate>
    </App>
    <Product ProductId="Pink">
      <IsActive>false</IsActive>
    </Product>

  </LicenseInformation>
</CurrentApp>
```

The listing contains the Pink product, and product id matches product id in your main `CatalogDataModel` collection. Basically, you link the two collections together: The store collection and the product listings collection with these models.

Purchasing a Product

When the user clicks the product in the main `GroupedItemsPage`, the user is redirected to `ItemDetailPage`, which shows the current product price and licensing information. Depending on whether the product is purchased, you present the purchaser with a button with the product's `FormattedPrice` or a message informing the user that this product is already purchased. Figure 11-6 shows detail page for the product.

FIGURE 11-6

`FormattedPrice` is a property of the `ProductListing` object in the store, and it comes in handy when your app sells in international markets: US users see US dollars and in Europe the information is presented in euros. Depending on the market the currency and price will be used in this field.

When the user clicks the Purchase button, you can use the `CurrentAppSimulator`'s `Request ProductPurchaseAsync` method to complete the transaction. When the product is purchased, its `IsLicensed` property is set to true. Listing 11-7 shows the code for the product detail page.

LISTING 11-7: ItemDetailPage.xaml.cs

```
using CatalogShoppingAppCS.Data;
using System;
using System.Collections.Generic;
using Windows.ApplicationModel.Store;
using Windows.UI.Xaml;

namespace CatalogShoppingAppCS
{
    /// <summary>
    /// A page that displays details for a single item.
    /// </summary>
    public sealed partial class ItemDetailPage
        : CatalogShoppingAppCS.Common.LayoutAwarePage
    {
        public ItemDetailPage()
        {
            this.InitializeComponent();
            this.DefaultViewModel["ProductLicenseData"]
                = (App.Current as App).ProductLicenseData;
```

```csharp
        }

        protected override void LoadState(Object navigationParameter,
            Dictionary<String, Object> pageState)
        {
            // Allow saved page state to override the initial item to display
            if (pageState != null && pageState.ContainsKey("SelectedItem"))
            {
                navigationParameter = pageState["SelectedItem"];
            }

            var item = CatalogDataModel.GetItem(
                (String)navigationParameter);
            this.DefaultViewModel["Group"] = item.Group;
            this.DefaultViewModel["Items"] = item.Group.Items;
            this.flipView.SelectedItem = item;
        }

        /// <summary>
        /// Preserves state associated with this page
        /// </summary>
        protected override void SaveState(Dictionary<String, Object> pageState)
        {
            var selectedItem = (CatalogDataItem)this.flipView.SelectedItem;
            pageState["SelectedItem"] = selectedItem.UniqueId;
        }

        /// <summary>
        /// Purchase the product
        /// </summary>
        /// <param name="sender"></param>
        /// <param name="e"></param>
        private async void purchase_Click(object sender, RoutedEventArgs e)
        {
            var selectedItem = (CatalogDataItem)this.flipView.SelectedItem;
            try
            {
                await CurrentAppSimulator.RequestProductPurchaseAsync(
                    selectedItem.Product.Listing.ProductId, false);
            }
            catch (Exception)
            {
                // handle this exception when the in-app purchase
                //  didn't succeed or the user decided to ignore the purchase
            }
        }
    }
}
```

NOTE *You should use asynchronous calls for any store-related operations to keep your UI from blocking. Exceptions such as any exceptions related to a purchase fit naturally in the asynchronous programming pattern.*

Adding Product Expiration

Some products may be a one-time purchase, for example levels in your game or themes of your app. These are *durable products*, or *durables*. You can design some products to expire after a period of time in a model similar to subscriptions. These *consumable* products may include gold or chips for your games or an expiring subscription to access some content.

The Windows Store enables you to decide what products you need in your app and offers choices to support both: lifetime or durable products as well as consumable products. The previous sections discussed an in-app purchase model for a one-time purchase. You can also make a consumable product by simply specifying an expiration date in the Windows Store and your proxy file for testing purposes.

To add an expiration date to a product in your proxy file, simply add the `ExpirationDate` element to the listing, like so:

```
<Product ProductId="product1">
    <IsActive>true</IsActive>
    <ExpirationDate>2013-01-01T00:00:00.00Z</ExpirationDate>
</Product>
```

Product expiration adds yet another dimension to your business model. Now you can design apps where users can use a feature for a certain period of time before the feature expires.

Adding Advertisements

Although ads may require a separate chapter to cover, they are also inseparable from monetization strategies; for that reason, ads are included in the example in this section.

In your Windows Store app, you can choose between Microsoft Advertising and third-party ads. Microsoft Advertising SDK, which comes with Windows 8 and Windows Phone, provides a quick way to add ads to your app. Advantages of using Microsoft ads are great integration of the SDK with Visual Studio, but if you have an established relationship with a third party ads provider, you can use it too.

While it's still in trial mode, Microsoft Ads can help you monetize your app, which helps you reach a wider audience by enabling trials — and you still get paid for your app.

Placing Ads

You can place ads on the application canvas. Ads in Microsoft Advertising SDK come in different sizes, and you can choose the best size for different pages of your app: 728×90 (great for top or bottom screen placement), 500×13, 300×250, 292×60, 250×250 (great for `GridView` control), 250×125, 160×600 (skyscraper). Bigger ads, such as skyscraper or 728×90, usually attract more publishers and may have higher revenue.

> **WARNING** *You must understand Windows Store policies for ads. For example, you cannot place ads on tiles, notifications, or swipe-from-edge surfaces, such as Settings or AppBar. You must have some additional content besides ads, and your ads must not execute any code.*

Referencing Advertising SDK

This section shows you how to add Microsoft Advertising SDK to your app. In Visual Studio in Solution Explorer:

1. Install Microsoft Advertising SDK.

2. In Visual Studio, right-click solution References ➪ Add Reference.

3. In the Reference Manager dialog that follows, check Microsoft Advertising SDK for XAML.

4. Click OK and you'll see a reference to Microsoft Advertising SDK added to your project. Figure 11-7 shows how to add Microsoft Advertising SDK reference to your project.

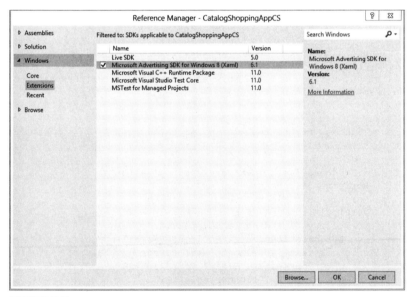

FIGURE 11-7

> **NOTE** *Your app has several pages, and ideally you want advertising to appear on all of them while the app is the trial mode. When the app is purchased, you want all ads to disappear. You must be fair with your users: Disabling ads in a purchased version is something everyone expects from a good quality app.*

4. After you have Microsoft Advertising SDK referenced in your project, add its namespace to GroupedItemsPage.xaml. In our example we used a yellow rectangle as a replacement for AdControl, but you can also add the real control:

```
xmlns:UI="using:Microsoft.Advertising.WinRT.UI"
```

5. Update your data template for the main `GridView`. In your `DataTemplate` make Microsoft `AdControl` visible or invisible depending on whether the `IsAdDisplayed` data model property is set to true or false. Listing 11-8 shows `DataTemplate` for grid items including `AdControl`.

LISTING 11-8: DataTemplate for grid items

```xml
<DataTemplate x:Key="Custom250x250ItemTemplate">
    <StackPanel>
        <!--
            In the actual application, instead of AdPlaceHolder
            grid, install and reference Microsoft Ads SDK
            and uncomment the AdControl code below
        -->
        <!--<UI:AdControl ApplicationId="test_client"
        AdUnitId="Image_250x250"
        HorizontalAlignment="Center" Height="250"
        Width="250" VerticalAlignment="Top"
        Visibility="{Binding IsAdDisplayed, Converter={StaticResource
        BooleanToVisibilityConverter}}"
        />-->
        <!--
        The grid below may be replaced with the AdControl
        in the real app
        -->
        <Grid x:Name="adPlaceHolder" Background="Yellow"
            HorizontalAlignment="Center"
            Height="250" Width="250"
            VerticalAlignment="Top"
            Visibility="{Binding IsAdDisplayed,
            Converter={StaticResource BooleanToVisibilityConverter}}">
            <TextBlock Text="Ad Placeholder" Foreground="Black"
                    FontWeight="Black" FontSize="28"
                    VerticalAlignment="Center"
                    HorizontalAlignment="Center" />
        </Grid>
        <Grid HorizontalAlignment="Left" Width="250" Height="250"
            Background="{Binding BackgroundColor}"
            Visibility="{Binding IsAdDisplayed,
            Converter={StaticResource BooleanOppositeConverter}}">
        <TextBlock Text="{Binding Title}" Foreground="White"
                FontSize="40"
                VerticalAlignment="Top"
                HorizontalAlignment="Left" Margin="15,15,0,0"/>
        <TextBlock Text="{Binding Price}" Foreground="Black"
                FontWeight="Black" FontSize="60"
                VerticalAlignment="Bottom"
                HorizontalAlignment="Right" Margin="0,0,20,15"/>
        </Grid>
    </StackPanel>
</DataTemplate>
```

6. Set the value of `IsAdDisplayed` to true for the last element of the first group in the data model. Listing 11-9 shows a method that changes ad visibility in the data model.

LISTING 11-9: SetAdVisibility method in CatalogDataModel.cs

```
/// <summary>
/// Set advertising group visibility
/// </summary>
/// <param name="groups">list of groups</param>
void SetAdVisibility(IEnumerable<CatalogDataGroup> groups)
{
    foreach (var group in groups)
    {
        // show the ad instead of the content
        group.Items.Last().IsAdDisplayed = true;
    }
}
```

Now the result page shows ads for the last element in the first group. Figure 11-8 shows the main page grid with the advertisement as the last element of the first group of items.

FIGURE 11-8

Supporting Trial Conversions for Ads

Finally, you need to instantly disable ads after the user converts from the trial to the full version. To complete the conversion, you must update the `IsAdDisplayed` property for the catalog data model in the `OnLicenseChanged` event of the app license data model. Listing 11-10 shows the method handler for the `LicenseChanged` event.

LISTING 11-10: AppLicenseDataModel.cs

```csharp
private async void OnLicenseChanged()
{
    if (!CurrentAppSimulator.LicenseInformation.IsTrial)
    {
        _licensed = true;
        CurrentAppSimulator.LicenseInformation.LicenseChanged
            -= OnLicenseChanged;

        // need this to the license change occurs on a different
        // thread to update UI bound elements from the data model
        CoreApplication.MainView.CoreWindow.Dispatcher.RunAsync(
            CoreDispatcherPriority.Normal, () =>
        {
            if (IsLicensed)
            {
                var groups = CatalogDataModel.GetGroups("AllGroups");
                foreach (var group in groups)
                {
                    foreach (var item in group.Items)
                    {
                        item.IsAdDisplayed = false;
                    }
                }
            }

            if (PropertyChanged != null)
            {
                PropertyChanged(this,
                    new PropertyChangedEventArgs(String.Empty));
            }
        });
    }
}
```

Summary: The Economics of Monetizing Your App

To estimate how to sell your apps, you can use a model from economics called *price optimization*, because the goal is to maximize return on sales. For example, as a developer, say you want to sell your app at the highest price, so you set the price to the maximum allowed in Windows Store: $999.99. You want to collect the full price for the download. But not surprisingly, there's little demand for your app at such a price. So you decide to lower the price and set it to $499. Unfortunately, this price point doesn't trigger any demand either. So, how should we price our app?

App Revenue with No Ad Support

Now you're curious; so you pull out Excel and decide to create a table to track your customer's demand by placing the price in the first column and the number of actual downloads in another column — see Table 11-4 for an example.

Note that the assumption from the previous section is that you didn't include any ads in your app. You also didn't have any in-app purchases in your first version. In terms of the Windows Store, you could have either a free app or a paid app (potentially with a trial offer).

TABLE 11-4: Sample App Price Sensitivity with No Ads

APP PRICE	DOWNLOADS
$999.99	0
$499.00	0
$199.00	0
$19.00	0
$7.99	1
$4.99	10
$1.99	100
$1.49	1,000
0	10,000

> **NOTE** *This is sample data; it does not represent the actual pricing of any app in the store but is given to illustrate how pricing affects the number of downloads.*

What you just did is *estimating elasticity of demand (Ed)*, or how responsive the number of downloads demanded is to changes in price. For the following equation, Q is the number of downloads, and P is the price:

$$E_d = \frac{\Delta Q}{\Delta P}$$

In economics, the results received in the example are called *elastic demand*: that is, as the price of the app grows, demand in the Color Shopping app goes to zero quickly, with the best results occurring somewhere in the range between $0 and $4.99 — the sweet spot for your app's price.

Ad-Supported App Revenue

In a second version of this example, you might decide to include Microsoft AdControl from the Advertising SDK to take advantage of two observations from the first version: you had a large number of downloads in the free tier of this app, and you want to make some money from the free version. Table 11-5 shows how ad revenue and downloads increase as your app price decreases.

TABLE 11-5: Sample App Price Sensitivity with No Ads

APP PRICE	ADS REVENUE	DOWNLOADS
$999.00		0
$499.00		0
$199.00		0
$19.00		0
$7.99	1.20	1
$4.99	12.00	10
$1.99	120.00	100
$1.49	360.00	1,000
0	1,200.00	10,000

> **NOTE** *This is sample data given to illustrate the ad-supported revenue model. The actual ad revenue, price, and number of downloads may vary.*

With the ad-supported version you may actually make more money in the long term because instead of a one-time purchase, ads keep generating revenue every month.

> **NOTE** *Monetizing your app may be an interesting journey, and the previous simple models can be a foundation for your analysis. But of course, in real life the success of your app also depends on whether you include a trial option, what price and products you include with your app, app quality, and marketing.*

APPLICATION PACKAGING

This section covers application packaging. You'll learn how to prepare your app in the Visual Studio and Windows Store, update the manifest and your Windows Store listing. You'll also see how to perform advanced packaging tasks, such as using the command line to package your apps. For the line of business (LOB) and enterprise apps, you'll learn about the tools Microsoft provided to package and deploy your apps in the enterprise.

You will learn how to test your app before deployment using Windows Apps Certification Kit.

When Visual Studio 2012 creates your project for the first time, it generates a manifest file `Package.appxmanifest` and adds it to your project. You need to update this manifest file, making sure that the name, description, images, supported orientations, and packaging information are correct. Package, name, and publisher information must exactly match your entry in the Windows Store. Figure 11-9 shows Visual Studio editor for the app manifest.

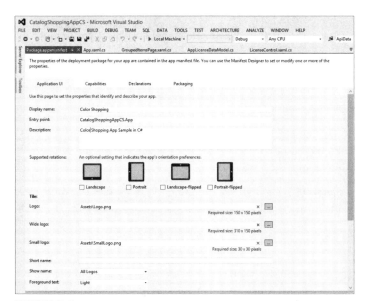

FIGURE 11-9

Preparing your app in Visual Studio

You must prepare your app before uploading it to the store. Remember that all development code in this example using `CurrentAppSimulator` must be replaced with the `CurrentApp`, or your app will fail certification.

In the store package, you also don't need to include any of the license XML files you used for testing. Instead create your in-app purchase products at the Windows Store website. Table 11-6 shows the various steps involved in preparing your app. These steps are discussed in greater detail in the following sections.

TABLE 11-6: Packaging Your App for Windows Store

STEP	DESCRIPTION
Open Developer Account.	You must get a developer account to submit your apps.
Reserve App Name.	One of the first steps to create your app in the store is reserving a name for the app. Names in Windows Store must be unique. Also, names are limited to 256 characters, but the space to display your app name may be even smaller, so plan for a shorter name.

continues

TABLE 11-6 *(continued)*

STEP	DESCRIPTION
Update Package. appxmanifest.	After you have the name of your app from the Windows Store, you must update your project's manifest file to match that name: Display Name, Package Name, Publisher ID, and Publisher Display Name in the manifest must correspond to your actual package.
Sell details.	Specifying your pricing tier actually has several parts in it: specifying the price for your app, or making it free, enabling trial mode, and adding any additional in-app products for purchasing.
Create screenshots and promotional images.	To submit your app, you must have at least one screenshot. Promotional images are optional, but as discussed earlier they are important to monetize your app.
Package your app for the store.	Right-click your project and select Store ➪ Create App Package; then follow the instructions to complete building the package for the store.
Upload package to the Windows Store.	You need to upload the .appxupload file to the store.
Submit app for certification.	After all the steps in the submission process are complete, click the Submit button and your app will be submitted for store certification. Store certification is a process of validating and publishing your app in the store, by Microsoft.

Opening Developer Account

Before you can submit apps to the Windows Store, you need to register a developer account. This account and publisher name will be used in your project's manifest when you associate your app with the app created in the Windows Store.

Reserving App Name

Even though the Windows Store enables long names, up to 256 characters, it's recommended to use shorter names for your apps. There are several reasons for this. It's harder for the user to read a long name, especially when it displays in a space-constrained search listing.

For example, the Windows Store limits its catalog search listing to only 15-wide characters displayed. The app listing is limited to 23-wide characters in full screen and fill mode, but when users view it in snapped mode, it's only 17-wide characters.

Tile size also limits what can display, and knowing these constraints may help you achieve a better reach for your apps.

You can reserve app names in other languages; then when you publish a localized version, you can use that name.

Pricing Your App

Remember when you initialized the app license in the Color Shopping example, your app was in trial mode? If you give an app any price, except Free in Selling Details, you can enable the Trial mode in your app. There are several options for trial: with expiration in 1, 7, 15, 30 days and a never-expiring trial.

Because your proxy license file has the same schema as the license object in the Windows Store, Price and IsTrial elements are what you effectively set in the Windows Store. Take a look at the InAppPurchaseLicense.xml and TrialLicense.xml included with your application example for a simulation of options available in the Windows Store.

```
<?xml version="1.0" encoding="utf-16" ?>
<CurrentApp>
  <ListingInformation>
    <App>
      <AppId>a8695030-29b8-45c4-8a5b-a1647a1bb104</AppId>
<LinkUri>http://apps.microsoft.com/app/a8695030-45c4-8a5b-a1647a1bb104
</LinkUri>
      <CurrentMarket>en-US</CurrentMarket>
      <AgeRating>3</AgeRating>
      <MarketData xml:lang="en-us">
        <Name>Catalog Shopping</Name>
        <Description>Catalog Shopping Sample App</Description>
        <Price>4.99</Price>
        <CurrencySymbol>$</CurrencySymbol>
      </MarketData>
    </App>
  </ListingInformation>
  <LicenseInformation>
    <App>
      <IsActive>true</IsActive>
      <IsTrial>false</IsTrial>
    </App>
  </LicenseInformation>
</CurrentApp>
```

Creating Screenshots and Promotional Images

The importance of screenshots and promotional images was previously discussed: Remember that the goal here is to make your app look good. Windows apps run at different resolutions. Images such as the store logo, splash screen, and wide and badge logo are required at 100 percent resolution. Optionally, you can provide images at different resolution factors: 80 percent, 100 percent, 140 percent and 180 percent. This is called *scaling to pixel density*.

For example, a square logo is required at 150×150 pixels. This is assuming a 100-percent resolution. Optionally, you can provide the logo at 80 percent: 120×120, and 140 percent: 210×210, and 180 percent: 270×270.

There's a naming convention for scaled images: You can either add a suffix to the image, for example, logo.scale-140.png, or use a folder naming convention and place scaled images in a folder, like so: \scale-140\logo.png.

In markup you can use the image without the naming suffixes.

```
<Image Source="logo.png" />
```

Packaging for the Store in Visual Studio

You've finally done most of the leg work for getting your app packaged. Now it's time to actually package it by following these steps:

1. Right click your project, and select Store ⇨ Create App Package.

2. Follow the instructions to complete building the package for the store.

3. You have two options when you build the package:

➤ For the store

➤ As a local package for sideloading or testing

If your package is created for the store, you need to sign into your Microsoft account. Figure 11-10 shows the packaging screen.

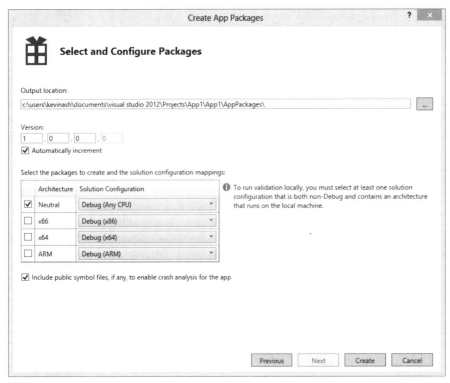

FIGURE 11-10

4. Remember that before you package your app, you must replace references of `Current AppSimulator` with `CurrentApp`. You can handle this in code by defining a conditional compilation symbol and then checking whether you're building it for the store.

```
#if !RELEASE

    using CurrentAppStore
        = Windows.ApplicationModel.Store.CurrentAppSimulator;
#else
    using CurrentAppStore = Windows.ApplicationModel.Store.CurrentApp;
#endif
```

Uploading Package to Windows Store

In your browser, log in to your developer account, and open the Packaging step in your application submission process. Simply drag your package on the dialog provided to begin the upload. Your package will be uploaded and analyzed by the Windows Store.

Submitting the App for Certification

Finally, you need to submit your app to begin the certification process in the Windows Store dashboard, by clicking Submit button in Windows Store. This is the final step that concludes your application submission. Now it's time to stretch and relax!

Windows Store takes your app through a number of internal tests: security, technical compliance, content compliance, signing and release. Each of these steps is important to ensure your app is delivered to the users, that the app doesn't contain any security violations or glaring technical problems, and is compliant with Windows Store content policy.

Your app will either pass or fail certification. If it passes, congratulations! Your users will be able to see your app in all its glory. Otherwise, you can check the reported issue, fix it and resubmit the app again.

Packaging Apps Using a Command Line

Most developers use Visual Studio to package apps. In some scenarios, when scripting or automation is required, you may need scripting tools and a command prompt. You can use App packager, CertMgr, and SignTool for scripted and automated tasks, and automate your packaging with PowerShell scripts. The follow shows the various command line scripting tools available to you for deployment and packaging:

➤ **App packager (MakeAppx.exe):** This creates app packages and extracts files from an app package to disk:

```
MakeAppx pack /d input_dir  /p filepath.appx
```

➤ **CertMgr:** This is a certificate, certificate trust lists, and certificate revocation list management tool:

```
CertMgr [-add|-del|-put] [Options] [ -s [ -r RegistryLocation ] ]
SourceName [ -s [ -r RegistryLocation ] ] [DestinationName]
```

➤ **SignTool:** This digitally signs files and verifies signatures:

```
signtool [Command] [Options] [FileName …]
```

To package apps you can use PowerShell or Developer Command Prompt for a Visual Studio command line. If you have a script that copies files into a build directory, make sure you copy all resources, assets, and graphics into the package directory. Then execute the following command:

```
MakeAppx pack /d input_dir /p MyPackage.appx
```

You can also use a mapping file that lists resources and assets outside of the package directory. To use a mapping file, you need to include a /f switch and include the path to the mapping file.

You also need to sign the package with your certificate and the SignTool:

```
SignTool sign /a /v /fd hashAlgorithm /c certTemplateName filepath.appx
```

Packaging Enterprise Line-of-Business (LOB) Apps

There's often a need in businesses for line-of-business (LOB) apps that are usually deployed by IT departments to user PCs. These apps may be sideloaded to the device by a local IT department.

Sideloading is the process of adding apps that bypass the Windows Store. You can add LOB apps to a Windows image with Windows PowerShell or the Deployment Image Servicing (DISM) platform. All Windows apps distributed by local IT departments using this method must be signed with a certificate connected with a trusted root certificate.

You can only use Dism.exe and PowerShell scripts to install WinRT apps; you cannot use them to install traditional desktop applications. The following shows tools for packaging, deployment, and LOB apps:

➤ **Add Apps (Add-AppxPackage); PowerShell cmdlet:** A line-of-business (LOB) app installation:

```
Add-AppxPackage C:\App1.appx
```

➤ **List Apps (Get-AppxPackage); PowerShell cmdlet.** Lists LOB Apps per user account:

```
Get-AppxPackage -AllUsers
```

➤ **Remove Apps (Remove-AppxPackage); PowerShell cmdlet.** Removes LOB app:

```
Remove-AppxPackage Package1
```

➤ **DISM.exe:** This is a Deployment Image Servicing platform for packaging LOB apps in Windows image.

Testing with Windows App Certification Kit

Before submitting your app to the store, you should test it with the Windows App Certification Kit. The tool automatically tests your app and detects problems before the app is submitted to the store.

Windows App Certification Kit tests your app thoroughly, by actually launching it, measuring the responsiveness, and testing for crashes and hangs. It also tests for compliance of the app manifest, security, supported APIs, performance, configuration, encoding, meta-data compliance, and many other parameters. The kit contains dozens of tests. Most of the conditions evaluate to Pass or Fail, but they may also include warnings. Figure 11-11 shows the Windows App Certification Kit app selection screen.

This may save you a lot of time and detect most common problems and issues. Your app will be validated and tested in the store as

FIGURE 11-11

well. It is recommended to use Windows App Certification Kit for pre-store testing to identify and fix problems before submitting to the store.

At the end of the testing, Windows App Certification Kit generates an HTML and XML report.

Windows App Certification Kit may be launched from an elevated command prompt as follows:

```
PS > appcert.exe test -apptype windowsstoreapp -packagefullname
    [package full name] -reportoutputpath [report file name]
```

Understanding Windows Store Certification Requirements

To pass certification, your app must pass automated tests and content compliance. You can test for automated compliance with the Windows App Certification Kit. Content compliance takes longer than the automated testing phase because it actually requires an engineer to look at your app. Microsoft wants good quality apps for the customers of the Windows Store.

I recommend using Windows App Certification Kit before every application deployment, and reviewing the most current certification requirements page available on the Microsoft site. Windows Store apps are available to millions and potentially billions of users, and therefore you must comply with the certification requirements and policies set for the store apps.

SUMMARY

In this chapter, you learned many aspects of Windows Store development, monetization, and the app life cycle. You can use the Color Shopping example to quickly use paid and trial apps, trial conversions, in-app purchases, and ad-supported apps. You learned how to package and test your apps from Visual Studio and the command line, and how to use Windows App Certification Kit to run tests before your app hits the store.

12

Putting It All Together: Building a Windows Store Application

WHAT'S IN THIS CHAPTER?

➤ Designing and creating a new Windows Store app from start to finish: Apply everything you have learned so far into a working sample

➤ Add support for `AppBar`, Tiles, splash screen, and MVVM

➤ Configuring and coding the home page

➤ Configuring and coding groups

➤ Taking care of detailed book information

➤ Integrate with the new SkyDrive API

➤ Keeping the Tile and splash screen up to date

➤ Get your app ready for deployment in the Windows Store

WROX.COM CODE DOWNLOADS FOR THIS CHAPTER

You can find the wrox.com code downloads for this chapter in code file 205709 C12.zip at www.wrox.com/remtitle.cgi?isbn=1118205707 on the Download Code tab. To illustrate handling data, files, and networking, several app examples are in DataSamplesCS.zip and Leaderboard.zip. In addition, NfcSimulatorDriver.zip contains a proximity device driver simulator for the Proximity section.

WELCOME TO THE FINAL CHAPTER OF THE BOOK

By getting this far you now have a solid grasp of important Windows Store app development concepts such as XAML, controls, contracts, tiles, and more. Now it's time to put all these things together to create a fully working sample app that is ready for Windows Store certification from concept to code to create a real-world, albeit limited, sample app that allows users to browse through various books that Wrox publishing has available for purchase. You add support for things such as the `AppBar`, custom Tiles, splash screen, and more. Now that you are an expert at Model-View-View-Model app design, you can utilize that design pattern to make full use of data binding. You can also limit the code in your code-behind files to the bare minimum required to perform user interface-specific functionality.

One topic this book has not covered yet is the new functionality available in Windows 8 for moving settings and files into the cloud and keeping your app in sync across multiple devices. In this chapter you see how to make use of the new Roaming Profiles to ensure application-specific settings apply across multiple devices. In addition, you see how to integrate the new SkyDrive Live service into the app to store a favorites list in the cloud and access that from any Windows 8 device with your app installed. Finally you will review what it takes to get the sample bookstore app ready for deployment in the Windows Store.

DESIGNING THE WROX BOOKSTORE APP

Before staring any new Windows 8 project, it's best you determine what you want to accomplish. So far in this book, you have been introduced to many new concepts and techniques that are different from traditional Windows desktop application development. That said, you need to think a bit outside the box with apps for Windows 8; because some of the things you are used to doing in the desktop world might not be the best for full-screen immersive Windows Store apps that can potentially be deployed to both PCs and tablets. In many cases you also want to factor in a Windows Phone version of your user interface so that you can run your app on all the available platforms. The first thing to remember is that the app needs to focus on content above everything else. Don't worry about toolbars, menus, or any other chrome when creating the initial design. If you find need a large number of menu commands to manipulate the content displayed, you probably don't have a great candidate for a Windows Store app. In this chapter, you build a book browsing app that can:

- ➤ Display the most recently available books
- ➤ Display all Wrox programming books according to various categories
- ➤ Provide users with the ability to filter/search for specific books
- ➤ Get additional information about a particular book
- ➤ Allow users to purchase the book directly from the Wrox website via a link in the app
- ➤ Save a wish list of books and access that list from any Windows 8 device

Displaying Wrox Press Books

The first requirement is to display the most recently available books. This also seems to go hand in hand with the second requirement that states users should browse for books by subject/category. As you have seen in several examples throughout the book, this type of user interface is easy to get working using some of the existing Windows 8 development templates and controls such as the `GridView` and `ListView`.

Using some of the standard templates available in Visual Studio 2012, it's easy to see how the display of books might shape up. You can envision the app loading a grouped view of books that contain most recently added, along with several categorized, books such as C# and ASP.NET. Figure 12-1 shows what this first page should look like.

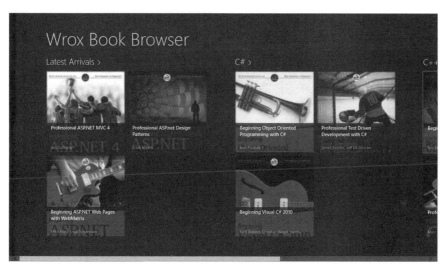

FIGURE 12-1

As you can see, users are presented with a standard `GridView` that has books grouped by category. This interface enables users to select either a group into which they can drill down further or an individual book. If users select a group, you should display a new page that presents the list of all books in that group and perhaps a description of the group. Figure 12-2 shows what this page might look like.

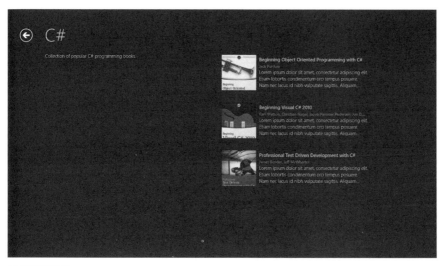

FIGURE 12-2

The next required page in the user interface is the detailed information page for a selected book. This page should show a larger cover image as well as a detailed description of the book. Because one of the requirements of the app is to enable users to purchase a book, you also want to provide a link that, when clicked/touched, fires up the default web browser and navigates directly to the page on the Wrox Press site, so users can make a book purchase. Figure 12-3 shows what the detailed book information screen should look like when complete.

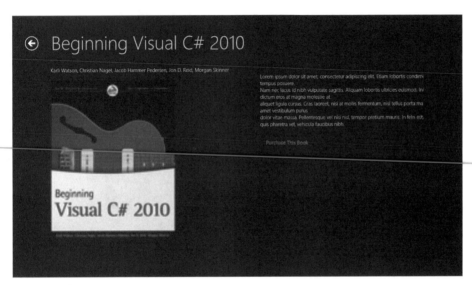

FIGURE 12-3

For the user interface, these three pages take care of the bulk of what you must accomplish. The only other necessary screen is one that enables users to manage books that they've added to a wish list. You just need to make this screen a checklist style screen so that it shows some thumbnails of books that users have added. Because you want to make the wish list available across all devices on which users run the app, you must ensure it's available in the cloud. Using the new SkyDrive API gives you the tools required to do so.

Adding a Wish List Across Devices

The final big requirement of this app is to provide users with a seamless experience should they download and run the app on an additional device. The main feature you want to make available across all devices is the user-created book wish list. Although Windows 8 provides support for roaming profiles that make it easy to share application-specific information across devices, these profiles are geared more toward saving application settings — not data. By using the new SkyDrive API, you can save/restore actual data files, or in this case a wish list, across devices in the cloud. You'll be surprised at how little code is required for this feature to work. The cool thing is that now if users run the book browser on a PC and add some books to a current wish list, they can instantly access that wish list from their tablet or even the phone version of the application. This provides a great user experience and makes users feel like they never left the app.

DIVING INTO THE CODE

Now that you have set some of the basic requirements, it's time to dive into some code. The goal of this chapter is to help you put together many of the concepts and techniques that you have learned throughout the book into a new Windows Store app, including all steps. Although conceptually this sample app is simple, the workflow you take to get to the end is most likely something you can reuse again as you develop your own successful Windows Store apps.

Start by following these general steps:

1. Fire up Visual Studio 2012 and select a new Windows Store project. For this project use the Blank app template, and call the project WroxBookStore. After the project loads, add the required user interface files.

> **NOTE** *The brief design session in the section "Designing the Wrox BookStore App" stated that you need a home page to display books filtered by various groups and a group drill-down page to show all the books included in that group. You should also give each book a detail page that shows additional information about the book and the purchase link. Finally, you need a page to let users manage the wish list stored and retrieved from the cloud. Many of these pages share characteristics of some of the pages automatically included in the* Grid *template projects. Although you created this project using the Blank App template, you still have access to all the individual page templates that help display grouped items.*

2. Begin by adding the home page. In Figure 12-1, you saw that the home page consists of a GridView and several groups of programming books. The best template to use for this page is the Grouped Items Page. Right-click the project node in Solution Explorer, and add a new page to the project called GroupedBooks.xaml. Be sure to use the Grouped Items Page template when creating the file. When that is complete you need to add the other pages to the project.

3. When users click a particular group, they should be redirected to a page that contains additional details about that group. In this case, you can use the Group Detail Page template in Visual Studio. This template supplies many of the things you need. Again, right-click the project node, and add a new page using this template. Call this file GroupDetailPage.xaml.

4. Next is the page that hosts additional information about a selected book. Again there is a great template that you can use in Visual Studio 2012 called the Item Detail Page. This presents you with the ability to show a larger image of the item along with a two-column display of additional, detailed information about the currently selected item. Add a new page to the project using this template, and name it BookDetailPage.xaml.

At this point you have all the user interface files required for this app to be added to the project. You also may have noticed several additional files were added to the project as you started using the item templates in Visual Studio. One of these, of course, is the StandardStyles.xaml file located in the Common folder. You may remember this from one of the earlier chapters. This file hosts a large collection of control templates and styles that you can choose from for custom `AppBar` buttons and more.

Getting Ready for MVVM

Before modifying any of the user interface XAML, you must first make a decision about how you architect your app. One method used throughout most of the book is to simply add XAML controls and corresponding control event handlers in the code-behind files — perhaps even segregating required business logic into a separate class. But for the most part, this results in direct manipulation of controls and calls into the business logic layer directly from the code behind. Although there is nothing fundamentally wrong with this approach, in this chapter, you should go the MVVM route that you saw in Chapter 10, "Windows Store Application Architecture."

MVVM provides a great separation of concerns and ensures that business logic stays out of your user interface. It also relies on data binding to update the user interface in real time without the need for any complex code in the code behind. What is great about this approach is that the visual states of various controls are toggled via data binding in the `ViewModel` class instead of needing to write a ton of boilerplate control manipulation code over various code-behind files. For example, rather than trying to ensure several controls are visible or hidden based on business logic and hoping you remember them all, binding the `Visibility` property to a `ViewModel` property means that the controls take care of that decision.

Chapter 10 shows that much of what you need to implement in MVVM already exists in WinRT. All `Button` controls support commanding, so you can easily bind `Button` actions to commands in a `ViewModel`. Also you can bind all XAML control properties to corresponding properties in the `ViewModel`. By using Data templates, you can easily create a reusable item template for the `GridView` and `ListView` that display images and properties from the `ViewModel` as required. The WroxBookStore app should use MVVM as the main design pattern for the application business logic rather than strictly the code behind. Remember, however, that just because you use MVVM does not mean that you cannot use any code behind. Actually, code behind isn't necessarily a bad thing if you use it only to manipulate something in the user interface that you simply can't accomplish with strict data binding.

Although a great deal of MVVM functionality is baked into WinRT, some nice-to-have features of MVVM are still missing. Chapter 10 introduces you to the free NuGet package called MVVMLight. This package includes several libraries that assist you with MVVM development from commanding to messaging, both of which you can use heavily in this demo app.

Because you use MVVM for this app, you obviously need a `ViewModel` for binding. If you install the NuGet package for MVVMLight in Visual Studio, you can see that several new files have been added to the project in a new `ViewModel` folder in Solution Explorer. You should see MainViewModel.cs and ViewModelLocator.cs. When you use MVVM, it is entirely legal to create a global instance of your `MainViewModel` class and start binding to it. However, that does not provide a friendly way to access the view model from multiple XAML files. The `ViewModelLocator` takes care of this problem by providing a static global instance of a locator class whose sole responsibility is returning the currently active view model instance. Listing 12-1 shows the `ViewModelLocator` class. Notice how the only logic here is to return a single instance of the `MainViewModel` class or instantiate one if it does not already exist.

LISTING 12-1: ViewModelLocator.cs

```
/*
    In App.xaml:
    <Application.Resources>
        <vm:ViewModelLocator xmlns:vm="clr-namespace:WroxBookStore"
        x:Key="Locator" />
    </Application.Resources>

    In the View:
    DataContext="{Binding Source={StaticResource Locator}, Path=ViewModelName}"

    You can also use Blend to do all this with the tool's support.
    See http://www.galasoft.ch/mvvm
*/

using GalaSoft.MvvmLight;
using GalaSoft.MvvmLight.Ioc;
using Microsoft.Practices.ServiceLocation;

namespace WroxBookStore.ViewModel
{
    /// <summary>
    /// This class contains static references to all the view models in the
    /// application and provides an entry point for the bindings.
    /// </summary>
    public class ViewModelLocator
    {
        /// <summary>
        /// Initializes a new instance of the ViewModelLocator class.
        /// </summary>
        public ViewModelLocator()
        {
            ServiceLocator.SetLocatorProvider(() => SimpleIoc.Default);

            ////if (ViewModelBase.IsInDesignModeStatic)
            ////{
            ////    // Create design time view services and models
            ////    SimpleIoc.Default.Register<IDataService,
            ////    DesignDataService>();
            ////}
            ////else
            ////{
            ////    // Create run time view services and models
            ////    SimpleIoc.Default.Register<IDataService, DataService>();
            ////}

            SimpleIoc.Default.Register<MainViewModel>();
        }

        public MainViewModel Main
        {
            get
            {
```

continues

LISTING 12-1 *(continued)*

```
                    return ServiceLocator.Current.GetInstance<MainViewModel>();
            }
        }

        public static void Cleanup()
        {
            // TODO Clear the ViewModels
        }
    }
}
```

In addition to this file, the MVVMLight NuGet package also updates the App.xaml file to add a single instance of the `ViewModelLocator` class that you can reference for data binding throughout the app. Listing 12-2 shows the updated App.xaml file.

LISTING 12-2: App.xaml

```xml
<?xml version="1.0" encoding="utf-8"?>
<Application x:Class="WroxBookStore.App"
    xmlns="http://schemas.microsoft.com/winfx/2006/xaml/presentation"
    xmlns:x="http://schemas.microsoft.com/winfx/2006/xaml"
    xmlns:local="using:WroxBookStore"
    xmlns:d="http://schemas.microsoft.com/expression/blend/2008"
    xmlns:vm="using:WroxBookStore.ViewModel"
    xmlns:mc="http://schemas.openxmlformats.org/markup-compatibility/2006"
    mc:Ignorable="d">
    <Application.Resources>
        <ResourceDictionary>
            <ResourceDictionary.MergedDictionaries>
                <!--
                    Styles that define common aspects of the platform
                    look and feel Required by Visual Studio project
                    and item templates
                -->
                <ResourceDictionary Source="Common/StandardStyles.xaml" />
            </ResourceDictionary.MergedDictionaries>
            <vm:ViewModelLocator x:Key="Locator" />
        </ResourceDictionary>
    </Application.Resources>
</Application>
```

You may have noticed in the comments of the `ViewModelLocator` class that to actually bind to a particular view model, you simply add the following lines in your XAML code to set the `DataContext` property of a particular page:

```
DataContext="{Binding Source={StaticResource Locator}, Path=ViewModelName}"
```

What this means is that you always bind to the `Locator` and then set the `Path` of the binding to the actual view model you want to reference. Although this particular app has only one actual view model class, the `ViewModelLocator` makes it simple to add additional view models to the app and easily reference them from your application pages through simple data binding.

Creating Sample Data

You have all the required XAML pages created, and you also have a view model ready to store application logic and properties. Now you need to start creating the actual user interface. When users fire up the WroxBookStore app, the first thing you want them to see is a grouped list of books. In a real-world app, you would most likely connect to an external data store through a web service and download the required data. In this sample app, you create a local data set of several books and categories. For the home page, you show books from the following categories: Most Recently Added, C#, ASP.NET, and SQL Server.

Adding a Corresponding Class

Each displayed book needs a corresponding class, so add that first:

1. Right-click the project node.

2. Add a new folder called Data.

3. Add a new class to this folder called WroxBook.

4. Update the WroxBook.cs file to look like Listing 12-3.

LISTING 12-3: WroxBook.cs

```
using System;
using Windows.UI.Xaml.Media;

namespace WroxBookStore.Data
{
    public class WroxBook
    {
        public string Title { get; set; }
        public string Author { get; set; }
        public string Subject { get; set; }
        public string Type { get; set; }
        public string Overview { get; set; }

        public ImageSource Thumbnail { get; set; }
        public Uri PurchaseLink { get; set; }
    }
}
```

Looking at the code you can see that each book is represented by several properties. The Title/Author/Subject properties are straightforward. The rest of the properties need a little explanation:

➤ Type: Determines what group the book belongs to.

➤ Overview: Displays additional information about the book — perhaps a table of contents or even an excerpt. For this sample app, all the books simply use basic lorem ipsum text as filler.

➤ `Thumbnail`: Used in the `GridView` and `ListView` controls. Again because you use MVVM, the plan is to customize the default Data template for the `GridView` item so that each book shows the `Title`, `Author`, and `Thumbnail` image.

➤ `PurchaseLink`: Provides a URI object that you can tie in with the `HyperlinkButton` control and redirect the user to the actual book purchase page on the `Wrox.com` website.

Adding a Grouped Collection

Now that you have a class to represent each displayed book, you need to support a grouped collection of these. If you remember in Chapter 3, "Enhancing your apps with Control Styles, Data Binding, and Semantic Zoom," you wanted to display a grouped version of content in a `GridView`, and you made use of the `CollectionViewSource`. The `CollectionViewSource` control is geared around binding its `Source` property to an `ObservableCollection` of objects that can provide both a group name and an internal collection of objects to display. In the following example, this is handled through a class called `GroupedBookList`:

1. Right-click again on the `Data` folder in Solution Explorer.

2. Add a new class called `GroupedBookList`.

3. Replace its contents with the code shown in Listing 12-4.

LISTING 12-4: GroupedBookList.cs

```
using System;
using System.Collections.Generic;
using System.Collections.ObjectModel;
using System.ComponentModel;
using System.Linq;
using System.Text;
using System.Threading.Tasks;

namespace WroxBookStore.Data
{
    public class GroupedBookList : INotifyPropertyChanged
    {
        public string Group { get; set; }
        public string Description { get; set; }

        private ObservableCollection<WroxBook> _bookList = null;
        public ObservableCollection<WroxBook> BookList
        {
            get
            {
                if (_bookList == null)
                    _bookList = new ObservableCollection<WroxBook>();

                return _bookList;
            }

            set
            {
```

```
                    _bookList = value;
                    RaisePropertyChanged("BookList");
                }
            }

            private ObservableCollection<WroxBook> _filteredBookList = null;
            public ObservableCollection<WroxBook> FilteredBookList
            {
                get
                {
                    if (_filteredBookList == null)
                        _filteredBookList = new
    ObservableCollection<WroxBook>(BookList);

                    return _filteredBookList;
                }

                set
                {
                    _filteredBookList = value;
                    RaisePropertyChanged("FilteredBookList");
                }
            }

            public event PropertyChangedEventHandler PropertyChanged;

            private void RaisePropertyChanged(string property)
            {
                if( PropertyChanged != null )
                    PropertyChanged(this, new PropertyChangedEventArgs(property));
            }
        }
    }
```

Because for the most part the GridView and ListView controls in this app bind to an
ObservableCollection of this class type, dig a little further to make sure you understand what all
the GroupedBookList properties are responsible for. Note the following about this code:

➤ To start you see two string properties called Group and Description. The idea here is
that when you bind to the CollectionViewSource, the Group property displays the group
heading that you can easily specify in the CollectionViewSource binding statement. Then
the Description property is used when a user drills down into a particular group and the
GroupDetailPage displays. This description, along with the collection of WroxBook items,
displays when that page loads.

➤ The last two properties are both ObservableCollection<WroxBook> types. The first
property is the BookList property. It is responsible for holding the entire list of books
that belong to the group. The FilteredBookList property holds a filtered version of
the original BookList. What having these two properties accomplishes is binding the
CollectionViewSource to the FilteredBookList at all times so that you can easily add
code to sort and filter the books in the collection without modifying or risking the loss
of the originally loaded collection of book objects for the group. This will make more
sense in a little bit when you start actually wiring up the CollectionViewSource to the
MainViewModel class.

➤ The `GroupedBookList` class is implementing the `INotifyPropertyChanged` interface. You need to implement this interface for the `FilteredBookList` property to work properly. Although the `ObservableCollection<T>` class notifies the user interface if there are changes to the underlying collection, it won't notify if the `ObservableCollection` is swapped for something else. For filtering and sorting you replace the entire `ObservableCollection<T>` with a new version sorted or filtered, and you want the user interface to refresh accordingly. Implementing `INofityPropertyChanged` and calling the internal `RaisePropertyChanged` method ensures the user interface updates to reflect the filtering/sorting.

Building Default Data

So now you have a `WroxBook` class to represent each book. You also have a `GroupedBooks` class to help you hold a filtered/sorted collection of grouped books. All you need to do is build up some default data before you work on the XAML code that will display it. Open up the MainViewModel.cs file and add the following code:

```
private ObservableCollection<GroupedBookList> _groupedBookCollection = null;
public ObservableCollection<GroupedBookList> GroupedBookCollection
{
    get
    {
        if (_groupedBookCollection == null)
            _groupedBookCollection = new
ObservableCollection<GroupedBookList>();

        return _groupedBookCollection;
    }

    set
    {
        _groupedBookCollection = value;
        RaisePropertyChanged("GroupedBookCollection");
    }
}
```

This property holds the entire list of groups and grouped books that need to display on the home page. Now you need to build up this initial list. Modify the constructor of the `MainViewModel` class, and also add the private `CreateMainDataSource` method shown in the following code:

```
public MainViewModel()
{
    if (IsInDesignMode)
    {
        // Code runs in Blend --> create design time data.
    }
    else
    {
        CreateMainDataSource();
    }
}

private ObservableCollection<WroxBook> _allBooks = null;

private void CreateMainDataSource()
```

```
{
    _allBooks = new ObservableCollection<WroxBook>();

    _allBooks.Add(new WroxBook
    {
        Type = "ASPNET",
        Subject = "ASP.NET",
        Title = "Professional ASP.NET MVC 4",
        Author = "Jon Galloway",
        PurchaseLink = new
Uri("http://www.wrox.com/WileyCDA/WroxTitle/Professional-ASP-NET-MVC-4.productCd-
111834846X.html", UriKind.Absolute),
        Thumbnail = new BitmapImage(new
Uri("ms-appx:///Assets/Artwork/aspnet4.jpg", UriKind.RelativeOrAbsolute)),
        Overview = "Lorem ipsum dolor sit amet, consectetur adipiscing elit.
Etiam lobortis condimentum orci tempus posuere. " + Environment.NewLine +
"Nam nec lacus id nibh vulputate sagittis. Aliquam lobortis ultricies euismod.
Integer dictum eros at magna molestie at" + Environment.NewLine +
"aliquet ligula cursus. Cras laoreet, nisi at mollis fermentum, nisi tellus
porta mauris, sit amet vestibulum purus" + Environment.NewLine +
"dolor vitae massa. Pellentesque vel nisi nisl, tempor pretium mauris. In
felis est, suscipit quis pharetra vel, vehicula faucibus nibh."
    });

    _allBooks.Add(new WroxBook
    {
        Type = "ASPNET",
        Subject = "ASP.NET",
        Title = "Beginning ASP.NET Web Pages with WebMatrix",
        Author = "Mike Brind, Imar Spaanjaars",
        PurchaseLink = new
Uri("http://www.wrox.com/WileyCDA/WroxTitle/Beginning-ASP-NET-Web-
Pages-with-WebMatrix.productCd-1118050487.html",
UriKind.Absolute),
        Thumbnail = new BitmapImage(new Uri("ms-
appx:///Assets/Artwork/beginaspnetmatrix.jpg", UriKind.RelativeOrAbsolute)),
        Overview = "Lorem ipsum dolor sit amet, consectetur adipiscing elit.
Etiam lobortis condimentum orci tempus posuere. " + Environment.NewLine +
"Nam nec lacus id nibh vulputate sagittis. Aliquam lobortis ultricies euismod.
Integer dictum eros at magna molestie at" + Environment.NewLine +
"aliquet ligula cursus. Cras laoreet, nisi at mollis fermentum,
nisi tellus porta mauris, sit amet vestibulum purus" + Environment.NewLine +
"dolor vitae massa. Pellentesque vel nisi nisl, tempor pretium mauris.
In felis est, suscipit quis pharetra vel, vehicula faucibus nibh."
    });

    _allBooks.Add(new WroxBook
    {
        Type = "ASPNET",
        Subject = "ASP.NET",
        Title = "Professional ASP.net Design Patterns",
        Author = "Scott Millett",
        PurchaseLink =
new Uri("http://www.wrox.com/WileyCDA/WroxTitle/Professional-ASP-NET-Design-
Patterns.productCd-0470292784.html", UriKind.Absolute),
```

```
                Thumbnail = new BitmapImage(new Uri("ms-
appx:///Assets/Artwork/aspnetdesign.jpg", UriKind.RelativeOrAbsolute)),
                Overview = "Lorem ipsum dolor sit amet, consectetur adipiscing elit.
Etiam lobortis condimentum orci tempus posuere. " + Environment.NewLine +
"Nam nec lacus id nibh vulputate sagittis. Aliquam lobortis ultricies euismod.
Integer dictum eros at magna molestie at" + Environment.NewLine +
"aliquet ligula cursus. Cras laoreet, nisi at mollis fermentum, nisi tellus
porta mauris, sit amet vestibulum purus" + Environment.NewLine +
"dolor vitae massa. Pellentesque vel nisi nisl, tempor pretium mauris.
In felis est, suscipit quis pharetra vel, vehicula faucibus nibh."
            });


        _allBooks.Add(new WroxBook
        {
            Type = "CSHARP",
            Subject = "C# Development",
            Title = "Beginning Object Oriented Programming with C#",
            Author = "Jack Purdum",
            PurchaseLink = new Uri("http://www.wrox.com/WileyCDA/WroxTitle/Beginning-
Object-Oriented-Programming-with-C-.productCd-1118336925.html", UriKind.Absolute),
            Thumbnail = new BitmapImage(new Uri("ms-
appx:///Assets/Artwork/beginoocsharp.jpg", UriKind.RelativeOrAbsolute)),
            Overview = "Lorem ipsum dolor sit amet, consectetur adipiscing elit.
Etiam lobortis condimentum orci tempus posuere. " + Environment.NewLine +
"Nam nec lacus id nibh vulputate sagittis. Aliquam lobortis ultricies euismod.
Integer dictum eros at magna molestie at" + Environment.NewLine +
"aliquet ligula cursus. Cras laoreet, nisi at mollis fermentum, nisi tellus
porta mauris, sit amet vestibulum purus" + Environment.NewLine +
"dolor vitae massa. Pellentesque vel nisi nisl, tempor pretium mauris.
In felis est, suscipit quis pharetra vel, vehicula faucibus nibh."
            });


        _allBooks.Add(new WroxBook
        {
            Type = "CSHARP",
            Subject = "C# Development",
            Title = "Beginning Visual C# 2010",
            PurchaseLink = new Uri("http://www.wrox.com/WileyCDA/WroxTitle/Beginning-
Visual-C-2010.productCd-0470502266.html", UriKind.Absolute),
            Author = "Karli Watson, Christian Nagel, Jacob Hammer Pedersen,
Jon D. Reid, Morgan Skinner",
            Thumbnail = new BitmapImage(new Uri("ms-
appx:///Assets/Artwork/begincsharp.jpg", UriKind.RelativeOrAbsolute)),
            Overview = "Lorem ipsum dolor sit amet, consectetur adipiscing elit.
Etiam lobortis condimentum orci tempus posuere. " + Environment.NewLine +
"Nam nec lacus id nibh vulputate sagittis. Aliquam lobortis ultricies euismod.
Integer dictum eros at magna molestie at" + Environment.NewLine +
"aliquet ligula cursus. Cras laoreet, nisi at mollis fermentum, nisi tellus porta
mauris, sit amet vestibulum purus" + Environment.NewLine +
"dolor vitae massa. Pellentesque vel nisi nisl, tempor pretium mauris. In felis
est, suscipit quis pharetra vel, vehicula faucibus nibh."
            });


        _allBooks.Add(new WroxBook
```

```
    {
        Type = "CSHARP",
        Subject = "C# Development",
        Title = "Professional Test Driven Development with C#",
        Author = "James Bender, Jeff McWherter",
        PurchaseLink = new
Uri("http://www.wrox.com/WileyCDA/WroxTitle/Professional-Test-
Driven-Development-with-C-Developing-Real-World-
Applications-with-TDD.productCd-047064320X.html",
UriKind.Absolute),
        Thumbnail = new BitmapImage(new Uri("ms-
appx:///Assets/Artwork/protestdriven.jpg", UriKind.RelativeOrAbsolute)),
        Overview = "Lorem ipsum dolor sit amet, consectetur adipiscing elit.
Etiam lobortis condimentum orci tempus posuere. " + Environment.NewLine +
"Nam nec lacus id nibh vulputate sagittis. Aliquam lobortis ultricies euismod.
Integer dictum eros at magna molestie at" + Environment.NewLine +
"aliquet ligula cursus. Cras laoreet, nisi at mollis fermentum, nisi tellus porta
mauris, sit amet vestibulum purus" + Environment.NewLine +
"dolor vitae massa. Pellentesque vel nisi nisl, tempor pretium mauris.
In felis est, suscipit quis pharetra vel, vehicula faucibus nibh."
    });

    _allBooks.Add(new WroxBook
    {
        Type = "CPLUSPLUS",
        Subject = "C++ Development",
        Title = "Beginning Visual C++ 2010",
        Author = "Ivor Horton",
        PurchaseLink = new Uri("http://www.wrox.com/WileyCDA/WroxTitle/Beginning-
Visual-C-2010.productCd-0470502266.html", UriKind.Absolute),
        Thumbnail = new BitmapImage(new Uri("ms-
appx:///Assets/Artwork/visualc2010.jpg", UriKind.RelativeOrAbsolute)),
        Overview = "Lorem ipsum dolor sit amet, consectetur adipiscing elit.
Etiam lobortis condimentum orci tempus posuere. " + Environment.NewLine +
"Nam nec lacus id nibh vulputate sagittis. Aliquam lobortis ultricies euismod.
Integer dictum eros at magna molestie at" + Environment.NewLine +
"aliquet ligula cursus. Cras laoreet, nisi at mollis fermentum, nisi tellus porta
mauris, sit amet vestibulum purus" + Environment.NewLine +
"dolor vitae massa. Pellentesque vel nisi nisl, tempor pretium mauris. In
felis est, suscipit quis pharetra vel, vehicula faucibus nibh."
    });

    _allBooks.Add(new WroxBook
    {
        Type = "CPLUSPLUS",
        Subject = "C++ Development",
        Title = "Professional C++ 2nd Edition",
        Author = "Marc Gregoire, Nicholas A. Solter, Scott J. Kleper",
        PurchaseLink = new Uri("http://www.wrox.com/WileyCDA/WroxTitle/
Professional-C-2nd-Edition.productCd-0470932449.html", UriKind.Absolute),
        Thumbnail = new BitmapImage(new
Uri("ms-appx:///Assets/Artwork/procplus.jpg",
UriKind.RelativeOrAbsolute)),
        Overview = "Lorem ipsum dolor sit amet, consectetur adipiscing elit.
Etiam lobortis condimentum orci tempus posuere. " + Environment.NewLine +
```

```
"Nam nec lacus id nibh vulputate sagittis. Aliquam lobortis ultricies euismod.
Integer dictum eros at magna molestie at" + Environment.NewLine +
"aliquet ligula cursus. Cras laoreet, nisi at mollis fermentum, nisi tellus porta
mauris, sit amet vestibulum purus" + Environment.NewLine +
"dolor vitae massa. Pellentesque vel nisi nisl, tempor pretium mauris. In felis
est, suscipit quis pharetra vel, vehicula faucibus nibh."
        });

    _allBooks.Add(new WroxBook
    {
        Type = "SQL",
        Subject = "SQL Server",
        Title = "Professional SQL Server 2012 Internals and Troubleshooting",
        PurchaseLink = new
Uri("http://www.wrox.com/WileyCDA/WroxTitle/Professional-SQL-
Server-2012-Internals-and-
Troubleshooting.productCd-1118177657.html", UriKind.Absolute),
        Author = "Christian Bolton, James Rowland-Jones, Glenn Berry,
Justin Langford, Gavin Payne, Amit Banerjee",
        Thumbnail = new BitmapImage(new Uri("ms-
appx:///Assets/Artwork/prosqltroubleshoot.jpg", UriKind.RelativeOrAbsolute)),
        Overview = "Lorem ipsum dolor sit amet, consectetur adipiscing elit.
Etiam lobortis condimentum orci tempus posuere. " + Environment.NewLine +
"Nam nec lacus id nibh vulputate sagittis. Aliquam lobortis ultricies euismod.
Integer dictum eros at magna molestie at" + Environment.NewLine +
"aliquet ligula cursus. Cras laoreet, nisi at mollis fermentum, nisi tellus porta
mauris, sit amet vestibulum purus" + Environment.NewLine +
"dolor vitae massa. Pellentesque vel nisi nisl, tempor pretium mauris. In felis
est, suscipit quis pharetra vel, vehicula faucibus nibh."
        });

    _allBooks.Add(new WroxBook
    {
        Type = "SQL",
        Subject = "SQL Server",
        Title = "Beginning Microsoft SQL Server 2012 Programming",
        Author = "Paul Atkinson, Robert Vieira",
        PurchaseLink = new Uri("http://www.wrox.com/WileyCDA/WroxTitle/Beginning-
Microsoft-SQL-Server-2012-Programming.productCd-1118102282.html",
UriKind.Absolute),
        Thumbnail = new BitmapImage(new Uri("ms-
appx:///Assets/Artwork/beginsqlprogramming.jpg", UriKind.RelativeOrAbsolute)),
        Overview = "Lorem ipsum dolor sit amet, consectetur adipiscing elit.
Etiam lobortis condimentum orci tempus posuere. " + Environment.NewLine +
"Nam nec lacus id nibh vulputate sagittis. Aliquam lobortis ultricies euismod.
Integer dictum eros at magna molestie at" + Environment.NewLine +
"aliquet ligula cursus. Cras laoreet, nisi at mollis fermentum, nisi tellus porta
mauris, sit amet vestibulum purus" + Environment.NewLine +
"dolor vitae massa. Pellentesque vel nisi nisl, tempor pretium mauris. In
felis est, suscipit quis pharetra vel, vehicula faucibus nibh."
        });

    _allBooks.Add(new WroxBook
    {
        Type = "SQL",
```

```
        Subject = "SQL Server",
        Title = "Professional Microsoft SQL Server 2012 Administration",
        Author = "Adam Jorgensen, Steven Wort, Ross LoForte, Brian Knight",
        PurchaseLink = new
Uri("http://www.wrox.com/WileyCDA/WroxTitle/Professional-Microsoft-SQL-Server-2012-
Administration.productCd-1118106881.html", UriKind.Absolute),
        Thumbnail = new BitmapImage(new Uri("ms-
appx:///Assets/Artwork/propowerpivot.jpg", UriKind.RelativeOrAbsolute)),
        Overview = "Lorem ipsum dolor sit amet, consectetur adipiscing elit.
Etiam lobortis condimentum orci tempus posuere. " + Environment.NewLine +
"Nam nec lacus id nibh vulputate sagittis. Aliquam lobortis ultricies euismod.
Integer dictum eros at magna molestie at" + Environment.NewLine +
"aliquet ligula cursus. Cras laoreet, nisi at mollis fermentum, nisi tellus porta
mauris, sit amet vestibulum purus" + Environment.NewLine +
"dolor vitae massa. Pellentesque vel nisi nisl, tempor pretium mauris.
In felis est, suscipit quis pharetra vel, vehicula faucibus nibh."
    });

    GroupedBookCollection.Add(new GroupedBookList { Group = "Latest Arrivals",
Description = "All of the latest programming books to arrive at Wrox.com",
BookList = new ObservableCollection<WroxBook>(_allBooks.Take(3).ToList()) });
    GroupedBookCollection.Add(new GroupedBookList { Group = "C#", Description =
"Collection of popular C# programming books", BookList = new
ObservableCollection<WroxBook>(_allBooks.Where(b => b.Type ==
"CSHARP").ToList()) });
    GroupedBookCollection.Add(new GroupedBookList { Group = "C++", Description =
"Collection of popular C++ programming books", BookList = new
ObservableCollection<WroxBook>(_allBooks.Where(b => b.Type ==
"CPLUSPLUS").ToList()) });
    GroupedBookCollection.Add(new GroupedBookList { Group = "ASP.NET",
Description = "Collection of popular ASP.NET programming books", BookList = new
ObservableCollection<WroxBook>(_allBooks.Where(b => b.Type ==
"ASPNET").ToList()) });
    GroupedBookCollection.Add(new GroupedBookList { Group = "SQL Server",
Description = "Collection of popular SQL Server programming books", BookList = new
ObservableCollection<WroxBook>(_allBooks.Where(b => b.Type == "SQL").ToList()) });

    RaisePropertyChanged("GroupedBooks");
}
```

The code here is straightforward. Basically all you do is create a grouped collection of WroxBook objects using the AllBooks ObservableCollection as a temporary holding place. After all the sample books are added to the collection, you can create groups of books based on the programming language or topic. This is simple to do using Linq because you can filter on the Type property to add the appropriate books to the various collections. At this point you have a basic view model class setup that contains sample data for the app. Now it's time to wire up some of these pages.

CREATING THE HOME PAGE

The home page for the app (refer to the design in Figure 12-1) should simply show the various GroupedBookCollection objects in a GridView or ListView if the user runs in Snapped Mode. You have already added a page using the appropriate template, so most of what you need is already in place. All you need to do is modify some of the templates to match the view model classes you use and also determine what type of actions need to occur when the user touches/clicks various groups or books.

Configuring the XAML

To start, open GroupedBooks.xaml and replace the current code with the code shown in Listing 12-5.

LISTING 12-5: GroupedBooks.xaml

```xml
<common:LayoutAwarePage
    x:Name="pageRoot"
    x:Class="WroxBookStore.GroupedBooks"
    xmlns="http://schemas.microsoft.com/winfx/2006/xaml/presentation"
    xmlns:x="http://schemas.microsoft.com/winfx/2006/xaml"
    xmlns:local="using:WroxBookStore"
    xmlns:common="using:WroxBookStore.Common"
    xmlns:d="http://schemas.microsoft.com/expression/blend/2008"
    xmlns:mc="http://schemas.openxmlformats.org/markup-compatibility/2006"
    xmlns:i="http://schemas.microsoft.com/expression/2010/interactivity"
    xmlns:mvvm="using:GalaSoft.MvvmLight"
    mc:Ignorable="d" DataContext="{Binding Main,
Source={StaticResource Locator}}">

    <Page.Resources>

        <!--
        Collection of grouped items displayed by this page, bound to a subset
        of the complete item list because items in groups cannot be virtualized
        -->
        <CollectionViewSource
            x:Name="groupedItemsViewSource"
            Source="{Binding GroupedBookCollection}"
            ItemsPath="BookList"
            IsSourceGrouped="true" />

        <x:String x:Key="AppName">Wrox Book Browser</x:String>
    </Page.Resources>

    <!--
    This grid acts as a root panel for the page that defines two rows:
    * Row 0 contains the back button and page title
    * Row 1 contains the rest of the page layout
    -->
    <Grid Style="{StaticResource LayoutRootStyle}">
        <Grid.RowDefinitions>
            <RowDefinition Height="140"/>
            <RowDefinition Height="*"/>
        </Grid.RowDefinitions>

        <!-- Horizontal scrolling grid used in most view states -->
```

```
<GridView
    x:Name="MainGridView"
    AutomationProperties.AutomationId="ItemGridView"
    AutomationProperties.Name="Grouped Items"
    Grid.RowSpan="2"
    Padding="116,137,40,46"
    ItemsSource="{Binding Source={StaticResource
groupedItemsViewSource}}"
    ItemTemplate="{StaticResource Standard250x250ItemTemplate}"
    SelectionMode="Single"
    SelectedItem="{Binding SelectedBook, Mode=TwoWay}"
    IsSwipeEnabled="false"
    Loaded="MainGridView_Loaded">

    <GridView.ItemsPanel>
        <ItemsPanelTemplate>
            <VirtualizingStackPanel Orientation="Horizontal"/>
        </ItemsPanelTemplate>
    </GridView.ItemsPanel>
    <GridView.GroupStyle>
        <GroupStyle>
            <GroupStyle.HeaderTemplate>
                <DataTemplate>
                    <Grid Margin="1,0,0,6">
                        <Button Command="{Binding
Main.SelectGroupCommand, Source={StaticResource Locator}}"
CommandParameter="{Binding}"
AutomationProperties.Name="Group Title"
Style="{StaticResource TextPrimaryButtonStyle}">
                            <StackPanel Orientation="Horizontal">
                                <TextBlock Text="{Binding Group}"
Margin="3,-7,10,10" Style="{StaticResource GroupHeaderTextStyle}" />
                                <TextBlock Text="{StaticResource
ChevronGlyph}" FontFamily="Segoe UI Symbol" Margin="0,-7,0,10"
Style="{StaticResource
GroupHeaderTextStyle}"/>
                            </StackPanel>
                        </Button>
                    </Grid>
                </DataTemplate>
            </GroupStyle.HeaderTemplate>
            <GroupStyle.Panel>
                <ItemsPanelTemplate>
                    <VariableSizedWrapGrid Orientation="Vertical"
Margin="0,0,80,0"/>
                </ItemsPanelTemplate>
            </GroupStyle.Panel>
        </GroupStyle>
    </GridView.GroupStyle>
</GridView>

<!-- Vertical scrolling list only used when snapped -->
<ListView
    x:Name="MainListView"
    AutomationProperties.AutomationId="ItemListView"
```

continues

LISTING 12-5 *(continued)*

```xml
                AutomationProperties.Name="Grouped Items"
                Grid.Row="1"
                Visibility="Collapsed"
                Margin="0,-10,0,0"
                Padding="10,0,0,60"
                ItemsSource="{Binding Source={StaticResource groupedItemsViewSource}}"
                ItemTemplate="{StaticResource Standard80ItemTemplate}"
                SelectionMode="Single"
                SelectedItem="{Binding SelectedBook, Mode=TwoWay}"
                IsSwipeEnabled="false"
                Loaded="MainListView_Loaded">

                <ListView.GroupStyle>
                    <GroupStyle>
                        <GroupStyle.HeaderTemplate>
                            <DataTemplate>
                                <Grid Margin="7,7,0,0">
                                    <Button
AutomationProperties.Name="Group Title"
Style="{StaticResource TextPrimaryButtonStyle}">
                                        <StackPanel Orientation="Horizontal">
                                            <TextBlock Text="{Binding Group}"
Margin="3,-7,10,10" Style="{StaticResource GroupHeaderTextStyle}" />
                                            <TextBlock Text="{StaticResource
ChevronGlyph}" FontFamily="Segoe UI Symbol" Margin="0,-7,0,10"
Style="{StaticResource
GroupHeaderTextStyle}"/>
                                        </StackPanel>
                                    </Button>
                                </Grid>
                            </DataTemplate>
                        </GroupStyle.HeaderTemplate>
                    </GroupStyle>
                </ListView.GroupStyle>
            </ListView>

            <!-- Back button and page title -->
            <Grid>
                <Grid.ColumnDefinitions>
                    <ColumnDefinition Width="Auto"/>
                    <ColumnDefinition Width="*"/>
                </Grid.ColumnDefinitions>
                <Button x:Name="backButton" Click="GoBack" IsEnabled="{Binding
Frame.CanGoBack, ElementName=pageRoot}" Style="{StaticResource BackButtonStyle}"/>
                <TextBlock x:Name="pageTitle" Text="{StaticResource AppName}"
Grid.Column="1" IsHitTestVisible="false"
Style="{StaticResource PageHeaderTextStyle}"/>
            </Grid>

            <VisualStateManager.VisualStateGroups>

            <!-- Visual states reflect the application's view state -->
```

```xml
                <VisualStateGroup x:Name="ApplicationViewStates">
                    <VisualState x:Name="FullScreenLandscape"/>
                    <VisualState x:Name="Filled"/>

                    <VisualState x:Name="FullScreenPortrait">
                        <Storyboard>
                            <ObjectAnimationUsingKeyFrames
Storyboard.TargetName="backButton" Storyboard.TargetProperty="Style">
                                <DiscreteObjectKeyFrame KeyTime="0"
Value="{StaticResource PortraitBackButtonStyle}"/>
                            </ObjectAnimationUsingKeyFrames>

                            <ObjectAnimationUsingKeyFrames
Storyboard.TargetName="MainGridView" Storyboard.TargetProperty="Padding">
                                <DiscreteObjectKeyFrame KeyTime="0"
Value="96,137,10,56"/>
                            </ObjectAnimationUsingKeyFrames>
                        </Storyboard>
                    </VisualState>

                    <VisualState x:Name="Snapped">
                        <Storyboard>
                            <ObjectAnimationUsingKeyFrames
Storyboard.TargetName="backButton" Storyboard.TargetProperty="Style">
                                <DiscreteObjectKeyFrame KeyTime="0"
Value="{StaticResource SnappedBackButtonStyle}"/>
                            </ObjectAnimationUsingKeyFrames>
                            <ObjectAnimationUsingKeyFrames
Storyboard.TargetName="pageTitle" Storyboard.TargetProperty="Style">
                                <DiscreteObjectKeyFrame KeyTime="0"
Value="{StaticResource SnappedPageHeaderTextStyle}"/>
                            </ObjectAnimationUsingKeyFrames>

                            <ObjectAnimationUsingKeyFrames
Storyboard.TargetName="MainListView" Storyboard.TargetProperty="Visibility">
                                <DiscreteObjectKeyFrame KeyTime="0" Value="Visible"/>
                            </ObjectAnimationUsingKeyFrames>
                            <ObjectAnimationUsingKeyFrames
Storyboard.TargetName="MainGridView" Storyboard.TargetProperty="Visibility">
                                <DiscreteObjectKeyFrame KeyTime="0"
Value="Collapsed"/>
                            </ObjectAnimationUsingKeyFrames>
                        </Storyboard>
                    </VisualState>
                </VisualStateGroup>
            </VisualStateManager.VisualStateGroups>
        </Grid>
    </common:LayoutAwarePage>
```

Although there is a lot of code here, you only have a few important parts to break down and look into further.

Pointing DataContext to the MainViewModel

Because you have set up a `ViewModelLocator` instance in App.xaml, you must ensure that the `DataContext` for the entire page points to your `MainViewModel`. You do this at the top of the page with the following code:

```
<common:LayoutAwarePage
    x:Name="pageRoot"
    x:Class="WroxBookStore.GroupedBooks"
    xmlns="http://schemas.microsoft.com/winfx/2006/xaml/presentation"
    xmlns:x="http://schemas.microsoft.com/winfx/2006/xaml"
    xmlns:local="using:WroxBookStore"
    xmlns:common="using:WroxBookStore.Common"
    xmlns:d="http://schemas.microsoft.com/expression/blend/2008"
    xmlns:mc="http://schemas.openxmlformats.org/markup-compatibility/2006"
    xmlns:i="http://schemas.microsoft.com/expression/2010/interactivity"
    xmlns:mvvm="using:GalaSoft.MvvmLight"
    mc:Ignorable="d" DataContext="{Binding Main, Source={StaticResource Locator}}">
```

Note that the `Binding` is set to `Main`, which, if you look in the ViewModelLocator.cs file `Main`, is the name of the view model returned. Also, the `Source` is set to just `Locator`, which is the key that was used in the App.xaml. At this point you can bind to any property or command that exists in the `MainViewModel` class.

Setting Up the CollectionViewSource

The next thing to take on is setting up the `CollectionViewSource` defined in the page. You want to ensure that it uses your `GroupedBookCollection` property and that for each object in that property, the individual book list is extracted from the `BookList` property. The following code in `Page.Resources` takes care of this:

```
<CollectionViewSource
        x:Name="groupedItemsViewSource"
        Source="{Binding GroupedBookCollection}"
        ItemsPath="BookList"
        IsSourceGrouped="true" />
```

Setting the Page Attributes

After setting the `CollectionViewSource` you can turn your attention to a simple fix, which sets the name that you want displayed at the top of the page. Because the title of the page is bound to a `StaticResource` called `AppName`, you can simply change that `String` setting to "Wrox BookStore" in the following code:

```
<x:String x:Key="AppName">Wrox Book Browser</x:String>
```

The `GridView` and `ListView` require a few modifications. By default, they are set to use an `ItemTemplate` and `HeaderTemplate` that looks for certain properties, which in your case do not exist in the `WroxBook` class. To get this to work, you can swap these properties for the ones relevant to your app. For example, in the `GridView.GroupStyle` declaration, the code for the `HeaderTemplate` has a `StackPanel` with two `TextBlock` controls. The first control is set to display the group name, and in this case the bound `GroupedBooks` class has a `Group` property containing that information. The following code ensures the binding is correct for this custom class.

```
<StackPanel Orientation="Horizontal">
    <TextBlock Text="{Binding Group}" Margin="3,-7,10,10"
Style="{StaticResource GroupHeaderTextStyle}" />
    <TextBlock Text="{StaticResource ChevronGlyph}" FontFamily="Segoe UI Symbol"
Margin="0,-7,0,10" Style="{StaticResource GroupHeaderTextStyle}"/>
</StackPanel>
```

Also the `GroupStyle.HeaderTemplate` has a declaration for a `Button` control that's bound to a command called `SelectGroupCommand`. Notice, however, that the entire `Binding` syntax points out both the `MainViewModel` and the `Locator` as the `Source`. This is required because the `GridView` has its `ItemSource` property bound to the `CollectionViewSource`. When that binding is complete, the individual header items no longer have access to the `MainViewModel` instance — only the actual bound `GroupedBooks` objects. Luckily, MVVM and data binding is flexible; at any time, you can set the `DataContext` of an individual control to something else and it overrides the current value. You can even do it down to the property level. So in this example, you still want the overall `Button` `DataContext` to stay bound to the `CollectionViewSource`, but you want the `Command` property bound to something else entirely. The following code takes care of setting this up:

```
<Button Command="{Binding Main.SelectGroupCommand,
Source={StaticResource Locator}}"
CommandParameter="{Binding}" AutomationProperties.Name="Group Title"
Style="{StaticResource TextPrimaryButtonStyle}">
```

At this point, there is no `SelectGroupCommand` in the *MainViewModel* class but that is fine, as you see in a sec. The purpose of this command is to let you know when the user has selected a specific group to drill down into. Then you can send a message to the user interface that it should navigate to the `GroupDetailPage`.

Another important detail to notice about the `GridView` code is that the `SelectedItem` property is bound to a property on the `MainViewModel` class called `SelectedBook`. This is important for a few reasons:

➤ You need a variable that can hold onto the selected book object.

➤ You need to know when a user has actually selected a book so that you can redirect to the `BookDetailPage`.

Because there is no `Command` property on the `GridView`, you can't simply bind to a command in the `MainViewModel` class like you did with the `Button`. Instead you must add your logic in the setter of the `SelectedBook` property. The other alternative is to add this logic to the code behind, but because you use MVVM, adding the logic to the setter is perfectly valid.

In addition to setting the `SelectedItem` property, you may also have noticed that the `Loaded` event is set to an event handler in the code behind. By default, when you bind to a `CollectionViewSource` as the page loads, the first item in the collection is automatically selected. The only time you can override this is in the `Loaded` event for the `GridView`. The plan is to cancel this initial item selection so that the user is presented with a list of grouped books with no predetermined selection made. Another reason to prevent this behavior is that if you allow the default selection, the `SelectedItem` property is set, and your setter logic in the `MainViewModel` fires causing the app to redirect to the `BookDetailPage` before the user even has a chance to make a selection, and you certainly don't want that to happen.

Modifying the Default ItemTemplate

The last thing you need to take care of in the XAML is to modify the default `ItemTemplate` used. Because you bind to `WroxBook` objects, the default template won't work for you. As you can see, the `ItemTemplate` property of the `GridView` is set to `Standard250x250ItemTemplate`. You can find this by searching the StandardStyles.xaml file. After you're there, replace the existing code for the template to the following:

```
<DataTemplate x:Key="Standard250x250ItemTemplate">
    <Grid HorizontalAlignment="Left" Width="250" Height="250">
        <Border Background="{StaticResource
ListViewItemPlaceholderBackgroundThemeBrush}">
            <Image Source="{Binding Thumbnail}" Stretch="UniformToFill"/>
        </Border>
        <StackPanel VerticalAlignment="Bottom" Background="{StaticResource
ListViewItemOverlayBackgroundThemeBrush}">
            <TextBlock Text="{Binding Title}" Foreground="{StaticResource
ListViewItemOverlayForegroundThemeBrush}" Style="{StaticResource TitleTextStyle}"
Height="60" Margin="15,0,15,0"/>
            <TextBlock Text="{Binding Author}" Foreground="{StaticResource
ListViewItemOverlaySecondaryForegroundThemeBrush}" Style="{StaticResource
CaptionTextStyle}" TextWrapping="NoWrap" Margin="15,0,15,10"/>
        </StackPanel>
    </Grid>
</DataTemplate>
```

Nothing is complicated here — just ensuring that the `Image` control is bound to the `Thumbnail` property and the `Title` and `Author` properties are used instead of the defaults.

Updating the ViewModel

Now that the XAML for the home page is complete, you must make some additions to the view model. Looking at the XAML, you know you need some properties to hold the selected group and selected book. You also need a command that selects the group and some setter logic that helps navigate to the appropriate page when a user selects a book. First tackle the properties. Open the MainViewModel.cs file and add the following code:

```
using GalaSoft.MvvmLight.Messaging;

private GroupedBookList _selectedGroup = null;
public GroupedBookList SelectedGroup
{
    get { return _selectedGroup; }
    set
    {
        _selectedGroup = value;
        RaisePropertyChanged("SelectedGroup");
    }
}

private WroxBook _selectedBook = null;
public WroxBook SelectedBook
```

```
        {
            get { return _selectedBook; }
            set
            {
                _selectedBook = value;
                Messenger.Default.Send<BookSelectedMessage>(new
        BookSelectedMessage(_selectedBook));
            }
        }
```

As you can see, when a book is selected you need to let the user interface know to navigate to the `BookDetailPage`. Chapter 10 shows that MVVMLight provides a great mechanism to communicate from the view model back to the code behind by making use of messages. Obviously, you need to implement MVVMLight because you can access only the main `Frame` object used for navigation from the code behind of the currently viewed page. You have tricks available to make the view model aware of the `Frame` and to let the view model handle the navigation, but that breaks one of the principals of MVVM, which is to keep view-specific logic out of the view model. In this case, navigating from page to page is view-specific and should stay in the code behind.

In the following code, you create a `BookSelectedMessage` and send that to whatever code-behind page happens to be registered for the message. Because this is not the only message passing around in your app, you should create a folder to hold the message classes:

1. Right-click the project node.

2. Add a new folder called `Messages`.

3. Add a new class called `BookSelectedMessage` and replace its contents with the code in Listing 12-6.

LISTING 12-6: BookSelectedMessage.cs

```
using System;
using System.Collections.Generic;
using System.Linq;
using System.Text;
using System.Threading.Tasks;
using WroxBookStore.Data;

namespace WroxBookStore.Messages
{
    public class BookSelectedMessage
    {
        public WroxBook Selected { get; set; }

        public BookSelectedMessage(WroxBook selected)
        {
            Selected = selected;
        }
    }
}
```

4. Add a `RelayCommand` for when a group is selected. All you need to do is send a message to the user interface so that the proper navigation can take place. Add the following code to MainViewModel.cs to handle group selection.

```
private RelayCommand<GroupedBookList> _selectGroupCommand = null;
public RelayCommand<GroupedBookList> SelectGroupCommand
{
    get
    {
        if (_selectGroupCommand == null)
            _selectGroupCommand = new
RelayCommand<GroupedBookList>(SelectGroup);

        return _selectGroupCommand;
    }
}

private void SelectGroup(GroupedBookList group)
{
    SelectedGroup = group;
    Messenger.Default.Send<GroupSelectedMessage>(new
GroupSelectedMessage(_selectedGroup));
}
```

5. You need another message class to handle this, so add a new class to the `Messages` folder called `GroupSelectedMessage`. Then replace its contents with the code in Listing 12-7:

LISTING 12-7: GroupSelectedMessage.cs

```
using System;
using System.Collections.Generic;
using System.Linq;
using System.Text;
using System.Threading.Tasks;
using WroxBookStore.Data;

namespace WroxBookStore.Messages
{
    public class GroupSelectedMessage
    {
        public GroupedBookList Selected { get; set; }

        public GroupSelectedMessage(GroupedBookList selected)
        {
            Selected = selected;
        }
    }
}
```

Finishing the Code Behind

The XAML is set, and the view model is ready. All that is left is to handle any messages coming in from the view model and ensure that the default CollectionViewSource is canceled. You must do all this from the code behind. Open the GroupedBooks.xaml.cs file and replace its contents with the code in Listing 12-8:

LISTING 12-8: GroupedBooks.xaml.cs

```
using GalaSoft.MvvmLight.Messaging;
using Windows.UI.Xaml;
using Windows.UI.Xaml.Navigation;
using WroxBookStore.Common;
using WroxBookStore.Messages;

// The Grouped Items Page item template is documented at
// http://go.microsoft.com/fwlink/?LinkId=234231

namespace WroxBookStore
{
    /// <summary>
    /// A page that displays a grouped collection of items.
    /// </summary>
    public sealed partial class GroupedBooks : LayoutAwarePage
    {
        private bool _initialLoad = true;

        public GroupedBooks()
        {
            this.InitializeComponent();
        }

        protected override void OnNavigatedTo(NavigationEventArgs e)
        {
            base.OnNavigatedTo(e);

            Messenger.Default.Register<BookSelectedMessage>(this,
HandleBookSelected);
            Messenger.Default.Register<GroupSelectedMessage>(this,
HandleGroupSelected);
        }

        protected override void OnNavigatedFrom(NavigationEventArgs e)
        {
            base.OnNavigatedFrom(e);

            Messenger.Default.Unregister<BookSelectedMessage>(this);
            Messenger.Default.Unregister<GroupSelectedMessage>(this);
```

continues

LISTING 12-8 *(continued)*

```
        }

        private void HandleBookSelected(BookSelectedMessage message)
        {
            if (_initialLoad == false && message.Selected != null)
                this.Frame.Navigate(typeof(BookDetailPage));
            else
                _initialLoad = false;
        }

        private void HandleGroupSelected(GroupSelectedMessage message)
        {
            this.Frame.Navigate(typeof(GroupDetailPage));
        }

        private void MainGridView_Loaded(object sender, RoutedEventArgs e)
        {
            MainGridView.SelectedIndex = -1;
        }

        private void MainListView_Loaded(object sender, RoutedEventArgs e)
        {
            MainListView.SelectedIndex = -1;
        }
    }
}
```

There are a few key points to take away from this code:

➤ The `MainGrid_Loaded` and `MainList_Loaded` event handlers are used to set the `SelectedIndex` to –1, which cancels that initial selection that the `CollectionViewSource` creates. This, however, does cause a problem. Just setting that index effectively fires a `SelectedItem` change, which in turn causes navigation to take place — which is not good. The previous code adds a variable that keeps track of whether this is the first time the `SelectedItem` is set and, if so, ignores it because you know it is –1 or null. Otherwise, the `HandleBookSelected` method performs the navigation to the `BookDetailPage`.

➤ The only other important code with which you should be familiar is when a user navigates to this page, you need to register for any required messages — in this case `BookSelectedMessage` and `GroupSelectedMessage`. The `GroupSelectedMessage` is handled by the `HandleGroupSelected` method and simply navigates to the `GroupDetailPage`.

➤ When the user navigates away from this page, you must unregister for any messages; otherwise, you run the risk of handling duplicate messages the next time the page loads.

If you now build and run the app in the Simulator, you should see groups of books loaded, as shown in Figure 12-4.

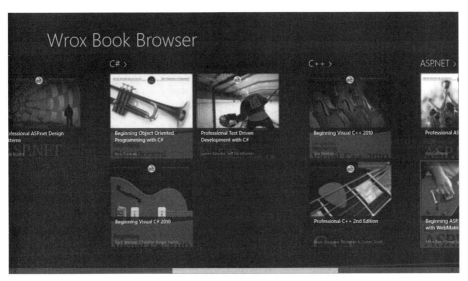

FIGURE 12-4

You can also click a group header or book and be redirected to the appropriate pages. Of course, those pages are blank at this point, but you are definitely heading in the right direction.

DRILLING DOWN INTO GROUPS

You now have the home page set, and the view model works to the point where you can see all the available groups and books. Now you need to work on some of these secondary pages. In this section, you start with the group drill down. This is a simple page, and the purpose is actually to allow a user to see only books that belong to a specific group. In addition, after this page loads, you should plan to allow users to sort and filter the results by using commands available in the `AppBar` for this page.

Configuring the XAML

The first thing to tackle is the required XAML for this page. Open up the GroupDetailPage.xaml file and replace the contents with the code in Listing 12-9:

LISTING 12-9: GroupDetailPage.xaml

```
<common:LayoutAwarePage
    x:Name="pageRoot"
    x:Class="WroxBookStore.GroupDetailPage"
    xmlns="http://schemas.microsoft.com/winfx/2006/xaml/presentation"
    xmlns:x="http://schemas.microsoft.com/winfx/2006/xaml"
    xmlns:local="using:WroxBookStore"
    xmlns:data="using:WroxBookStore.Data"
```

continues

LISTING 12-9 *(continued)*

```
    xmlns:common="using:WroxBookStore.Common"
    xmlns:d="http://schemas.microsoft.com/expression/blend/2008"
    xmlns:mc="http://schemas.openxmlformats.org/markup-compatibility/2006"
    mc:Ignorable="d" DataContext="{Binding Main,
Source={StaticResource Locator}}">

    <Page.Resources>

        <!-- Collection of items displayed by this page -->
        <CollectionViewSource x:Name="itemsViewSource" Source="{Binding
SelectedGroup.FilteredBookList}" />
    </Page.Resources>

    <Page.BottomAppBar>
        <AppBar>
            <Grid>
                <Grid.ColumnDefinitions>
                    <ColumnDefinition Width="50*" />
                    <ColumnDefinition Width="50*" />
                </Grid.ColumnDefinitions>
                <StackPanel Orientation="Horizontal" Grid.Column="1"
HorizontalAlignment="Right">
                    <Button x:Name="FilterBooks" Style="{StaticResource
FilterAppBarButtonStyle}" Command="{Binding FilterListCommand}" />
                    <Button x:Name="SortBooks" Margin="20,0,0,0"
Style="{StaticResource SortAppBarButtonStyle}" Command="{Binding
SortListCommand}" />
                </StackPanel>
            </Grid>
        </AppBar>
    </Page.BottomAppBar>

    <!--
    This grid acts as a root panel for the page that defines two rows:
    * Row 0 contains the back button and page title
    * Row 1 contains the rest of the page layout
    -->
    <Grid
        Style="{StaticResource LayoutRootStyle}">

        <Grid.RowDefinitions>
            <RowDefinition Height="140"/>
            <RowDefinition Height="*"/>
        </Grid.RowDefinitions>

        <!-- Horizontal scrolling grid used in most view states -->
        <GridView
            x:Name="MainGridView"
            AutomationProperties.AutomationId="ItemGridView"
            AutomationProperties.Name="Items In Group"
            TabIndex="1"
            Grid.RowSpan="2"
```

```
                    Padding="120,126,120,50"
                    ItemsSource="{Binding Source={StaticResource itemsViewSource}}"
                    ItemTemplate="{StaticResource Standard500x130ItemTemplate}"
                    SelectionMode="Single"
                    IsSwipeEnabled="false"
                    SelectedItem="{Binding SelectedBook, Mode=TwoWay}"
                    Loaded="MainGridView_Loaded">

                    <GridView.Header>
                        <StackPanel Width="480" Margin="0,4,14,0">
                            <TextBlock Text="{Binding SelectedGroup.Description}"
    Margin="0,0,18,0" Style="{StaticResource BodyTextStyle}"/>
                        </StackPanel>
                    </GridView.Header>
                    <GridView.ItemContainerStyle>
                        <Style TargetType="FrameworkElement">
                            <Setter Property="Margin" Value="52,0,0,10"/>
                        </Style>
                    </GridView.ItemContainerStyle>
                </GridView>

                <!-- Vertical scrolling list only used when snapped -->
                <ListView
                    x:Name="MainListView"
                    AutomationProperties.AutomationId="ItemListView"
                    AutomationProperties.Name="Items In Group"
                    TabIndex="1"
                    Grid.Row="1"
                    Visibility="Collapsed"
                    Padding="10,0,0,60"
                    ItemsSource="{Binding Source={StaticResource itemsViewSource}}"
                    ItemTemplate="{StaticResource Standard80ItemTemplate}"
                    SelectionMode="None"
                    IsSwipeEnabled="false"
                    IsItemClickEnabled="True"
                    Loaded="MainListView_Loaded">

                    <ListView.Header>
                        <StackPanel>
                            <TextBlock Text="{Binding Author}" Margin="10,0,18,20"
    Style="{StaticResource TitleTextStyle}" MaxHeight="60"/>
                            <Image Source="{Binding Thumbnail}" Margin="10,0,18,0"
    MaxHeight="160" Stretch="UniformToFill" AutomationProperties.Name="{Binding
    Title}"/>
                            <TextBlock Margin="10,20,18,30" Text="{Binding Overview}"
    Style="{StaticResource BodyTextStyle}"/>
                        </StackPanel>
                    </ListView.Header>
                </ListView>

                <!-- Back button and page title -->
                <Grid>
                    <Grid.ColumnDefinitions>
                        <ColumnDefinition Width="Auto"/>
                        <ColumnDefinition Width="*"/>
```

continues

LISTING 12-9 *(continued)*

```xml
                </Grid.ColumnDefinitions>
                <Button x:Name="backButton" Click="GoBack" IsEnabled="{Binding
Frame.CanGoBack, ElementName=pageRoot}" Style="{StaticResource BackButtonStyle}"/>
                <TextBlock x:Name="pageTitle" Text="{Binding SelectedGroup.Group}"
Style="{StaticResource PageHeaderTextStyle}" Grid.Column="1"
IsHitTestVisible="false"/>
            </Grid>

        <VisualStateManager.VisualStateGroups>

        <!-- Visual states reflect the application's view state -->
            <VisualStateGroup x:Name="ApplicationViewStates">
                <VisualState x:Name="FullScreenLandscape"/>
                <VisualState x:Name="Filled"/>

                <!-- The entire page respects the narrower 100-pixel margin
convention for portrait -->
                <VisualState x:Name="FullScreenPortrait">
                    <Storyboard>
                        <ObjectAnimationUsingKeyFrames
Storyboard.TargetName="backButton" Storyboard.TargetProperty="Style">
                            <DiscreteObjectKeyFrame KeyTime="0"
Value="{StaticResource PortraitBackButtonStyle}"/>
                        </ObjectAnimationUsingKeyFrames>

                        <ObjectAnimationUsingKeyFrames
Storyboard.TargetName="MainGridView" Storyboard.TargetProperty="Padding">
                            <DiscreteObjectKeyFrame KeyTime="0"
Value="100,126,90,0"/>
                        </ObjectAnimationUsingKeyFrames>
                    </Storyboard>
                </VisualState>
                <VisualState x:Name="Snapped">
                    <Storyboard>
                        <ObjectAnimationUsingKeyFrames
Storyboard.TargetName="backButton" Storyboard.TargetProperty="Style">
                            <DiscreteObjectKeyFrame KeyTime="0"
Value="{StaticResource SnappedBackButtonStyle}"/>
                        </ObjectAnimationUsingKeyFrames>
                        <ObjectAnimationUsingKeyFrames
Storyboard.TargetName="pageTitle" Storyboard.TargetProperty="Style">
                            <DiscreteObjectKeyFrame KeyTime="0"
Value="{StaticResource SnappedPageHeaderTextStyle}"/>
                        </ObjectAnimationUsingKeyFrames>

                        <ObjectAnimationUsingKeyFrames
Storyboard.TargetName="MainGridView" Storyboard.TargetProperty="Visibility">
                            <DiscreteObjectKeyFrame KeyTime="0"
Value="Collapsed"/>
                        </ObjectAnimationUsingKeyFrames>
                        <ObjectAnimationUsingKeyFrames
```

```
Storyboard.TargetName="MainListView" Storyboard.TargetProperty="Visibility">
                                <DiscreteObjectKeyFrame KeyTime="0"
Value="Visible"/>
                                        </ObjectAnimationUsingKeyFrames>
                                </Storyboard>
                        </VisualState>
                </VisualStateGroup>
        </VisualStateManager.VisualStateGroups>
    </Grid>
</common:LayoutAwarePage>
```

Although the default code generated from the Visual Studio template is close to what you want, it's not quite exactly what you need. The previous code makes a few important modifications. First, just as you did with the home page of the app, you set up the overall DataContext of the page to the MainViewModel. Then you declared an instance of an AppBar along with a few commands. In the following code, two Button controls in the AppBar handle filtering and sorting the books that display as part of the selected group.

```
<Page.BottomAppBar>
    <AppBar>
        <Grid>
            <Grid.ColumnDefinitions>
                <ColumnDefinition Width="50*" />
                <ColumnDefinition Width="50*" />
            </Grid.ColumnDefinitions>
            <StackPanel Orientation="Horizontal" Grid.Column="1"
HorizontalAlignment="Right">
                <Button x:Name="FilterBooks" Style="{StaticResource
FilterAppBarButtonStyle}" Command="{Binding FilterListCommand}" />
                <Button x:Name="SortBooks" Margin="20,0,0,0"
Style="{StaticResource SortAppBarButtonStyle}"
Command="{Binding SortListCommand}" />
            </StackPanel>
        </Grid>
    </AppBar>
</Page.BottomAppBar>
```

In both cases you bind the Command property to a RelayCommand that needs to be implemented in the MainViewModel. Next, you need to slightly modify the CollectionViewSource so that it points to the list of books belonging to the SelectedGroup property of the view model. The following code takes care of this:

```
<Page.Resources>

<!-- Collection of items displayed by this page -->
<CollectionViewSource
    x:Name="itemsViewSource"
    Source="{Binding SelectedGroup.FilteredBookList}" />
</Page.Resources>
```

With the CollectionViewSource setup and pointing to the FilteredBookList, you can now update the GridView. Again you have the issue of a default selection being made from the CollectionViewSource, so you must handle that with the Loaded event handler. Again, you bind to the `SelectedBook` property of the `MainViewModel` so that when a user makes a selection, the user interface properly navigates to the `BookDetailPage`. Finally, this `GridView` uses a slightly different `ItemTemplate`. Now it uses the `Standard500x130ItemTemplate`, so you need to modify that in the StandardStyles.xaml file to reflect binding to a `WroxBook` object. Find the style declaration and replace it with the following code:

```
<DataTemplate x:Key="Standard500x130ItemTemplate">
    <Grid Height="110" Width="480" Margin="10">
        <Grid.ColumnDefinitions>
            <ColumnDefinition Width="Auto"/>
            <ColumnDefinition Width="*"/>
        </Grid.ColumnDefinitions>
        <Border Background="{StaticResource
ListViewItemPlaceholderBackgroundThemeBrush}" Width="110" Height="110">
            <Image Source="{Binding Thumbnail}" Stretch="UniformToFill"
AutomationProperties.Name="{Binding Title}"/>
        </Border>
        <StackPanel Grid.Column="1" VerticalAlignment="Top" Margin="10,0,0,0">
            <TextBlock Text="{Binding Title}" Style="{StaticResource
TitleTextStyle}" TextWrapping="NoWrap"/>
            <TextBlock Text="{Binding Author}" Style="{StaticResource
CaptionTextStyle}" TextWrapping="NoWrap"/>
            <TextBlock Text="{Binding Overview}" Style="{StaticResource
BodyTextStyle}" MaxHeight="60"/>
        </StackPanel>
    </Grid>
</DataTemplate>
```

Now when each book displays in the `GridView`, the `Title`, `Thumbnail`, `Author`, and `Overview` text displays. That just about takes care of the user interface code for this page, so now you can move on to implementing some of the commands and properties required in the `MainViewModel` class.

Updating the View Model

A couple changes are required in the view model to support the group details page. The first is creating a few `RelayCommand` objects to handle the filtering and sorting enabled in the `AppBar`. Because the display of the filter and sort menu contains user interface-specific logic, you need to place that code in the code behind. This simplifies the view model quite a bit because all these commands actually need to do is to fire a couple new messages to the code-behind file to let it know that the pop-up menus should display. Open the MainViewModel.cs file and add the following command code:

```
private RelayCommand _sortListCommand = null;
public RelayCommand SortListCommand
{
    get
    {
        if (_sortListCommand == null)
            _sortListCommand = new RelayCommand(SortList, () => {
return SelectedGroup != null; });

        return _sortListCommand;
    }
```

```
    }

    private void SortList()
    {
        Messenger.Default.Send<SortListMessage>(new SortListMessage(_selectedGroup));
    }

    private RelayCommand _filterListCommand = null;
    public RelayCommand FilterListCommand
    {
        get
        {
            if (_filterListCommand == null)
                _filterListCommand = new RelayCommand(FilterList, () => {
    return SelectedGroup != null; });

            return _filterListCommand;
        }
    }

    private void FilterList()
    {
        Messenger.Default.Send<FilterListMessage>(new
    FilterListMessage(_selectedGroup));
    }
```

Clearly these commands require the use of two new messages. Add two new class files to the
`Messages` folder called `SortListMessage` and `FilterListMessage`. Then replace the contents with
the code in Listing 12-10 and 12-11, respectively.

LISTING 12-10: SortListMessage.cs

```
using System;
using System.Collections.Generic;
using System.Linq;
using System.Text;
using System.Threading.Tasks;
using WroxBookStore.Data;

namespace WroxBookStore.Messages
{
    public class SortListMessage
    {
        public GroupedBookList Selected { get; set; }

        public SortListMessage(GroupedBookList selected)
        {
            Selected = selected;
        }
    }
}
```

LISTING 12-11: FilterListMessage.cs

```
using System;
using System.Collections.Generic;
using System.Linq;
using System.Text;
using System.Threading.Tasks;
using WroxBookStore.Data;

namespace WroxBookStore.Messages
{
    public class FilterListMessage
    {
        public GroupedBookList Selected { get; set; }

        public FilterListMessage(GroupedBookList selected)
        {
            Selected = selected;
        }
    }
}
```

Surprisingly, that is all that is required in the view model for this page. As you can see, because of data binding and MVVM, you are drastically reducing the code that would normally be required in this app. Now you are sending filter and sort messages back to the user interface pages that have registered for these messages. All that is left is to write the logic to display these menus in the code behind.

Finishing the Code Behind

You need to handle the filter and sort messages as well as cancel that default `GridView` selection. Open the GroupDetailPage.xaml.cs file and replace its contents with the code in Listing 12-12:

LISTING 12-12: GroupDetailPage.xaml.cs

```
using GalaSoft.MvvmLight.Messaging;
using System;
using System.Collections.ObjectModel;
using System.Linq;
using Windows.Foundation;
using Windows.UI.Popups;
using Windows.UI.Xaml;
using Windows.UI.Xaml.Media;
using Windows.UI.Xaml.Navigation;
using WroxBookStore.Common;
using WroxBookStore.Data;
using WroxBookStore.Messages;
using WroxBookStore.ViewModel;

// The Item Detail Page item template is documented at
```

```
http://go.microsoft.com/fwlink/?LinkId=234232

namespace WroxBookStore
{
    public sealed partial class GroupDetailPage : LayoutAwarePage
    {
        private bool _initialLoad = true;

        public GroupDetailPage()
        {
            this.InitializeComponent();
        }

        protected override void OnNavigatedTo(NavigationEventArgs e)
        {
            base.OnNavigatedTo(e);

            Messenger.Default.Register<BookSelectedMessage>(this,
HandleBookSelected);
            Messenger.Default.Register<FilterListMessage>(this,
HandleFilterList);
            Messenger.Default.Register<SortListMessage>(this,
HandleSortList);
        }

        protected override void OnNavigatedFrom(NavigationEventArgs e)
        {
            base.OnNavigatedFrom(e);

            Messenger.Default.Unregister<BookSelectedMessage>(this);
            Messenger.Default.Unregister<FilterListMessage>(this);
            Messenger.Default.Unregister<SortListMessage>(this);
        }

        private void MainGridView_Loaded(object sender, RoutedEventArgs e)
        {
            MainGridView.SelectedIndex = -1;
        }

        private void MainListView_Loaded(object sender, RoutedEventArgs e)
        {
            MainListView.SelectedIndex = -1;
        }

#region Message Handlers

        private void HandleBookSelected(BookSelectedMessage message)
        {
            if (_initialLoad == false && message.Selected != null)
                this.Frame.Navigate(typeof(BookDetailPage));
            else
                _initialLoad = false;
        }

        private async void HandleFilterList(FilterListMessage message)
```

continues

LISTING 12-12 *(continued)*

```
        {
                PopupMenu filterMenu = new PopupMenu();
                MainViewModel vm = this.DataContext as MainViewModel;

                filterMenu.Commands.Add(new UICommand("ALL BOOKS", (command) =>
                {
                    _initialLoad = true;
                    vm.SelectedGroup.FilteredBookList = new
ObservableCollection<WroxBook>(vm.SelectedGroup.BookList.ToList());

                    MainGridView.SelectedIndex = -1;
                    MainListView.SelectedIndex = -1;
                }));

                filterMenu.Commands.Add(new UICommand("BEGINNER SERIES",
(command) =>
                {
                    _initialLoad = true;
                    vm.SelectedGroup.FilteredBookList = new
ObservableCollection<WroxBook>(vm.SelectedGroup.BookList.Where(b =>
b.Title.ToUpper().IndexOf("BEGINNING") >= 0).ToList());

                    MainGridView.SelectedIndex = -1;
                    MainListView.SelectedIndex = -1;
                }));

                filterMenu.Commands.Add(new UICommand("PROFESSIONAL SERIES",
(command) =>
                {
                    _initialLoad = true;
                    vm.SelectedGroup.FilteredBookList = new
ObservableCollection<WroxBook>(vm.SelectedGroup.BookList.Where(b =>
b.Title.ToUpper().IndexOf("PROFESSIONAL") >= 0).ToList());

                    MainGridView.SelectedIndex = -1;
                    MainListView.SelectedIndex = -1;
                }));

                await filterMenu.ShowForSelectionAsync(GetMenuRectangle
((FrameworkElement)
FilterBooks));
        }

        private async void HandleSortList(SortListMessage message)
        {
                PopupMenu sortMenu = new PopupMenu();
                MainViewModel vm = this.DataContext as MainViewModel;

                sortMenu.Commands.Add(new UICommand("SORT BY TITLE", (command) =>
                {
                    _initialLoad = true;
                    vm.SelectedGroup.FilteredBookList = new
ObservableCollection<WroxBook>(vm.SelectedGroup.BookList.OrderBy(b =>
```

```
                  b.Title).ToList());

                                  MainGridView.SelectedIndex = -1;
                                  MainListView.SelectedIndex = -1;
                          }));

                          sortMenu.Commands.Add(new UICommand("SORT BY AUTHOR", (command) =>
                          {
                                  _initialLoad = true;
                                  vm.SelectedGroup.FilteredBookList = new
          ObservableCollection<WroxBook>(vm.SelectedGroup.BookList.OrderBy(b =>
          b.Author).ToList());

                                  MainGridView.SelectedIndex = -1;
                                  MainListView.SelectedIndex = -1;
                          }));

                          await sortMenu.ShowForSelectionAsync(GetMenuRectangle
          ((FrameworkElement)
          SortBooks));
                  }

          public static Rect GetMenuRectangle(FrameworkElement element)
          {
                  GeneralTransform transform = element.TransformToVisual(null);
                  Point point = transform.TransformPoint(new Point());
                  Rect finalRect = new Rect(point, new Size(element.ActualWidth,
          element.ActualHeight));

                  return finalRect;
          }

      #endregion
          }
      }
```

Now you have quite a bit of work going on in the code behind — more so than on any other page of the app. So break down some of the more important points. First, you are handling the OnNavigatedTo and OnNavigatedFrom methods so that you can properly Register and Unregister for the Sort/Filter/Selection messages sent from the view model. You have seen that code before, so it should not need further explanation. The MainGrid_Loaded and MainList_Loaded event handlers again simply take care of canceling out the initial selection made from the CollectionViewSource. This leaves only the sort and filter code as the only remaining items to explain.

Chapter 4 — in particular the AppBar topic in that chapter — introduced you to much of the sorting code. Just as in that chapter, you need to add UICommand objects to the Commands property of the PopupMenu control. These commands require having their logic declared inline using a lambda expression. What is interesting about this is the following line:

```
vm.SelectedGroup.FilteredBookList = new ObservableCollection<WroxBook>(
vm.SelectedGroup.BookList.OrderBy(b => b.Title).ToList());
```

This line basically grabs the full unfiltered/unsorted list of books from the current view model and creates a new `ObservableCollection<WroxBook>` instance to replace the current `FilteredBookList`. Because this property has a `RaisePropertyChanged` call in the setter, the `GridView` automatically refreshes to display only the newly filtered items in the list, once again demonstrating the power of MVVM and data binding. In Chapter 4, you didn't write any additional code to refresh the `GridView`. Simply updating the underlying content was enough to get the screen to change. For sorting it's the same deal. You just replace that `FilteredBookList` with a sorted version of the books matching the selected group. Data binding takes care of the rest. Now if you build and run the app in the Simulator, you can click one of the programming topics from the main page, and you see the newly updated `GroupDetailPage`, as shown in Figure 12-5.

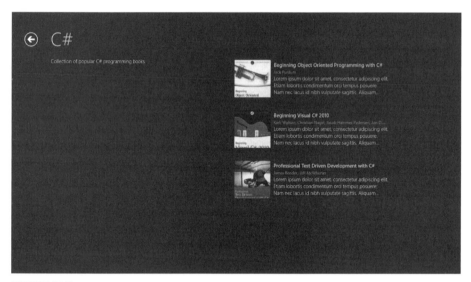

FIGURE 12-5

SHOWING DETAILED BOOK INFORMATION

Now you have the home page and group details page finished. Next on the agenda is tackling what happens when a user selects an individual book. The design calls for a detailed information page for the selected book. This should display a large version of the book cover along with title, author, and a brief overview of the book's content as well as an option to purchase the book directly from the Wrox website. You've already created the BookDetailsPage.xaml file using the appropriate Visual Studio item template, so you need to update the XAML to display the required information.

Configuring the XAML

The `ItemDetailPage` template that you use to create the `BookDetailPage` file is interesting in that it makes use of the new `RichTextColumns` XAML control in Windows 8. This control enables you to add rich text to any XAML page while controlling how text wraps around images and how text overflows into additional columns. For this example, users arrive on this page when they touch/click an individual book from the `GridView` control either on the main home page or the `GroupDetailPage`. When here, you need to present a large version of the book cover and some overview text about the book. The goal is to display the title/author/thumbnail on the left side of the screen and push the overview text (in this case just lorem ipsum text) over to the right side or second column. To get this to work, you need to make some adjustments to the XAML generated from the template. Open the BookDetailPage.xaml and replace it with the code in Listing 12-13:

LISTING 12-13: BookDetailPage.xaml

```xaml
<common:LayoutAwarePage
    x:Name="pageRoot"
    x:Class="WroxBookStore.BookDetailPage"
    xmlns="http://schemas.microsoft.com/winfx/2006/xaml/presentation"
    xmlns:x="http://schemas.microsoft.com/winfx/2006/xaml"
    xmlns:local="using:WroxBookStore"
    xmlns:common="using:WroxBookStore.Common"
    xmlns:d="http://schemas.microsoft.com/expression/blend/2008"
    xmlns:mc="http://schemas.openxmlformats.org/markup-compatibility/2006"
    mc:Ignorable="d" DataContext="{Binding Main,
Source={StaticResource Locator}}">

    <Page.BottomAppBar>
        <AppBar>
            <Grid>
                <Grid.ColumnDefinitions>
                    <ColumnDefinition Width="50*" />
                    <ColumnDefinition Width="50*" />
                </Grid.ColumnDefinitions>
                <StackPanel Orientation="Horizontal" Grid.Column="0"
HorizontalAlignment="Left">
                    <Button x:Name="AddToWishList" Style="{StaticResource
WishListAddAppBarButtonStyle}" Visibility="{Binding IsAddWishListVisible}"
Command="{Binding WishListAddCommand}" />
                    <Button x:Name="RemoveFromWishList" Style="{StaticResource
WishListRemoveAppBarButtonStyle}" Visibility="{Binding IsRemoveWishListVisible}"
Command="{Binding WishListRemoveCommand}" />
                </StackPanel>
            </Grid>
        </AppBar>
    </Page.BottomAppBar>

    <!--
    This grid acts as a root panel for the page that defines two rows:
    * Row 0 contains the back button and page title
    * Row 1 contains the rest of the page layout
    -->
    <Grid Style="{StaticResource LayoutRootStyle}">
        <Grid.RowDefinitions>
            <RowDefinition Height="140"/>
            <RowDefinition Height="*"/>
```

continues

LISTING 12-13 *(continued)*

```xml
        </Grid.RowDefinitions>

        <Grid Grid.Row="1">

        <!-- Content is allowed to flow across as many columns as needed -->
            <common:RichTextColumns x:Name="richTextColumns"
Margin="117,0,117,47" DataContext="{Binding SelectedBook}">
                <RichTextBlock x:Name="richTextBlock" Width="560"
Style="{StaticResource ItemRichTextStyle}" IsTextSelectionEnabled="False">
                    <Paragraph>
                        <Run FontWeight="Normal" Text="{Binding Author}"/>
                    </Paragraph>
                    <Paragraph LineStackingStrategy="MaxHeight">
                        <InlineUIContainer>
                            <Image x:Name="image" MaxHeight="480"
Margin="0,20,0,10" Stretch="Uniform" Source="{Binding Thumbnail}" />
                        </InlineUIContainer>
                        <LineBreak />
                        <LineBreak />
                        <LineBreak />
                    </Paragraph>
                    <Paragraph>
                        <Run FontWeight="SemiLight"
Text="{Binding Overview}"/>
                        <LineBreak />
                        <LineBreak />
                        <LineBreak />
                        <InlineUIContainer>
                            <HyperlinkButton DataContext="{Binding Main,
Source={StaticResource Locator}}" Command="{Binding PurchaseBookCommand}"
Content="Purchase This Book" />
                        </InlineUIContainer>
                    </Paragraph>
                </RichTextBlock>

                <!-- Additional columns are created from this template -->
                <common:RichTextColumns.ColumnTemplate>
                    <DataTemplate>
                        <RichTextBlockOverflow Width="560" Margin="80,0,0,0">
                            <RichTextBlockOverflow.RenderTransform>
                                <TranslateTransform X="-1" Y="4"/>
                            </RichTextBlockOverflow.RenderTransform>
                        </RichTextBlockOverflow>
                    </DataTemplate>
                </common:RichTextColumns.ColumnTemplate>
            </common:RichTextColumns>
        </Grid>

        <!-- Back button and page title -->
        <Grid>
            <Grid.ColumnDefinitions>
                <ColumnDefinition Width="Auto"/>
                <ColumnDefinition Width="*"/>
```

```
                </Grid.ColumnDefinitions>
                <Button x:Name="backButton" Click="GoBack"
    IsEnabled="{Binding Frame.CanGoBack, ElementName=pageRoot}" Style="{StaticResource
    BackButtonStyle}"/>
                <TextBlock x:Name="pageTitle" Text="{Binding SelectedBook.Title}"
    Style="{StaticResource PageHeaderTextStyle}" Grid.Column="1"
    IsHitTestVisible="false"/>
            </Grid>

            <VisualStateManager.VisualStateGroups>

                <!-- Visual states reflect the application's view state -->
                <VisualStateGroup x:Name="ApplicationViewStates">
                    <VisualState x:Name="FullScreenLandscape"/>
                    <VisualState x:Name="Filled"/>

                    <!-- The back button respects the narrower 100-pixel margin
                    convention for portrait -->
                    <VisualState x:Name="FullScreenPortrait">
                        <Storyboard>
                            <ObjectAnimationUsingKeyFrames
    Storyboard.TargetName="backButton" Storyboard.TargetProperty="Style">
                                <DiscreteObjectKeyFrame KeyTime="0"
    Value="{StaticResource PortraitBackButtonStyle}"/>
                            </ObjectAnimationUsingKeyFrames>
                        </Storyboard>
                    </VisualState>
                    <VisualState x:Name="Snapped">
                        <Storyboard>
                            <ObjectAnimationUsingKeyFrames
    Storyboard.TargetName="backButton" Storyboard.TargetProperty="Style">
                                <DiscreteObjectKeyFrame KeyTime="0"
    Value="{StaticResource SnappedBackButtonStyle}"/>
                            </ObjectAnimationUsingKeyFrames>
                            <ObjectAnimationUsingKeyFrames
    Storyboard.TargetName="pageTitle" Storyboard.TargetProperty="Style">
                                <DiscreteObjectKeyFrame KeyTime="0"
    Value="{StaticResource SnappedPageHeaderTextStyle}"/>
                            </ObjectAnimationUsingKeyFrames>
                        </Storyboard>
                    </VisualState>
                </VisualStateGroup>
            </VisualStateManager.VisualStateGroups>
        </Grid>
    </common:LayoutAwarePage>
```

Now break down some of the key parts of this XAML code update starting with the page-level binding. As you have with each page so far, you set the main DataContext of the page to the MainViewModel instance using the following code:

```
<common:LayoutAwarePage
    x:Name="pageRoot"
    x:Class="WroxBookStore.BookDetailPage"
    xmlns="http://schemas.microsoft.com/winfx/2006/xaml/presentation"
    xmlns:x="http://schemas.microsoft.com/winfx/2006/xaml"
    xmlns:local="using:WroxBookStore"
```

```
        xmlns:common="using:WroxBookStore.Common"
        xmlns:d="http://schemas.microsoft.com/expression/blend/2008"
        xmlns:mc="http://schemas.openxmlformats.org/markup-compatibility/2006"
        mc:Ignorable="d" DataContext="{Binding Main,
    Source={StaticResource Locator}}">
```

With that complete, all the properties and commands in the `MainViewModel` class are available for binding. Next, add an `AppBar` to the screen, as shown in the following code:

```
<Page.BottomAppBar>
    <AppBar>
        <Grid>
            <Grid.ColumnDefinitions>
                <ColumnDefinition Width="50*" />
                <ColumnDefinition Width="50*" />
            </Grid.ColumnDefinitions>
            <StackPanel Orientation="Horizontal" Grid.Column="0"
HorizontalAlignment="Left">
                <Button x:Name="AddToWishList" Style="{StaticResource
WishListAddAppBarButtonStyle}" Visibility="{Binding IsAddWishListVisible}"
Command="{Binding WishListAddCommand}" />
                <Button x:Name="RemoveFromWishList" Style="{StaticResource
WishListRemoveAppBarButtonStyle}" Visibility="{Binding IsRemoveWishListVisible}"
Command="{Binding WishListRemoveCommand}" />
            </StackPanel>
        </Grid>
    </AppBar>
</Page.BottomAppBar>
```

The `AppBar` on this page needs only one command to add/remove the currently viewed book to/from the wish list. Each `Button` also makes use of a few new control Style assignments. First, the `AddToWishList` button uses the `WishListAddAppBarButtonStyle`. This style is a copy of the `CopyAppBarButtonStyle` with the text below the icon changed — the same thing goes for the `RemoveFromWishList Button` control. In this case, the `CutAppBarButtonStyle` is copied with some replacement text. The benefit of this is that you can easily utilize the copy/cut icons that are already defined, but because you create new styles with them, you don't run the risk of breaking the existing styles should you need them elsewhere in your app. Add the following code in the StandardStyles. xaml file to implement these two new `AppBar Button` styles:

```
<Style x:Key="WishListAddAppBarButtonStyle" TargetType="ButtonBase"
BasedOn="{StaticResource AppBarButtonStyle}">
    <Setter Property="AutomationProperties.AutomationId"
Value="PasteAppBarButton"/>
    <Setter Property="AutomationProperties.Name" Value="Add To Wishlist"/>
    <Setter Property="Content" Value="&#xE16D;"/>
</Style>
<Style x:Key="WishListRemoveAppBarButtonStyle" TargetType="ButtonBase"
BasedOn="{StaticResource AppBarButtonStyle}">
    <Setter Property="AutomationProperties.AutomationId" Value="CutAppBarButton"/>
    <Setter Property="AutomationProperties.Name" Value="Remove From Wishlist"/>
    <Setter Property="Content" Value="&#xE16B;"/>
</Style>
```

Also included in this XAML code is content for the `RichTextColumns` control that creates several `Paragraph` declarations. In the following code, the first `Paragraph` simply presents the `Author` of the book.

```
<Paragraph>
    <Run FontWeight="Normal" Text="{Binding Author}"/>
</Paragraph>
```

Next is a paragraph that includes an `InlineUIContainer` for an Image control. You can use the `InlineUIContainer` whenever you need to embed a XAML control in the middle of a rich text paragraph. In this case, the `Image` control displays a larger version of the book cover thumbnail. The following code shows the second `Paragraph` declaration.

```
<Paragraph LineStackingStrategy="MaxHeight">
    <InlineUIContainer>
        <Image x:Name="image" MaxHeight="480" Margin="0,20,0,10"
Stretch="Uniform" Source="{Binding Thumbnail}" />
    </InlineUIContainer>
    <LineBreak />
    <LineBreak />
    <LineBreak />
</Paragraph>
```

You might wonder why you have three additional `LineBreak` tags after the `Image` displays. These `LineBreak` tags force all the `Overview` text for the book to display on the right column. Without these, the default overflow behavior of the `RichTextColumns` control is to simply start the next paragraph below the `Image` and then wrap any overflow text into the next available column. In this example, you don't want any of this text to appear in the same column as the image, so a few extra line breaks ensure that they don't.

The next and final `Paragraph` tag contains both the `Overview` text for the book along with another `InlineUIContainer`. In the following code, notice how an added `HyperlinkButton` control is responsible for navigating the user to the Wrox website, so they can purchase the book if they choose to do so:

```
<Paragraph>
    <Run FontWeight="SemiLight" Text="{Binding Overview}"/>
    <LineBreak />
    <LineBreak />
    <LineBreak />
    <InlineUIContainer>
        <HyperlinkButton DataContext="{Binding Main,
Source={StaticResource Locator}}" Command="{Binding PurchaseBookCommand}"
Content="Purchase This Book" />
    </InlineUIContainer>
</Paragraph>
```

Now you have everything you need for the user interface of this page. You've seen a couple new commands declared; however, you need to jump back to the `MainViewModel` class and take care of the `PurchaseBookCommand`, the `WishListAddCommand`, and `WishListRemoveCommand`.

Updating the View Model

In the view model for this page, you have several commands to implement and you must use properties to determine which of the two `AppBar Button` controls should display. Now tackle the commands first by looking at the `PurchaseBookCommand`. The goal of this command is to tell the app to navigate to the Wrox.com page that provides the user with an option to actually purchase the book. The best place to handle the navigation is in the code behind; all you need to do here is set up a message to be sent that triggers the navigation. Add the following code to the MainViewModel.cs file to implement this command:

```
private RelayCommand _purchaseBookCommand = null;
public RelayCommand PurchaseBookCommand
{
    get
    {
        if (_purchaseBookCommand == null)
            _purchaseBookCommand = new RelayCommand(PurchaseBook, () =>
{ return SelectedBook != null; });

        return _purchaseBookCommand;
    }
}

private void PurchaseBook()
{
    Messenger.Default.Send<PurchaseBookMessage>(new
PurchaseBookMessage(_selectedBook));
}
```

When that is complete, you need to create the class for the PurcahseBookMessage. In the Messages folder add a new class called PurchaseBookMessage, and replace the contents with the code in Listing 12-14:

LISTING 12-14: PurchaseBookMessage.cs

```
using WroxBookStore.Data;

namespace WroxBookStore.Messages
{
    public class PurchaseBookMessage
    {
        public WroxBook Selected { get; set; }

        public PurchaseBookMessage(WroxBook selected)
        {
            Selected = selected;
        }
    }
}
```

Because the actual navigation is handled in the code behind, this is all the code you need in the view model. The two remaining commands are somewhat complex in nature and require an understanding of the new SkyDrive API (which requires its own explanation), so rather than adding that code now, get the book purchasing code set in the code behind and come back to the wish list feature.

Finishing the Code Behind

You have the command ready to go for purchasing a book. Now you simply need to register for the PurchaseBookMessage and take care of the actual navigation. Open up the BookDetailPage.xaml .cs file and replace its contents with the code in Listing 12-15:

LISTING 12-15: BookDetailPage.xaml.cs

```csharp
using GalaSoft.MvvmLight.Messaging;
using System;
using Microsoft.Live;
using Windows.System;
using Windows.UI.Xaml.Navigation;
using WroxBookStore.Common;
using WroxBookStore.Messages;

// The Item Detail Page item template is documented at
// http://go.microsoft.com/fwlink/?LinkId=234232

namespace WroxBookStore
{
    /// <summary>
    /// A page that displays details for a single item within
    /// a group while allowing     gestures to
    /// flip through other items belonging to the same group.
    /// </summary>
    public sealed partial class BookDetailPage : LayoutAwarePage
    {
        private LiveConnectSession session = null;

        public BookDetailPage()
        {
            this.InitializeComponent();
        }

        protected override void OnNavigatedTo(NavigationEventArgs e)
        {
            base.OnNavigatedTo(e);
            Messenger.Default.Register<PurchaseBookMessage>(this,
HandlePurchaseBook);
        }

        protected override void OnNavigatedFrom(NavigationEventArgs e)
        {
            base.OnNavigatedFrom(e);
            Messenger.Default.Unregister<PurchaseBookMessage>(this);
        }

        private async void HandlePurchaseBook(PurchaseBookMessage message)
        {
            await Launcher.LaunchUriAsync(message.Selected.PurchaseLink);
        }
    }
}
```

Looking at this code a little further, you can see the usual `Register` and `Unregister` calls for the `PurchaseBookMessage`. Then in the handler for the message, you see that to send the user to the appropriate page you need to fire up an instance of Internet Explorer using the correct `Launcher`. Again, because this action must be asynchronous, you must mark the handler as `async` and call the `LaunchUriAsync` method using the `await` keyword. If you fire up the app in the Simulator and navigate to any particular book, you can click the purchase `HyperlinkButton` and see Internet Explorer 10 launching with the correct book page from `www.wrox.com` loaded, as shown in Figure 12-6.

FIGURE 12-6

PROVIDING A WISH LIST FEATURE WITH SKYDRIVE

The goal of this feature is to allow users to simply create a wish list file that is saved across all the devices they may own having the `WroxBookStore` app installed. In this version of the app, you simply allow users to add/remove single books from the wish list. Ultimately, you have endless possibilities for implementing such a feature, but in this example, you simply add/remove the title of the selected book to a plain text file. Because you want this file to be accessible across multiple devices, you can easily accomplish this using Microsoft SkyDrive. The available SkyDrive API makes it simple for you to upload/download files to the cloud and access them via the SkyDrive Windows Store app or the browser. SkyDrive is not solely a .NET product by any means either. The SkyDrive API is a REST-based web service that you can access through Java/JavaScript/Objective C/.NET or any programming language that can make a simple REST-based call. The SkyDrive API is based on end users having a Windows Live ID with which they use to log in to SkyDrive. For the `WroxBookStore` app, you use the credentials of the current Windows 8 user.

Making Files Available Locally

In addition to using SkyDrive to sync the wish list across multiple devices in the cloud, you also want to make the file available locally. For this app, you store the wish list in the Documents Library.

The workflow follows:

1. Load the wish list from SkyDrive.

2. If the file is successfully downloaded from the SkyDrive directory, copy it locally to the Documents Library.

3. To make use of the contents, load each of the books listed in the file into an in-memory data structure from which you can add/remove items until it's time to sync the changes back to SkyDrive.

With a basic understanding of how this overall wish list feature should work, dive into some code.

1. You need a data structure to hold the entire in-memory wish list. An `ObservableCollection<string>` can do the trick here. So in the MainViewModel.cs file, add the following code:

```
private ObservableCollection<string> _wishListTitles = null;
public ObservableCollection<string> WishListTitles
{
    get
    {
        if (_wishListTitles == null)
            _wishListTitles = new ObservableCollection<string>();

        return _wishListTitles;
    }
}
```

2. Back when the `AppBar` was declared, you had two `Button` controls and the `Visibility` of each was to be determined by two additional properties in the view model. With the `WishListTitles` property existing, you can safely add these two additional properties. Add the following code to MainViewModel.cs:

```
public Visibility IsAddWishListVisible
{
    get
    {
        if( WishListTitles.Where(b => b.ToUpper() ==
SelectedBook.Title.ToUpper()).Count() > 0 )
            return Visibility.Collapsed;

        return Visibility.Visible;
    }
}

public Visibility IsRemoveWishListVisible
{
    get
    {
        if (WishListTitles.Where(b => b.ToUpper() ==
SelectedBook.Title.ToUpper()).Count() > 0)
            return Visibility.Visible;

        return Visibility.Collapsed;
    }
}
```

As you can see the `Add Button` control becomes visible only if the selected title is not found in the wish list collection. Consequently, the `Remove Button` control is invisible unless the selected book is found in the wish list collection. This is straightforward so far; now you need to actually create/save the wish list file.

> **NOTE** *Because you want to keep the actual add/remove command logic as simple as possible, you must ensure that the wish list file exists when the application starts up and any additional books load into the* `WishListTitles` *property. This requires the use of file IO and SkyDrive. Before using either of these, however you need to take care of a few simple prerequisites.*

3. To read/write application specific files to the Documents Library on Windows 8, you need to configure your app to request access to the Library. You do this by opening up the Package.appmanifest file and selecting the Capabilities tab. After that tab is open, be sure to select the Documents Library check box in the list, as shown in Figure 12-7.

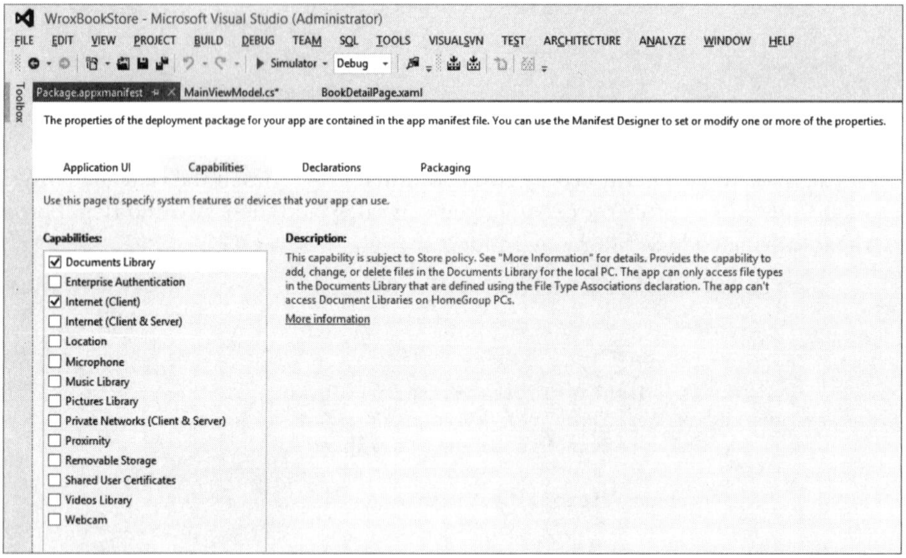

FIGURE 12-7

4. Set the default file extension for the file you want to write. This should be an application-specific file extension, so for the wish list file, simply use .wslst.

5. Before reading/writing .wslst files, you need to open the Declarations tab of the manifest and select a new File Type Association. Be sure to add the file type of .wslst and set the Edit flags to the Always Unsafe check box option, as shown in Figure 12-8.

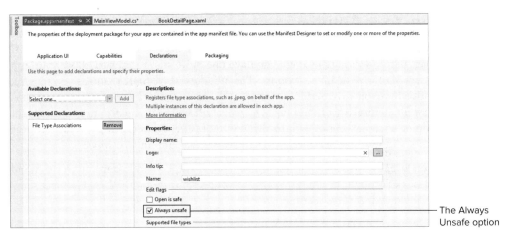

FIGURE 12-8

6. You now have everything you need configured for reading/writing your new wish list file to the Documents Library in Windows 8. All that is left before coding is to configure your app so that it can access the SkyDrive API. To start you need to actually download and install the SkyDrive API. At the time of this writing, the latest version of the API can be downloaded here: `http://msdn.microsoft.com/en-US/live/ff621310`.

7. When the install is complete, you need to right-click the project reference node in Solution Explorer and add a reference to Live SDK, which is found under the Windows/Extensions tab, as shown in Figure 12-9.

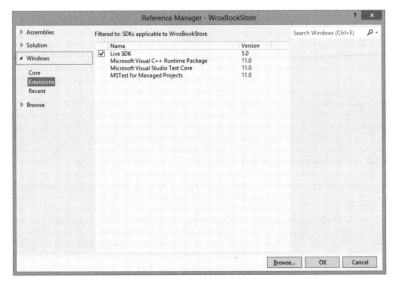

FIGURE 12-9

Registering Your App

Now that the references have been updated you have full access to the .NET SkyDrive API in your app. However, before writing any code you have one more step to take to allow your app to actually access the users SkyDrive or Live accounts. The Windows Live SDK requires you to actually register your app with Microsoft Live Services and upon doing so enter the confirmation information into your manifest file before any of the Live SDK calls will work. If you attempt to access the SkyDrive API before doing so, an exception will be thrown to the effect that the app has not yet been configured to work with Windows Live Services. You can register the app in two ways:

➤ If you already have a Windows Store account, you can add your app to the Windows Store and work through the configuration of your app to set up the Live Connect services under the Advanced features section.

➤ If, however, you do not have a Windows Store account set up, you can also get SkyDrive integration setup by visiting https://manage.dev.live.com/build?wa=wsignin1.0 and following the detailed instructions on the site. Ultimately, if you follow this URL, you need to enter the Package Name and Publisher information, and in turn you receive a confirmation code to add in your manifest file. The website is straightforward and gives you detailed screenshots to walk you through the rest of the configuration.

Assuming you have everything set up correctly, you can finally use the SkyDrive API and get the wish list code working. The first step in the process is to make sure the wish list file exists at startup and the `WishListTitles` property is set to modify the `MainViewModel` constructor to look like the following:

```
public MainViewModel()
{
    if (IsInDesignMode)
    {
        // Code runs in Blend --> create design time data.
    }
    else
    {
        CreateMainDataSource();
        LoadWishList();
    }
}
```

Loading/Creating the Wish List File

The only difference here is that you add a call to `LoadWishList`, which you need to implement next. By putting this in the constructor of the `MainViewModel`, you're ensured that the wish list file is created/read on application startup because one single instance of this view model is instantiated in the App.xaml file by the `ViewModelLocator` class.

Adding the LoadWishList Method

Now you need to add the `LoadWishList` method, so insert the following private method to the MainViewModel.cs file:

```
private async void LoadWishList()
{
    StorageFile wishList = await GetWishListFromSkyDrive();
    _wishListTitles = new ObservableCollection<string>();

    if (wishList == null)
    {
        StorageFolder docsFolder = KnownFolders.DocumentsLibrary;
        wishList = await
docsFolder.CreateFileAsync("WroxBookStore\\WroxBookStoreWishList.wslst",
CreationCollisionOption.ReplaceExisting);
    }

    if (wishList != null)
    {
        IList<string> titles = await FileIO.ReadLinesAsync(wishList);

        foreach (string title in titles)
            _wishListTitles.Add(title);
    }
}
```

The method starts by attempting to load the wish list from the current users' SkyDrive account. If the file does not exist in SkyDrive, the soon-to-be-implemented GetWishListFromSkyDrive method returns a null instance of the StorageFile class. You should be familiar with the StorageFile class from Chapter 6, "Handling Data, Files, and Networks." Ultimately, if you cannot load the file from SkyDrive, you simply get a reference to the DocumentsLibrary and create the WroxBookStoreWishList.wslst file in the WroxBookStore directory.

Adding Files to the WishListTitles Property

After the file is loaded/created, each line — in this case simply the title of the book — is read. Each title line is then added to the WishListTitles ObservableCollection<string> property. Doing all this ensures that the WishListTitles property is ready to go when the user navigates to any particular book details page. Then the correct Add/Remove AppBar Button control should be visible depending on the contents of the file. You can easily verify that the file is created by building and running the app at this point. Just be sure to insert a skeleton method to represent the GetWishListFromSkyDrive method or simply set wishList to null before running to avoid compilation errors. When the app runs, you can navigate to one of the book details pages, load up Explorer, and navigate to the Documents library. You should have a folder called WroxBookStore and in that folder the WroxBookStoreWishList.wslst file. The file will be empty, but at least you can see that the actual file I/O is occurring correctly.

The only thing still missing from this load method is the implementation for the GetWishListFromSkyDrive method, which you can start on now. In MainViewModel.cs, add the following code:

```
using Microsoft.Live;

private async Task<StorageFile> GetWishListFromSkyDrive()
{
    LiveAuthClient client = new LiveAuthClient();
```

```
          LiveLoginResult result = await client.LoginAsync(new List<string>()
     { "wl.signin", "wl.basic", "wl.skydrive" });
          LiveConnectSession session = null;
          LiveConnectClient skyDrive = null;

          if (result.Status == LiveConnectSessionStatus.Connected)
          {
               session = result.Session;
               skyDrive = new LiveConnectClient(session);

               LiveOperationResult cloudResult = await
     skyDrive.GetAsync("me/skydrive/files");
               IDictionary<string, object> files = cloudResult.Result;
               List<object> fileData = (List<object>)files["data"];
               string fileID = "";

               foreach (dynamic fileDetails in fileData)
               {
                    if (fileDetails.name == "WroxBookStoreWishList.wslst")
                         fileID = fileDetails.id;
               }

               if (!String.IsNullOrEmpty(fileID))
               {
                    StorageFolder docsFolder = KnownFolders.DocumentsLibrary;
                    StorageFile wishList = await
     docsFolder.CreateFileAsync("WroxBookStore\\WroxBookStoreWishList.wslst",
     CreationCollisionOption.ReplaceExisting);

                    await skyDrive.BackgroundDownloadAsync(String.Format("{0}/content",
     fileID), wishList);
                    return wishList;
               }
          }

          return null;
     }
```

After adding this code, in addition to the `using` statement, you also need to add a reference to the SkyDrive API libraries in the project. To do this, follow these steps:

1. Right click the References folder in solution explorer and select the Add Reference option.

2. Select the Windows ⇨ Extensions tab.

3. You should see an entry for the Live SDK option. Be sure to select this check box.

4. Click OK.

Now looking back at the code there is a good amount of information that needs to be reviewed a little further:

➤ The using statement ensures that all of the .NET Live SDK features are available and ready for IntelliSense.

➤ In the following code you are essentially creating a Windows Live client object and performing a log in.

```
LiveAuthClient client = new LiveAuthClient();
LiveLoginResult result = await client.LoginAsync(new List<string>()
{ "wl.signin", "wl.basic", "wl.skydrive" });
```

➤   The `LoginAsync` requires the `await` keyword because it is performed asynchronously. Because you can use the Live SDK for more than just SkyDrive, you must pass the `LoginAsync` method a few parameters telling it what you need to access.

➤   The `wl.signin` parameter essentially tells the SDK to grab the currently logged in Windows 8 users' Live credentials and pass them on through. This creates a single sign-on type experience.

➤   The `wl.basic` parameter requests access to the users basic profile information as well as any contacts.

➤   The `wl.skydrive` feature requests read access to all documents located on the users' SkyDrive account.

> **NOTE** *You can pass many other parameters to the log-in and can find the full list at* `http://msdn.microsoft.com/en-us/library/live/hh243646.aspx`*. If you visit this site you can learn how to get permissions for additional Live SDK features such as the Calendar.*

The first time you call this log-in method, you see an additional pop-up message appear on the simulator, and your users will as well. Because you ask for access to the user's SkyDrive account, the user must add your app to the permissions list for SkyDrive/Windows Live. In Figure 12-10 you can see the pop-up that appears the first time you log in. Simply agree to give the `WroxBookStore` access, and you are on your way. You need to do this only one time because the permissions are stored on the users' account settings online. If for some reason users want to remove that permission, they can simply log in to their live account and go to Preferences/Manage Apps to remove the `WroxBookStore`.

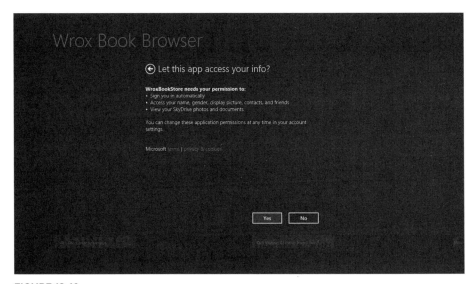

FIGURE 12-10

Ensuring a Successful User Log-in

After the log-in is complete, you need to ensure that the log-in succeeded and that the user can connect with a valid Live Session. Because you need the Session for other calls to the SDK, the following line just stores it in a `LiveConnectSession` variable.

```
session = result.Session;
```

The next line of code creates a new `LiveConnectSession` that accesses any SkyDrive methods.

```
skyDrive = new LiveConnectClient(session);
```

Accessing User File Data

Now things get interesting. Because you can use this SDK for multiple languages, the .NET Wrapper is basically a wrapper around the REST-based communication that goes on. Because of this, you'll find that when you make some of the calls to SkyDrive, you do not have the advantage of using typed objects. This means no IntelliSense. Many of the return values are simply of the type `DynamicDictionary`, which means you must make use of the new C# 4 dynamic keyword to access the data you need. In the following code you ask SkyDrive for a list of all the files the user has in the root SkyDrive directory and ultimately put the list of files into a `List<object>` variable. You need to grab the entire list of files because to access any single file on SkyDrive, you must use a SkyDrive generated `ID`, and unfortunately the first time you run it, you simply won't know that `ID`. The only way to find the WroxBookStoreWishList.wslst file is to cycle through all the files until you find one with the matching name property. Here is the code that grabs the list and searches for the correct file:

```
LiveOperationResult cloudResult = await skyDrive.GetAsync("me/skydrive/files");
IDictionary<string, object> files = cloudResult.Result;
List<object> fileData = (List<object>)files["data"];
string fileID = "";

foreach (dynamic fileDetails in fileData)
{
    if (fileDetails.name == "WroxBookStoreWishList.wslst")
        fileID = fileDetails.id;
}
```

If the file is found (and it won't be the first time you run the app) you simply store the id of the file so that you can reference it later when you attempt to download the content.

If the file `id` is found, that means it exists on SkyDrive, so you want to pull the latest version down locally and store it in the Documents Library. In the following code, you use some of the new WinRT file I/O methods to create the actual file, and then you use the SkyDrive `BackgroundDownloadAsync` method to pull the contents of the wish list into the instance of the `StorageFile` you created:

```
if (!String.IsNullOrEmpty(fileID))
{
    StorageFolder docsFolder = KnownFolders.DocumentsLibrary;
    StorageFile wishList = await
docsFolder.CreateFileAsync("WroxBookStore\\WroxBookStoreWishList.wslst",
```

```
CreationCollisionOption.ReplaceExisting);

    await skyDrive.BackgroundDownloadAsync(String.Format({0}/content",
fileID), wishList);
    return wishList;
}
```

An important thing to note in the path for the `BackgroundDownloadAsync` method is that you specify "/content" after the file id. If you do not do this, you retrieve a shell of the file containing all the file attributes and properties but not the actual content. This gives you a way to create a file explorer without actually taking the time to download the content of all the files you want to see. In your case, you actually want the contents immediately so that you can add that "/content" syntax to ensure that happens.

Saving the Wish List File

Now you have the code that creates a default wish list. You also have the code that is ready to load the most current version of the wish list from a SkyDrive account. All that is left to do is to write some code to store the current wish list to SkyDrive, so any other device with this app installed can pick up the data.

```
private async void SaveWishList()
{
    StorageFolder folder = KnownFolders.DocumentsLibrary;
    StorageFile wishList = await
folder.CreateFileAsync("WroxBookStore\\WroxBookStoreWishList.wslst",
CreationCollisionOption.OpenIfExists);

    await FileIO.WriteLinesAsync(wishList, WishListTitles.ToList());
    SaveToSkyDrive(wishList);

    RaisePropertyChanged("IsRemoveWishListVisible");
    RaisePropertyChanged("IsAddWishListVisible");
}

private async void SaveToSkyDrive(StorageFile wishList)
{
    LiveAuthClient client = new LiveAuthClient();
    LiveLoginResult result = await client.LoginAsync(new List<string>()
{ "wl.signin", "wl.basic", "wl.skydrive", "wl.skydrive_update" });
    LiveConnectSession session = null;
    LiveConnectClient skyDrive = null;

    if (result.Status == LiveConnectSessionStatus.Connected)
    {
        session = result.Session;
        skyDrive = new LiveConnectClient(session);

        await skyDrive.BackgroundUploadAsync("me/skydrive",
"WroxBookStoreWishList.wslst", wishList, OverwriteOption.Overwrite);
    }
}
```

Adding the Commands

You can now create/open/save a wish list file both locally in the Documents Library and in the cloud via SkyDrive. All you need to do is actually implement the AppBar commands that the Button controls are bound to. You already have all the logic you need, so simply add the following code to implement both the Add and Remove wish list commands:

```
private RelayCommand _wishListAddCommand = null;
public RelayCommand WishListAddCommand
{
    get
    {
        if (_wishListAddCommand == null)
            _wishListAddCommand =
new RelayCommand(AddToWishList, () => { return SelectedBook != null; });

        return _wishListAddCommand;
    }
}

private void AddToWishList()
{
    WishListTitles.Add(SelectedBook.Title);
    SaveWishList();
}

private RelayCommand _wishListRemoveCommand = null;
public RelayCommand WishListRemoveCommand
{
    get
    {
        if (_wishListRemoveCommand == null)
            _wishListRemoveCommand =
new RelayCommand(RemoveFromWishList, () => { return SelectedBook != null; });

        return _wishListRemoveCommand;
    }
}

private void RemoveFromWishList()
{
    WishListTitles.Remove(SelectedBook.Title);
    SaveWishList();
}
```

There is nothing too complicated here. When you add a book to the wish list, you simply add to the collection and call the SaveWishList method you implemented previously. Then when you want to remove a book, simply remove it from the collection and call the same SaveWishList method.

At this point you have everything you need to try it out. If you build and run the app and navigate to a specific book details page, you should freely add/remove that book to/from your wish list. Also, if you navigate to your local Documents library, you should find the wish list file and open it up to see if it reflects changes as you make them. Finally, if you log in to your SkyDrive account, you should also see a copy of the file sitting out there. Figure 12-11 shows the file in a SkyDrive account using the Windows 8 default SkyDrive app that is installed.

Nick's SkyDrive ˅ 1 item

WroxBookStoreWishList.wslst
11:05 PM 47 bytes

FIGURE 12-11

UPDATING THE TILE AND SPLASH SCREEN

All the application features are set, so before deploying the app to the Windows Store, you just want to ensure you tidy up a few loose ends. Obviously, you don't simply want to throw an app into the store without its own tile or splash screen. You want your app to have a logo suitable for display in the store; otherwise you run the risk of the app getting rejected. Although this app won't make use of Live Tiles, you should still plan to use an image other than the default that Visual Studio supplies. For the WroxBookStore app, the sample code has already supplied all the required images. The following list shows image samples along with the list of required images and sizes. You can open any of these in your favorite image editing program, such as Fireworks or Photoshop. Just be sure not to change the dimensions because they've all been created using the standard Windows Store app logo settings:

FIGURE 12-12

➤ Logo.png (150 × 150), as shown in Figure 12-12.

FIGURE 12-13

➤ SmallLogo.png (30 × 30), as shown in Figure 12-13.

➤ StoreLogo.png (50 × 50), as shown in Figure 12-14.

➤ WideLogo.png (310 × 150), as shown in Figure 12-15.

FIGURE 12-14

After you update all the tile images and logos, you now need to do something about the default splash screen. The sample code for this chapter includes a pretty basic splash screen, but again like Figures 12-12 through 12-15, you can simply open it in any image editor and modify it to suit your needs. The file is located under Assets\SplashScreen.png. Figure 12-16 shows the splash screen in action when the application is first loaded.

FIGURE 12-15

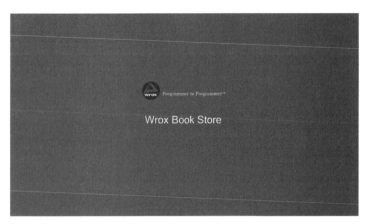

FIGURE 12-16

With all these images updated and ready to go, you have only one thing left to do: Get your app ready for deployment in the Windows Store.

GETTING READY FOR THE STORE

Chapter 11 introduces the Windows Store and has a solid primer on how everything works, including the various monetization strategies available. This chapter won't get into too much detail — simply a quick walkthrough to refresh your memory and familiarize you with the process you should follow every time you want to deploy a new app to the Windows Store.

Much of this work doesn't even involve leaving Visual Studio. Visual Studio gives you a pseudo checklist that you can use to ensure that you meet all the required steps. You can easily access this menu by clicking the Project Menu and selecting the Store submenu. Figure 12-17 shows the Visual Studio Store menu along with the checklist of tasks you need to walk through before your app is ready for deployment.

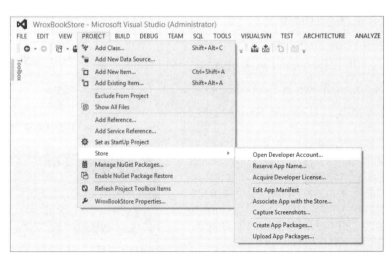

FIGURE 12-17

Opening a Developer Account

The first step in the checklist is to open a developer account. If you do not have one already, you need a Windows Live ID. After you decide on which Live ID you want to register, click the link in the Visual Studio Store menu. You are redirected to the Windows Store Developer Center. The current home page for the Developer Center is shown in Figure 12-18.

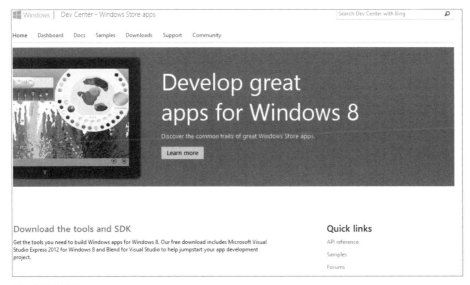

FIGURE 12-18

You are asked a series of questions along with verification steps to complete your registration. You are also charged $99 to enroll in the program. Even if you currently have a valid enrollment in the Windows Phone Developer Center, you still need to pay an additional $99 to register as a Windows Store app developer. When this step is complete, you are taken to the dashboard where you can move onto the next step in the process.

Reserving an App Name

This is the second step in the Visual Studio Store menu, and when you type in a name for your app and click the Reserve App Name button, you're redirect to the Windows Store Developer center page where you can start filling out some basic details about your app. Figure 12-19 shows the name reservation process.

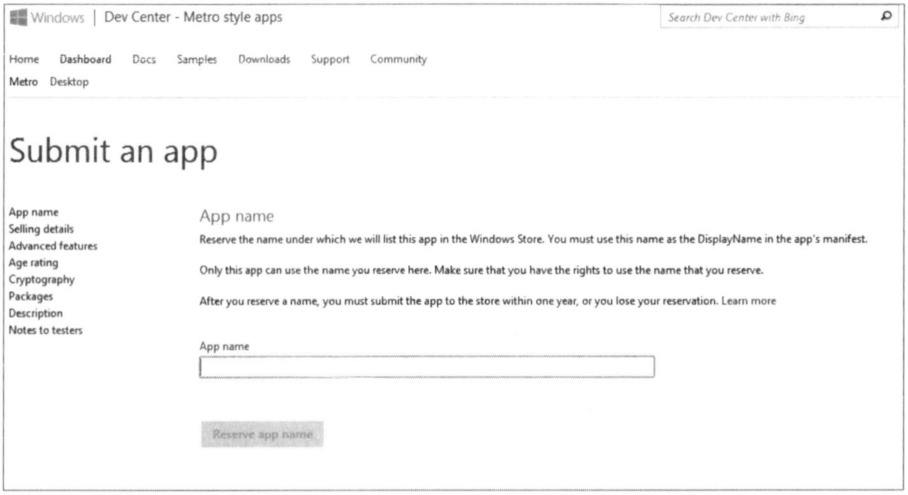

FIGURE 12-19

Even if you have not completed your app, you should reserve an app name sooner rather than later. After you reserve the app name in the Windows Store, you have up to one year to actually deploy the code before the reservation is lost.

Acquiring a Developer License

The next step in the menu is to acquire a developer license. When you first created the project using the Blank App project template, more than likely you were asked to retrieve a valid Windows 8 developer license. However, if for some reason your license is expired, you can still click this menu option, and you are presented with the option to renew your license, as shown in Figure 12-20. If you do not need to renew your license, you can skip this step.

Editing the App Manifest

Next on the agenda is to edit the application manifest.

FIGURE 12-20

If you haven't already specified the various Capabilities and Declarations required by your app, this is the time to do so before you create any deployment package. For the WroxBookStore app, you've built up the manifest as you worked through the development, so no additional step is required here. Even so, going through this step in the process at least gives you another chance to review the manifest and make any last minute changes before you move on.

Associating the App with the Store

The next step in the process and the fifth item on the Store submenu is to associate your app with the Windows Store developer account you registered. If you simply use this Visual Studio option, you are presented with a screen asking you to sign in to your Windows Store account. Then Visual Studio syncs required information, such as Package Display Name, Package Name, Publisher ID, and Publisher Display Name, to your app's Windows Store entry. This step is required and can also be done online by visiting the Dashboard entry for your app in the Windows Store Developer Center. Figure 12-21 shows the login screen that displays when you select this menu option.

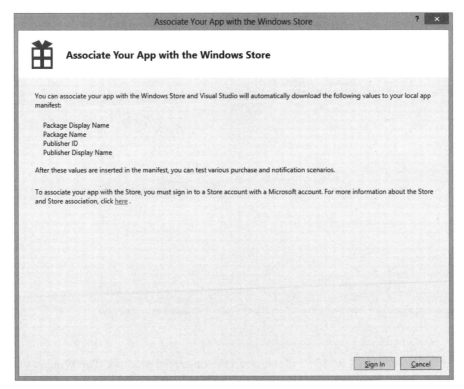

FIGURE 12-21

Capturing Screenshots

After setting up your app in the store, you must capture some screenshots that show off your app to potential buyers. This menu option in Visual Studio simply fires up a copy of the Simulator and runs your app in the debugger. While the app runs, you are instructed to make use of the Capture Screen button in the Simulator to extract high-quality images that you can upload to the Windows Store entry for your app. After you capture as many images as you think you need, you can head over to your app entry on the Windows Store Developer Center dashboard and upload the screenshots so that they are available to any prospective buyers.

Creating App Packages

There are only two simple steps left before your app is ready for final configuration in the Windows Store. First, you must build and create the deployment package for your app. If you select the Create App Packages menu option in Visual Studio, you are presented with the screen in Figure 12-22.

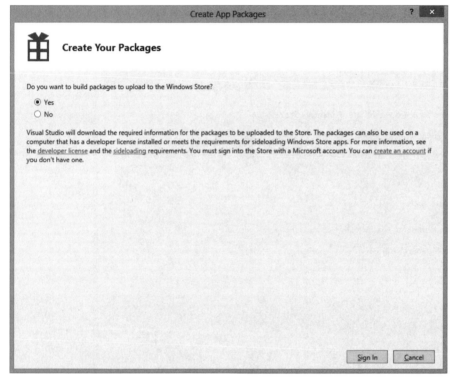

FIGURE 12-22

Sign in using your Windows Store Live ID, and follow all the on-screen prompts. The Windows Store wizard downloads the necessary information from the Windows Store that is required in your application package. After this step is fully complete, you can move on to the final step in the process.

Uploading App Packages

Now you have your application package built and configured. The only thing left to do is upload it to the Windows Store and then sit back and wait for the money to start rolling in. Select the Upload App Packages menu option in Visual Studio, and you are redirected to the Windows Store Developer Center Dashboard. From there, you can select your package and upload it to the Store. Simply follow all the onscreen prompts that you see to complete the process. Once the package is updated you then need to wait for the Microsoft application certification process to complete. This process simply allows Microsoft to scan your app for any potentially malicious code or other techniques that don't follow Windows 8 development guidelines.

Concluding Remarks on the Store Checklist

Although this was a quick primer on the deployment process, you can always refer to Chapter 11 for more detailed information on any of these steps, including the application certification process. One of the best ways to understand the application deployment process, however, is to simply create a new Windows Store app and walk through the entire process start to finish. After you complete one submission you'll have a good handle on it and can see just how easy the process is.

SUMMARY

This chapter covered a lot of information and summarized many of the topics presented throughout this book. Although this sample app may not reflect what you do in the real world to create a Windows Store app, it does demonstrate the process you should use when you develop your Windows Store apps. If you've gotten this far, you should have a solid understanding of all the critical Windows 8 development skills including the following:

➤ Creating content-driven user interfaces using XAML

➤ Making use of all the XAML and Windows 8 user interface controls

➤ Properly using Data Binding and MVVM patterns to reduce code

➤ Interacting with the Windows 8 ecosystem through Contracts

➤ Enriching your apps by using hardware features such as sensors and geolocation

➤ Solidly understanding the application life cycle and how it differs from traditional Windows Desktop application development

➤ Using WinRT for File operations, Network Access, and Cloud Storage through the SkyDrive API

➤ Understanding all the various monetization options for Windows Store apps and how to properly configure your application for deployment in the Windows Store

Hopefully you have extracted all the information you need to start writing rich, content-driven Windows Store apps that can not only enrich users of Windows 8 devices but also make you some money in the process. Remember, for the latest information on Windows 8 development and API changes, visit `http://msdn.microsoft.com`.

INDEX